The Bitterroot and Mr. Brandborg

The Bitterroot & Mr. Brandborg

*Clearcutting
and the Struggle
for Sustainable Forestry
in the Northern Rockies*

Frederick H. Swanson

The University of Utah Press
Salt Lake City

The Defiance House Man colophon is a registered trademark
of the University of Utah Press. It is based upon a four-foot-tall,
Ancient Puebloan pictograph (late PIII) near Glen Canyon, Utah.

15 14 13 12 11   1 2 3 4 5

LIBRARY OF CONGRESS CATALOGING-IN-PUBLICATION DATA
Swanson, Frederick H. (Frederick Harold), 1952-
  The Bitterroot and Mr. Brandborg : clearcutting and the struggle for
sustainable forestry in the northern Rockies / Frederick H. Swanson.
    p.   cm.
  Includes bibliographical references.
  ISBN 978-1-60781-101-5 (cloth : alk. paper)
  1. Forest conservation—Bitterroot National Forest (Mont. and
Idaho)—History—20th century. 2. Clearcutting—Bitterroot National
Forest (Mont. and Idaho)—History—20th century. 3. Sustainable
forestry—Bitterroot National Forest (Mont. and Idaho)—History—20th
century. 4. Brandborg, G. M. (Guy Mathew), 1893-1977. 5. Conservationists—United
States—Biography. 6. Bitterroot National Forest (Agency : U.S.)—Officials and
employees—Biography. 7. Bitterroot National Forest (Mont. and Idaho)—History—
20th century. 8. Bitterroot National Forest (Mont. and Idaho)—Environmental conditions. 9. Environmental protection—Bitterroot National Forest (Mont. and
Idaho)—History—20th century. I. Title.
  SD413.B48S93 2011
  634.9092—dc22
  [B]
                                                    2010044444

Printed and bound by Sheridan Books, Inc., Ann Arbor, Michigan.

Contents

Illustrations

Photographs follow page 252

Maps

Figures

Acknowledgments

.

Any writer who wades into the thick brush of the past century's forest management controversies needs a bearing tree every few hundred yards, and fortunately I have been able to sight in on several giants in the field. My brief course work under Dr. Arnold Bolle at the University of Montana during the mid-1970s gave me a steady point of reference for the policy issues that populate this book. Dean Bolle opened his classroom and office to interested outsiders and helped me gain a better appreciation for the enormous difficulties that public policy makers face every day. During those same years Gordon Robinson was giving seminars for environmental activists through his consulting work with the Sierra Club, and I enjoyed his impish wit and his insights into how forestry used to be (and perhaps still ought to be) practiced. For decades Bud Moore shared his insights into land management with students at the Wilderness Institute at the University of Montana. It is with sadness and great respect that I note his passing in November 2010.

More tall timber: I am indebted to Stewart and Anna Vee Brandborg for opening their home, their files, and their photograph collection to me and for numerous enjoyable and wide-ranging interviews and telephone conversations. Stewart continues to give heart to many Bitterroot Valley activists with his command of both the spirit and the language of land conservation.

Dale Burk spent many hours sharing his memories of Guy and Ruth Brandborg and offered his insights into the Sturm und Drang of the Bitterroot controversy. It was Dale, a master of in-depth reporting, who insisted that Guy's legacy deserved fuller treatment than daily journalism could provide. He also contributed numerous photographs from his own collection, which forms the most complete documentation of the issue. Mavis McKelvey performed an invaluable service with her 1975 oral history interviews of Guy Brandborg and Doris Milner, as well as her biographical research into Brandy's early life and career, all of which I have drawn upon extensively. Betsy and Dan Brandborg helped greatly through their recollections of their grandfather's life and character.

It was a notable privilege to be able to talk with a number of Forest Service retirees who worked on the Bitterroot or in the Northern Region during the tumultuous years of the clearcutting controversy. Ray Abbott, Orville Daniels, Mick DeZell, John Grove, Jerry Hinman, Ray Karr, Sonny LaSalle, Jack Losenky, Bud Moore, and Bill Worf shared many useful insights and helped me to understand this difficult yet exciting time in the agency's history. I have tried to accurately depict their work, which has often been misunderstood and unfairly castigated. Ron Trosper gave helpful insights into his father's role as supervisor of the Bitterroot National Forest from 1955 to 1960.

A special thanks to Mary Williams of the Bitterroot NF for offering good advice, answering many questions, and helping me locate archival materials. Her assistant, Gene Grifo, also provided able help. Thanks also to Carlie Magill and Shandy Lemperlé for invaluable assistance in locating materials and photographs from the Northern Region's historical collection; likewise, I thank Vicki MacLean, formerly of the Helena NF, Cindy Schacher of the Nez Perce NF, Kelsey McCartney of the Lewis and Clark NF, and Sarah Nelson in the Seattle office of the National Archives, Pacific Alaska Region.

Donna McCrea of the Archives and Special Collection Department at the University of Montana's Mansfield Library (the K. Ross Toole Archives) gave me access to the Brandborg family papers while they were still unprocessed, a special privilege for any researcher and one that considerably expedited this book. Her staff, especially Amy Casamassa and Teresa Hamann, assisted me in locating materials from this important collection and many others. Appreciation also to the staffs of the Montana Historical Society, Idaho State Historical Society, Albertsons Library of Boise State University, Denver Public Library, Marriott Library of the University of Utah, University of Washington Libraries, and Ravalli County Museum, who together curate a significant number of collections important to the history of conservation.

Scott Bischke and Joanna Tenney conducted valuable oral histories of Stewart Brandborg, Clif Merritt, and Doris Milner and answered my questions about their work. Dennis Baird, Richard Behan, Bill Cunningham, Brock Evans, and Teddy Roe, key players in forest management and wilderness issues in the Northwest during that era, added their insights about the battles over clearcutting, the Magruder Corridor, and the Timber Supply Act. Bob Gilluly recalled the exciting days when he reported from the center of the storm. Larry Campbell and Matthew Koehler showed me some aspects of recent timber management on the Bitterroot, a subject that deserves more extensive treatment than the short discussion here.

Drs. Martin Nie, Char Miller, and James Burchfield brought their expertise to bear on reviews of all or portions of the text, as did Stewart and Anna Vee Brandborg, John Grove, and Mavis McKelvey. I deeply appreciate their willingness to spend many hours poring over the manuscript. Errors that remain, of course, are mine. Portions of this book were adapted for use in articles for the 2009 issue of *Forest History Today*, the journal of the Forest History Society, and the Autumn issue of *Montana: The Magazine of Western History*.

It has been a pleasure to work with the staff of the University of Utah Press through the production of this book. Peter DeLafosse, the press's acquisitions editor for western history, possesses a sharp understanding of his field and gives much encouragement to those of us who try to bring its stories to light. The late Bruce Roberts, marketing and sales director for the press, was well known to booksellers all across the Rocky Mountain states and was an indispensable source of advice and encouragement; he is sorely missed. Annette Wenda performed a comprehensive and skillful manuscript edit, and Jessica Booth carried the illustrations to completion.

Travel costs for my initial research were defrayed by a generous grant from the Matthew Hansen Endowment, a fund of the Montana Community Foundation. Laurie Yung and Laurie Ashley of the Wilderness Institute at the University of Montana, which administers the endowment, also deserve thanks for their assistance.

My close colleagues in the writing business, Jennifer Anderson and David Schleicher, bestow their welcome advice and encouragement as we each continue our quest for a paragraph that truly works. Bill Bisbee, Valerie Hoynacki, and Pat Murdo have been gracious Montana hosts. And as always, Bessann keeps me from getting lost in the underbrush.

If there ever stood oversize figures among Montana's conservationists, it would have to be Lee Metcalf and Guy Brandborg. I never met Senator Metcalf, but shortly after I arrived in Montana in 1974 my aunt Helen, who served in the Hamilton Women's Club, introduced me to Guy and Ruth. More should be written about the roles that Ruth Melendy Brandborg and Edna Stevenson Brandborg played in these battles. Finally, even though we were not able to touch upon past events, it was a tremendous gift to have one last conversation with Doris Milner before her passing, and for this I am grateful to her and to her sons, Kelsey and Eric. Through the better part of five decades Doris's leadership, passion, and humor inspired and delighted wilderness supporters throughout the Northern Rockies. We treasure her memory.

Abbreviations

BNF: USDA Forest Service, Bitterroot National Forest, Hamilton, Montana

GB: Guy M. Brandborg

GBP: G. M. Brandborg Papers, K. Ross Toole Archives, Maureen and Mike Mansfield Library, University of Montana, Missoula (container and folder numbers in this and other collections are separated by a slash, as in "GBP 2/3")

IHS: Idaho State Historical Society, Boise

KRTA: K. Ross Toole Archives, Mansfield Library, University of Montana, Missoula

LMP: Lee Metcalf Papers, Montana Historical Society, Helena

MHS: Montana Historical Society, Helena

mmbf: million board feet

NAS 95: Record Group 95, USDA Forest Service, National Archives, Pacific Alaska Region, Seattle, Washington

SBP: Stewart Brandborg Papers, K. Ross Toole Archives, Mansfield Library, University of Montana, Missoula

TWS: The Wilderness Society Records, Denver Public Library, Denver, Colorado

USFS-NR: USDA Forest Service, Northern Region history files, Missoula, Montana

Maps

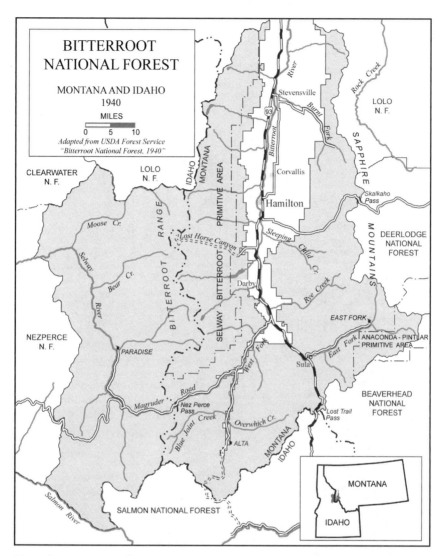

MAP 1. Bitterroot National Forest, 1940

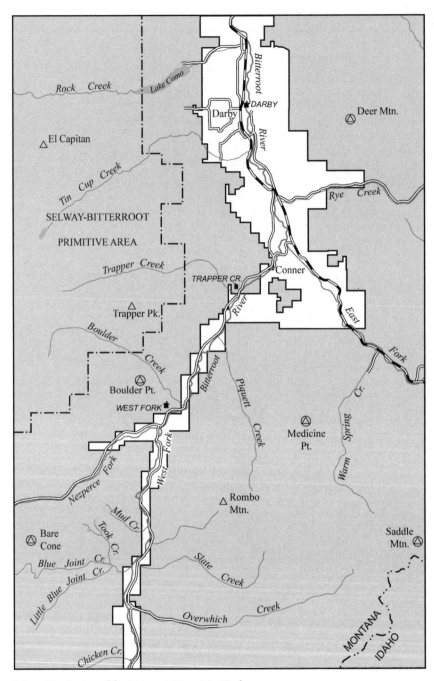

MAP 2. Headwaters of the Bitterroot River, West Fork, 1940

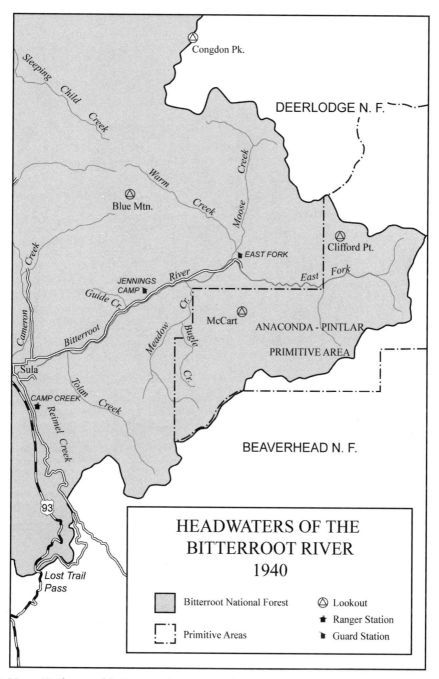

Congdon Pk.

Sleeping Child Creek

DEERLODGE N. F.

Warm Creek

Moose Creek

Blue Mtn.

Clifford Pt.

EAST FORK

River

East Fork

JENNINGS CAMP

Guide Cr.

Cameron Creek

Bitterroot

Meadow Cr.

Bugle Cr.

McCart

ANACONDA - PINTLAR

PRIMITIVE AREA

Sula

Tolan Creek

CAMP CREEK

Reimel Creek

BEAVERHEAD N. F.

93

Lost Trail Pass

HEADWATERS OF THE BITTERROOT RIVER 1940

Bitterroot National Forest △ Lookout

Primitive Areas ☗ Ranger Station

☗ Guard Station

MAP 3. Headwaters of the Bitterroot River, East Fork, 1940

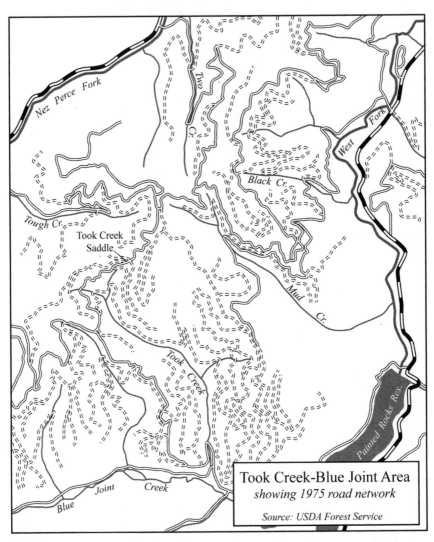

Nez Perce Fork

Two Cr.

West Fork

Black Cr.

Tough Cr.

Took Creek
Saddle

Mud Cr.

Took Creek

Painted Rocks Res.

Took Creek-Blue Joint Area
showing 1975 road network

Source: USDA Forest Service

Joint Creek

Blue

MAP 4. Took Creek–Blue Joint Area, 1975

Introduction

Took Creek Saddle, Southwestern Montana, August 1971

To the five men who stood by the side of a logging road in the headwaters of the West Fork of the Bitterroot River, the scene was one of appalling wreckage. The forest cover was missing from most of the hillside, felled and hauled off five years earlier to supply the sawmills of the southern Bitterroot Valley. Burned stumps and leftover logs attested to the pine, fir, and spruce that once covered the slopes. Most startling were the ranks of bulldozed terraces that ran across the mountainside in neat, parallel rows, an alien pattern superimposed upon the landscape.

Two of the men, former forest supervisor Guy M. "Brandy" Brandborg and his onetime subordinate, a ranger named Champ Hannon, pointed out features in the gouged and upset terrain to their guest, Senator Gale McGee of Wyoming, who had interrupted his family's summer vacation to examine forest practices in western Montana's Bitterroot National Forest. His assessment was blunt: of all the clearcuts he had viewed in the national forests of the Rocky Mountains, this one was "the shocker of them all." Vowing to bring such practices to a halt, McGee said that "what has taken place on the Bitterroot is a crime against the land and the public interest." He had already introduced legislation to place

1

a moratorium on the practice of clearcutting, based on the examples he had seen in his home state, but the denuded hillside at Took Creek gave him what he considered irrefutable ammunition.[1]

McGee's angry words would soon be read throughout western Montana, thanks to two reporters accompanying this day's tour. Miles Romney Jr. had for years railed against contemporary forest practices in the pages of his *Western News,* a family-owned weekly from the Bitterroot Valley. Much wider coverage came from a young outdoorsman named Dale Burk, who worked for the *Missoulian,* western Montana's largest daily. Over the past two years he had authored numerous articles on the crisis gripping the national forests of Montana; later that fall, his photograph of McGee and Brandborg examining the terraces of Took Creek made the front page of the *New York Times,* marking the ascent to a national stage of what might have remained a parochial issue from Montana's backwoods.[2]

Guy Brandborg, who led this day's tour, understood the critical role the news media played in modern environmental controversies and was in almost daily contact with Burk and other reporters. At the age of seventy-eight, tall, white-haired, and sturdily built, Brandy maintained an imposing presence in the Bitterroot Valley, his home for nearly half of his life. His weathered face recalled a forty-year Forest Service career, much of it spent on horseback in the company of backwoods rangers, trappers, and firefighters. Brandborg formed his philosophy of forest management during the last years of the Progressive Era, when, as he put it, he and his fellow rangers "considered ourselves servants of the people and were imbued with the spirit that all wealth comes from the good earth."[3] To him, the clearcut hillsides appearing throughout his old forest were symptomatic of a lost connection to the land.

Senator McGee's comments at Took Creek added weight to the complaints of citizens from West Virginia to Oregon who believed that the Forest Service had become subservient to the timber barons and was committing folly on a grand scale. But the scene he condemned on the Bitterroot holds a more complex story than that of a federal agency captured by the industry it was supposed to regulate. Scarcely visible in Dale Burk's photographs were ranks of spindly, foot-tall ponderosa pine seedlings, planted three years earlier after the bulldozers completed the terraces. The nursery-grown plants were still developing their root systems and would only later begin to shoot skyward. Today those trees cover the once desolate slopes like thirty-foot cornstalks, laying on cellulose thick and fast, just as the government's foresters intended. Walking among their evenly spaced trunks, one listens to the wind sing in the high branches, the music of a forest come back to life.

To the silvicultural experts in the Forest Service, the scene at Took Creek in 1971 was anything but devastation; things were proceeding exactly as planned. As employees of the U.S. Department of Agriculture, their vision for this forest was based on the renewal, growth, and harvest of a future crop. The men of the modern Forest Service were not without feeling for the beauty of growing trees; in their eyes, the young plantations growing in clearcuts all across the Bitterroot were redeeming the forest from the destructive agents of fire, insects, and decay.

Large-scale clearcutting was introduced to the Bitterroot National Forest in the late 1950s as a means of regenerating timber stands afflicted by dwarf mistletoe, a parasitic plant that slows tree growth. One of the foresters' first experiments with the practice came in 1957 on relatively gentle terrain at the head of Guide Creek, a minor tributary of the East Fork of the Bitterroot River. To reach the area, one turns off the main road near the vanished homesite of Felix Guidy, who settled his family there in 1882 and gave his name (pronounced "guy'-dee") to the nearby creek. The graveled logging road, one of dozens that lace this forested region, ascends smartly and tops out at a saddle where clearcuts of various vintages are regrowing to ponderosa pine. The reproduction here surpasses that at Took Creek—in fact, it is overdue for a thinning cut.[4]

It does the personnel of the Forest Service no injustice to liken the clearcut patches at Took Creek and Guide Saddle to an Iowa hillside farm; it was their intention, as one of their timber planners put it in 1946, to "demonstrate silviculture as the agriculturalists have demonstrated scientific farming."[5] On the Bitterroot they even tried a version of contour cropping, cutting eight- to twelve-foot terraces into the mountain slopes after the trees had been harvested. Along these rows they ran specially designed planting machines whose operators dropped seedlings into the waiting furrows, as efficient a setup as any farmer steering a tractor. The terraces captured runoff and contained erosion, a fact known to hillslope farmers since antiquity. Seedling survival—a problem in earlier clearcuts—improved dramatically, permitting the agency to continue its aggressive cutting program and fuel a boom in lumber processing in the southern Bitterroot Valley.

By 1967 foresters were clearcutting and terracing more than three square miles of the Bitterroot National Forest every year.[6] Its personnel took pride in these results, but they were not quite ready to display their work before the public. The Bitterroot National Forest's annual report for the 1967–1968 fiscal year featured feel-good stories about forest thinning, fire-control efforts, and enhanced wildlife habitat, with little mention of clearcutting. Only the report's announcement that 126 million board feet (mmbf) of timber had been harvested from the forest in the past year suggested the scale of change that was occurring.[7]

Without knowing it, these enterprising forest farmers were coming to the end of their row. Alarmed Bitterroot Valley citizens soon were stopping by Guy and Ruth Brandborg's home with accounts of devastation up in the hills. In the fall of 1968, after Champ Hannon took him on a hundred-mile tour of newly logged high-elevation watershed lands, Brandy decided to haul his agency back to its former course. He and his close friends unleashed a campaign that would kneecap the Bitterroot's carefully planned logging program and propel its staff into an unaccustomed public spotlight.

Brandborg accomplished this without filing a single lawsuit or timber-sale appeal, relying instead on skillful use of the news media and careful tending of Montana's progressive grassroots. Bitterroot Valley residents grew used to hearing Brandy's prophetic voice at public forums on forest management, warning of devastated streams and wildlife habitat, depleted timber supplies, and eventual economic ruin. But most of his work was done offstage. Richard Behan, who served on a University of Montana faculty committee that investigated the Bitterroot's logging practices, described Brandy as a "consummate operative" who recruited scientific experts and powerful political allies to back up valley residents' claims of resource damage. "He kept all his contacts fresh and flattered," Behan recalled.[8]

Significantly, Brandborg insisted that the problem was not clearcutting itself, which if properly applied was a useful forest management tool, but the long-term overcutting of both public and private forest lands. New sawmills had been built and others expanded in anticipation of ever-increasing timber cuts. The intensive logging could not be sustained, in his view, and the mills' eventual closure was sad but inevitable. The only answer was to reduce the cut and build a permanent forest economy based on sustained-yield timber harvesting, regardless of landownership.

The Bitterroot clearcutting controversy is often depicted as a textbook case of the environmental awakening of the 1960s and 1970s, and indeed that era's concern over land abuses allowed Brandborg and his allies to gain wide publicity for their campaign.[9] But the horrific appearance of the Bitterroot's bulldozed clearcuts, though they gave rise to sensational news stories and prompted Congress to adopt significant reforms in forest practices, tended to obscure Brandborg's chief concern—the century-old, still unresolved issue of sustained-yield forestry. The nation had never settled the question of the fundamental purpose of its national forests. Whose interests would these trees serve? Which generations would benefit from their bounty? Was it still possible to develop a wood products–based economy that sustained local communities far into the future while keeping the forest healthy and beautiful?

Guy Brandborg and his rangers believed they had worked out a solution to these questions during the 1940s, when they placed these woods under a program of careful selective harvesting of large-diameter, high-value ponderosa pine. As supervisor of the 1.6 million–acre Bitterroot National Forest from 1935 to 1955, Brandy saw his program as a way to provide a modest but steady flow of timber, forage, and irrigation water for Bitterroot Valley residents. An agrarian populist by upbringing and temperament, he held a consistent vision of the Forest Service as the protector of the valley's independent loggers, farmers, ranchers, and small sawmill operators, many of whom faced competition from larger firms located outside the valley, including those allied with the powerful Anaconda Copper Mining Company. To Brandy, forestry was an adjunct to permanent agriculture, not a primary source of export goods. Everything in his experience, reading, and instincts told him that logging booms did not create vital communities.

His heroes were the founders of the conservation movement, including the Forest Service's first chief, Gifford Pinchot, and his political sponsor, Theodore Roosevelt, both of whom believed that protection and use of the national forests were fully compatible. These men had not been afraid to oppose monopoly and exploitation of publicly owned resources, setting an idealistic direction for government forestry that has not been matched since. When Pinchot toured the Bitterroot with Brandborg in 1937, the former chief instructed Brandy to defend sound forest practices against those who would exploit the public's timber—a message the young supervisor took to heart.

Following World War II Brandborg felt a growing sense of betrayal of his agency's mission. Its leaders in Washington repeatedly handed down directives to increase timber cutting, sometimes overruling the objections of local rangers. Political appointees transferred conscientious land managers at the behest of livestock interests. Scientific investigations of land abuses were shelved and ignored. Promotions depended upon whether one got out the cut. To a few dissidents within the agency, it appeared that the green uniform had become indistinguishable from a timber executive's business suit.[10]

In truth, the emerging dominance of the agency's timber branch reflected another Progressive ideal—that of scientifically managed production for the good of the nation. Silviculturalists and timber planners in Missoula and Washington wanted to bring public forestry into the modern era and integrate their agency's operations into the booming postwar economy. It was not greed, malfeasance, or even the desire for larger budgets that drove them to adopt ever-higher cutting levels—only their insistence that timber be treated as a crop.

On the Bitterroot, however, the advocates of modernization ran into an unyielding obstacle in supervisor Brandborg, who held a much different vision of what the public's forests were about. He insisted that watershed, wilderness recreation, and big-game habitat be given at least equal priority with timber. Brandy's superiors made repeated efforts to get him to step up the cutting, but he held to the limited harvest program he had implemented on the eve of World War II. The impasse might have ended with Brandborg's retirement in 1955, when he could have pursued the many options for outdoor recreation in the mountains and streams around his home in Hamilton, Montana. But having spent twenty years trying to create a grassroots coalition for conservation action in the Bitterroot Valley, he refused to yield to the new approach. He counseled his successor to continue the old practices, and through his efforts to promote conservation education among sportsmen's clubs and in Montana's schools and universities, he mentored a new generation of activists who opposed encroachments upon Montana's and Idaho's superb wildlands.

By the time Senator McGee stood on the hillside at Took Creek, Brandy had conducted a dozen or more media tours in which he contrasted his selectively cut stands with the stark, intensively managed clearcuts. His influence extended nationwide as well, for he played a key role in persuading Idaho senator Frank Church to hold hearings on timber practices in Washington, D.C., earlier that year, at which witnesses from across the country (including Brandborg and Burk) served notice to the agency's leaders that they would no longer have a free hand in managing the nation's public woodlands.

Guy Brandborg passed away in 1977, just as new restrictions on logging and clearcutting, a legacy of his years of work on the issue, were transforming the

Forest Service's operations in the Northern Rockies. His name was given to a jagged mountain peak visible from the main Bitterroot Valley, commemorating his role as a lightning rod for controversy. Yet his views on forestry and public affairs were complex and far-reaching, as relevant to our time as they were to a desperate Montana in the 1930s. The Bitterroot clearcutting controversy helped inaugurate a contentious new era in forest management, but it was a battle with roots deep in the soil of rural Montana, where farsighted men and women struggled to find a lasting means of living off the land.

CHAPTER 1

The Forests of the Bitterroot

1878–1930

Few Americans enjoy as intimate a connection to forested land as the forty thousand residents of Montana's mountain-rimmed Bitterroot Valley, who can gaze up at sylvan peaks from almost any point in their spacious river basin. Trails, campgrounds, and fishing holes lie only a few minutes' drive from the valley's main highway, U.S. 93; for those with more time, adventure awaits in the Selway-Bitterroot Wilderness Area, the eastern boundary of which reaches almost to the valley floor, or in the smaller Anaconda-Pintler Wilderness, which lies in the headwaters of the Bitterroot River's East Fork. Little wonder, then, that local real estate has for decades commanded some of the best prices in the Big Sky country.

The Bitter Rooters, as they often call themselves, also deal with the legacy of more than four decades of disagreement over how the surrounding forests ought to be managed—a conflict that Guy Brandborg helped instigate through his determined advocacy for locally based, sustained-yield forestry. Decades after his passing, conversations and friendships are still weighed down with talk of management plans, timber-sale appeals, and court appearances—all of which come with living next to a publicly owned forest. These are crucial issues for those who live in western Montana, but at times it seems that conflict lies on the Bitterroot like the heavy wool blanket of a trapper burdened with a long winter.

It helps to step outside the cabin and take a look at the surroundings, for there is much to admire in this forest—and much that is worth protecting, in whatever way one chooses to use the term.

The Bitterroot National Forest encompasses many distinct mountain landscapes, each with its characteristic tree cover. Most obvious to the visitor is the classic alpine scenery of the Bitterroot Range, whose abrupt mountain face forms the western margin of the Bitterroot Valley. Its sheer granitic cliffs are set off with a garland of wind-twisted subalpine fir, whitebark pine, and the gloriously gnarled Lyall's larch, a deciduous conifer that flaunts dusky-gold needles in the autumn.

These jagged summits steal attention from the less imposing but deceptively rugged Sapphire Range to the east of the valley, which shelters elk and moose within its deep, heavily forested valleys. Farther south, the two ranges merge to form the headwaters of the Bitterroot River, including nearly forty miles of the Continental Divide, which here makes its westernmost run in the forty-eight contiguous states. A continuous cover of lodgepole pine blankets the higher reaches of these mountains, the legacy of millennia of recurring wildfires. The mundane, scaly-barked lodgepole gets little respect from timbermen or recreationists, but stand amid this forest up on the Divide when the autumn winds promise snow and you will feel the sweep of wildness as surely as on any high Bitterroot crag.

Farther down the slopes, Douglas firs grow as rugged, isolated specimens on exposed ridges, unlike the unbroken canopies they form in the Pacific Northwest. The Douglas fir is also a common understory tree in stands of ponderosa pine that have been protected from fire, another ecological variation from its western sister. Grand fir, western larch, and Engelmann spruce occupy moister sites at these middle elevations, providing thermal cover for large game during the summer. These forests form a vital watershed for the Bitterroot River, fulfilling one of the original purposes of the national forest.

Below about six thousand feet in elevation, where soils reach greater depths and the wintertime winds are blunted, there flourish extensive stands of ponderosa pine—the Bitterroot's emblematic tree and the one that valley residents most often associate with their forest. In favored places it reaches heights of well over a hundred feet, with a trunk three or more feet in diameter—not a forest giant like the redwood or sequoia, but stately and impressive in this setting. In places where repeated ground fires have cleared out underbrush and other trees, it will form nearly pure stands of mature specimens spaced at five paces or more.[1]

With their heavy branches beginning twenty or thirty feet above the ground, the mature ponderosa forest in these localities takes on an irresistible likeness to a well-groomed park, a scene that may even evoke the savannas of our human origins. Sit underneath these trees on a warm day, and a sense of well-being almost palpably surrounds you. The ponderosa's five-inch needles carpet the forest floor, which is strewn with its open, attractive, toothy cones. On sunny days the trees' jigsaw-cut bark yields a fine aroma, most often described as vanilla—the same scent that real estate agents deploy at open houses. If there is a breeze high up in the forest canopy, the effect is complete—no other tree sounds as delightful as it combs the air.

One could get possessive about such a forest. No doubt the Salish people who once lived here felt that way about these woods, which they, like the Nez Perce to the west, helped craft over the centuries by lighting fires to clear travel lanes and promote the growth of grasses. Modern residents of the Bitterroot also came to feel a special affinity for their backyard woods. Whether as hunters, anglers, picnickers, hikers, or horse packers, they joined the prospectors, trappers, and timbermen who were the original Anglo users of the forest. Their desires would sometimes clash, and the forest would not always present a benign aspect, but only a place of surpassing beauty could elicit the passions that have surrounded this very public forest.

That Americans have national forests to contend over is the result of a happy coincidence of several historical forces in the late nineteenth century. The forest conservation movement that emerged by the 1870s in response to the extensive depletion of timber in the East and Midwest was a precondition for the establishment of the first federal forest reserves in the West. This movement gained strategic support from farmers and irrigators who feared the loss of their sources of water—the unsullied rivers and streams that emerged from the mountain fastness of the interior West and made agriculture possible hundreds of miles distant. Protecting headwater forests from fire, logging, and grazing was thought to secure these stream flows. Perceived threats to irrigation supplies would emerge again in the 1960s as one of the chief reasons behind the Bitterroot clearcutting controversy—reprising concerns expressed in such forums as the National Irrigation Congresses of the early 1900s.[2]

Conservation as an identifiable program was nearly indistinguishable from its chief political sponsor, the Progressive movement. The men most visibly behind

Progressivism, Theodore Roosevelt and Gifford Pinchot, loved forests and the things they contained: raw materials for building a new society as well as wild plants and creatures to study, catch, or hunt. These two men did not originate the idea of reserving America's remaining forests against further exploitation, but by 1905, with Pinchot installed as the chief forester of the newly created Forest Service, they took the concept to new heights. Pinchot would visit the Bitterroot at least three times, lending his prestige and influence to the cause of forest protection in western Montana and deeply influencing its most outspoken forest supervisor.

The Progressives stood for carefully managed, rational use of resources—what historian Samuel P. Hays calls "the transformation of a decentralized, nontechnical, loosely organized society, where waste and inefficiency ran rampant, into a highly organized, technical, and centrally planned and directed social organization which would meet a complex world with efficiency and purpose." Many of the movement's adherents, including Pinchot, also brought a strong sense of social equity to their work, seeking to curb the enormous power then vested in the country's industrial and financial combines. Managerial efficiency and social reform did not always dovetail comfortably, which created a fault line within the conservation movement. During the rest of the twentieth century, the Forest Service would waver between these twin aims, torn between those who favored the strict application of scientific principles that would maximize resource production and a more egalitarian wing that hoped to rein in the power of corporations and distribute the benefits of forestry to ordinary Americans. Here, too, lay the seeds of the Bitterroot controversy and the crisis in national forest management of the 1960s and 1970s.[3]

The Bitterroot National Forest derives from the system of reservations established under the 1891 Forest Reserve Act, Congress's first attempt to retain significant timbered areas in public ownership. Soon after, President Benjamin Harrison established the first of these withdrawals, the Yellowstone Timber Land Reserve, whose major purpose was to protect the watersheds east and north of Yellowstone Park and safeguard the herds of bison and elk that wandered in and out of the park.[4]

It took another six years to set aside more of the Northern Rockies' forests. On February 22, 1897, President Grover Cleveland signed a proclamation creating thirteen new reserves under the Sundry Civil Appropriations Act of

1897, including the Bitter Root, Flathead, Lewis and Clarke (as it was initially spelled), and Priest River, which together sprawled across a huge area of western Montana and northern Idaho. At 4.1 million acres, the Bitter Root was the largest of the so-called Washington's Birthday reserves, reaching from the western margin of the Bitterroot Valley almost to the Snake River in Idaho.[5] Although this withdrawal would appear to be the action of a distant federal government with little connection to Montana or Idaho, it actually got a boost from some Bitterroot Valley settlers who were upset with the unbridled logging taking place on the valley's margins. In 1891 residents of a small community near scenic Lake Como, located between Hamilton and Darby below the high peaks of the Bitterroot Range, grew concerned about extensive logging that was visible from the shore of the lake. The residents, which included future forest ranger Than Wilkerson, petitioned the General Land Office to set aside a forest reserve encompassing sixteen thousand acres along the pine-covered slopes below the mountain face from Tin Cup Creek to Lost Horse Creek.

Lt. George Ahern, an army explorer who was lecturing on forestry at the Montana Agricultural College in Bozeman, took up their cause with the Interior Department and met with Bernhard Fernow of its Bureau of Forestry. In 1896 Ahern accompanied Gifford Pinchot and Henry Graves of the federal Forest Commission, a blue-ribbon advisory group, on a tour of a larger proposed reserve encompassing much of the Bitterroot Range. Their favorable report overcame opposition from timber interests within the state, including the Anaconda Copper Mining Company, and helped persuade Cleveland to take his sweeping measure establishing the Bitter Root reserve.[6]

Only about one-sixth of the reserve lay in Montana, and it included no lands east of the Bitterroot Valley. In 1907 its name was changed to the Bitter Root National Forest, and on July 1, 1908, President Roosevelt signed Executive Order 883, which apportioned its Idaho acreage to form the Nezperce and Clearwater national forests and added lands in the Sapphire Range from the Hellgate and Big Hole reserves, which had been created in 1905. The order also changed the forest's name to one word, although some local residents would continue to favor the older spelling. The Bitterroot National Forest did not assume its present configuration until 1934, following the dissolution of the Selway National Forest and the return of lands in the upper Selway River drainage and Salmon River Breaks to the Bitterroot.[7]

Reaction from western lumber and livestock interests to the forest reserves was hostile from the start. Seeking to bolster its position, Interior dispatched Richard Goode, an experienced geographer and topographic surveyor, and J. B.

Leiberg, a geologist, to make reconnaissance surveys of the new reserves in the Northwest and report on the resources they contained. To attempt to survey such a large region was a daunting assignment, to say the least, for, as Goode reported in an 1898 article for *National Geographic,* "there is probably no portion of the country, exclusive of Alaska, about which there was so little known as the territory included in the Bitter Root Reserve."[8]

Goode's assignment was to establish rough boundaries and begin topographic surveys of the reserve, but he also used his report to paint a bleak picture of the devastating forest fires set by hunters and other forest users since the arrival of the white man. Extensive burns had occurred in the headwaters of the West Fork of the Bitterroot River as well as in many of the side canyons along the front of the mountain range. "Reaping where he has not sown and failing to restore where he has destroyed, a noble heritage is slipping away through carelessness and cupidity," Goode wrote. Leiberg, charged with making an economic survey of the reserve, contrasted the Anglo misuse of the forest with what he regarded as the careful husbandry practiced by its former Indian inhabitants.[9]

Both men warned that attempting to grow crops or graze cattle in the subalpine meadows of the Bitterroot Range would be ruinous; according to Goode, this would amount to a "dangerous experiment" that would "throw into the valley the season's drainage much more rapidly than now, and thus diminish still further the available irrigation water during the growing season." Timbering in mountainous areas such as the upper West Fork of the Bitterroot River also posed a threat, Leiberg believed, inasmuch as the heavy forest cover "prevents the free circulation of warm air and screens the snow banks from the direct rays of the sun and too rapid melting."[10] This concern for the water-retaining capacity of the high-elevation forests would guide management on the Bitterroot for more than a half century.

The immediate goal of advocates for the Bitter Root reserve was to end decades of timber trespass upon the federal domain. In 1885 the Department of the Interior filed suit against the Anaconda Company for illegally cutting 45 million board feet of dimension lumber, as well as railroad ties, shingles, cordwood, and posts from public lands.[11] But with no real federal presence in the forests, let alone boundary surveys and signs, such trespass was almost inevitable. The case against Anaconda dragged on for years and became enmeshed in the company's larger struggle to retain control of political affairs in Montana. At one point the

Northern Pacific Railroad, one of the company's chief allies, threatened to withdraw its deposits from a bank owned by Governor Samuel Hauser unless he took steps to block the federal government's suit.[12]

Against this background Leiberg examined squatter claims that had been located under the 1878 Timber and Stone Act along the fringes of the forest, particularly in the lower reaches of the East and West forks of the Bitterroot River. He found only three that showed active use as homesteads. "A great many others were abandoned as soon as the timber growing on them was cut and disposed of," he observed. Logging companies often paid squatters to file claims in their stead. Leiberg noted that "only the choice portions of the logs were taken.... [T]rees were felled, sawn up into proper logging lengths, and left to rot." Logging slash was left in place, creating a fire hazard. Extensive cutover areas suggested to him that perhaps 50 mmbf were being taken annually from private lands in the valley—a rate he did not believe could be sustained for more than twenty years.[13]

By far the largest timber user in the state was the Anaconda Copper Mining Company, which Montanans often referred to as the ACM, or simply "the company."[14] To supply mine-support timbers and building lumber for its Butte copper workings, Marcus Daly, the company's founder, opened a sawmill in Hamilton in 1891. The elegant ponderosa pines that ringed the Bitterroot Valley were ideal for this purpose. Called yellow pine at the time, this tree was second in value only to the fabled white pine of the Northern Rockies' river valleys. By the turn of the century Daly's mill was processing 18–20 mmbf of Bitterroot pine annually, shipping the lumber by rail to Missoula and on to Butte and other destinations. Much of this timber appeared to have been illegally logged from the forest reserve; investigators for the General Land Office claimed that the company had removed in excess of 100 mmbf without permit from 1897 to 1899.[15]

Even more ponderosa came from private tracts in the Bitterroot Valley, including the extensive land-grant holdings of the Northern Pacific Railroad, on which Anaconda either purchased stumpage rights or bought the land outright. Part of the railroad's original 1864 grant had since reverted to the federal government and become part of the national forest system, but the railroad still owned some of the best timberlands in the Clark Fork and Bitterroot valleys. In 1905 the ACM acquired the Montana Improvement Company's mill in Bonner, just east of Missoula, which was ideally situated on rail lines at the confluence of the Big Blackfoot River and the Clark Fork. Two years later it completed a deal with the Northern Pacific to acquire nearly a million acres of timberlands to feed its Bonner and Hamilton mills. Over the next decade the company contributed half of all the timber cut in the entire state.[16]

Numerous small mills also operated in the Bitterroot Valley, some no more than open-air single-blade outfits designed to produce rough lumber for ranchers' use. Railroad ties, which could be cut almost like cordwood from otherwise useful trees, were also in demand. Clarence Strong, who went on to head the Northern Region's operations division, recalled that in the early 1900s, "these mills were ripping out ties and lumber from the choicest ponderosa and Douglas-fir trees that ever stood in that valley."[17] Liquidation of private timber stocks motivated Forest Service policy makers to husband the public's timber against the day it would be needed, as well as to try to prod industry to adopt more conservative practices that would stretch out its supply.

The Bitterroot's first rangers worked under the loose control of the Interior Department and had their hands full patrolling the Montana portion of the reserve; designing timber sales was not in their purview. It took until 1899 for two enterprising rangers, Than Wilkerson and H. C. Tuttle, to build the first patrol cabin anywhere in the forest—and perhaps in the whole system of reserves. This was a single-room structure fashioned from lodgepole-pine logs and finished with a sod roof, located near the mining camp of Alta in the upper West Fork drainage. The rangers paid for materials out of their fifty-dollar monthly salary—as Wilkerson recalled, "Uncle Sam wasn't putting out a good cent for a pair of hill-billy rangers to live while they took care of the woods."[18] The cabin was restored in the 1960s as a historic site—a local effort that had Brandborg's enthusiastic support. Visitors can easily imagine the smell of wood smoke and the creak of bedsprings as the ranger, who usually worked alone, rose to put on the day's coffee and outfit himself for another day's patrol in these remote mountains.

The Forest Service is often depicted as taking a custodial approach to management during its early decades, but the Bitterroot's first supervisors worked assiduously to develop a harvesting scheme for their more accessible pine stands. Gifford Pinchot's directions to his field staff were clear: they would undertake a program of scientific forestry as soon as possible, applying principles such as balancing cutting with growth, improving the stock resource, and minimizing losses from fire, insects, and disease. Pinchot placed his Forest Service firmly within the Progressive movement's utilitarian aims: the resources found on the national forests would be made available for use, not just husbanded against future contingencies.[19]

Planning was essential to this program. No other aspect of Forest Service management so well illustrated the Progressives' managerial approach as their attempts to implement a timber harvesting program. Over the years the Forest Service would spend countless man-days inventorying its timber and forage and computing how much could be used at any one time. In their early years the national forests operated under a so-called limitation of cut that was set by the secretary of agriculture upon the advice of the chief of the Forest Service. In 1910, for example, chief forester Henry Graves recommended that the Bitterroot's maximum annual harvest level be set at 37 mmbf—1 percent of the forest's estimated volume of standing timber.[20] If carried out over the long term, this approach would have yielded an average rotation age (the age of a typical timber stand at harvest) of one hundred years for all species in the forest.

This figure was overly optimistic, given the inaccessibility of most of the national forest, yet within two years the Agriculture Department upped it to 55 mmbf, using a more precise method of calculation based on the annual growth from an estimated eight hundred thousand acres of productive timberland in the forest. Twenty million feet of this total were to come from ponderosa pine, which at the time was the only commercially viable species on the forest and constituted an estimated 1 billion board feet of merchantable standing timber. The foresters noted that they could safely cut up to 25 mmbf of lodgepole pine, 7 million more than the estimated annual growth, because so much of it was mature or overmature. In all, they figured that the forest contained 2.3 billion board feet of merchantable lodgepole pine, 1.5 billion of Douglas fir, 150 million of spruce, and 50 million of larch.[21]

These crude calculations were meant to serve as an upper bound and never reflected the Bitterroot's actual harvest levels. The closest the forest came to its permissible harvest in those years was during 1908–1911, when an average of 14.5 mmbf were removed from several drainages northwest of Darby, including the well-documented Lick Creek area, where the Bitterroot was conducting one of the largest sales in the region. In 1905 the Anaconda Company's lumber division expressed interest in buying national forest timber in a great belt of ponderosa pine forest extending from Lost Horse Creek south to Tin Cup Creek. Forest officials were unsure how to proceed; they wanted to put this timber to use before it fell prey to fire or insect attack, but they were concerned lest they appear to favor the company over smaller operators. E. A. Sherman, the forest supervisor at the time, advised Gifford Pinchot that Anaconda would likely pay fifty to seventy-five thousand dollars for the stumpage rights to this area, which was, he said, "a higher figure than would be paid by the settlers who would take up the land and sell the timber to the same lumber company."[22] Although the proceeds would be welcome to his agency, which was trying to show it could be fiscally solvent, Sherman told Pinchot that the sale would not be popular locally. They proceeded nonetheless, having no other means of implementing timber management on so large a scale.

Harvesting began at Lick Creek in the fall of 1907 under the direction of Elers Koch, who had replaced Sherman as supervisor, and continued through 1911. Anaconda's contractor selectively cut almost two thousand acres of ponderosa pine as well as several hundred acres in the Douglas fir and spruce types. Logs were yarded by horse and by steam "donkey" engines; wooden skids were laid down to form chutes for sliding the logs. Temporary rail spurs were constructed to haul the timber to the main branch and thence to the Hamilton mill. The foresters laid out the sale without any specific marking guidelines, although they were instructed to reserve younger healthy trees for a future cut, taking out most of the older pines. In all, about 70 percent of the overall volume was cut—a fairly heavy removal for a selective harvest. In September 1906 Gifford Pinchot visited the sale area while marking was under way and added his own instructions, calling for a somewhat lighter cut than had been planned.[23]

Subsequent foresters were able to study how the cutting in Lick Creek affected forest regrowth, thanks to a set of glass-plate images of the original sale area that were taken by a photographer sent from the agency's Washington office. In 1925 K. D. Swan, a photographer for the District 1 office, relocated these photo positions with help from forest supervisor Wilfred White, who had worked on the sale. Guy Brandborg had the locations permanently marked in 1938, allowing scientists to follow natural succession in the sale area and observe the effect of later cuttings. They measured substantial improvement in growth on the remaining trees, but careful observers also saw how Douglas fir seedlings, along with forage shrubs such as willow and bitterbrush, filled in many of the openings—undercutting the early-day foresters' hopeful intentions to perpetuate the valuable pine. These changes were occurring throughout the Bitterroot's ponderosa pine belt, to the point that by the year 2000 researchers estimated that logging and fire control had reduced the pine's overall stand composition to half of what it had been in 1900.[24]

In 1907 the Anaconda Company also obtained rights to 13 mmbf of timber in the Bunkhouse Creek drainage, which it cut concurrently with Lick Creek. Subsequent sales were made in 1916 and 1917 in the Lost Horse and Shannon Gulch drainages, which removed nearly 20 mmbf of ponderosa pine and Douglas fir.[25] In making these sales the Forest Service was fortunate to have a large company with a considerable need for timber already established in the Bitterroot Valley, a situation that did not yet exist in many parts of the West. But agency officials also did not want to see Anaconda use the public's land as a bargain basement while keeping its own holdings in reserve. This uneasy interplay between the Bitterroot National Forest and the large private timber owners in the valley continued into the 1940s and beyond. The approach the agency took in balancing these competing needs was more than simple custodianship, yet it was far from a lockstep relationship with industry, as environmentalists would later allege. The agency's foresters wanted to make their sales serve larger goals under the Progressive program of fostering competition and promoting productive employment for local men. Until the early 1970s, when public opinion would begin to play a decisive role in the Bitterroot, the foresters had a fairly free hand to establish their cutting program—limited only by the local market and the interest of regional players such as Anaconda.

After Anaconda closed its Hamilton mill in 1915 in favor of its Bonner operation, much of the Bitterroot's public timber lay too far from markets to be profitable; following completion of the sales in the Lake Como district, harvests from the national forest dropped to 2.5 mmbf in 1912, none in 1913, and between 1 and 2 mmbf from 1914 to 1916. Not until World War I did demand again develop for the forest's timber. Harvest levels climbed to 7.5 mmbf by 1919, reflecting cutting from the Lost Horse and Shannon Gulch sales, then dropped again below 2 mmbf with the onset of depressed economic conditions in 1921–1922. After making additional surveys of forest-stand conditions, supervisor White decided in 1922 to lower the annual cutting limit to 35 mmbf, still well beyond any realistic chance of fulfillment.

By 1925 John Lowell, the new forest supervisor, recommended that the annual sales ceiling on the Bitterroot be reduced to 27 million board feet, in line with a further reduction in the estimated acreage of commercial lodgepole pine—411 mmbf compared to the 2.3 billion they had charted so hopefully in 1912.[26] Even this level of harvest was not reached until the 1960s, when the forest began clearing firebreaks along the Continental Divide and Sapphire Range. An outbreak of the mountain pine beetle in the 1920s and early 1930s decimated lodgepole pine stands on the Bitterroot and the adjoining Beaverhead National Forest, further dampening interest in this species for commercial production.

Most of the action during this time was taking place on privately owned forests in northern Idaho and northwestern Montana, where workers in lumber camps on the Clark Fork, Kootenai, Flathead, and Clearwater rivers were felling large-diameter white pine, Douglas fir, and western red cedar. The total cut from District 1 peaked in 1926 at 123 million board feet, most of which came from these lower-elevation forests. The Great Depression brought an end to this expansion as regionwide timber volumes, both cut and sold, fell to less than 30 million in 1933.[27]

Both the measurement of standing timber on the Bitterroot and the method of calculating the cut would be refined considerably over the years, but these early plans indicate a desire on the part of Forest Service staff to fully utilize the available timber and convert stands of overmature trees to more productive young growth—a goal that would take on paramount importance following World War II. To the early-day foresters, custodial management might be necessary for a time, but it was never their ultimate goal. It would take a half century, however, before the Bitterroot would produce timber at the level its first foresters dreamed of achieving.

CHAPTER 2

Pinchot's Corps

1881–1924

The roots of the Bitterroot clearcutting controversy draw upon some of the key themes in national forest history, including the agrarian populism of the late nineteenth century, whose adherents looked to the forest reserves as sources of timber, forage, and water that remained beyond the control of eastern monopolists. Populism, in turn, emerged from fertile midwestern soil—including the lake country of west-central Minnesota, where in 1881 Charles and Betsy Brandborg, a farming couple of Swedish extraction, took up a homestead on a half-section of mixed prairie and woodland a few miles west of the town of Henning.

It was a propitious year to begin farming in Otter Tail County; the Northern Pacific, Fergus, and Black Hills Railway was constructing a branch line westward through the county seat of Fergus Falls with the intention of reaching the booming town of Deadwood in Dakota Territory. The hundreds of Scandinavian farmers who were growing wheat in the surrounding prairies were less interested in Black Hills gold than in gaining a vital connection eastward to markets in Minneapolis and Chicago.

The new line was a mixed blessing to the settlers, since its parent company, the Northern Pacific Railroad, also controlled many of the grain elevators and flour mills on which the small landsman relied. To counteract the company's monopoly, Charles organized a local chapter of the Farmer's Alliance, a loose-knit organization of farm cooperatives that had sprung up in the 1880s in localities from New York to Texas and the Dakotas. Over the next decade Brandborg and his fellow Alliance men in Henning started a newspaper and built a grain elevator, with Brandborg managing the latter. Thus pitted against the merchants, purchasing agents, and railroad men living in Fergus Falls and other towns, confrontation was perhaps inevitable.

At Henning's Fourth of July celebration in 1891, Alliance supporters mixed patriotic oratory with antimonopoly sentiments while their detractors in the audience shouted their disapproval. When one man leaped up on the stage to state his views, he was promptly arrested. His friends, angered by this peremptory insult, were soon after Brandborg. Fearing for his life and unable to elude his attackers, Charles picked up a loose fence rail and swung, fatally injuring one of the men. Brandborg was acquitted of murder at trial, but the incident became a family legend.[1]

Guy Mathew Brandborg—who went by "Brandy" for most of his life—was born on March 3, 1893, the ninth of Charles and Betsy's ten children. If Charles made a strong impression on the little town (he twice ran for governor of Minnesota on the Socialist Labor ticket), less is written of Brandy's mother or other family members. In a 1975 interview with his friend Mavis McKelvey, Brandy spoke of how his parents left Sweden to seek freedom of thought and religion as well as economic opportunity. Along with their desire to escape Old World strictures, they brought with them a heritage of careful husbandry and a strong aversion to waste. "If Mother saw us throwing away bread," Brandy told McKelvey, "she said it was a sin. And if our Dad saw us destroying things, you know, breaking shovel handles and things like that in our work, he called it to our attention, what those kind of things meant."[2]

Brandy remembered his father showing him the traditional Swedish ways of farming and building in which skilled hands often served better than machinery—and, not incidentally, kept one in touch with the soil. "They always impressed upon us that if we'd abide by the law of nature, we'd be all right," he said. Decades later, when he was managing a forest instead of a farm, Brandy was inclined to accept the growth that nature provided on its own—aided only by judicious thinning of trees—rather than undertake drastic measures such as large-scale clearcutting and terracing to force it into unnatural productivity.[3]

The older children were schooled at home by a hired teacher, who made use of the Brandborgs' extensive library, which included works by Victor Hugo, Alexander Dumas, Mark Twain, Karl Marx, Henry Fielding, and Leo Tolstoy. Guy attended school in town through the tenth grade, but his home environment remained the stronger influence. Politics was a frequent topic of dinner conversation; Charles wanted his children to understand that every citizen had a right and a duty to organize against powerful economic interests. He customarily gave his children a subscription to the *New York Times* upon graduation, expecting that they would continue to follow world affairs as they earned their bread.[4]

In his 1975 interview Brandy did not linger on his Minnesota origins, although his voice preserved the musical lilt and extended vowels of his Scandinavian heritage. Still, Charles's dedication to the cause of the small farmer left an impression: throughout his career Brandy felt that the Forest Service must keep foremost in mind the men who worked in the woods and small mills, as well as the farmers who ran sheep and cattle up in the high meadows and depended upon continuous flows of irrigation water.

McKelvey visited Henning a few years after Brandy's death and talked with a handful of old-timers who had known him as a boy; one woman spoke of him as a good student with a serious attitude, while others remembered the Brandborg boys as a rambunctious lot. Growing up on their hilltop farm, the children would have had close contact with the natural world, and there were ponds and sloughs that supported abundant bird and animal life. Yet Brandy seems not to have been drawn to natural history, nor did he take up the difficult work of farming. Instead, he would head farther west, as many young men and women did in the early 1900s, to find adventure in the forests and mountains of the Big Sky country.

In the early years of the twentieth century the railroads carried many hopeful farmers to Montana, where they faced an uncertain future in the drought- and depression-prone state. The rails also brought tourists seeking a path to the state's shining mountains and mysterious thermal basins. James J. Hill's Great Northern Railroad led straight to Glacier National Park, one of the nation's alpine jewels, which had been established in 1910 with no small assistance from Louis Hill, James's son and heir to the railroad operation.[5] The park, Louis realized, would lure tourists away from Yellowstone, the rival Northern Pacific's chief tourist attraction. He undertook at once to build a series of backcountry camps designed to smooth the tourist's path among Glacier's remote crags. In 1913, at a spectacular site overlooking a glacial cirque beneath the western flank of Gunsight Mountain, his workers built a dining hall and laid the foundation for a stone-walled, European-style hostel. This opened in the summer of 1914 as the Sperry Chalets, named for a glacier spilling off the north side of the peak.

Brandy's sister Ellen worked as the manager of the Sperry camp in its prechalet years; her husband, Ernie Lanneau, led the pack strings that brought supplies into this refuge and to other wilderness camps and chalets in the park. Brandy had no experience with horse packing in the mountains, but Ellen was able to find him work as a roustabout during the summer of 1913. For a young man from the topographically subtle prairies of Minnesota, it was a stunning introduction to one of the most scenic mountainscapes in the Rockies. Likely, he also gained experience bringing up the rear of Ernie's pack strings, making sure the animals survived Glacier's dizzying mountain trails that switchbacked up flower-strewn hillslopes and clung to limestone ledges.[6] He may also have met a few of Glacier's park rangers, whose duties included looking for poachers, fighting fires, checking on the packers, and posing for tourists. Experience with stock in mountainous terrain was a prerequisite for the job, whether in the national parks or the newly designated national forests, and the chance to work outdoors appealed to many young men. Perhaps it was in Glacier's high alps that Brandy first considered spending a life in the mountains. He returned first to Minnesota to complete his high school education, staying in Bemidji with his older brother Carl and his wife, Pearl Sanderson. There he met Pearl's brother Stanley Sanderson, who worked as a national forest ranger at a remote outpost at the foot of the Rockies south of Glacier. Brandy asked about job possibilities, and after returning to the farm in Henning in January 1914, he received a letter from Stanley offering work as a laborer that summer.

Sanderson's Lewis and Clark National Forest encompassed three million acres of wild country athwart the spine of the Rocky Mountains, forming the headwaters of the eastward-draining Sun, Teton, and Marias rivers as well as the uppermost reach of the Flathead River, part of the Columbia system. Only two other forested regions in the Rockies compared to it in sheer wild grandeur— the Shoshone-Yellowstone country of northwest Wyoming and the Bitterroot–Salmon River mountains in Idaho.[7]

Controlling fire loomed high on the rangers' task list. The three million–acre conflagration of 1910, although centered in northern Idaho, also burned through extensive areas in the upper Flathead and added to the sense of urgency. The job of devising a fire-control plan for the forest fell to ranger E. A. Woods, who called for a network of trails, backcountry cabins, telephone lines, and observation sites, linked together to permit rapid reporting and triangulation of fires. Absent proper lookout cabins and towers, many fire spotters lived out of tents and performed their duties atop crude observation platforms perched improbably upon lopped-off trees.

Woods needed men to build this infrastructure, prompting Sanderson's letter to Brandborg. Early in the summer of 1914 Brandy rode the Great Northern back to Montana, making his way from East Glacier Station to the Lewis and Clark's headquarters in the small town of Choteau. He was assigned to Sanderson's ranger station below Ear Mountain, an imposing limestone wedge visible for miles to the east. There he set to work stringing thirty miles of telephone line up from Choteau as well as constructing trails in the mountains. Years later Sanderson told Brandy's son, Stewart, that he had laid his father off twice that summer, but Brandy, having nothing else to do, simply returned to the mountains and continued building trails. The young worker returned to headquarters at the end of the season to collect his pay.[8]

During that first summer Brandy fell in with several young men from the Choteau area who also had Forest Service jobs, including two brothers, Duff and Frank Jefferson, who lived on a horse ranch along the Sun River. "They were great horsemen, tremendous horsemen," Brandy told Mavis McKelvey in 1975. "And Duff, especially, talked to me a lot about horsemanship." Brandy listened and learned, developing his skills and cultivating a love for fine riding stock. The two men practiced their cowboy skills while riding the foothills to check on livestock, roping calves out of sight of their owners. On one of these jaunts they decided to emulate the Montana cowboy artist Charlie Russell by lassoing a black bear. "I got the rope on the bear, first," Brandy remembered. "I'd no sooner got him around the neck than my horse started to buck. Duff was hollerin' for me, he was a real cowboy, he was hollering for me to keep pulling and everything else, which I did." Jefferson managed to get a rope on the bear's hind leg and "choked him down until we just about caught him out." After they released their hold, "the bear just laid there for a while, and took off."

Years later, Brandy attributed his chronically painful knees to stunts such as this. Further damage probably occurred at the rodeo grounds in the neighboring town of Augusta, where the boys sometimes put their talents on display. At that time the Forest Service included a number of former frontiersmen within its ranger corps, whose horsemanship and woodcraft counted more than a college degree. Still, the agency wanted its new crop of rangers to be grounded in the fundamentals of forest and range management. In January 1915, after spending part of the winter at home, Brandy enrolled in the Forest Service's ranger school in Missoula, which had opened the previous year as an adjunct to the School of Forestry at the State University of Montana (then known as MSU).[9]

The three-month program was headed by Dorr Skeels, dean of the forestry school, who was assisted by several university faculty and Forest Service supervisors and ranger staff. Classes were held in a two-story building on campus known as "the old shack" and covered such topics as silviculture, forest mensuration and inventory, botany, civil engineering, range science, and animal husbandry. Brandy bunked with the Jefferson brothers and Stanley Sanderson at the University Apartments west of campus, throwing their sheepherder beds and camp gear on the floor and paying for room and board by working in local restaurants.

Dean Skeels, Brandborg recalled in 1975, emphasized the social utility of good forestry, instructing his students that the public's forests should be managed for the benefit of ordinary citizens, not large corporations. "He always used to tell us that Lincoln said, that the government of the United States is a foster child of the special interests, capitalists, and manufacturers of the United States. Not the true government of the people." Skeels brought in a lecturer from Germany who told of the land abuses that had occurred in Europe and cautioned them that the same despoliation could happen here unless the public and its appointees were on guard. The dean took a close interest in the young Forest Service men, Brandy recalled, believing them to be the real force for better land management.[10]

Such sentiments were also common among the ranger staff of the Lewis and Clark, whose conversations often turned to the ideals of the Forest Service's founder. "My God, all they were talking about was Gifford Pinchot and the direction and leadership that he was giving," Brandy recalled. President Taft had dismissed Pinchot in 1910, but his former employees still referred to him as the chief, and his influence on the Forest Service remained profound. Many Progressives regarded the agency as a bulwark against the monopolistic tendencies of the nation's timber and railroad interests. "We were lectured on that to no end," Brandy remembered.[11] His father had primed him for this lesson, which stuck somewhere deep in his psyche. For the remainder of his career he assumed that his primary duty was to improve social conditions in forest-dependent communities, and not necessarily by making resources available to industry. Pinchot's Progressivism advocated both agendas, but Brandborg always placed the former first.

His schooling gained him a formal appointment as a forest guard on the Lewis and Clark beginning June 1, 1915, marking the start of his forty-year career with the Forest Service (not counting his summer as a temporary laborer). He was assigned to a ranger station on the South Fork of Dupuyer Creek, to which

Stanley Sanderson had been transferred. This outpost lay at the eastern edge of the forest where the Rocky Mountains gentled down to the plains amid the gravelly outpourings of vanished glaciers. Immediately to the west rose the stair-stepped limestone cliffs of the Rocky Mountain Front, through which ran the only trails to the interior. Brandy's duties that summer sometimes kept him near the station repairing pack saddles, roofing buildings, herding lost cows and horses, or scaling timber at the sawmill on Dupuyer Creek, but soon he packed for greater adventures in the backcountry, riding into a wilderness that stretched for fifty miles to the west.

The mountain interior presented new challenges for the young recruit, since the fledgling agency, stretched thin in the vast woods of the Northern Rockies, expected its personnel to be highly self-reliant. Brandy worked out of field camps for much of the season, helping to build cabins, repair and improve trails, and haul supplies to fire lookouts. His usual route led into the South Fork of Birch Creek via a seven thousand–foot pass and a descent down a corrugated ridge known as Bloody Hill. At the head of the South Fork, another pass intervened before the rider entered the enormous basin of the Middle Fork of the Flathead River, then known as the Big River. A short distance below the pass the forest parted to reveal Big River Meadows, a grassy expanse where he and his coworkers built a log cabin that served as a base of operations for decades.

Even as late as 1915 the pioneer era lingered on in the Big River country. Lacking the stunning alpine peaks that drew tourists to Glacier, these mountains remained the domain of a handful of trappers, hunters, and woodsmen who enjoyed plenty of solitude—not the most welcome gift for an eager young man. At one evening's lonely campfire in Big River Meadows, Brandy's thoughts were on a certain Choteau girl with whom he had struck up a friendship. He described the scene in his 1975 interview with Mavis McKelvey: "I was just cooking supper, and I saw my horses throwin' their heads up, lookin' up the meadow—there was a bend in it. So I thought, well, there must be somebody up there. And I was sure pleased, because I was getting to think I—Well, I had a girl outside the mountains too, you know, a telephone operator, and I was thinkin' about her and getting out of the mountains."[12]

His visitor was a veteran woodsman named Griff Jones, who E. A. Woods had mentioned was in the area. Woods had described Jones (Brandy recalled) as "a tremendously large man, he's got a big white flowing mustache, a man with the longest arms you've ever seen." The old trapper was known to procure his meat whenever he needed it, and not necessarily in season; Woods advised Brandy to overlook these transgressions. Indeed, when Jones introduced himself that evening, he offered a fresh deer liver for their meal. While Brandy baked Dutch-oven biscuits over the coals, "Griff had cut the liver, and it was ready to fry. Never said a word, got the skillet, and put the skillet on the fire, and fried the liver. And boy was that wonderful."

Ranger Woods, realizing that a young man could have a tough time back in this country, had asked Jones to be on the lookout for Brandy. After spending the night in camp, Jones asked if Brandy would like to come along while he checked his trapline. He accepted eagerly and followed the woodsman as they headed up the trail. "I think we'd gone a mile or so," Brandy remembered, when "he turned around and asked me what I'd seen. I didn't know what he was talkin' about. So, he said, 'Did you see this? Did you see that?' And he told me what he'd observed, walking up that trail."

They came to a well-used game trail that led down to a small slough. "He said, 'Have you ever been down to that elk lick?' And I said, no, I hadn't. I didn't know that was an elk lick. He said, 'Now, you've gotta look at these things, see, find out what they mean.'" Jones led the way down to a blind he had improvised out of some stacked logs. After watching the animals for an hour, he told Brandy, "'Let's get up and spook 'em.' So we jumped up and started hollering, and I didn't know what he meant by him spookin' 'em, but I found out, and now I know."

Jones, like many such men, moved in and out of the Rocky Mountains' shadows, sometimes running traplines in the interior of the range, other times raising cattle on ranch land he rented near Dupuyer. He was sixty-seven years old when he met Brandborg, had never married, and was a well-known character in the villages of Pondera County. Griff's long arms had connected with more than one unfortunate man in Dupuyer and nearby towns. County sheriff Carl Embody remembered that "anyone who said a word contrary to Griff's got it. That was when Griff was in his glory as a fighting man."[13] Fortunately, Jones took a liking to young Brandy, tutoring him in the intricate workings of the natural world. "Everyplace he went, so long as he was in the country, back there picking up traps, I was with him," Brandy recalled. "I just learned so much, about living in that kind of an environment."

Brandborg returned to ranger school early in 1916 to complete his formal training. It was the last time he would take college-level classes, although he valued education highly and later served on the Montana Board of Education, which oversaw the state's public schools and university system. The technical aspects of forestry that he learned under Dorr Skeels were of less interest to him than social policy: Pinchot's future rangers and foresters were taught that their job was not simply to control cattle and sell logs; they were to be vanguards in a national effort to bring better conditions of life to all Americans. Timber on the stump and meat on the hoof were vital resources, to be sure, but the rangers' greater mission was to prevent the undesirable social consequences that accompanied unbridled exploitation of forests and rangelands.

Pinchot was careful to distinguish proper use from preservation, which he felt represented waste the nation could not afford. "I am not a preserver of trees. I am a cutter down of trees," he told the delegates to the 1905 American Forest Conference in Washington, D.C. "It is the essence of forestry to have trees harvested when they are ripe, and followed by successive crops.... Yet it by no means follows that the face of the land shall be denuded, so that the character of the watersheds shall be altered, with the resulting injury to streams and to agricultural lands depending upon them."[14]

It made sense to Brandborg, with his Midwest farm background, to consider commodity production and protection of the land as fully compatible. His fellow rangers, he recalled, "had the same sense, the same attitude, the same ethics towards resources and land" that he had learned. He would retain for the rest of his life a faith in the ability of conscientious land managers to produce vital goods while leaving the landscape and watershed intact. This respectful interplay between man and the land would advance human culture, which, he would come to believe, was conservation's ultimate purpose.

Following his second winter at ranger school, Brandborg returned to his patrol duties in the Big River country. That fall he took the agency's ranger exam, which was held at the forest headquarters in Choteau. This consisted of a written test and brief oral examination with the forest supervisor, followed by a demonstration of his ability to handle livestock and pack a horse. Duff Jefferson had tipped him off that he was to be given a particularly high-strung animal, so Brandy was prepared for the worst as he roped it and managed to slip a halter over its head. "I could see he was snorty," he recalled, "so I led him over to where they wanted me to pack, and I was wearing a jacket, so I just pulled my jacket off, and tied it over his eyes and head, and that was all there was to it." He passed the exam, and on October 20, 1916, he received his assignment as district ranger on the Helena National Forest at its Glendale station, located on the east slope of the Elkhorn Mountains, 120 miles to the south. Years later Brandy told his family that the news "made my heart soar like the eagle." He rode south from Choteau with a second horse in tow, following the edge of the Rockies to Radersburg, a mining camp at the edge of the Elkhorn's dry, windswept foothills.

In 1866 miners fanning out from the workings around Helena discovered placer gold in creek beds east of the Elkhorns, inaugurating a busy new mineral district. The camps along Crow Creek consolidated into a more permanent village, which was named after Reuben Rader, a nearby rancher who donated land for the townsite. By the time Brandborg arrived, ore production from the district was at its peak, supporting a general store, school, horse stables, and a hotel. Stockmen opened ranches along lower Crow Creek, pasturing large herds of sheep and cattle in the extensive open foothills of the Elkhorns.[15]

The Glendale Ranger Station, located under a limestone cliff where Crow Creek exited the mountains, administered a grazing-oriented district with only an occasional small timber sale to supervise. Brandy and his fellow rangers worked assiduously to win the ranchers' respect and support while trying to forestall overgrazing. Brandy seemed to relish this task, and with his love of riding he spent considerable time monitoring the allotments. In later years he would point to his successors' work on the Crow Creek allotment as an example of how cooperative relations with stock growers could promote better range conditions. Today these slopes support flourishing grass and forb communities, providing important winter range to a large elk herd.[16]

America's entry into the European war cut into the forest's manpower while simultaneously increasing demand for beef and wool. Brandy's logbooks for 1917 and 1918 record difficulties with controlling excessive grazing and lack of support from the forest headquarters.[17] He received his own draft call in June 1918. Assigned to Camp Lewis, Washington, he worked his way into a job breaking horses and supervising the clearing of a firebreak around the camp. He returned to the Glendale station following his discharge in March 1919, never having served overseas.

While stationed at Glendale, Brandy partook in the social life available in Radersburg and in the county seat of Townsend, where he joined the Masonic fraternity. He also met his first serious love interest. The rangers' telephone line led to a switchboard at Charles R. Stevenson's general store in Radersburg, whose daughters Edna and Mary homesteaded at Lone Mountain south of town. Edna was an accomplished rider, according to Stewart Brandborg, and she had an easy laugh and an appreciation for the sundry characters that did business at the store. Brandy was likewise a playful, jovial fellow, yet in his ranger uniform he made a good impression when on errands in town. The year their romance blossomed is not recorded, but by the early 1920s he was making trips with Edna to her Lone Mountain homestead. Edna had a young child of her own, Becky, by a previous marriage.

Two years later Brandy was promoted to assistant supervisor of the Helena National Forest, necessitating a move to Montana's Queen City. He continued to focus on grazing matters, spending many days in the field examining range conditions and counting cows. In April 1924 he was transferred to the Nezperce National Forest, headquartered in Grangeville, Idaho. Here he would continue to ride the range in the dry hills above the Salmon and Snake rivers, gaining further experience in dealing with the diverse people who made their living directly from the land. The move prompted Guy to propose to Edna, and they were married in Butte on their way to Idaho. Edna gave birth to their own child, Stewart, the following February, while Brandy adopted Becky in 1926. Edna's ranch remained in the family, although they would never again live on the east side of the Rockies. Henceforth the Brandborgs would live at the edges of another great wilderness region—the Selway River country—a landscape that would enthrall Brandy and motivate much of his conservation work.

CHAPTER 3

From the Snake to the Selway

1924–1935

The Nezperce National Forest, one of four created out of the original Bitter Root reserve, stretched across the entire width of north-central Idaho, begin-ning in the sunbaked depths of Hells Canyon on the Snake River and culminat-ing in the lofty mountain headwaters of the Selway River far to the east. More than a vertical mile separated the Snake from the dark crags of the bordering Seven Devils Mountains, from which the land plunged again into the canyon of the lower Salmon River, one of the Snake's main tributaries. Close by this pre-cipitous topography lay the town of Grangeville, a service center for wheat farm-ers and cattle ranchers living in the broad upland called Camas Prairie. The town also served the mining camps of Elk City and Dixie in the mountains to the east, both of which enjoyed boom times during the nineteenth century before settling into desultory attempts at ore production. The Brandborgs would spend almost eleven years in Grangeville, Brandy's duties taking him down to the grasslands along the Snake and into the most remote parts of the Bitterroot Range. Within this wilderness he and Edna introduced their children to Idaho's breathtaking mountain peaks, rushing streams, and subalpine lakes—experiences that would shape their understanding of one of the West's wildest landscapes.

J. B. Leiberg, who surveyed the Bitter Root reserve in 1898 for the U.S. Geo-logical Survey, described the western slope of the Bitterroot Range as "a vast mass of curving, winding, peak-crowned spurs constituting the watersheds of the Clearwater basins…a perfect maze of bewildering ridges."[1] The vertical extent of these mountains—beginning at less than two thousand feet along the Salmon and lower Selway rivers to more than nine thousand feet at their summits—created a wide array of forest types, from grasslands interspersed with ponderosa pine along the stream bottoms to subalpine fir and whitebark pine on the high divides. The handful of forest rangers in charge of this region had a vast territory to patrol, their paths typically following ancient Indian travel routes such as the Lolo Trail, which for centuries was the main hunting and trading route for Nez Perce and Flathead (Salish) Indians.

The equally steep but much drier topography south and west of Grangeville was mostly a stockman's province, with as many as fifty-five thousand sheep and six thousand cattle grazing its grassy flats and mountain meadows. Brandborg often drew the pleasant springtime duty of inspecting these extensive rangelands, riding fine five-gaited horses supplied by his employer. During these tours he would stop by the region's scattered ranches to discuss range conditions and point out the forest's administrative requirements, sometimes staying for a dinner of rich Snake River sturgeon. On one of these visits he acquired a bridle studded with silver coins, a memento of seemingly idyllic times.[2]

As on the Helena, a cooperative approach proved most effective with forest users. Ranchers' associations sometimes complained about grazing restrictions and fees, and occasionally a dispute over allotment boundaries would require the attention of supervisor Leon Hurtt or his successor, Roy Phillips. Years later Brandy recalled how "whistling Roy," who became his boss in 1928, would assume a humble attitude and not profess to know all the answers regarding range use or protecting wildlife habitat. Phillips backed up his rangers in disputes, preferring to let them "sit pretty much as judge, present each case, and give the decision that he thought was just and proper."[3] Although Brandy learned much from Phillips and other experienced hands such as Tom Lommasson of the district office in Missoula, he brought his own enthusiastic good nature to his interactions with stockmen, sportsmen, and other forest users.

Brandborg's notebooks from the period, though not extensive, show his belief in the agency's role in weighing competing uses and ensuring that none harmed the land. "Forest administration provides for control and regulated use," one entry reads. "Only by this method [will] forage, timber, water, wildlife, continue to yield their benefit to mankind. If various controls had not been established we would have endangered our existence years ago." Sportsmen, he observed, were able to enjoy Idaho's tremendous wildlife resources because of regulations put in place to maintain game and fish populations. Most residents of the state, while generally deeply conservative, accepted some encumbrances upon their freedom in order to protect their wild heritage. The particulars would be hotly debated, though, especially when it came to preserving large areas of wilderness in the central part of the state.

As his family settled into life in Grangeville, Brandy tried to expand the townspeople's understanding of forestry and grazing issues. A favorite method was to hold informal discussion forums at which he would present his views on conservation practices. He also was elected to the local school board, an interest that would expand in the coming years to encompass citizen training and education in many fields. The Forest Service in the 1920s still bore Gifford Pinchot's evangelistic fervor, a quality Brandy exhibited even more than most of his colleagues.

It was still a close-knit outfit, too, especially in an isolated town such as Grangeville. The entire permanent staff of the Nezperce numbered only fourteen individuals, which shrank to eleven during the Depression years. The men and their families played cards with each other, attended community dances, and headed into the nearby hills for summer picnics. Dorothy McConnell, the wife of district ranger Earl McConnell, recalled Brandy's ardent personality in a letter to Mavis McKelvey. "Anyone who met him never forgot him," she wrote. "He was very hearty, bluff, was always making jokes, particularly practical jokes."[4]

As soon as Stewart was old enough to ride, the family took summertime horse-packing trips into the lake basins of the Seven Devils Mountains. To reach the mountains involved a long descent down the hairpin switchbacks of the White Bird Grade, then, after crossing the Salmon River, following another steep track into the high country. "I recall very distinctly the long rides up that road," Stewart said recently, "with our dog Bob, the old Model T boiling, and the very, very narrow circuitous route on those bald hills where you knew that if the car rolled it wouldn't stop for a thousand or two thousand feet."[5] The trails into the Seven Devils were equally precarious, with thrilling views of the canyon beneath one's knees. The family also took spring and fall outings along the Salmon River to fish and hunt small game; during the summer's heat the tall forests of the Clearwater River offered campouts by its deep, clear pools.

The Clearwater, formed from the confluence of the mountain-spun Lochsa and Selway rivers, was also the locus of the region's burgeoning timber industry.

Harvests of valuable white pine were coming out of the river's North Fork, where the Clearwater Timber Company, part of the great Weyerhaeuser lumber empire, was logging on private lands. Springtime log drives down the North Fork to the main stem of the Clearwater began in 1927 to supply the company's new mill at Lewiston. White pine was scarce on the Nezperce, but the forest did support an estimated 5 billion board feet of merchantable ponderosa pine, lodgepole pine, and Douglas fir—enough to supply a large mill on the annual growth alone, the agency calculated, if the trees could be brought to market.[6] Lacking both roads and strong demand, the forest was able to offer only occasional small sales in more accessible areas. Brandborg thus had little exposure to the timber side of the agency's operations during those years.

These stands, meanwhile, were susceptible to loss from insects, disease, and especially fire. The west slope of the Bitterroot Range bred frequent thunderstorms as Pacific moisture drifted into the warm interior valleys; what rangers most feared were the dry lightning storms that sparked fires but brought little rain. Rising afternoon winds could fan even small fires into dangerous, unpredictable blazes. Such conditions gave the Nezperce the reputation as the most fire-prone forest in Region 1. During the 1920s lightning strikes accounted for as many as a hundred fires every summer on the Nezperce, according to Brandborg's notes, although the forest guards held most of the burns to an acre or less.

Better roads, more trails, and an expanded system of lookouts were the only solution. When Brandborg arrived on the forest, crews were improving the wagon road along the South Fork of the Clearwater to Elk City, but no funds were allocated for construction in other parts of the forest.[7] To reach the ranger station at Red River Hot Springs in the South Fork's headwaters required a twelve-hour drive by truck along sixty miles of rough road. Ranger stations and lookouts farther into the Selway could be reached only by trail. To supply these outposts Brandy would head out on weeklong patrols during the summer and fall on his favorite horse, Sage King, taking with him the thick Swedish bedroll his mother had given him—"damn near half a load for a mule," Stewart recalls. With his friend Clyde Blake, the forest's fire-control officer, he would help erect sturdy four-posted lookout towers and cabins to complete the overlapping network of lookout stations. By the end of 1930 Blake's crews had erected twenty-five of these structures, some assembled from prefabricated kits packed in from a Forest Service warehouse in Spokane, others crafted from the timber at hand. Supplementing these were twenty lookout trees—mere arboreal platforms left over from the early days.[8] When assisting Blake with cabin construction, Brandy employed the painstaking Swedish log-scribing method he had learned as a youth in Minnesota. He and Blake engaged in friendly competition to see who could be most useful, whether by getting up first to make the morning coffee or hewing a log and swinging it into position.

Smoke chasers were kept busy during the parched summer of 1929, when the Bald Mountain fire in the Lochsa River drainage burned through 30,000 acres of the adjacent Selway National Forest. Another severe season in 1931 saw Brandy and Clyde Blake rescuing a trapped firefighter on Blacktail Mountain at the edge of the national forest east of Grangeville. District forester[9] Evan W. Kelley, whom chief Robert Stuart had assigned to Missoula specifically to prevent a repeat of the disastrous blowup of 1910, understood that early detection and rapid response offered the only hope of controlling fires during the region's periodic dry summers. "Major" Kelley, as he was known in tribute to his work with the French Engineer Corps during World War I, sought to sharpen his agency's response times by instilling thorough training and discipline in his men.[10]

William R. "Bud" Moore, a longtime Forest Service officer who began his career in 1935 as a seasonal employee on the Powell District of the Lolo National Forest, wrote in his book *The Lochsa Story* that "Kelley tolerated no mediocre performance" and required an in-depth review of each fire that his field crews were not able to put out immediately. Moore recalled recently that Kelley would sometimes show up at his ranger station unannounced to check on the men and that "a certain amount of fear was part of his management technique."[11] Kelley immediately pushed for infrastructural improvements to aid firefighting efforts, notably the construction of crude truck roads deep into the Selway backcountry. These generally followed ancient Nez Perce migratory trails that the Forest Service had cleared out and signed for packers. First to be completed was the Lolo Trail road, which bounced along the ridges north of the Lochsa River through topography that had nearly defeated the Lewis and Clark expedition.

The second route roughly followed the aboriginal trade and hunting route that led from the southern Bitterroot Valley over Nez Perce Pass and descended into the upper Selway. Forest Service planners had long sought a road to connect Elk City with the Bitterroot Valley; the journey by car involved a lengthy trip through Wallace, Idaho. Construction of a narrow truck trail along the Nez Perce route began in 1920; by 1936 workers from the Civilian Conservation Corps (CCC) camp on the West Fork of the Bitterroot River met crews working from Elk City near Observation Point, completing the long-sought connection.[12] The road was named after Lloyd Magruder, a packer who was murdered with his companions in 1863 while returning to Lewiston from the gold diggings at Bannack, Montana. The Magruder road split in two the largest remaining wildland expanse in the Lower 48, a stronghold of lonely forests and wild rivers that stretched from the Sawtooth Range to the mining camps of Coeur d'Alene.

Another severe fire season hit the Selway during the dry and windy summer of 1934. Early in the morning of August 11, lightning storms started nineteen small fires in the lower Selway and Lochsa drainages. Major Kelley's forces reacted as they had been drilled: lookouts spotted the fires within hours and smoke chasers were dispatched. Even with the new truck trails, though, most of the fires had to be located by crews on foot or horseback. Several were already burning through deadfall and dry brush, too hot to put out with shovels and moving too fast to encircle with fire lines. Before long embers were wafting over the firefighters' heads, forcing retreat. Within the first day two major fires, one in the drainage of Pete King Creek and another near McLendon Butte, had spread to more than 9,000 acres. Word quickly reached Brandy, who was enjoying a camping vacation with his family along the Clearwater River. He reported to the nearby Fenn Ranger Station and was assigned to head a team based at the Pete King Station, located a short distance above the Selway-Lochsa confluence. Edna took Becky and Stewart home to Grangeville; they would not see their father for a month.

On August 17 adverse winds blew the fires out of control, merging the two largest blazes and burning an additional 53,000 acres in a single day. Onlookers as far away as Spokane and Walla Walla, Washington, observed the smoke column reaching 40,000 feet in the sky to the east.[13] Survival, not control, was on the minds of the men struggling underneath it. At the Pete King Station, the rising afternoon wind blew firebrands across the Lochsa and started spot fires on the slopes above them. Brandy assembled a hundred men to go after the new blazes, but the fire quickly coalesced and locked them in a battle for their lives. The crews set backfires to consume the intervening timber and wet down the buildings using gasoline-powered Pacific pumps, each capable of shooting thirty-eight gallons per minute of river water. They saved the station and lost no men, but their efforts had no effect on the fire's course.

At the fire's peak more than five thousand men were clearing lines and providing support, many of them civilians who had been working on blister rust–control projects in Idaho under the National Industrial Recovery Act (NIRA). It was, according to B. A. Anderson, Brandy's successor on the Nezperce, "the largest body of organized firefighters ever employed on a single fire in the history of the Forest Service."[14] But even with these resources the inferno continued until the start of fall rains in the third week of September. In all, 252,250 acres burned. "I remember when he [the elder Brandy] finally got home," Stewart recalled. "He filled the bathtub, and I'd never seen the bathtub filled right to someone's chin."

Major Kelley convened a review board in Missoula that September to determine what, if anything, could have been done. Attending was the chief of the agency's fire-control division, Roy Headley, who advised Ferdinand Silcox (the new chief forester) to double firefighting expenditures, if necessary, to "keep every acre green," as he put it. New tools such as aerial attack with water and retardant, which had been used experimentally on the Pete King fire, offered hope of more complete control, and Headley believed that the rewards in preserving timber and watersheds justified the expense.[15]

But throwing untrained men at large fires, according to Brandborg, would solve nothing. Following the Selway burn he was placed in charge of a review board consisting of the assistant supervisors from the Clearwater, Nezperce, and Lolo national forests, along with Clarence Sutliff, a senior ranger involved in the fire. They concluded that agency manpower had been stretched thin fighting other fires in the region and that the fast-spreading Selway blazes simply overwhelmed the tired, often inexperienced firefighters. They cited "long hours of exhaustive physical and mental strain" as well as "moving men to new sectors or even assignment to new fires, always keeping them on hot-line work, with no opportunity to relax. Men working in this condition eventually become little more than robots and [are] not sufficiently productive." They faulted the regional office for not providing the manpower they had requested before August 11 and said that the untested NIRA workers and CCC youths were not up to the task. "After a few days on the Selway lines," the reviewers wrote, "crews reached that stage of physical exhaustion where all efforts...were directed towards maintenance of a too often mere pretense of work."[16]

Some officials in the regional office viewed the report as a whitewash; exhausted or not, their men were expected to throw everything they had at a fire. But Brandborg was inclined to back his employees. He cited "a tremendous volume of increasing activities and projects managed by an ever decreasing permanent Forest overhead. Forest officers are buried under a mass of problems incident to project management." He wanted to see better staff training before the fire season began—a theme that he would continue to propound throughout his career. He cited the "false economy" of keeping too few skilled hands available on staff. In a truly efficient organization, "the chief in charge of the fire project will not be required to hunt for able assistants, camp bosses, timekeepers and sector foremen when the second-line defense moves in. Nor will camp bosses and superintendents spend valuable time searching for saw-filers, tool sharpeners, and kitchen help." As he assumed positions of greater responsibility, Brandborg defended the lower ranks of the organization against what he perceived as a bureaucratic structure that tended to lose sight of on-the-ground needs.

The Selway disaster, coming after severe burns in the Pacific Northwest the year before, led Silcox to look for ways to prevent more unmanageable blowups that threatened the safety of his firefighters as well as the forest. In 1935 he and his staff promulgated the so-called 10 a.m. policy, which stressed early attack and control of all fires by the morning following their discovery. Field personnel would report their progress each day, with the objective of control by the following morning, not at some distant date. Some officials wanted to take a more situational response, but the new policy served to ratify Major Kelley's emphasis on quick fire control. It seemed to work: over the next quarter century, the Northern Region stopped any single fire from spreading over more than 41,000 acres.[17]

Brandborg readily assented to the Service-wide obsession with halting wildfire. At the time neither he nor the regional office leadership understood the lasting consequences of this policy for the land and for Forest Service budgets. It would take almost forty years after the Pete King debacle before a handful of pioneering officials (including Bud Moore, the Lochsa River veteran) would introduce a new policy allowing some wildfires to burn under limited conditions in the Selway wilderness. Until then, Major Kelley's full-attack program would set the direction for the entire region. Within the remote Selway and Lochsa country, rangers and road crews would replace the old Indian trails with truck routes, knock down trappers' cabins to build new ranger stations, and create outposts of civilization in what had been a dark and sometimes dangerous woods.

Brandy's narrow escape from the Pete King fire brought his season's work in the Selway country to a close, but he would have many more occasions to return. That fall Major Kelley promoted him to supervisor of the adjacent Bitterroot

National Forest, headquartered in Hamilton, Montana, across the mountains in the beautiful Bitterroot Valley. A good portion of the Selway River drainage would go with him, transferred over with the dissolution of the Selway National Forest that year. He would continue to enjoy horseback travels along the stony ridges of the Bitterroot Range and make camps among its sheltering pines, growing steadily more attached to the pleasures of primitive travel in this huge, undeveloped country. In the years to come he would join the ranks of those who protested the coming of modern ways to these remote mountain basins.

For now, Kelley wanted him to get a handle on livestock use around the margins of the Bitterroot Valley, applying his long experience working with ranchers to improve range conditions both on and off the forest. He would take charge at the start of the new year. His agency's mission was evolving, however, and Brandy would increasingly be dealing with new resource development goals—an assignment that would take him beyond building trails, constructing lookouts, and riding herd on wool growers. While on the Bitterroot, he and his employees would enter the modern age of road building, timber cutting, and increasing recreational use of the forest. Many of his colleagues were eager to ride this new trail, but for Brandy and his closest associates, these changes portended a dangerous shift from the ideals he had embraced when he first came to Montana.

CHAPTER 4

Protection Forest

1935–1939

The move to Hamilton brought the Brandborgs to Montana's lovely, pastoral Bitterroot Valley, one of the few places in the West where temperate agricultural land lay next to a large expanse of forested wilderness. The bold mountain front of the Bitterroot Range was punctuated by steep-walled canyons that funneled snowmelt down to irrigation works along the west side of the valley; hay fields on the more expansive but dryer east side were fed by streams flowing out of the Sapphire Range. Most of the flow of the Bitterroot River came from the mountainous headwaters to the south, which boasted no spectacular high crags yet were no less vital to the life of the valley. These waters helped valley ranchers and farmers escape the worst ravages of the Dust Bowl, which had brutally punished farmers and homesteaders east of the Rockies since the 1920s.

By 1935, according to historian Joseph Kinsey Howard, a fourth of Montana's population was on relief. Farm foreclosures were rising in the Bitterroot Valley, though, and more land was going vacant. Cattle rustling became prevalent, and forest rangers were on guard against unemployed men setting fires in order to procure temporary work.[1] Depression-era work programs such as the CCC and NIRA could ameliorate unemployment in the short term, but Brandborg's ultimate goal was to promote steady employment by maintaining all of the valley's forests, streams, and grasslands in their most productive condition. His national forest could offer a steady supply of forage, water, and wildlife, as well as wood products ranging from fence posts and corral logs to high-quality close-grained sawtimber. No resource yield could be sustained, however, if private ownerships were laid waste. Over the next two decades Brandborg would devote almost as much effort toward placing the Bitterroot's private lands on a more productive course as he lavished on his own jurisdiction.

On New Year's Day 1935 Brandy and Edna moved with their two children into the vacated home of John Lowell, the former forest supervisor. By June they had settled into their own home on South Third Street, in which the couple would spend the rest of their lives. Hamilton was a community of some two thousand residents whose businesses served the surrounding farms and small towns of the still rural Bitterroot Valley. Founded in the 1880s to house workers for Marcus Daly's sawmill and stock operations, it survived the mill's closure in 1915 and the end of a brief orchard boom, diversifying with government employment from the Forest Service and the Rocky Mountain Laboratory. The latter was a government-sponsored biological research facility initially set up to study Rocky Mountain spotted fever, which was endemic among the forest's considerable tick population. Over the years the "Lab," as it was called, attracted dozens of scientists to live in the Bitterroot's idyllic setting—some of whom would . number among Brandy's strongest allies in his conservation battles.

Major Kelley's charge to improve grazing practices on the forest was welcome to Brandy, who enjoyed riding the ranges as he had on the Nezperce and Helena forests. Meeting permittees on their own territory allowed him to explain how careful control of their herds would be profitable in the long run. Every operator who ran cattle or sheep on the national forest was subject to regulation and fees, but Brandborg believed that his responsibilities as a conservation leader did not stop at the forest boundary. "We tried to establish the fact in the stockmen's mind," he said in his 1975 interview, "that the continued overgrazing of either the national forest lands or the private lands outside of the national forest would be to their detriment. We established these pastures, and grazed them properly, and in the course of very few years, it was very easy to see the results of proper land use."[2]

He was fortunate to have the support of several prominent stockmen, including Stanley Antrim and Ed Reed from the northern end of the Bitterroot Valley, who had already organized a group called the Ravalli County Improvement

Association and were attempting to create a countywide soil-conservation district. They invited Brandy to attend their meetings, through which they induced ten Bitterroot Valley ranchers to cooperate in managing livestock numbers and grazing seasons on the forest allotments. These ranchers formed the nucleus for Brandy's decades-long efforts to promote agricultural land conservation in the Bitterroot Valley.

Not all questions of grazing use were easily resolved. Some operators would bring their herds or flocks up to the forest too early in the spring, when the ground was soft and grasses were insufficiently developed, or they might load on stock in excess of their allotment, trespass onto adjoining allotments, or leave their animals out too late in the fall. Range reform took a bit longer than Brandy seems to have recalled, as shown in a range examiner's photo taken in 1938 in the Burnt Fork drainage east of Stevensville. On one side of the fence, on private land, the grass grows lush and tall, while on the Forest Service side palatable grasses are grazed to the nub. This was the classic dilemma of the commons, in which there was greater incentive to overuse land belonging to all.

Sheep grazing had begun several decades before the forest reserves were established, when ranchers and drovers found ample business supplying Montana's busy mining camps. Competition for forage was keen, and ranges were quickly depleted. Some ranchers, such as Edgar Wetzsteon of the Bitterroot's East Fork, embraced Forest Service regulation of mountain pastures after they found themselves being edged out by herds from Marcus Daly's Bitterroot Stock Farm. Wetzsteon told range examiner K. D. Swan that "if it hadn't been for the Forest Service we'd been starved out."[3] But Major Kelley directed Brandborg to eventually phase out sheep use on the Bitterroot, reflecting an informal partitioning of Region 1 forests along the Continental Divide. Timber would take precedence on the west side, while forage for cattle and sheep would predominate on the forests to the east. Nature aided the reduction program in the 1920s and 1930s when a bark-beetle epidemic killed a high proportion of lodgepole pine in the high country. As the trees fell, they created interlocking piles that closed sheep driveways and made it difficult to utilize mountain pastures. Some valley ranchers turned to cattle for their livelihoods, while others, such as Stanley Antrim, continued raising sheep through the 1940s. During his twenty-year tenure as supervisor, Brandborg was able to reduce the number of sheep using the national forest by about thirty thousand, leaving only one band of about five hundred in Charles McDonald's Stevensville district, which was retired a few years after 1955.[4]

To offset the removal of sheep from the mountain ranges, Brandborg encouraged ranchers such as Antrim and Reed to improve their own pastures and to acquire and rehabilitate overused lands within the valley. He was joined in these efforts by several regional office staffers, including assistant regional forester Earl Sandvig (whom Brandy had met in the Elkhorns in the 1920s) and Leon Hurtt, his former boss from the Nezperce who went on to become a range inspector for Region 1. In the 1940s Hurtt directed a reseeding program in Reimel Creek in the lower East Fork that replaced a thistle-infested bottomland with rye, brome, and crested wheatgrass. "They saved the country from really eroding," recalled East Fork rancher John McClintic. All of these efforts benefited from Evan Kelley's strong support—a necessity when dealing with the politically powerful livestock industry. Sandvig recalled that "when we needed help and backing in a range reduction or similar problem the 'old man' was right behind us all the way. We got many things done without too much problem because of a positive approach."[5]

Brandy's efforts paid off; in 1949 range examiner Paul Roberts commended him and his rangers for "an outstanding piece of work in advancing range management both outside and inside the national forest." Roberts recalled a rangeland tour involving some 250 people during which rancher Edward O'Hare gave Brandborg "full credit for the imagination and vision that stirred him into buying tax delinquent lands and the reseeding of wornout sagebrush land." The result, Roberts said, was "a prosperous ranch of which he is very proud. He says Brandy showed him his duty to society; to convert unproductive to productive acres."[6] Brandy's exhortations on conservation practices annoyed some of the stockmen, but others recalled his efforts with respect. Antrim, in fact, would almost literally ride to Brandy's rescue in 1949, taking time from a sheep drive to defend his friend before a McCarthy-era investigative hearing.

In later years reformers such as Sandvig and McDonald ran into difficulties carrying out stock reductions and blamed the Forest Service's top leadership for lack of support—a problem Brandborg would also encounter with the timber program. He had found ways to improve and stabilize Ravalli County's agricultural sector so that ranchers were less dependent upon public pastures; he saw no reason this approach could not be applied to timber as well. When the Northern Region began to ramp up its logging program in the late 1940s and 1950s, a split quickly emerged between Brandy and other advocates of a locally based steady-state, rural agricultural economy and the backers of a new resource-production imperative that lent itself to rapid industrial expansion, increasing payrolls, and greater dynamism in employment. These were anathema to Brandborg, another manifestation of capitalism's uninterest in the cultural life and economic well-being of rural areas.

In the midst of regulating grazing, monitoring timber-stand conditions, and offering a variety of small timber sales, the Bitterroot paid what attention it could to other resources such as recreation and wildlife. The Forest Service had no statutory directive to promote recreational uses or safeguard wildlife habitat, but many of its personnel in Montana were anglers and hunters who understood the value of the state's outstanding trout streams and big-game herds. In 1933 the Bitterroot staff worked up a detailed plan for managing the forest's elk herds, which had doubled in size from an estimated six hundred animals in 1921. More elk were killed by predators than by hunters, it stated; neither, however, was subject to direct Forest Service control.

What the agency could do was to try to provide more winter range, particularly in the Skalkaho Creek and East Fork drainages where timber stands thinned out into grasslands. Here, too, lay conflicts with established grazing uses. Leon Hurtt noted during a range inspection of the East Fork in 1920 that in the early winter about a hundred head of elk would drift down from the higher forests into open, windswept slopes in the drainages of Tolan and Reimel creeks. "This band of elk furnish a great deal of sport and recreation for the upper Bitterroot," he wrote. "Precautions should be taken in allotting the range to allow them sufficient leeway. For this reason I feel that no effort should be made to fully utilize all the available sheep range on the East Fork."[7]

Reducing livestock grazing in the remote and politically conservative East Fork valley would prove to be a difficult undertaking, requiring decades of cooperative efforts among sportsmen, ranchers, and the state Fish and Game Department. Brandborg encouraged his district rangers to take the lead in these discussions, but he did not hesitate to offer his own views. Fred Wetzsteon, Edgar's brother, thought that Brandborg was too willing to favor sportsmen against the ranchers in pursuit of his range program. "He was playing one against the other, keeping [up] an agitation that could have been solved, but wasn't solved.... [I]t was always the stockman that did the most surrendering."[8]

Brandy, for his part, encouraged the stockmen to form cooperative grazing associations to work out disputes among themselves and consider larger issues such as wildlife. By 1941 Sula district ranger Arlen Gundersen was reporting success, but Brandy advised him that "aggressive follow-up" would be needed to keep the association moving forward. This was typical of his approach, which favored the common effort over laissez-faire individuality. Left to their own, Brandy feared, the East Fork ranchers would continue to maximize their herds to the detriment of range conditions, thus his constant agitating for better practices.[9]

Major Kelley's second charge to Brandborg was to protect the forest from fire. The Bitterroot's prized ponderosa stands and its high-elevation watershed forests must be guarded against the day (not long off, the foresters hoped) when they could be more fully utilized. Quick access, as always, was essential to fire-control efforts. Brandborg's staff plotted concentric outlines on maps to show how many hours crews would need to reach a fire in the backcountry. Delays mounted quickly in remote, steep terrain—time that was crucial to reach lightning-caused fires before they spread. Pack trails, guard stations, and lookouts in the backcountry were a first line of defense, but only by building new roads could they bring large portions of the forest within an hour's reach.

An ambitious plan drawn up by the West Fork district in 1935 envisioned roads up the entire lengths of Overwhich, Piquett, Blue Joint, and Chicken creeks, as well as a spur leading from the new truck trail over Nez Perce Pass to Castle Rock and on to the lookout station atop Bare Cone, with another route following the Idaho-Montana divide from Hughes Creek to the lookout at Blue Nose. These were to be built with federal Emergency Recovery Administration (ERA) funds, but when the money was not forthcoming, many of the planned roads had to be postponed. The wild country of the upper West Fork would remain largely undisturbed for another decade, although following the war Brandy would punch roads into a few of the drainages in order to broaden his timber-management base.[10]

Additional help came from the Civilian Conservation Corps, which employed younger, less experienced men in building roads, trails, lookouts, and bridges as well as fighting fires. The Bitterroot's first CCC camp opened in 1933 as a summertime operation based out of the Allen Ranger Station on the West Fork. A permanent camp was erected in 1938 at Trapper Creek, which operated until 1942. Its most notable project was to improve and extend the primitive truck trail over Nez Perce Pass and on toward Elk City. Both this and the Lolo Trail were bladed to a width of only seven feet, but that was enough to bring in fire crews and supplies in a hurry.[11]

The main Bitterroot massif remained the most serious barrier to reaching the Idaho interior. Pack trails extended up several canyons along the mountain front, including one in Blodgett Canyon that climbed over a high pass into the drainage of Big Sand Creek in the Lochsa River's headwaters. While reconstructing this trail around 1911, ranger Carl Weholt watched as his pack horses "clawed their way up the rock bluffs" past "the bleached bones of rolled animals" from previous hunting and trapping parties.[12] Firefighters' response times over such trails were counted in days, not hours. Blodgett Canyon did not appear suitable for a road, but a few miles farther south, the long, deep trench of Lost Horse Canyon offered better prospects. Glaciation had scoured the valley clear of major cliffs, and its location was convenient to the towns of Hamilton and Darby.

Work on the Lost Horse road began in the summer of 1934. Crews soon ran into huge rock fields that reached down the north face of the canyon clear to the creek bottom, necessitating arduous drilling and blasting to dislodge boulders that blocked the way. Major Kelley grew dissatisfied with the lack of progress and hoped that Brandborg would move things along. Brandy tapped thirty thousand dollars in federal ERA funds to hire the necessary labor and machinery for the project. Dynamiting a path through each rock slide required drilling an average of fifty shot holes for each blast, thirty blasts per slide. Excavating machines and Cletrac bulldozers were brought in to clear the route of rubble and trees. The project was one of the larger construction efforts valley residents had seen, bringing a welcome payroll to the Depression-struck county. Just supplying the commissary was an undertaking: an inventory of camp supplies listed "6 bales of flour, 3 sacks of graham flour, 9 lb. soda, 30# [lb.] rice, 80# ham, 60# bacon, 50 cans lard, 53 tins butter, etc."[13]

Construction continued through the 1936 and 1937 seasons. Kelley's plan was to take the road clear to the Bitterroot Divide along the Idaho-Montana border, enabling fire crews to disembark and follow trails westward into the upper drainages of Moose Creek and Bear Creek. Brandborg was reluctant to see a road go to the very top of the canyon, and as construction approached Twin Lakes, located in an attractive subalpine basin below the crest of the range, he halted work and ordered the equipment taken off. When F. E. Thieme, an assistant regional forester, discovered this during a project inspection in September 1937, he informed Brandborg that Major Kelley wanted the road finished to the upper lakes and on to the divide. Upon checking progress a month later, Thieme learned that no further work had been done, and he sent a terse memo to Brandborg asking why.

Brandy's response, which he sent directly to Kelley, was revealing. "I naturally assumed," he wrote, "that this project was like all other jobs in that it was my duty and responsibility to determine the most satisfactory and proper terminus." He had decided to halt the road a quarter mile below Twin Lakes, believing it offered a better parking site than up on the divide. But that was not all: "I considered if farther extension was to be made of the Lost Horse project, some very careful consideration should be given by landscape and recreational experts because of encroachment upon recreational possibilities around the upper lake before undertaking more work. I am sure you will agree that circumstances on the ground required such action."[14]

As a devoted backcountry horseman, Brandborg enjoyed riding in the remote Selway country lying beyond the Bitterroot crags. He was signaling his feeling that the high country ought not to be made too accessible to automobiles and the concentrated human use they would bring. It was a minor discrepancy from plans, but that was enough to touch off another curt note from Thieme, reminding him that he was to complete the project to the letter. Besides showing Brandborg's concern for recreational values (and for the newly designated Selway-Bitterroot Primitive Area, into which the road ran), here was an indication that he felt quite able to make decisions affecting his forest without interference from above. Brandy completed the road, but it would not be the last disagreement he would have with development-oriented individuals in the regional office.

The new road up Lost Horse Canyon would prove popular with campers and anglers in the Bitterroot Valley, but its deep incursion into wild country left some devotees of primitive travel feeling bereft. Ernst Peterson, a Hamilton writer and photographer, was one of the occasional folks who liked to shoulder a pack and head for the high country without benefit of automobile or even a horse and pack string. In September 1931, while still in high school, he and a buddy hiked the sixteen miles up the canyon, taking six days to savor "the sight of many elk, deer, and moose.... Around our campfires the fascination of this awe-inspiring country and our remoteness from civilization were embedded in our minds for a lifetime."[15]

Five years later Peterson returned to find his trail obliterated. "I was shocked by the realization of the drastic change this one road made in the Lost Horse drainage. The elk and deer had moved back deeper into the canyons. Local automobile-minded fishermen, eager to be in on the kill, had depleted the fish from

Twin Lakes. In one short year the beauties and the inspiration of that country had been destroyed." His was a minority view in 1936, but as the agency's road-building program continued, others would mount a more forceful opposition. Robert Marshall, the Forest Service's most frenetic wilderness explorer and conservationist, placed the Bitterroot Range high on his list of personal favorites. In 1927, while stationed at Idaho's Priest River Experiment Station, he experienced a frightening encounter near Grave Peak with a "colossal grizzly" that was defending its cubs, putting the indelible stamp of the primeval on this landscape.[16]

Such experiences were a prime reason Marshall wanted to set aside wild areas such as the Selway-Bitterroot. On July 3, 1936, following several years of Marshall's determined lobbying, acting chief Earle Clapp formally established the 1,875,300-acre Selway-Bitterroot Primitive Area, the nation's largest.[17] It stretched from Lolo Peak on its northeasternmost edge to the Salmon River on the south, enclosing the Magruder road, the Elk Summit road off of the Lochsa, and the new road coming up Lost Horse Canyon. Even with these incursions, it formed a magnificent wild region in which the Bitterroot Range's endless ridges and valleys dwarfed the foresters' efforts to render them accessible.

While the Selway primitive area designation pleased wilderness supporters, the regulation under which it had been established, known as L-20, left the specifics of management largely up to the regional foresters. Timber, forage, and water resources could still be developed, subject only to being "properly regulated," a decidedly loose standard. Irrigation dams had been built on many of the small lakes below the Bitterroot crest to regulate stream flows for valley ranchers, who had built primitive maintenance roads up the rocky canyons. On the other side of the crest, airstrips were bulldozed at several locations in the Selway drainage, allowing wealthy hunters and fishermen to access remote camps in the backcountry. All of these uses compromised the feeling of raw nature that Marshall and his supporters extolled, and foreshadowed the difficult decisions that lay ahead over the management of this area.

Brandy's duties included occasional inspection visits to the upper Selway; on some of these trips he would bring Stewart along, leaving him in the care of the CCC superintendent at Deep Creek camp. In the mid-1930s this outpost was becoming less isolated as road crews constructed a spur off the Magruder road down the Selway River to White Cap Creek. Stewart would watch from a safe distance as crews lit off a hundred sticks of dynamite at a time to blast open the rock faces along the river. He recalled recently that if World War II had not intervened, "that damn road would have gone right down the river to Selway

Falls."[18] If his father objected to the road construction at the time, no record remains in his files.

In the summer of 1937, while touring the western states, Bob Marshall undertook another of the prodigious day hikes for which he was known. After catching a ride to Paradise Guard Station along the Selway River, he set off up Canyon Creek to the Bitterroot Divide, then strolled down Boulder Creek to the West Fork Ranger Station—a mere forty-one-mile-long saunter, counting a lengthy diversion up White Cap Creek. The following day he paid a visit to the Brandborgs' home in Hamilton. Stewart, then twelve years old, listened to the enthusiastic conversation that was shared over Edna's dinner. "I remember [Marshall's] face still being as red as a beet," he recalled. "He was sunburned to the point of having cooked himself."[19]

Marshall had recently taken a position as director of recreation and lands in the agency's Washington office, where he had considerable influence over wilderness policy. Among the issues he likely discussed with Brandborg was the need to halt any further truck trails from sullying the Selway country. By then Brandy was coming to hold similar views on the need to protect wild country. He evidently impressed Marshall enough that he was one of five agency men Marshall listed as his possible replacement.[20] When Marshall died unexpectedly in November 1939, however, he was replaced by his assistant, fellow wilderness explorer John Sieker.

The Selway-Bitterroot Primitive Area was one of Marshall's greatest legacies in the Northern Rockies, an area in which the agency's "protection forest" concept generally took precedence over other uses. But for Evan Kelley, more roads such as the one up Lost Horse Canyon were needed for fire protection. His successors, moreover, eyed the vast timber stands within the primitive area and wondered why they should not be managed for production. Brandborg's resistance to this move, along with the opposition of a growing number of local sportsmen, hikers, and campers, would help trigger the clash over cutting practices across the entire Bitterroot National Forest. By the time of Marshall's visit, Brandy had come to believe that the art of primitive travel needed to be kept alive and that a growing society would find wilderness strongholds such as the Selway more useful than the timber they contained.

CHAPTER 5

Forests for the People

1937–1941

For all his interest in rangeland conservation, Brandborg displayed a Forest Service bias in advocating that Bitterroot Valley farmers grow trees on marginal lands instead of grain, hay, or cattle. Long-term forestry, he believed, would increase farm income and alleviate overproduction on lands ill-suited to heavy grazing. To outline the path toward permanent forestry on all ownerships, he recruited a local businessman named Warren Pollinger to make a comprehensive inventory of Ravalli County's forest stands—an approach parallel to the agency's Copeland Report, a nationwide evaluation of forest problems the Forest Service had prepared in 1933. Pollinger completed his report in 1939 and presented it to a joint committee of Congress during a public hearing on forest legislation in Portland, Oregon, that December.[1]

Pollinger stressed the close relationship between the forested lands of Ravalli County and the lives of its residents. With more than 127,000 acres of commercial timber land in private ownership within the county—nearly as much as on the national forest—how those stands were managed would have a major bearing on the valley's economy. More than 80 percent of the timber harvested in the valley came from large private owners such as Anaconda and the Northern Pacific—a situation he believed could not be sustained, as much of the cutover land had been left "in such a condition that a merchantable crop cannot be produced short of 150 years." The remaining private timber, Pollinger stated, would be exhausted in ten years. With the forest-product sector directly and indirectly supporting some nineteen hundred county residents, more effort was needed to acquire and restock those lands. He also called for more federal funds to administer national forest timber sales, promote the ongoing CCC program, and keep temporary employees such as firefighters on the payroll longer.[2]

Brandborg contributed heavily to Pollinger's report and adopted its goals as his own. In his talks to civic groups in Ravalli County, he warned that a disastrous economic dislocation would occur once Anaconda had cut through the old growth on its lands, leading to a repeat of the emptied-out towns and horrendous slash fires on cutover areas in the East. The key to avoid this, he felt, was greater oversight of cutting on private lands, preferably through regulation, or, if that was not possible, outright purchase. As radical as this approach may seem today, Brandy was not going it alone within his agency. The Forest Service had long promoted a sustained-yield program on private lands as a means of preventing the social ills that accompanied the cut-and-get-out timbering of the previous century. But where previous chiefs had emphasized voluntary cooperation from landowners, mostly by offering planning assistance, seedlings, fire protection, and similar help through the agency's State and Private Forestry branch, Ferdinand Silcox saw a stronger role for his agency. In his 1937 Christmas message to his employees, he called for new action to "revitalize the forest movement in relation to human beings." The nation's forested regions suffered from serious social problems, he said, citing low incomes, substandard housing, and poor education. "Forests are vital tools in the service of mankind and we, as foresters, must wield them," he insisted.[3]

Silcox's philosophy made its way into a special message that Franklin Roosevelt sent to Congress in 1938, in which the president called for new government measures to ensure continuous cropping on privately owned forest lands, greater public ownership of those lands, and, most controversially, creating "such public regulatory controls as will adequately protect private as well as the broad public interest in all forest lands."[4] FDR's support led to a Senate resolution in June 1938 that established a joint congressional committee to study the forest situation. This was the cue Silcox needed to promote his agenda. He detailed associate chief Earle Clapp to prepare a report for the committee, which was issued in June 1939 as a 296-page preliminary draft. Titled *A National Forest Economy: One Means to Social and Economic Rehabilitation,* it cited continuing unemployment, a "sick" agricultural sector, lowered national income, and "a paradox of serious want in the midst of plenty" as reasons to expand the federal forestry program.

Letting industry police itself had failed, Clapp and Silcox claimed. More than three-fourths of the nation's original stands of sawtimber were now gone, and current harvest levels exceeded annual growth by nearly one-half. "Forest industries are still steadily cutting out and closing down," they warned, "with a disastrous aftermath of unemployment, wrecked communities, and stranded populations." Preventing such dislocations through continued forest-related employment was essential and would provide "the opportunity for millions of people to escape degrading relief rolls and to regain and maintain self-respect," as well as to restore hope for young people who had been "trained for jobs which do not exist. Something to take boys off the streets and away from crime. The opportunity for a normal family life."[5]

Brandborg was no stranger to these concerns. He had rubbed shoulders with the footloose men of the logging camps of Idaho and western Montana long enough to know what a difficult life they led. He could not hire loggers directly, but he could employ young men and older, more experienced hands in the kind of work he had known early in his career, such as building trails, fighting fires, and stringing phone lines. He tried to find additional work for these seasonal employees during the fall and winter, ensuring them of a paycheck into the lean months. He formalized this effort in early 1939 by writing a comprehensive employment plan for the forest, which he described as "an earnest and aggressive plan to do something towards stabilizing the employment of the seasonal organization." Brandy valued his seasonals' "labor, loyalty, and cooperation [that] too often remain unobserved and unsung." His formative experiences on the Lewis and Clark led him to regard woods work as healthful and constructive; he would continue to advocate work programs such as the CCC throughout his life, observing in his later years that it was "the making of these men in more cases than not."[6]

Silcox's national plan went even further, proposing that the time had come for active regulation of private forest land. "The liquidation philosophy is too old and too deeply intrenched [sic] to be changed overnight by purely voluntary action," his report stated. This was a swipe at the policies of former chief William B. Greeley, who believed that cooperation with industry would achieve the desired results. Anticipating objections from Congress, the report asserted that "nearly every other civilized country which has any real forestry program now regulates private forests. It is an old, not a new exercise of sovereignty."[7] Silcox had been raising this alarm for several years; in a provocative address to the Society of American Foresters in 1935 titled "Foresters Must Choose," he called on his profession to return to the "aggressive, crusading spirit" of the Pinchot years to bring the ideals of good forestry to more land.[8] The chief's message was particularly meaningful to Brandborg, coming during his first year on the Bitterroot. He regarded *A National Forest Economy* as a blueprint for how his forest could foster better practices on Ravalli County's private lands. But proposals for active regulation never passed muster in Congress, and by the end of World War II, when free-market approaches again gained primacy, Silcox's and Clapp's ideas were no longer being actively considered. In 1953 chief Richard McArdle officially disavowed the report and ordered all copies of it destroyed. Brandy saw this as a betrayal of his agency's principles, and it was a factor in his deciding to retire two years later.

An integrated approach to managing public and private forests seemed well within reach during the Depression years. Major Kelley shared Silcox's concerns and saw an active role for his supervisors in combating poor logging practices outside of the national forests. In March 1938, probably at Brandy's invitation, Kelley drove to Hamilton to give a speech to representatives of Ravalli County's combined Chambers of Commerce, urging the businessmen to take an interest in how private forest lands were managed. Such land, Kelley said, "represents a material part of the actual and potential wealth-producing capacity of your commonwealth." It mattered, therefore, "whether seed trees are left, and of what species; how the slash is treated; how the residual stands are exposed to or protected from destruction in slash-disposal processes."[9]

The business leaders of Ravalli County, Kelley stated, must not passively accept whatever the Anaconda Company chose to do with its Bitterroot holdings. "You needs must exercise public pressure in trying to secure reasonably good treatment of those lands by present-day and future owners. In other words, you need a county forest-land policy." But to truly ensure sustained yield for the long term, he felt that much of the private timber should pass into public ownership, where the Forest Service could manage it for continuous production. "I know of no owners of forest lands who have any plans whatsoever of permanent possession for growing successive crops of timber," he said.[10]

Kelley and Brandborg enjoyed a generally friendly relationship and often visited each other's homes to socialize and discuss such matters.[11] The Major's support gave Brandy running room to pursue his dual agenda for the public and private forest ownerships in the Bitterroot Valley. The key to a sustained-yield program in Ravalli County lay primarily with the Anaconda Company, but the problem also extended to smaller landholders, particularly ranchers who were clearing forest land to grow grass. Brandborg and his staff believed that growing trees was the highest and best use for marginal agricultural land, since it not only provided sawlogs and other wood products but also fostered watershed and wildlife habitat as well.

Practices on the smaller timber holdings, he asserted, were little better than Anaconda's: "Under present private land management practices, these lands from the standpoint of future crops' growth rate, are barely holding their own. In many instances they have been, or are being, denuded of all reproduction and residual timber growth through wood cutting, broadcast burning, overgrazing and other forms of exploitation and misuse after removal of the mature timber crop."[12] Getting small landowners to pursue timber cropping proved more elusive than improving their grazing practices, however. Grass was of more immediate use than trees, which were a decidedly long-term project. The federal government had no means to compel ranchers to become tree farmers. Despite his agency's interest in social forestry, Brandborg could do little more than exhort them to think in terms of future generations.

Unable to regulate practices directly, Major Kelley urged Brandborg to work out what were known as indemnity-stumpage deals to acquire company lands in Rye Creek, located southeast of Darby, in exchange for national forest timber in the West Fork of the Bitterroot River. Under these agreements the landowner was required to follow Forest Service logging standards, including selective cutting, while the acquired lands could also be placed under sustained-yield management. Such trades were usually done under the provisions of the General Exchange Act of 1922 and allowed the agency to block up its ownership at the fringes of the national forests without huge federal outlays.

Brandy was initially reluctant to pursue this approach. "I question whether it would even serve as a palliative in creating interest in selective cutting on the part of the A. C. M. Company," he replied to Kelley. The giant landowner, he was certain, "must first feel the pressure of public regulation before we can ever get beyond the muddling stage and really accomplish something." Kelley and his staff believed that the alternative was to see the Anaconda and Northern Pacific lands logged without any controls, so he instructed Brandborg to proceed. Company officials were willing to grant the forest 1,674 acres in Rye Creek in exchange for West Fork stumpage. Once the agreement was consummated, timber staffers and engineers from both organizations met in the field to determine marking procedures—perhaps the first instance of the Forest Service exerting its influence on Anaconda's own ground.[13]

By 1945 Brandborg and the Northern Region staff had negotiated sixteen indemnity-stumpage deals that brought 32,674 acres of private land, mostly Anaconda's, into the Bitterroot National Forest.[14] Although this was a significant accomplishment, the lengthy negotiations required for these kinds of deals (including advance approval from the Interior Department) meant that the foresters could not acquire most of the extensive private holdings on the east side of the valley that Brandborg hoped to bring under public oversight. Interest in such exchanges waned after the war, as the agency focused on maximizing production from its own lands.[15]

The Anaconda Company remained the chief timber producer in the Bitterroot Valley throughout the 1930s, harvesting an estimated 30–40 mmbf annually from its holdings and from the Northern Pacific's checkerboard-pattern sections. Twenty or more small mills also operated in the valley, coming and going as markets warranted, most of them processing 50 thousand to 1 million board feet per year. These mills presented a dilemma to Forest Service leaders, who realized that only larger firms had the staying power to handle large volumes of timber in multiyear contracts, rather than scattershot sales offered to whoever might show up at the door.

Larger operators such as Anaconda also had the wherewithal to utilize smaller trees, pile and burn slash, and observe such niceties as keeping a pumper truck handy to fight fires. But distrust of the company ran deep in Montana, reflecting decades of its political and economic influence that sifted into every corner of the state, from its newspapers to legislative and judicial bodies. Anaconda had propelled the state out of the wilderness to become a leading supplier of raw materials for the nation. But the price it demanded was high: with as many as three-fourths of the state's wageworkers getting a paycheck from businesses allied with Anaconda, the citizens of Montana no longer ran their own affairs.[16]

Community leaders in the Bitterroot Valley might take satisfaction at seeing loaded log cars heading up the Northern Pacific's tracks to Bonner, but the more farsighted among them openly wondered how much longer this bounty could be extracted. The Bitterroot's foresters warned of a day fast approaching when the company would finish cutting out its lands and come clamoring for national forest timber. The liquidation would take longer outside of the Bitterroot Valley, but toward the end of the twentieth century the Forest Service and the public could only watch as the bulk of western Montana's private timber was carried off to the mills. By then, with public timber already heavily cut, they could do little to soften the impact on the state's economy.

Timber harvesting in Region 1 was beginning to rebound from its near stand-still at the start of the Great Depression, reaching 71 mmbf in 1935 and rising to around 100 mmbf during the following three years. The Bitterroot, however, contributed a minuscule 2 mmbf of the region's total in 1935. Under Brandborg's management (and with a slowly recovering economy), the cut increased to 6 mmbf by calendar year 1941, almost all of it from the forest's ponderosa pine stands.[17] To continue this progress, Brandborg and his ranger staff hoped to expand timber management beyond the readily accessible areas close to Darby, Hamilton, and Stevensville. They believed that a turnabout was imminent once privately owned timber stands were depleted, whereupon industry would be willing to pay the extra costs involved in cutting public timber under agency oversight.

Over the next three years Brandborg detailed his staff to review the forest's existing timber-stand data and conduct a new cruise covering 77,000 acres in the ponderosa pine type. Clarence Sutliff, who had transferred to the Bitter-root as assistant supervisor, headed the effort. Within accessible areas that could practically be logged, they came up with a total standing volume of 496 mmbf of ponderosa pine growing on 73,000 acres—a little more than half of the volume that his predecessors had listed in 1925. Additional stands farther from road access brought the total volume to 565 mmbf on 118,900 acres. In line with Major Kelley's desire to place private stands under sustained-yield management, Elers Koch, now head of timber management for the region, asked Brandborg to inventory the timber that was left on private lands in the valley, using the same standards as for the forest inventory.[18]

The inventory occupied the Bitterroot's staff for several years. Brandy assembled student crews from the forestry school in Missoula to run cruises under the direction of Professor Hayes Clark. With a great deal of ground to cover, Clark worked them hard. "They left in the dark and sometimes returned in the dark," recalled Edward Morris, a staff engineer. Brandy liked to cultivate and train new talent, Morris noted, using students for range surveys and fire-lookout mapping.[19]

Sutliff, with much input from Brandborg, worked up a draft of the timber plan in 1940 and sent it to Missoula the following March for review. Major Kelley signed off on the document in June 1941; approval from the chief's office followed three months later. The plan set the forest's allowable harvest level at 7.5 mmbf of ponderosa pine per year, based on selective harvests within the estimated 565 mmbf of commercial ponderosa pine over a somewhat arbitrary stand-entry interval of fifty years. The initial timber sales within these stands would remove about two-thirds of the volume, taking the older slow-growing trees of two to three hundred years or more in age. These yielded the finest lumber, including the prized No. 1 Select boards that came from trees twenty inches or more in diameter, and left the younger, healthier growing stock to put on fiber for a second cut a half century later.[20]

The 7.5 mmbf annual cut was a considerable reduction from previous limits, but still allowed for a good deal more harvesting than had been done since the big sales around Lake Como. About 1,400 acres would be cut each year, allowing some drawdown of the initial stock of old-growth timber by the end of the cutting cycle. By then the foresters anticipated that better road access would allow them to make up the difference from other areas of the forest. The plan set no cutting limits for other species, since there was as yet little demand for them. The vast stands of lodgepole pine in the high country of the Bitterroot and Sapphire ranges would be retained as a protection forest, to serve primarily as an undisturbed watershed. With this plan Brandborg let go of his predecessors' dreams of bringing the entire forest under silvicultural control. He would focus on carefully managing the ponderosa pine stands that had some actual value to industry.

Instead of providing a backstop for Anaconda once it finished logging its lands, Brandborg intended to supply the valley's small mills with enough timber to supplement their private stocks. In all, these mills were processing about 12 mmbf annually and ranged from what the Darby district ranger described as "small ramshackle outfit[s]" that produced only 150–200 mbf (thousand board feet) per year to the G. F. Shook mill in the West Fork with an annual capacity of 6 mmbf. Other significant producers included the Storer and Flightner mill in Darby, which was shut down at the time, and the Charles Hughes mill at Charlos Heights, north of Darby, which mostly served area ranchers. The latter, he observed, filled "a much needed place in the local community, much the same kind of a place the old grist mill filled and still fills in certain communities. Locals take their logs to this mill, sometimes help run them through and the finished product serves their needs and costs them less."[21] This was the kind of operation Brandy most wanted to support, even though it lacked the efficient machinery and trained workers of larger concerns.

Small sales of choice timber would serve these outfits best: in the West Fork, for example, ranger Samuel Billings recommended that he advertise only one or two sales per year, totaling perhaps 4 mmbf. "There are many blocks of timber containing over-age stuff that is deteriorating rapidly," he reported to Brand-borg. "It is my thought that some of these chances could be sold on a very selective basis—that is, only those areas that are clearly on the down-grade to be marked. Those trees are mostly those containing high-grade lumber—a large percentage of select and shop and the operator should be able to handle these chances profitably."[22]

Timber sales of this sort served Brandborg's goals in several ways. The mills in the Darby–West Fork area would be well positioned to bid on them, unlike Anaconda and other large operators that were located eighty miles or more away in Missoula County. Thinning the aging ponderosa stands would improve their growth, and marking trees would employ agency personnel during most of the year. Quality stumpage would fetch higher bids, with the lumber thus derived selling for premium prices, benefiting the local economy. This approach became the cornerstone of the Bitterroot's timber program in the 1940s and early 1950s, reflecting Brandborg's desire to keep local men employed and retain as much of the timber's value as possible in Ravalli County's economy.

Selective high-value harvesting formed an important part of Forest Service doctrine at the time and was central to the agency's efforts to bring about so-called permanent forestry on all ownerships. To further this cause the Bitterroot's 1941 timber plan featured an extensive discussion of the social and economic situation in Ravalli County. Brandborg and Sutliff expected their agency to exert considerable influence toward better timbering practices beyond the forest boundary. "National forest timber resources cannot be evaluated on a strictly monetary basis," they stated in a foreword to the plan. "Their true value is not reflected so much by the revenue they bring into the National treasury, as by the material benefits they are made to contribute to the permanent social and economic welfare of society. The commercial timber resources of the Bitterroot Working Circle must therefore be managed and utilized so as to contribute their utmost towards stabilization of social and economic conditions of the community at a satisfactory level."

The key was "stabilization"—and with this preamble Brandborg and his staff announced their intention to make national forest timber an instrument of social policy. The forest's stumpage would not necessarily go to the highest bidder, nor would it simply feed into the national economy. The goal was to help a struggling local industry by providing a steady, reliable supply of fine logs and—as the plan would also detail—protect those enterprises from competition at the hands of more powerful outside interests.

This role was necessary, the plan asserted, because there was no assurance of continued timber supplies from private lands. "The crest of the lumbering era is past," it stated. "Since 1890 this industry has filled an important place in the social and economic structure of the Bitterroot Valley. Private timber holdings are now 85% cutover and at the present cutting rate will be entirely so within the next five years." Private firms were cutting, on average, about 45 mmbf annually, but the Forest Service expected this to soon decline to 10 mmbf. With the valley's small mills growing more dependent on public timber, there was the prospect of a bidding war in which Anaconda would be at a clear advantage. Rather than allow stumpage prices to rise (which would have increased the forest's revenues and allowed it to get on with its road-building program), Brandborg chose to bail out the local operators, believing that they contributed more in economic and social benefits to the valley.

To cement the local firms' advantage, Sutliff and Brandborg inserted an unusual clause into their plan that allowed the Forest Service to reject any bid that came from a mill located outside of the forest's working circle, which by that time had been consolidated to include all of Ravalli County. This requirement generally excluded mills in the Missoula area, although they were able to obtain occasional sales that local outfits chose not to bid on. The local milling requirement engendered much controversy as demand for timber increased among mills outside of the valley. But the notion that Bitterroot timber should go to Bitterroot mills had a solid underpinning in Forest Service policy. In the 1907 version of the Forest Service's *Use Book,* Gifford Pinchot exhorted his supervisors to usurp monopoly by favoring local buyers. Supervisor E. A. Sherman observed in 1908 that harvesting and milling federal timber could provide year-round work for "the men of small communities...the bulwark of manly and sterling independence." The Bitterroot, however, appears to be the first national forest to explicitly give priority to local firms.

Elers Koch noted that there was "a good deal of well-justified difference of opinion" on the local milling question, although he was willing to approve the plan for the time being. Koch forwarded to Brandy an analysis by Phillip Neff, a logging engineer on the region's staff, that showed that Harper Brothers (Anaconda's logging contractor in the Bitterroot Valley) paid 50 percent higher wages than the best of the valley's smaller mills and utilized a greater percentage of timber. With its many subsidiaries in western Montana, the company sold or otherwise made use of "slab wood, hog fuel, sawdust, wedges, boxes, etc., as well as mine stull," according to Neff. "The small mills get little if any overrun and cannot utilize by-products to any extent. More than this, most of them butcher the logs and produce an inferior product."[23]

But Brandy was charting a course for his forest that downplayed economic efficiency. He found support from the chief of the agency's timber management division in Washington, E. E. Carter, who was "strongly in accord" with the local milling requirement. Carter thought that Brandborg's approach could well be a model for other forests in the country and ought to be given "wide distribution as a broad hint for others."[24]

It is unlikely that any forest-level plan in the agency's history has made so bold a claim for public control of private timber. But it fitted the climate in Washington, where New Deal bureaucrats had established unprecedented federal oversight of American industry.[25] With the backing of Evan Kelley and ultimately the chief forester, Brandborg thought he was in a position to push the citizens of Ravalli County off the track laid by the Anaconda Company. Looking back on this effort more than three decades later, he told his friend Mavis McKelvey that "we were supposed to take a position, because subserviency to the corporate interests, everyone knew where that's gonna lead us."[26] In the coming years he would return often to this theme of grassroots control of the county's affairs, much as his father had exhorted the farmers of Otter Tail County to take charge of their future. Brandy saw the federal role as a corrective to the moneyed interests whose influence ran deep in the Treasure State.

The 1941 timber plan was a milestone for the Bitterroot National Forest, setting realistic cutting goals after decades of pie-in-the-sky assumptions. Under its guidance, Brandy's rangers applied the best silvicultural practices known at the time to the magnificent ponderosa stands that fringed the valley. The plan guided cutting for more than a decade and underlay Brandborg's activist forest management philosophy. But as demand for timber grew during World War II, Major Kelley's successors would favor the larger, better-equipped operators who could handle greater volumes of timber. To them, the Bitterroot's plan was a millstone that held the forest to a social program they would just as soon leave behind. By 1950 the forest would stand alone in the region, and to an increasing degree so would Guy Brandborg.

However constituted, the goal of achieving a sustained yield of forest products assumed an almost mythic importance within the Forest Service. The concept was rather malleable and depended upon what the agency was trying to accomplish at the time. In its first formulation, which came to America with Progressive foresters such as Gifford Pinchot, the goal was to balance harvests with the natural growth of the forest. Pinchot learned his trade in the thoroughly regulated forests of France and Germany, where the object was to take only the annual increment of wood fiber from a designated area. The area of forest under consideration—what was known as the working circle—influenced this calculation, as did the age and condition of the trees within it.

The agency later modified the strict cut-equals-growth policy to allow older, less productive stands to be harvested at a more rapid rate, encouraging new growth and permitting a higher overall harvest. Various formulas were advanced to balance these variables. A timber-management plan could emphasize regulating the forest to produce certain age classes of sawtimber, which might mean varying the cut over time, or it could stabilize harvests to benefit certain mills or operators. As agency leaders came and went, so too did various flavors of forest practice. Much of the later controversy on the Bitterroot can be chalked up to opposing notions of the sustained-yield concept. Brandborg positioned his forest to cooperate with the valley's small producers, opting for a relatively unvarying supply of high-quality logs, each laboriously selected, marked, and cut. Although this approach may have maximized the long-term yield from the ponderosa stands, it left the rest of the forest to its own devices, including a high rate of mortality from insects and disease.

In pursuing this course Brandborg broke with his predecessors' goal (unrealistic though it may have been at the time) of bringing more of the forest under silvicultural control in order to maximize wood-fiber production. When his associates in the regional office reasserted this doctrine in the late 1940s, Brandy would stubbornly resist, forcing them to delay implementing their plans until after he retired. Throughout this conflict he would refer to his 1941 timber-management plan and his conservative version of sustained yield. To him, efficient production was less important than preserving a way of life in the Bitterroot Valley—a vision in which supporting small mill owners and backwoods loggers counted more than supplying logs to the nation's emerging industrial economy.

CHAPTER 6

To Manage and Conserve

1941–1954

Many Forest Service employees consider the position of forest supervisor to be one of the most rewarding on the agency's career ladder, since it brings real authority over operations while still offering a chance to work with field personnel. Brandborg managed to keep this balance during his two decades at the Bitterroot's helm, finding frequent excuses to examine ponderosa stands with his timber staff or ride the range along the margins of the Bitterroot Valley. Pausing at any high point in the foothills, Brandy could have pondered how publicly owned timber, water, and grass sustained the life of Ravalli County. Federal land virtually surrounded the valley, but he was less inclined than most forest officers to regard a national forest boundary sign as a limit to his influence.

He enjoyed his position as a community leader, yet as a respite from work he would often head down to the Elks Lodge for a drink with friends or shoot a game of pool at the Brunswick establishment on Hamilton's main street. Card games at Haigh's beer parlor were pleasant affairs that drew old-timers from around the valley. Stewart Brandborg would sometimes accompany his father on these occasions, where he would watch what he called "this great snoose-chewing fraternity" enjoying their homespun humor. Talk of weather, hunting, and crops would be punctuated at intervals by Brandy's explosions of laughter, which Mavis McKelvey described as akin to the buildup and sudden release of steam from a boiler. While he could command attention with stories from his days on the fire lines, he also listened closely if a friend had a concern to express. Fools and reactionaries he suffered less gladly.

The senior Brandy also enjoyed the company of his fellow Masons and had risen to the thirty-second degree within that organization. "He had an ability to enjoy fellowship with people without reference to social issues," Stewart said. "These guys weren't social activists, these were just good old guys." Stewart also met some of the woodsmen who formed the backbone of the Forest Service in its early days. Raised in the Bitterroot Valley or other rural locations, fine crafts-men with ax or saw, they knew how to handle stock and comport themselves in rough country. As supervisor, Guy Brandborg felt an allegiance to all of these citizens and believed that his agency ought to look out for them.

Most forest supervisors took pains to cultivate public support, but Brandy brought a missionary zeal to his outreach efforts, organizing classes and reading groups, giving talks, meeting with community leaders, and taking any opportu-nity to draw connections between land health and economic prosperity. Gov-ernment planning, he emphasized, was essential if valley residents hoped to prosper over the long haul. He assembled much of his thinking into a speech he gave to civic organizations in the Bitterroot Valley starting around 1940. Titled "Can We Manage and Conserve Our Forests?" it envisioned sustained yield as a social issue as well as a conservation imperative. The title was more than rhetor-ical; he was not altogether sure that the American public was willing to support permanent forestry. Achieving a stable supply of timber and other resources would require swift action to control overcutting and overgrazing on the valley's private holdings. "Ever since I came to Montana," he stated, "I have heard that the timber in Ravalli County was being cut far faster than it was growing. I have heard that young pine pole stands were being cut for cordwood just at the age when its high value growth was starting. I have heard that permanent-type grass-lands were so overgrazed, and badly managed, they now support less than half the cattle that could be maintained thereon. Yet to this day I have not heard one Ravalli County citizen express concern over the condition of these resources." He would try to change that situation in the ensuing years, helping to start var-ious citizen and intergovernmental organizations to grapple with problems of excessive use. "I do not believe Democracy can work otherwise," he concluded.[1]

Although he joined Major Kelley in advocating government regulation of timber cutting on privately owned forest lands, Brandy now believed that so much had been cut that it was too late to have much effect, at least until the sec-ond growth came of age. He would tell Kelley in 1948 that "there is no use in locking the barn on the Bitterroot, the horse has already been stolen. Practically all private timber is in small holdings and has been cut over at least once. The last large holdings are on Gird Creek and that timber will be cut within the next two years."[2] There was still a useful role for both the national forest and private landowners, he believed, if they would adopt the long-term thinking that he had helped instill in some of the valley's ranchers. "Sound forestry requires planning far beyond the lives of the planners," he said. "As individuals we all plan. The better the planner, the more successful the citizen." Social planning was no different, he believed, but among many people it was regarded as "un-American, Communist, or Fascist."

Brandborg regarded planning as an outgrowth of what he called the natural laws of a democracy, which included self-restraint and respect for the land. To arrogate excessive wealth to oneself was to shortchange those who followed:

> If each youngster growing up could be taught to treat his environment so that it would be better at his death than at his birth, we would be on the way toward solving our toughest national problem. The astonishing result of properly treating one's environment is to obtain in the long run more rewards than come to the heedless exploiter. Most of you know it pays to handle farm land in accordance with the best principles of soil conservation. A farmer who can turn over his soil to his son more fertile than he had found it has followed the natural laws to the benefit of himself, his son, and the community.[3]

These were principles Brandy had learned on the farm from his Swedish parents. Now he applied them to his national forest, where he needed support to forestall a raid on the public's timber. "You could have abundance for this generation but poverty for your children," he warned, "if the remaining old growth national forest timber were to be cut at the same rapid rate, and in the same wasteful manner, as the private timber has been cut in the past." His objective on the Bitterroot was to ensure "permanency and stability of timber supply and its accompanying forest values at the highest level our country can afford. This means abundance for our children and a reasonable supply for this generation."[4]

He made an eloquent call for a longer perspective on local land-use issues. "We Americans have not yet learned to live in the same environment, generation after generation," he observed. "As individuals we have been able to move on to new land when the old farm wore out. As a nation we have moved on to exploit new frontiers. Whether this generation can be its own doctor and prescribe for its own ills remains a serious question." To him, the reservoir of old-growth timber on the Bitterroot was a resource to conserve, not to squander needlessly. It was a thoroughly Old World outlook—the antithesis of the exploitative mentality so long in evidence in America.[5]

In an agency that customarily transferred its personnel every few years, Brandborg gave himself the luxury of time on the Bitterroot, passing up any chance of promotion to the regional office or to Washington.[6] He was thus able to build the kind of organization he felt was needed to carry out his social agenda. Under his leadership the Bitterroot gained a reputation for effective in-service training in topics such as firefighting, timber-sale marking, and log scaling, as well as his favorite issue, the conservation of natural resources. Victor Sandberg, who headed Region 1's training program, regarded him as a "staunch counselor and helpmate in carrying out the regional effort....Brandy recognized early in his Forest Service career that it was not enough to be a skilled technician. In addition, the fledgling forester had to master the skills of communication so that the public in turn could be informed effectively of conservation programs. He constantly brought into his forest training program the breadth of the humanities—psychology, speech, sociology, the philosophy of management, public relations."[7]

These were lofty ambitions, certainly, but his coworkers sometimes bridled under Brandy's authoritarian approach to running a forest. Charles McDonald, who came to the forest in 1944 as the district ranger at Stevensville, recalled in 1978 that his boss was inclined to give orders rather than negotiate agreement. "Brandy was more like a drill sergeant than a supervisor," he said, although "he was fair and gained the men's respect." This approach, while it grated on some of his employees, stemmed from his strong beliefs in the vital mission of the agency. McDonald, who became one of Brandy's close friends and most trusted subordinates, went so far as to say that Brandy at first seemed to have a "Christ complex," which he was able to moderate as time went on. Evan Kelley, in particular, coached him in better human relations, advising him that a leader who gave himself ulcers was likely to give them to others as well.[8]

Brandborg's long interest in education led in 1941 to an appointment to the Montana State Board of Education (now the Board of Regents), on which he served for ten years. The eleven-member board, which included the governor, the state superintendent of public instruction, and the attorney general, set policy for the state's educational institutions, including its colleges and universities. Governor Sam Ford, a progressive Republican, wanted a citizen member who would help fight the heavy influence that the state's major corporations had long wielded over its university system, including the hiring and firing of professors. The position brought Brandy in touch with Montana's top political leaders as well as various professors in the natural sciences from Montana's university system, many of whom he invited to the Bitterroot to examine range and timber conditions and share their expertise with his staff. That year Brandborg helped MSU-Missoula (later the University of Montana) organize a four-week short course for government resource agency personnel, called the School of Public Administration, which drew primarily on professors from the humanities. Victor Sandberg served as the Forest Service's liaison to the school, which served hundreds of agency staffers during its first decade. Sandberg called it "one of the best informed university liberal arts groups on resource management in the Nation."[9] In its later incarnation as the School for Administrative Leadership, Brandy would form a cordial working relationship with its director, forestry school professor (later dean) Arnold Bolle, who would go on to become a key figure in the Bitterroot clearcutting controversy.

Brandborg conducted a homegrown version of this course at the supervisor's office in Hamilton during the second decade of his tenure, which drew agency personnel from throughout the region to learn his unique philosophy of management. He called the program "The Wheel of Progress," a metaphor he used for the crucial relationship between the national forests and local communities. A handout for the class featured a drawing of a dynamo representing the national forest, which spun off public benefits in the form of clean water, wood fiber, recreation, wildlife habitat, and other goods. In its depiction of the humming energy that powered American progress it could have illustrated a Works Progress Administration mural and hardly suggested a radical at work. Ray Karr, who went on to head the Northern Region's public information division in the 1970s, took the course in 1954 and recalled it as "excellent in content and presentation." Karr described Brandborg as "enthusiastic, sincere, friendly and dedicated. I just wished my college professors were as skilled."[10]

Brandborg's conservation views echoed those of Walter Lowdermilk, a former acquaintance in the Forest Service who went on to become the assistant director of the Soil Conservation Service. In the 1930s and 1940s Lowdermilk lectured extensively on the relationship between agricultural practices and land health, warning that civilizations from North Africa to the Far East had come to ruin after cutting down their forests and overgrazing their ranges. The problem was not limited to the classic Dust Bowl states of Texas, Oklahoma, and Kansas; a 1934 survey of western agricultural lands showed that 4.4 million acres in Montana had undergone severe erosion, meaning they were no longer economically capable of growing crops or supporting livestock.[11]

Ravalli County had thus far escaped the worst of these ravages, but Forest Service surveys had found that much of the Bitterroot Valley's agricultural land was infested with cheatgrass and other weeds.[12] Brandborg wanted federal and county agents to offer more demonstration programs for good conservation practices, ranging from proper soil tillage and crop rotation to his own brand of conservative forestry. Results were needed that people could see and emulate. "The Department of Agriculture, without slackening its search for scientific facts, should devote even more attention than it has to the matter of getting the facts applied," he wrote. This was the key, ultimately, to public support: "If any effort to improve the productivity of Ravalli County is to be completely successful it must be understood and supported by laboring, professional, and business people,

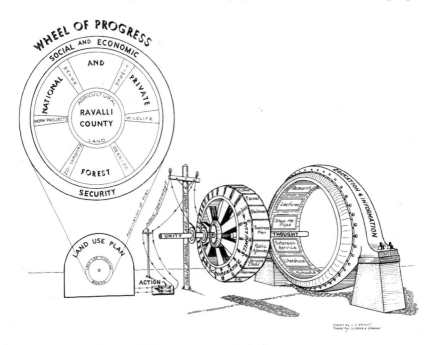

FIGURE 1. Guy Brandborg used his "Wheel of Progress" as a handout for his in-service training classes to illustrate how the national forests spun off multiple benefits to the surrounding communities. Courtesy of USDA Forest Service, BNF Archives.

farmers and ranchers, and government agencies."[13] As a land manager, he was not content to see Agriculture's bureaucrats compile crop reports and issue bulletins; what counted was keeping weeds out of farmers' fields and silt out of streams.

He also tried to get the New Deal's various government agencies working on common conservation goals by sponsoring educational outreach programs, films, reading libraries, teacher training, and show-me trips. An umbrella group called the USDA Council was supposed to coordinate the work of its many programs within Ravalli County, including the MSU Extension Service and State Experiment Station, Farm Credit Bureau, Forest Service, Production Marketing Administration, and Soil Conservation Service.[14] Immediately following the war, Brandborg and Stanley Halvorsen, the Ravalli County extension agent, organized a show-me tour and conference that attracted some of the state's more progressive thinkers, including Montana State College president Roland Renne and writer Joseph Kinsey Howard. The group examined instances of abused lands as well as demonstration areas such as grass-reseeding plots and selective-harvest sites.[15]

Despite good intentions, the conference did not ignite the lasting cooperation Brandborg envisioned. Some county residents looked upon planning efforts as socialistic or worse, while federal agencies saw to their own jobs without much reference to each other or to the overarching conservation principles Brandborg wanted to promote. The new focus was on economic expansion, which better fitted the interests of individuals acting on their own. The result would be the steady attrition of Ravalli County's agricultural lands as thousands of new residents settled in the Bitterroot Valley during the postwar decades.

If Brandborg's approach to agricultural conservation and private forestry was expansive and (as some would say) grasping, he wanted nothing more than to achieve a degree of productivity that individual efforts rarely produced. Acquiring cutover lands and placing them under Forest Service management would detract little from tax revenues, he said, since many such properties were currently in delinquency. Once they were producing timber and forage again, they would contribute 25 percent of federal receipts to Ravalli County's coffers. He also promised that by acquiring significant stands of young growth, the national forest could cut its older stands more heavily—an application of the working-circle theory that lay behind the Sustained Yield Forest Management Act of 1944. More roads would be built into stands of mature timber, allowing the agency to harvest "more old, fine, ripe trees…which would otherwise die." This, he said, would permit a lighter overall cut, since more acres would be growing timber. He took neither a preservationist nor an industrial approach; his goals were predominately social, and only secondarily meant to enhance residual-stand growth and reduce mortality. Even less important, in his mind, was the need to return the maximum dollars to the federal Treasury or to supply large volumes of sawtimber to the nation's economy.

Successful forestry, Brandborg said in another of his talks during the 1940s, required "planning and a lot of perspiration and time." He described how each year his field personnel would mark forty-five thousand individual trees for cutting. A sample of trees was scaled and examined for decay in order to determine how much the purchaser would pay for stumpage. In all, his timber cruisers and check scalers spent some nine hundred man-days each year in this labor-intensive process. Champ Hannon, who worked on the Bitterroot as the West Fork district ranger before the Depression and as a timber cruiser afterward, epitomized the boots-on-the-ground style of forestry practiced in the days before computerized timber-stand analyses. Marking ponderosa pine stands took days of fieldwork for each timber sale. "Each tree that was cut had to be marked with a U.S. brand on both the stump and the log," Hannon recalled in a 1970 interview. "And the brush had to be trimmed up, the main large limbs had to be trimmed out and the brush had to be piled in the open in little tee-pee piles so it could be burned easily."[16] Such practices were envisioned under the agency's Organic Administration Act of 1897, which required that national forest timber be marked and designated before being sold—a stipulation that would have enormous consequences for the agency in future years.

Hannon, who grew up on a ranch outside of Darby, typified the early-day forester whose career did not always advance along the usual lines. As the West Fork ranger from 1925 to 1928, he was mainly responsible for firefighting efforts on his largely uncut district. He left his position to study at Montana State College in Bozeman, but did not complete the requirements for a forestry degree, and following the war he had to start over as a timekeeper on the Lost Horse road project. As cutting increased he found plenty to do in the forests' timber-management branch, often working under Clarence Sutliff, the author of its 1941 timber-management plan. Hannon described Sutliff's approach to selective cutting in the ponderosa pine:

> We marked according to the Keen classification and that is what you call a high risk classification, the classes 4 and 5 are old and overmature yellow

pine [that] we attempted to take out. Now the number three class was
a tree that had reached the full canopy height of the forest. But it has a
pointed top, the needles were darker, the needles were heavier.... [W]e
left [these] younger ones that were healthy trees.... Now the purpose of
this policy, the object of the Forest Service at that time was to get over all
the yellow pine land in the forest. And get these big overmature trees out,
because that's where the loss is occurring.[17]

Stewart Brandborg, who spent the summer of 1944 as Hannon's assistant,
attested to the sweat it took to follow him up and down the West Fork's hills
with marking ax in hand. But all this labor paid off with improved growth. There
was a romance to this kind of forestry, examining individual pines with a trained
eye, spotting the best candidates for future growth, and harvesting the old
giants that yielded a high percentage of quality wood. Historian Alfred Runte
describes this as classical forestry in the European mold—a hands-on approach
that was "both beautiful and functional.... Even as some trees were coming
down, many more were always growing. By being consistently selective, in other
words, the forester could not help but remain sensitive to the natural environment."[18] Nor was it difficult for the public to understand classical forestry as a
kind of landscape gardening, harvesting the land's bounty even as the future forest was left standing. As Hannon mentioned, crews would even lop off the lower
branches of the "leave" trees in order to promote the growth of clear lumber.
Selective cutting, to most observers, improved the appearance of the forest—
often making it easier to walk, ride, and see through. If done properly, the forester had little explaining to do.

To bolster his selective-cutting program and track silvicultural changes in the
forest, Brandborg installed a series of photo locations in the Lick Creek drainage, where his predecessors had conducted a large timber sale from 1906 to
1911. Repeat photography at these locations showed the growth of the remaining large pines and the development of a new stand. In 1946, thirty-five years or
more after the original harvests, the leave trees had put on an average of sixty-six
board feet per acre per year. The new pines that reproduced underneath the old
trees were growing even faster.[19]

Hannon and Brandborg remained strongly attached to selective cutting,
believing it was the best way to handle ponderosa stands despite increasing evidence that pine was not a climax species on the Bitterroot. The young Douglas
fir and grand fir that sprouted under the canopy would present a problem for
future foresters concerned with fire control and maintaining presettlement forest

conditions. The Bitterroot's staff was aware that forest succession in the absence of fire would eventually supplant the pines, and at one point Brandy even had crews girdle the young firs to prevent their crowding the pines, using funds left over at the end of summer seasons—another example of his favoring labor-intensive forestry that would employ local men. The emphasis on removing old, overmature trees also meant that less habitat would be available for cavity-nesting birds; to foresters of that generation, dead snags were an indication of inefficient forest management. Leaving wildlife trees and downed logs—and allowing fire a role—is now an important part of forestry practice, but ecological considerations remained in the background for decades until it became obvious that whole stands were drastically changing in character.

Lick Creek became a showcase for the Forest Service's timber-management methods, leading to a visit in 1937 from Brandborg's old hero, Gifford Pinchot, long since dismissed from the Forest Service but still active in conservation affairs. Summer rains fell as Brandy toured Pinchot and a group of agency foresters around the Lick Creek sale area, viewing cutting units the chief had inspected in 1906. Pinchot still regarded selective cutting as the best way to harvest a stand's accumulated wood fiber while allowing for continued forest growth. Brandy agreed with his former boss. In later years he delighted in telling friends how after their tour he, Pinchot, and Evan Kelley retired to his and Edna's home, where the old forester (who had recently completed a second term as governor of Pennsylvania) recounted conservation battles as he stood drying his backside in front of a blazing fire. Pinchot, Brandy recounted, told him that democracy could survive only through the maintenance of a productive natural resource base. To deplete those resources, Pinchot said, created "poverty and lack of advantages for the common man."[20]

The chief's visit was a turning point for the young supervisor. "Pinchot charged me then and there [that] if I wanted to be a good forester, I'd better defend sound practices" like those used at Lick Creek, he recalled. "Major Kelley was present, and he said, 'Goddamit Brandy, you'd better do it.'" Coming from two men he admired, the advice made a deep impression. Brandborg adopted Pinchot's words as his personal instructions and attempted to carry them out for another four decades.

Forest officers had long recognized that recreation and wildlife were among the Bitterroot's most important resources. Elk, deer, and trout garnered the most interest among sportsmen, but local residents also enjoyed seeing moose in the upper forks of the Bitterroot River. George Hollibaugh, who conducted a game census for the forest in 1942, noted that roadside sightings would invariably stop traffic and that residents were "terribly worked up" over poaching of these bottomland dwellers. Fred Wetzsteon recalled that ranger Clyde Shockley, who was deputized as a game warden, "had a special love for moose and he put a stop to the monkey business."[21] Hollibaugh also attempted to assess more elusive species such as mountain goat and grizzly bear. By the 1920s only a handful of the latter were believed to be on the forest, all of which had migrated over the divide from the Selway River region. The last of these was reported killed in 1931. By the mid-1940s the grizzly was gone even from that stronghold.[22] Mountain goats were more numerous and found ideal habitat among the high Bitterroot crags; the 1942 census estimated that more than four hundred were roaming those rocky slopes.

Brandy had enjoyed hunting and fishing throughout his early years in Montana and Idaho, although as time went on he took less interest in pursuing big game, deriving as much enjoyment from watching creatures in the wild. His damaged knees also limited his outdoor activities, but he would often take Stewart out to the Bitterroot's orchards to hunt pheasants. He believed that sportsmen should understand the ecological interdependence of game species and their habitats (a field that Stewart, not coincidentally, pursued as his first career), and to that end he arranged in 1949 for members of the Ravalli County Sportsmen's Association to meet with his friend Joseph Severy, a professor of biology at the state university in Missoula, to design an adult education program on wildlife-management issues.

Both Severy and Brandborg wanted sportsmen to move beyond their usual concerns about hunting seasons and bag limits and take on the more difficult question of improving the care of private and public lands. Severy developed a ten-lesson series that focused on basic principles of wildlife biology; the course proved popular in several Bitterroot Valley towns and attracted as many as thirty participants. Panel discussions and field trips ensued to discuss sportsmen-landowner relations, grazing practices, and other issues involving national forest lands.[23]

In his position as chairman of the Montana Wildlife Federation's education committee, Brandborg commended Severy's program to the group's local affiliates, leading a number of them to host the lecture series in their communities. The committee formalized the program during the winter of 1950–1951 and arranged a three-day course for Severy to train additional lecturers. By 1954, with demand for the program growing, the federation reached an agreement with the Montana State Fish and Game Commission to fund the program. Dr. Les Pengelly, a former colleague of Stewart Brandborg, took over from Severy as director, and a second lecturer, Dr. Eldon Smith of Montana State College, joined the following year. Severy and Pengelly credited the Wildlife Extension program with substantially raising support for scientific wildlife-management efforts among Montana sportsmen. Both the senior Brandy and his fellow sportsmen in Hamilton continued their close involvement with the program, conducting follow-up discussions in community forums and stocking the local library with wildlife-related books and pamphlets.

Their efforts paid off in an active community of sportsmen in the Bitterroot; in 1954, for example, members of the Ravalli County Fish and Wildlife Association met with Sula district ranger Vern Hamre and the local stockmen's association to discuss drought conditions and resulting poor forage on the important winter range along the East Fork of the Bitterroot River. Hamre got the stockmen to agree to take their cattle off the range by October 1, one and a half months earlier than usual, and to reduce numbers by 25 to 35 percent on the ranges they used. The fish and game commissioners authorized an extended deer and elk season to help bring their numbers into balance with the range.[24]

Not every national forest experienced similar success dealing with grazing issues during the 1940s and early 1950s. Powerful western politicians made sure that their ranching constituents received preferential treatment in case of disputes with the agency, to the consternation of range managers who were trying to limit excessive use. Complaints from some livestock operators led to the introduction of legislation by Senator Patrick McCarran of Nevada and Congressman Frank Barrett of Wyoming to define grazing privileges as a right, as well as to permit the transfer of grazing lands in the national forests to the states and eventually to private owners. They promoted their program at a series of well-publicized hearings in 1947. Congressman Wesley D'Ewart of Montana, a rancher with his own Forest Service grazing permits, tried to stoke his constituents' anger at hearings in Glasgow and Billings, but to little effect. "Montana was, on the whole, well satisfied with the Forest Service," wrote Bernard DeVoto in his 1948 essay "Sacred Cows and Public Lands," which was among the many pieces he wrote for his Easy Chair column in *Harper's Magazine* to defend the federal agencies' conservation work.[25] DeVoto, more than any conservationist group, was responsible for marshaling public opinion against the so-called land-grab bills of this period.

A few prominent individuals in the Forest Service risked their careers to cultivate support from conservationists on the range issue. Chet Olsen, head of the Intermountain Region in Ogden, Utah and a strong conservationist, had been urging his field staff to come to grips with decades-old overgrazing and erosion in Utah's mountain ranges. The prospect of congressional interference rankled, so he set about organizing a clandestine network of agency cooperators. In 1946 he invited DeVoto to come to Utah and see the results of devastating floods originating in the stripped mountains, supplying the author with much of the inside information and contacts he would use in his columns.[26] Olsen also referred DeVoto to supporters in Montana, including assistant regional forester James K. Vessey, who helped arrange several tours for DeVoto in Montana and Idaho. Vessey knew of Brandborg's strong feelings on conservation issues and put the two men in touch; that June Brandy discussed grazing issues with DeVoto for an hour in Hamilton and in a subsequent visit may have accompanied the author in the field. Details of his involvement were not publicized, since no federal employee was supposed to directly influence legislation. With additional advice from Joseph Kinsey Howard and A. B. Guthrie Jr., two Montanans DeVoto knew through literary circles, the writer had plenty of ammunition for his crusade against western development interests and their allies in Congress. Wallace Stegner, DeVoto's biographer, credited him with holding off the stockmen's efforts to hamstring the Forest Service's regulatory program.[27]

Charles McDonald developed a reputation as the most assertive of Brandy's rangers, serving trespass notices on ranchers who overloaded their allotments and achieving local fame for shooting and injuring an inebriated logger who had attacked him without provocation.[28] This incident, known as the Battle on Bass Creek, ended without a conviction, but McDonald did not have any further difficulties with logging contractors on his district. In 1954 a rancher objected to McDonald's proposed reductions in his allotment, taking his concerns over Brandborg's head. McDonald presented his case at a review meeting in the regional office at which Congressman Lee Metcalf appeared in support of his actions. The regional forester backed McDonald, but following Brandy's retirement the soft-spoken ranger found less support for his actions.

Brandborg, McDonald, Hannon, and Metcalf would have occasion to work together when timber-management issues came to the fore on the Bitterroot in the 1960s. Until then, flare-ups over logging contracts or grazing permits remained the exception. In the 1940s and 1950s Ravalli County may not have achieved the degree of cooperation in conservation work that Brandy hoped for, but he and his rangers had made great strides in correcting the excesses of the past. He remained hopeful that with enough education and prodding, many more of Ravalli County's citizens and land users would want to see their resources managed for long-term health and sustainability.

CHAPTER 7

Timber Boom

1941–1955

America's entry into World War II put the Bitterroot National Forest's ponderosa pine stands into full production for the first time, as demand soared for everything from ammunition boxes to mine-support timbers. Its silvicultural staff soon cast aside the annual cutting limit of 7.5 mmbf of ponderosa pine timber that had been set scarcely three months before Pearl Harbor. Harvests at first rose gradually, then reached 10.8 mmbf in 1943 and peaked at 17.4 mmbf in 1944. Averaged over five years, the volume cut only slightly exceeded the annual limit, and after a new timber study showed more ponderosa pine on the forest than had earlier been estimated, the overrun did not appear so alarming. George Haynes, an assistant forester on the Bitterroot, probably expressed many staffers' feelings in an April 1944 memo to Brandborg: "These are not normal times and conditions. We are at War. About all that can be done at present is to make whatever sales that are necessary for this emergency. When the urgency of the emergency is past, bring the management plan up to date and do the other things necessary to practice the best forestry possible."[1]

Haynes's comments suggest that his boss may have been reluctant to put too much pressure on his valuable pine stands. Brandy instead proposed to begin cutting more of the forest's Douglas fir, then considered an inferior species on the Bitterroot owing to mistletoe infection, fire scars, and pitch seams. By

1944 the forest was selling 6 mmbf of this species, as well as some Engelmann spruce, which found application in light-airplane construction. Brandy was also concerned about the firs' tendency to grow back underneath the big pines—"apparently as the climax type," he told Major Kelley, "and presumably brought about by the control of forest fires."[2] Here was a chance to do the forest some good as well as supply raw materials for the war effort.

To suppress the fir he proposed to undertake what he called "clean cutting followed by controlled burning and planting" in areas of heavy regrowth. This may have been the first time that clearcutting was purposefully advocated as a silvicultural method on the Bitterroot, and it is noteworthy that the suggestion came from the man who would later roundly criticize the agency's application of the practice. He told Kelley that the method should first be field-tested, but he and his timber staff understood that they had a problem on their hands in the mixed ponderosa-fir type. Outside of a handful of experimental patch cuts, including a seven-acre unit along the West Fork road below Painted Rocks Dam in 1944, he never used the method widely, and fir became solidly established in the pine stands.[3]

Following the war western Montana's sawmills were reluctant to give up their newly increased production capacity. Fred Stell, one of Brandy's timber staffers, noted in 1946 that Ravalli County's mills were now "keyed to a much larger production than the 7-½ million feet of ponderosa pine now fixed as the cut limitation in the Bitterroot Working Circle plan." He suggested that the cut be raised to 13.7 mmbf by using a somewhat lighter selection harvest at twenty-year intervals instead of the fifty years contemplated in the 1941 plan. This would allow the forest to put all of its commercial ponderosa pine stands into production instead of limiting the harvest to readily accessible areas. The silvicultural staff in Hamilton and Missoula wanted to seize this chance, but instead there ensued a protracted dispute with Brandborg over how fast and how far to increase the Bitterroot's cutting levels.[4]

A higher cut, Stell admitted, would draw down stocks of old-growth ponderosa pine, resulting in a future reduction in sale offerings. "At first glance," he wrote, "the drop in the proposed annual cut between the first and second cutting cycles would appear to be disturbing to the stability of employment in the Bitterroot Valley." He noted, however, that "the history of the lumbering industry in the Bitterroot does not indicate that there has ever been much stability of employment. The quantity cut per year and the seasonal cuts have varied and the mills that have started up and shut down after a short time have been too numerous to recount." The regional office decided to split the difference, setting the cutting limit for ponderosa at 10 mmbf, with another 15 mmbf of other species added to the overall allowable cut, based on the prospect of better road access to remote stands using newly available federal road-construction funds. Although he acceded to the new ceiling, for the next five years Brandborg limited his annual sales to about 18 mmbf.[5]

With Anaconda's operations winding down in the Bitterroot Valley, and with smaller private timber holdings also significantly depleted, the valley's sawmills grew ever more dependent on federal timber. The prospect of a log shortfall was reinforced in a study issued in late 1943 by the Intermountain Forest and Range Experiment Station at Missoula. Titled *The Forest Situation in Ravalli County, Montana*, it backed Brandy's frequent assertions about the timber drain from private lands. Its authors, Lawrence Zach of the agency's Division of Forest Survey and S. Blair Hutchison of the Intermountain Station, pointed out that an average of 40 mmbf of ponderosa pine was being cut from all holdings in the valley, compared to only 7 mmbf of growth. "At the past rate of cutting and with the present plan of the owners," they wrote, "the private and State timber will be exhausted within a relatively few years, and the annual cut of pine in the Bitterroot Valley may be expected to drop to 7-½ million feet—the calculated sustained yield of the national forest."[6]

Lawrence Zach put the problem in more accessible terms in a news release issued in January 1944. He recalled "the golden stream of ponderosa pine" that had "poured out of the Bitterroot Valley beginning with the first large mill built at Hamilton in 1891":

> Now another chapter is about to be written in the lumbering history of Ravalli County. The big time cutting is about at an end; soon the long train of fine long logs that grew in the valley will no longer comprise the big part of the load as the train comes whistling for the crossing past Fort Missoula. Perhaps the lighter load will make it less difficult for the engine to climb the rise before crossing the Missoula River. Lighter also will be the revenue for the railroad. Gone will be some of the jobs that for over 50 years flowed from the pine forests of the Bitterroot.[7]

Complicating the picture in the ponderosa stands was the severely unequal distribution of age classes, consisting of a relatively small number of large, old pines on the national forest and a preponderance of young reproduction and pole-size stands on private lands—the leftovers from decades of heavy cutting. Much additional land lay unstocked or was being converted to range. "Too often," Zach wrote, "this results in changing good forest land capable of growing 100 board feet or more of saw timber per acre per year to grazing land that becomes progressively poorer and soon supports only a skimpy growth of weeds and unpalatable shrubs." Cuttings for poles and fuelwood also prevented establishment of mature stands, which was analogous, Zach claimed, to "butchering the milk cow right after freshening."[8]

Brandy had been making these points for years and agreed that something needed to be done. In his discussions with Major Kelley he noted that the fall-off in cutting would have a serious impact on the economy of the entire valley. He even made the startling suggestion of relaxing restrictions on logging within the Selway-Bitterroot Primitive Area to permit access to some stands of merchantable timber along its eastern edge. "These areas are in no one place of great magnitude but, on the whole, will be of such importance to the economy of the Bitterroot Valley that they should be used commercially."[9] There is no indication that he authorized any incursions into the primitive area, other than completing the Lost Horse road, but the need to maintain log supplies and keep local men employed clearly weighed on him.

Other than the modest increase in cutting approved by the regional office, Brandborg stuck to the stipulations of his 1941 plan: with few exceptions the pine would be hand marked and harvested using the single-tree selection method. Logs would be milled primarily within the Bitterroot Valley, leaving out of the picture the newer and rapidly expanding mills located in and around Missoula. He was willing to build roads into the remaining lower-elevation timber stands to put them into production, but only at a measured pace. Above all, he would try to avoid any major increases in cutting that would encourage industry to expand beyond what he believed was the long-term productive capacity of the forest. His focus was on maintaining employment in the county's small mills, not creating a new, modernized timber industry. But forces were at work that would require western Montana's timber operators to integrate into the larger economic picture. To remain competitive industry needed to bring in new equipment, adopt more efficient harvesting methods, and market its products to a wider area. These demands would place the valley's small operators in a difficult position during the postwar years.

After riding the wave of wartime demand, the timber industry was poised to take advantage of a surge in new home construction as hundreds of thousands of GIs returned from service. Beginning in 1946 the Forest Service's assistant chief, C. M. Granger, issued a series of directives to the regional offices urging them to immediately ramp up their timber-sale programs to meet the demand. "Road construction and betterment activities for at least the next twelve months should be set up to develop the immediate cutting of as large a volume of saw-logs and peelers as possible," he stated that June. Extending the forest-road network back into the mountains was critical, he said, to avoid overcutting stands closer to the mills. The Northern Region was allotted three million dollars in road-construction funds that year from the National Housing Administration, supplemented by two million dollars from regular appropriated funds. Because it would take time for the forests to build more long-haul roads to access remote stands, "any benefit of doubts should be given to the shorter term project this year," Granger emphasized.[10]

The leadership in Region 1 saw the Washington office's directive as both a challenge and an opportunity. Here was the long-awaited chance to bring its forests closer to full utilization of the timber resource—a goal they had sought since at least the 1920s. During the Depression and continuing into wartime, timber-sale levels on most of the forests in the region languished well below their allowed ceilings. That needed to change, according to regional forester P. D. "Pete" Hanson, who replaced Evan Kelley in 1944. In 1946 Hanson submitted substantial upward revisions in the annual allowable cuts for all of his west-side forests. The Flathead, a productive forest in northwestern Montana with extensive Douglas fir and larch stands, saw its ceiling raised from 40 mmbf in 1939 to 60 mmbf, while the Kootenai, also a rich timber producer, jumped from 18.4 mmbf to 44.6 mmbf. The Idaho national forests within the region—the Clearwater, Coeur d'Alene, Kaniksu, Nezperce, and St. Joe—collectively had their allowable cut raised from 157 mmbf to 254 mmbf.[11]

The new allowable cuts were no longer to be regarded as distant, unattainable ceilings but seen as clear objectives, Hanson told his forest supervisors. "We are obligated to push the regional cut up to 360 million this calendar year, 578 million in calendar year 1947, and about 600 million in calendar year 1948. By forests your production objective is to obtain actual production of not less than about 95 percent of your allowable cut during calendar year 1947."[12] Here was the clearest indication yet that a new era in public forestry had begun. The rapid acceleration in cutting would require hundreds of miles of new access roads and far more manpower devoted to laying out and administering timber sales. Each forest, Hanson said, was to examine its budget and tell the regional office where it needed more money, especially for timber surveys.

Hanson understood that accelerating harvests would make it harder to properly design timber sales. "We want [this] policy clearly understood," he instructed his field personnel in a curiously mixed message. "We do urge that each unit do its best to cut the maximum possible under sustained yield. But we do not want lowering of standards in sales preparation, marking, sales contract compliance, scaling, slash disposal, etc." Conspicuous by its absence was an expressed concern for other forest values, from aesthetics to wildlife habitat. "Obviously we should short-cut on methods wherever economy of effort without lowering standards will result," Hanson continued. "What we aim for is the maximum cut that can be obtained to acceptable standards." His message strongly implied that although field personnel should try to follow the rules, getting the timber out had priority. Occasional lapses in road construction, slash disposal, or log scaling, Hanson seemed to be suggesting, would be tolerated. In the rush to meet national housing goals, the agency's former insistence upon strict harvesting and cleanup requirements, a hallmark since Pinchot's time, was about to slip from its grasp.

It is unlikely that these requests caught the region's forest supervisors by surprise; many of their staffers, as on the Bitterroot, had been arguing for just such increases. The agency derived its cutting projections not in a top-down manner, as the regional forester's memo seemed to suggest, but from the bottom up: each forest, and indeed each ranger district, was required to periodically survey its merchantable timber stands and determine how much they could cut, given the available budget. They also were to indicate how much *more* they could cut if extra funds were made available for roads and sale preparation. Considerable encouragement in this direction came from Washington and the regional offices, but most field staff were ready and eager to get going. So was Brandborg, to a degree—but his concerns would mount steadily as the region's cutting program continued to advance.

Axel G. Lindh, who in 1944 replaced Elers Koch as Pete Hanson's chief of timber operations, was the principal architect of the Northern Region's stepped-up harvest program. In late 1946 he sent Brandborg his overview of the timber situation in the region, working from notes that he had prepared for Congressman Mike Mansfield.[13] The new objective was to harvest timber in each of the region's forests to the allowable limit. "The nation needs its timber," Lindh wrote. "Two-thirds of our production is exported....All parts of all these 85 working circles must be made to produce." Lindh remarked that the accelerated cutting "is vital if we are to achieve full production in minimum time.... [The current] rate of cutting is not enough and in fact will have to be approximately doubled if we are to achieve full production by 1948." Lindh noted that because of the growing demand for timber, nearly all of the sales they were offering in the region were being bid at ceiling prices set by the federal Office of Price Adjustment. These were due to be removed, promising greater revenues for the federal Treasury.

The Forest Service, in turn, required larger appropriations from Congress in order to hire and train staff to mark and advertise sales, lay out roads, and conduct the myriad aspects of a full timber program. Timber purchasers could build logging spur roads through credits applied against the price of stumpage, but the Forest Service felt it had to shoulder costs for the main haul roads—$10.5 million nationally for fiscal year 1947 alone.[14] "We believe the western congressional delegations do understand something of the need for a more aggressive program to facilitate production of timber from the national forests," Lindh told Brandborg. "Real timber crop management has had little place in the history of America. We have been custodians and protectors. We have had little opportunity to really demonstrate silviculture as the agriculturalists have demonstrated scientific farming. Yet the need to do so is everywhere apparent in an America of dwindling forest resources."[15]

Historians and other analysts have argued that the postwar timber boom on the national forests was fueled by a bureaucratic drive to expand the agency's budgets and authority.[16] There is much to support this idea: as federal appropriations increased, the Forest Service hired more timber staff and became almost completely oriented toward meeting production goals. Correspondence between the Washington office, the Northern Region, and the Bitterroot during the 1940s and early 1950s shows that the foresters were quite willing to take advantage of federal largesse in order to accomplish their goals, but funding alone does not seem to have been their primary motivation. For decades the personnel on the Bitterroot and in the regional office had tried to bring more timber stands under silvicultural control—a goal as important to them as contributing to local and national needs for timber. Achieving full forest regulation would represent a victory over nature's forces of decay and destruction—"stand mortality," in their term. Forest Service staff from the planners in the Hamilton office on up the line were as interested in applying their knowledge and skills as any trained professional. Money from Washington simply gave them the means to implement a program that had been too long in waiting.

Nor do the attitudes of regional office staffers such as Axel Lindh suggest that industry was handing down timber-cutting targets through the Congress. The Forest Service certainly saw itself as a key supplier of raw materials for the nation's growing economy, but within the Northern Region, and especially at the forest and district level, the relationship with individual lumber companies was often uneasy. The foresters were concerned about cutting too much from easily accessible areas where logging costs were lowest, and disagreements commonly occurred over wood utilization, log scaling, and road-construction standards. Far from being a response to outside pressure, the new emphasis that was evident in Hanson's and Lindh's directives reflected the deep-seated interests of forestry professionals at every level. The agency had been waiting since 1905 for this opportunity. The economic stars had aligned at last, and they were not about to miss their chance.

Lindh continued to prod Brandborg to step up his timber-management activities in line with the new emphasis. The Bitterroot's 1941 timber-management plan was the only one approved thus far in Region 1, but even it was outdated, Lindh thought. The plan addressed the regulation and development of 120,000 acres of ponderosa pine, but an additional 236,000 acres of the Bitterroot were considered commercial timberland. "With the local growing dependence it is urgent that this plan be revised and greatly intensified," Lindh wrote.[17]

The Bitterroot's timber staff continued to look for ways to utilize species other than ponderosa pine, including the lodgepole pine that covered the higher elevations of the forest. By 1954 they were encouraging local mills to install horizontal band-saw rigs that could handle trees down to five-inch tops. Brandborg told Pete Hanson that "in view of the large amount of Lodgepole material available, which, under present circumstances, is absolutely static or is even losing ground, we have encouraged the operator to go ahead. We believe we have an opportunity here to turn a liability into an asset provided we are able to encourage other operators into this field."[18] He stopped short of inviting Missoula-area mills to open new operations in the Bitterroot Valley, however, believing they would unduly compete with the local firms.

Outbreaks of insects such as the spruce bark beetle, spruce budworm, and Douglas fir bark beetle gave the foresters in Region 1 extra incentive to build roads into formerly undeveloped areas. These insects were attacking Douglas fir stands in the East Fork of the Bitterroot River and in the Deer Creek–Thunder Mountain area in the West Fork. By 1954 additional federal road-building funds were forthcoming, prompting the foresters to propose an extensive road network in the West Fork drainage to permit harvest of more than 250 mmbf of Douglas fir and ponderosa pine. On July 2, 1954, they held a public hearing at the Darby Ranger Station (as required under the terms of the federal grant) to present their rationale for the program. The initial phase of the project involved building or reconstructing twelve miles of road along the West Fork and in the Warm Springs and Blue Joint Creek drainages. Eighteen people, most of them sawmill owners, logging contractors, and stock growers, attended.[19]

The West Fork was a popular stream for anglers and campers, some of whom were concerned about losing the larger old trees that shaded their favorite spots, as well as increased log-truck traffic. The project drew what was probably the first formal citizen protest of a timber development project on the Bitterroot. Miles Romney Jr., who published a valley newspaper called the *Western News*, made his protest "in the most friendly terms," he wrote, but he felt that the road construction would prove as detrimental to the backcountry as the Lost Horse Canyon road. Romney's father had established the *Western News* in the 1890s as a quirky, progressive paper independent of the Anaconda-owned press. In a lengthy editorial, which he attached to his protest letter, Romney stated that the project would turn the West Fork into "a cigarette flipper's paradise with a maze of roads where trails should be built." His main concern, however, seemed to be that the foresters would not stop with the West Fork, and that "after the Bitter Root's recreation areas are despoiled will come an attack upon the Selway region.... I possess no doubt but that certain interests have their eye upon the Selway, are thirsting to 'harvest those ripe stands of timber' and turn that wonderful district into an American Gobi."[20]

To press their case in the face of this controversy, mill owners in the Darby area hired Sam Billings, who had recently retired from his job as the West Fork district ranger. Billings submitted a statement on behalf of his clients stating that the three roads under consideration were needed to efficiently manage the forest resources in the area. But he went to some length to acknowledge concerns about potential damage to recreation and wildlife areas:

> We realize that many individuals abhor the idea of having roads built into or near their favorite hunting, fishing or camping areas. They love the natural scene as God made it and through use of a favorite spot year

after year they acquire a sense of proprietorship over that particular site or area.... However, we hold that the recreational and wildlife and esthetic values in the drainages to be penetrated by these road and logging operations will not be materially reduced. There is very little evidence that roads and logging operations reduce game herds but a lot of prejudiced opinion that it does. Virgin fishing streams and lakes admittedly take a beating although there is still some mighty fine fishing in the Bitterroot River in spite of many roads. Logging roads do change the beauty of the natural scene in the immediate area of the road, but they also open up vistas for all to see that few if any people could see before.[21]

Billings's statement, which was as good a summary of the recreationists' concerns as any, seemed to indicate a degree of conflict in his own mind. The ranger probably spoke for many of his former colleagues who felt a close attachment to the Bitterroot's forests and waters and did not want to see them harmed. These men did not believe that they were exploiting a resource; they felt that the fine old trees in such places as the West Fork and the Selway were in jeopardy from destructive influences, and unless the stands were renewed through harvest they would soon lose their attractiveness and utility.

As an additional justification for expanding cutting into the West Fork, Billings cited problems from a needle blight called *Elytroderma,* which was spreading among ponderosa pine in the Blue Joint Creek drainage and, he feared, could become as devastating as the mountain pine-beetle epidemic of the 1930s. The harvest projected from this area, he said, would provide an annual payroll of nearly a million dollars and directly employ 237 men. "That's not hay," he concluded, pointing out that many of those who objected to the plan also financially benefited from the local timber industry.

Miles Romney's protest over the West Fork road project did nothing to slow the Bitterroot's logging program. It was a minor skirmish, but it foretold the contentious disputes that were to come in a few more years over the disposition of timber stands in the upper Selway River drainage. If Guy Brandborg harbored any doubts over timbering in the West Fork, he appears to have kept them to himself. His son, Stewart, recalled that "he never objected to good logging done on good sites." His public statements in the forest's annual reports show his desire to arrest the ongoing insect and blight epidemics and ensure better growth in the district's ponderosa pine and Douglas fir stands. The new roads, he noted in his report for 1954, would also improve access to this recreational area. "Scenic beauty, hunting and fishing chances and uncongested spots along cool, clear streams—these are the real recreation opportunities afforded on national forests," he wrote. "To preserve and enhance them, considerable thought is going into location and construction of roads whether they be short log haul roads or trunk lines up the West Fork."[22]

Despite his staff's push for more active management, Brandborg charted a middle course for the Bitterroot during his last ten years as supervisor. He insisted on having better timber inventories before undertaking any further expansion of cutting, as well as a well-trained staff to carry out the program and a strong public education effort. All of this took manpower away from laying out roads and preparing timber sales. His attempts to influence cutting practices on the Anaconda Company's land and other private holdings absorbed much of his staff's efforts. Selective cutting also was hardly conducive to high production goals. His conservation philosophy countenanced some new roads and a modest increase in logging, but not at the rapid rate his superiors demanded.

Brandy's "wheel of progress" concept depended upon balancing many factors of production, with no single program getting undue emphasis. Some of his colleagues wanted him to crank up the voltage from his metaphorical dynamo, at least in terms of timber production, but to the dismay of foresters like Axel Lindh, Brandy kept one foot on the brake. Lindh represented the managerial, production-oriented wing of Progressive thought, which sought to coax the maximum output of timber through the application of scientific forestry principles. But Brandy's conservative nature mistrusted any sudden explosion of activity, however well grounded in science. His policies hewed more to New Deal social concerns than to this latest manifestation of Progressive utilitarianism. He would not set his forest off-limits to logging, but he would limit harvests to the most productive sites and ensure that his rangers carefully monitored sales, cleanup, and road-construction work.

The limited amount of timber the Bitterroot offered for sale also brought it into conflict with mills in the Missoula area that wanted to take part in the region-wide expansion, including the Intermountain Lumber Company and its affiliate, Tree Farmers, Inc. Intermountain had acquired an interest in the Jess Edens mill in Darby and was cutting timber on State of Montana and Northern Pacific land as well as from the national forest. In 1954 Cameron Warren of Tree Farmers met with John Castles, a senior planner in the regional office, to complain about the Bitterroot's meager offerings. He said that the forest could offer an annual sustained yield of 61.8 mmbf if all species, including lodgepole pine, were factored in. At that time the forest was operating under an overall limit of 25 mmbf but was selling only 16 mmbf.

Brandy, when contacted by Castles, responded indignantly that in recent years he had offered sales that had gone without bids or had been sold to a single bidder and claimed that Intermountain had been trying to stir up opposition to the forest's policies among other mills in the Bitterroot Valley. "We fully anticipate a considerable amount of pressure from both Mr. Warren and Mr. [Horace] Koessler [a co-owner of Intermountain] to double our planned cut since their main source of timber in the very near future will be entirely from national forest lands," he replied. "With the completion of their mill the entire allowable cut of the Forest could very well be absorbed by their operations."[23] In later years both Brandborg and Koessler would recall these conversations in very different terms as each attempted to paint a picture of systematic malfeasance on the part of the other. By the 1950s the Bitterroot National Forest was one of the few sources of old-growth ponderosa pine in the region, which was at least partly the result of Brandborg's conservative harvesting policies. In trying to change those policies, both the Intermountain Lumber Company and its friends in the regional office were willing to put at risk the long-term supply of these golden trees.

During his last year on the forest, Brandy's staff began a second revision of the 1941 timber-management plan with an eye to increasing harvests of species other than ponderosa pine—a possible means of relieving the pressure on that species. A new timber-stand inventory showed 127,000 acres of merchantable Douglas fir that they thought could support an annual cut of 14 mmbf. Ponderosa pine harvests could be increased to 12 mmbf, for an overall sawtimber cut of 26 mmbf—barely above the 1946 agreement. Nearly 300,000 acres of lodgepole pine could provide some 70,000 cords of so-called roundwood for a prospective pulp mill in the Missoula area.[24] But industry officials saw even greater potential in the forest's untapped resources and continued to press the Bitterroot to make more sales available. After encountering Brandy's resistance, they employed the familiar tactic of taking their concerns to the state's congressional delegation. In February 1955 Cameron Warren complained to Mike Mansfield, now Montana's junior senator, that the Bitterroot still was offering only 18 mmbf per year, when local sawmills needed more than 30 mmbf. These mills, he said, "had to draw heavily on state and private timber to keep their mills operating. It is of great importance to the economy of the Bitterroot Valley that the allowable cut on a sustained yield basis be put up for sale each year, as the timber other than Federally owned is becoming scarcer and scarcer."[25]

Conflicts over timber policy were inevitable under the agency's competitive bidding system, and most forest supervisors expected complaints about their sale offerings. Warren's statement regarding the depletion of private timber stocks in the Bitterroot Valley was more serious and bore out one of Brandborg's frequent assertions: that industry would first cut through its lands and then turn to the national forests for relief. Brandy's clashes with the Intermountain Lumber Company would have repercussions lasting well beyond his retirement, when he would contend that they should never have located in the Bitterroot Valley given the limited amount of timber the national forest could produce. But despite this developing conflict, the Bitterroot would remain for a few more years a quiet backwater in Region 1's determined march into the industrial age.

CHAPTER 8

The Life of the Community

1943–1952

Even as Region 1 directed its west-side forests to focus on timber management, Guy Brandborg remained concerned for the health of Ravalli County's agricultural economy and the rural communities it supported. Before the war, the New Deal's economic stabilization programs had brought hundreds of Civilian Conservation Corps youths to Montana and employed local men in building roads into federal wildlands, but these programs did little to stem the outflow of residents from rural areas. World War II worsened the situation as military service drew off Montana's young men; factory jobs in West Coast cities promised better wages for workers fed up with the moribund agricultural sector.

Brandborg supported federal work programs, but he also believed that rural Montanans needed to do a little bootstrapping in their own communities. "It is not surprising that many of our young people want to get away from such places and into an atmosphere of enterprise, achievement, and at least apparent prosperity," he said in one of his talks from the 1940s. "To many young people the farm is becoming a dull place to live, and I believe that to many of them the small town looks even worse. In some areas of the state its appearance is barren, trees are few, buildings are often unpainted, many stand abandoned and in a state of decay. The very physical state of many of these smaller towns is a reminder of blasted hopes and thwarted ambitions."

There was a higher purpose to life, he believed, than scratching out an existence from a sometimes hostile land. "We must, to be sure, be able to make a living, but it is equally important that we be able to live richly. For unless life itself can be made challenging and satisfying, no economic opportunity in the way of a chance to make money will keep our young people in the state and give to our state the fullest development."[1] These opportunities, he believed, could be found only in stable communities that emphasized education at all levels, including for adults. Rapidly industrializing boomtowns were not conducive to such goals, nor were depopulated rural areas where men had to leave for jobs in cities—another reason he resisted the development paradigm instituted during World War II that relied on a mobile, follow-the-jobs workforce. Such thinking lay behind his resistance to increasing timber sales. Instead of finding ways to justify higher cutting levels, he would join Montana's liberal intellectuals in setting a backfire against too rapid industrial progress.

During the mid-1940s Brandy acquired some influential friends for his cause of community betterment. They came from the academic world, a region Brandy had set foot in during his service on the Montana State Board of Education. He frequently prodded his fellow board members to make the university system more relevant to the citizens of Montana's small towns and rural areas, who he believed deserved as many educational opportunities as the residents of Missoula and Bozeman. The chancellor of the state's university system, Ernest O. Melby, also wanted his colleges and universities to play a role in revitalizing Montana's smaller communities. City life, Melby observed, made followers of its citizens, who could then be "herded politically," as he put it, especially in times of war. To promote a vital rural life, Melby had helped direct a short-lived program of adult education and community affairs called the Northern Plains Study, which focused on the potential for regional planning and development in the upper Missouri River Basin. Funding for the project came from the Rockefeller Foundation, whose director, David Stevens, took an active interest in the welfare of the nation's rural areas.

In 1943 Stevens proposed to Melby that he set up a program with broader reach that emphasized local involvement in community planning and the humanities. The result was the Montana Study, a unique experiment in fostering self-awareness and community betterment in eleven of the state's small towns.

According to Melby, the study was to "find out so far as possible how the lives of the people in Montana and of their families and communities, may be stabilized and enriched." Since national forest lands formed an important part of the economic life of western Montana, the study aimed to cooperate closely with the Forest Service.[2]

With a grant of twenty-five thousand dollars from the Rockefeller Foundation, Melby hired Baker Brownell, a professor of philosophy at Northwestern University who had a deep interest in rural problems, to direct the study. Brownell in turn brought in Paul Meadows, a professor of sociology at Northwestern, and Joseph Kinsey Howard, the news editor of the *Great Falls Leader*, who had recently written a popular but controversial exposition of Montana history titled *Montana: High, Wide, and Handsome*. In it Howard made a case for regional planning as a means of coping with the harsh conditions of agriculture on the Great Plains—a position that would get him in trouble with some Montana politicians. His views on the subject paralleled Brandborg's. "Planning—grass-roots planning, the only kind that can ever succeed, was born in the agony of the northwestern drouth," Howard wrote. "The new farm practices [such as large-scale contour-strip farming] wouldn't work for just one farmer in a district or a county. There had to be cooperation, agreed upon in advance. It was cooperate or perish, and with cooperation, there was planning."[3]

The study leaders met with a citizen steering committee in Bozeman in 1945 to outline the projected work, producing a document that depicted the current state of Montana's economic and social life. It suggested that the state operated largely as a colonial economy in which raw materials were shipped outside its borders in exchange for manufactured goods—a situation the authors thought was not viable over the long run. "We look with pride upon figures that reflect the results of our high-powered, mechanized effort," its authors wrote, "taking little heed in what obviously is a stark reality, namely, that too often 'figures of production are figures of exhaustion.'" The answer, they believed, was for citizens to "institute plans of land utilization that will mean an enduring economy." To the notion of greater economic self-sufficiency, Brownell added the goal of social stabilization—helping Montanans create the cultural and economic institutions that would encourage permanent communities. He drew a parallel to the idea of sustained-yield forestry: by stabilizing economic life, both young and old could find work that would contribute to a lasting society. "Our booms, depressions, wars, our migratory workers, our disintegrating families and small communities, all show this lack of balance and stability," he said.[4]

Brownell, Meadows, and Howard traveled around the state to locate likely towns in which to set up community study groups. Eleven communities responded favorably, including five in the Bitterroot Valley. The project staff assisted the groups' discussions and research but made it clear that these must be community-led efforts. Each decided on its own approach, which might take the form of historical studies and interviews, community dramatic productions (as favored by another Montana Study staffer, dramatist Bert Hansen of Montana State College in Bozeman), or hands-on projects such as building recreational centers and locating new businesses.

Brandy and Edna took a leading part in a discussion group in Hamilton along with twenty-seven other residents, including his timber staff officer Fred Stell and West Fork ranger Sam Billings. Brandy presented reports on family affairs and wildlife; other committees addressed school issues and relations between towns and rural areas.[5] In Darby, Champ Hannon chaired a study group that examined employment conditions in the southern Bitterroot Valley and encouraged local businessmen to start new ventures in town. Darby residents credited the study with sparking a development boom of sorts, according to Richard Poston, a former Montana State University student who interviewed Montana Study participants for his book *Small Town Renaissance*. Fifteen new businesses opened their doors in or near Darby within a few years of the study, including a small sawmill, a planing mill that employed twenty-six men, a restaurant, grocery, auto garage, machine shop, and well-drilling outfit. These enterprises mitigated the decline in private-land timber harvests and made it possible for more high school graduates to put down roots.[6]

The Darby group also wrote and presented an allegorical play titled *Darby Looks at Itself.* In an episode about the demise of the logging industry in the valley, the Anaconda Company is loosely portrayed as the Devil. Here he is depicted alongside an old lumberjack, both of them surveying the aftermath of destructive logging on private lands:

DEVIL: Well, well, old lumberjack, old pal, it looks like you've done a pretty good job around Darby. Pretty good indeed.

OLD LUMBERJACK: This here is the last big tree on the last big job. Logging around here is about finished and so am I who logged it.

DEVIL: Well, that's fine. Good Work. Good Work. You've been a faithful servant.

OLD LUMBERJACK: Don't know of a logging job in sight for anybody, to tell the truth. She's all gone.

The Devil points out that there are trees still standing in the nearby forest reserve, to which the lumberjack retorts, "Them woods is under selective logging practices which means you can't cut them all out, only a certain percentage of them. And I ain't no fool, not any more I ain't." The Devil rallies the other lumberjacks and urges them to raid the government land, branding as a communist anyone who demurs. A second lumberjack raises a club and brains the Devil, ending the debate. A forest ranger appears and assures the men that there will always be trees to cut in the reserve—"more and more as time goes on."[7] This over-the-top production may not have expressed everyone's sentiment in Darby, but it accurately depicted the views of a contingent of old-time loggers and foresters who approved of the Bitterroot's approach to forest management. Several of them, including Hannon, would form a nucleus for the timber protests of the 1960s.

In Stevensville Charles McDonald, Brandy's district ranger, helped plan a community-wide reenactment of the Anglo settlement of the Bitterroot Valley and the eviction of its Salish inhabitants. The pageant drew twenty-five hundred viewers from up and down the valley and featured the grandson of Charlo, the Salish chief, in that role. McDonald tried to build on the success of the pageant by starting a study group devoted to analyzing land-use practices, a topic he addressed frequently in his work as district ranger. According to Poston, McDonald "had preached good management of natural resources for so long that people were sick of listening," but he found a small group that was willing to pursue the idea. Looking back on their work in a 1970 interview, McDonald lamented the lack of support for the Montana Study among some townspeople. "I think the people had a great opportunity there, and they muffed it," he said. "They had this fear of being called a Communist, see, and they just run from it, and plugged their ears. It's a great shame, I think the valley's the poorer because of missing out on that."[8]

The Forest Service was officially involved with the Montana Study in Lincoln County, Montana, where it was considering a cooperative sustained-yield unit with the J. Neils Lumber Company of Libby, through which public and private timberlands would be managed under a single plan. Baker Brownell engaged sociologists Harold and Lois Kaufman to survey county residents' attitudes about the proposal. The tall forests of northwestern Montana had supported a robust logging economy for decades, but the depletion of its private timber stocks told a story akin to that taking place on the Bitterroot, in which many residents feared for the continued existence of smaller independent logging and milling operations. While the Kaufmans agreed that the J. Neils mill could stabilize local industry because of its size and efficiency, they noted widespread distrust of the company. "From the standpoint of the community members interviewed," they wrote, "the basic issue with respect to forest policy is not so much one of technical forestry as one of social control and economic reward"—in other words, who stood to benefit from the concentration of managerial and economic power in one company.[9]

Axel Lindh, as head of the Northern Region's timber management division, welcomed the Kaufmans' study, but he came down on the side of the larger business concerns. "The Forest Service believes that at least one reasonably sized mill is essential as a mainstay of industry in Lincoln County," he wrote in a separate section of the report. "Small mills are commonly wasteful of timber and their products are of such low quality as to be the first to weaken in declining markets." Such mills, he said, served primarily to absorb workers who for various reasons might not want to work for a larger outfit.[10] He would take much the same position in regard to the Bitterroot's historically scattered and evanescent sawmills.

Lindh suggested that Montanans needed to grapple with the social consequences of logging by themselves, as his staff was quite occupied with the technical aspects of forestry. "Frankly," he wrote, "the forest planners are still engaged in the basic job of shaping the forest management and timber disposal plans and have a number of unsolved major problems."[11] By this he evidently meant that his staff would work out how to supply the timber, but they could not deal effectively with diffuse, intractable community issues. It was an attitude that would haunt his successors once powerful grassroots concern developed in opposition to the Northern Region's heavy emphasis on timber production.

Other officials in the Northern Region saw more promise from the Montana Study. Meyer Wolff, an assistant regional forester in charge of operations, suggested that a study similar to the Kaufmans' be done for Ravalli County. He believed that it would show that the Bitterroot Valley was as dependent on irrigation water from the forest as it was on timber. Recreational needs and livestock forage also needed attention. Wolff, a self-described Progressive who had worked in the Northern Region since 1911, advised regional forester P. D. Hanson that "we should never slight these other uses and services of forest lands when considering the influence on local welfare."[12]

Brandborg was the Montana Study's biggest cheerleader in the agency, since it seemed to offer the best chance to get citizens in Ravalli County and elsewhere in Montana truly involved in their future. He fought for continued funding for the study through the State Board of Education, defending it against attack from politicians who saw the program as overly idealistic and left-leaning. At a meeting of the state board in Missoula in December 1945, debate broke out over whether to sponsor the program for a third year. The *Great Falls Tribune* quoted Governor Sam Ford as saying he did not "believe in turning a lot of foreigners loose with wild ideas," but he would support the program with certain safeguards.[13] Some of the board members objected to Joseph Howard's support for regional planning ventures such as the Missouri Valley Authority—Senator James Murray's proposal for a coordinated program of water power, flood control, and irrigation development patterned after the controversial Tennessee Valley Authority. Many Republican lawmakers in the state, including Ford, feared the program would give the federal government power to condemn land for reservoir projects, as had happened in Tennessee. Taking note of these attacks, Baker Brownell assured Brandborg that he had not used his position to advance his personal agenda. "The staff has not attempted to promote any cause whatever through the Montana Study," he said, "except that of preserving the small Montana community, the family farm, and the family. We do not regard these as 'wild ideas.'"[14]

The lack of support for the Montana Study among the state's leaders spelled its demise. During the initial two-year study Stevens made it clear that the state, especially its university system, would have to get behind the project and eventually supply most of its funding. That proved difficult to obtain. College enrollments were booming following the war, and administrators favored funding their own institutions in preference to an extracurricular program in which few students participated. It did not help that most of the project's staff had plans to move on. Ernest Melby resigned his chancellorship in 1944 to assume the presidency of MSU; he left this position the following year to become dean of New York University. He was replaced by George A. Selke, the president of St. Cloud College in Minnesota and a former teacher of Melby. Baker Brownell, who was on leave of absence from Northwestern, signaled his intention to return to his duties during the study's second year. Brandy tried to dissuade him, but

Brownell resigned in September 1946 and was replaced by Ruth Robinson, a teacher from Conrad, Montana, who had served on the project's staff. Howard resigned a few months later to return to his writing career.

Brandborg made two trips to Helena to urge Selke to submit a new funding proposal to Rockefeller, but in August 1948 Stevens informed Selke that the foundation had denied further support. Brandborg, Howard, and Robinson continued to press Selke and Stevens for some kind of interim funding, to no avail. Brandy let his frustration show in a letter to Howard following a state board meeting in the fall of 1948. "I told the educators that educationally speaking they were cooking on a cold stove and as far as I could see they didn't really want to tackle some of our educational problems," he wrote. Most of the board members, he said, felt "rather unkind over some of my comments."[15] Having tasted several years' worth of community action in Ravalli County, including two spectacular dramatic productions, Brandy was loath to let the program go. Soon after receiving the news from Stevens, he got Selke to sign off on a plan to resurrect the Montana Study for a six-year period. Ravalli County would serve as a pilot program to establish as many study groups as possible, continue the drama program, and set up university short courses in small communities. Selke and Brandborg were able to get the state board to add $80,000 to the pot, but the $127,000 they requested from Rockefeller was turned down.[16] Nothing seemed to work, and Brandy resigned himself to the loss of his dream for an effective community-action program in the Bitterroot.

The demise of the Montana Study turned out to be a loss for the Forest Service as well; the discussion forums Brandborg was so fond of might have given its leaders early warning of discontent over its timber program. Ravalli County's citizens could have actively shaped the Bitterroot's overall management program, perhaps by underscoring the critical importance of irrigation water, as Meyer Wolff had suggested. When the Montana Study closed its doors, no clear avenue remained for citizens to report their concerns to the agency, other than through isolated complaints about practices in particular drainages. It would take another grassroots committee two decades thence to call attention to the larger implications of forest management practices—information the Forest Service needed much earlier in order to adjust its timber program. The Montana Study was idealistic, certainly, and probably unrealistic in its goals, but in limiting themselves to traditional educational concerns, the state's leaders lost a chance to forge a more participatory democracy.

Despite the successes of the Darby and Stevensville study groups, many valley residents still considered the Montana Study to be a source of subversive thinking. They were not alone; the postwar environment nationwide was growing much less hospitable to liberal thinking. In March 1947 President Truman signed Executive Order 9835, which required each federal department to set up loyalty boards to investigate suspicious employees. The investigations were conducted in secret, generally by the FBI, and in a gross inversion of justice they required suspected individuals to prove their innocence. A master index kept by the Civil Service Commission ensured that no employee found to be disloyal would ever again find work with the federal government.

Brandy's support for the Montana Study reinforced his reputation as a controversial figure in the Bitterroot Valley, one already well established through his frequent statements on the importance of government planning and acquisition of private forest lands. It nonetheless came as a shock when in January 1949 he received a registered letter from the executive secretary of the Department of Agriculture's loyalty board, informing him that the FBI had conducted an investigation of him and had supplied its findings to the department. A detailed interrogatory was enclosed that he was to fill out under oath and return in quadruplicate. It included such questions as "Were you acquainted with the late Robert 'Bob' Marshall?" and asked whether he had ever subscribed to or regularly read *In Fact, New World, New Republic, Russia Today,* or *People's Voice.* There were the usual questions about whether he advocated the overthrow of the government, had been a Communist Party member, attended party meetings, had known or associated with known communists, had belonged to any group listed as sympathetic to communism, or ever "cursed the United States Government."[17]

Brandy answered "no" to each of these questions without elaboration, which was likely a mistake. His answers would be processed by a faceless functionary in Washington who had his own reasons (or directions) for pursuing the investigation and was not inclined to give him the benefit of the doubt. By not amplifying his answers or taking an aggressive stand against his accusers, Brandy had little chance of derailing the investigation. Two months later a second letter arrived, informing him that he stood accused of disloyalty. Its tone was chilling:

> The record discloses that you have indicated that you favor the overthrow
> of the present form of government of the United State [*sic*]; that you have
> espoused the Communist form of government; that you have associ-
> ated on a friendly basis with a person reliably reported to be a member
> of an organization designated as Communist; that you have subscribed to
> and regularly read publications which follow the Communist Party line;
> and that you have distributed these publications among fellow employ-
> ees.... You are directed to show cause why you should not be removed
> from your position in this Department.[18]

No evidence for these accusations was given. Brandborg was allowed fifteen days to answer the charges in writing and was given the right to request a
hearing. His reply was earnest, heartfelt, and reasonable, indicating that he still
did not fully understand the nature of the game he was in. "It's indeed regretta-
ble," he wrote, "that the Department subjects its employees to such embarrass-
ment without first making a thorough administrative investigation." The charges
arose, he said, as a result of differences of opinion over his advocacy of land-use
planning to improve forest management on private lands—a program developed and encouraged by an agency of the Department of Agriculture. This, he
said, "gave cause to such criticism that I was advocating Communism or something aside from Americanism."

Yes, he had met with Bob Marshall, a Forest Service employee who had
toured Region 1 in 1937. Yes, he subscribed to *People's Voice*, a publication of the
National Farmer's Union, a rural populist group. No, he had never requested any
employee to read the publications in question. "Besides," he offered, "reading
different points of view on any subject is no cause for judging anyone disloyal."
He asked his investigators to look instead into those who had anonymously
accused him and requested a hearing to clear his name. "It appears," he said,
"that we are experiencing a stage in our development where anyone striving to
strengthen Democracy becomes branded as an enemy."[19]

His efforts to reason with the loyalty board were fruitless. He was dealing
with an enormous engine of suspicion and power that cared nothing for individual Americans, and had terrorized the staffs of government departments into
following its blind agenda. An atmosphere of hysteria gripped many members
of Congress; a committee set up to investigate the loyalty boards' excesses made
only the mildest protest of their methods. "Disloyal and subversive elements in
our Government constitute a dangerous and malignant growth which must be
promptly and effectively removed," its report stated. "Considering the insidious

cunning and deceit of a Communist, any reasonable doubt as to the loyalty of a person should be resolved in favor of the Government."[20]

Brandborg suspected that the initial accusations had come from one or two former employees who were upset by his advocacy of social forestry. Earlier, one of these employees had filed a complaint with the regional office in Missoula, triggering an in-house investigation from which Brandy was exonerated without much fuss. It hit him hard, though, that an old grievance had been lifted out of some file drawer and dressed up as a serious federal charge. He resolved not to tell Edna, who was unwell with a heart condition, about the matter, denying himself her support through the coming ordeal. Instead, he found a well-recommended attorney in Missoula to help him fight the charges.[21]

Joseph Kinsey Howard was among those outraged by the affair, and he asked Senator James Murray to intercede on Brandy's behalf. "To question his loyalty, I can testify from close association with him for some years, is absurd," he wrote. "Like the Senator, myself and thousands of others, he has been a lifelong liberal; as such he has been a tower of strength in Montana. He has been by long odds the most progressive member of the State Board of Education, an outstanding friend of higher education and, even more important in my opinion adult education. He has originated or inspired important moves to bring the problems of resource conservation and wise use home to the citizens—demonstration tours, countywide study groups, etc." Howard, no stranger to controversy, told Murray that he, too, read *People's Voice*. "I happen to be a stockholder in that paper to the extent of $10. That hardly makes my loyalty suspect, or does it?"[22]

The hearing was held in Missoula on June 3, 1949. The men who spoke on Brandy's behalf were a who's who of Montana's liberal elite. They included three Montana Supreme Court justices, who suspended court for the day in order to testify: Chief Justice Hugh Adair, Associate Justice Vic Bottomly, and a progressive attorney from Stevensville named Lee Metcalf. Joseph Kinsey Howard testified, as did two former regional foresters—likely Evan Kelley and possibly Elers Koch—as well as a dozen of Brandy's other Forest Service friends (their names, unfortunately, are not on record). MSU president James McCain spoke of Brandborg's service to higher education. A telegram of support from Governor John Bonner and a letter from Ernest Melby added to the list. Stanley Antrim, a Bitterroot Valley rancher who had worked with Brandy since 1935 on range conservation programs, took time from his summer sheep drive to testify. Howard reported that Antrim "paid Brandy high tribute as stimulating him to adopt many of the practices which had made him a highly successful rancher."[23]

Brandy's supporters managed to turn the tables on the investigative committee, accusing it of bringing a baseless case against an esteemed public servant. Taken aback by this show of force, the committee members asked whether they or Brandborg were the subject of the hearing. Both Howard and Brandborg understood that this was an exceptional case and worried that accusations brought against junior government employees could well be made to stick. "There's something at work in our democracy," Howard wrote to Ernest Melby after the hearing, "which appears to me to be even more deadly than the witch hunt after World War I—that was unreasoning hysteria which, though it wrecked the labor movement at the time, burned itself out and died in disgrace. There seem to be cooler and smarter heads behind this present business. . . . I don't know what the result is going to be and it scares me."[24]

Given the weight of testimony in Brandborg's favor, the hearing panel had little choice but to exonerate him. Even that took six months, with the results finally appearing in Brandy's mailbox as a form letter. It announced that a favorable decision had been reached and the case would be closed. The department offered no further explanation or apology.[25] He retained his job, but in the minds of some of his associates, his reputation had been tainted. The secrecy of the proceedings ensured that no others would hear the testimony on his behalf.

Chief Justice Adair was sufficiently exercised by the tribunal that while waiting outside the hearing room (each witness was ushered in separately), he composed letters of protest to President Truman and the members of Montana's congressional delegation. "Who is trying to get Guy Brandborg's job? And why are they trying to do it?" he asked Senator Zales Ecton. "Who and what has inspired this investigation and hearing? Is it the stock growers who desire to put more cattle on the public domain? Is it the lumber and timber interests who desire to have less rigidly enforced rules and regulations governing the taking of timber from the public domain?"[26]

Adair's questions could not be answered, but in pointing his finger at the state's resource users, he was displaying a fear long held among Montana's progressives, who knew the state's history of political domination by the Anaconda Company, Montana Power Company, and Northern Pacific Railroad. Brandy's belief that the charges had originated with former employees was probably closer to the mark. Given the climate of the times, it hardly required behind-the-scenes manipulation on the part of resource interests to bring about such an affair. Brandy, for his part, never laid blame at Anaconda's doorstep.

The affair still rankled, though, when he recounted it for Mavis McKelvey in 1975. "Can you imagine yourself going up into an attorney's office and hafta ask somebody to defend you in this kinda stuff?" he said, his voice betraying emotion twenty-six years later. "You can imagine what you're livin' under in those kind of circumstances."[27] On several occasions he described the experience as humiliating, but why it would be so is not clear. As Joe Howard remarked to Ernest Melby, "The demonstration of friendship was so striking and such glowing testimony was given on his behalf that I think his memories of the incident will, after a short time, be grateful ones." That would not happen, unfortunately. More than one of his friends noticed that Brandy seemed a changed man after his loyalty hearing—disillusioned, perhaps; certainly disappointed in the state of American democracy. He believed, as did most liberals, in the forward progress of democratic institutions. He survived his grueling inquisition, but his faith in his government was seriously weakened.

A further blow came early in 1952, when P. D. Hanson completed a round of personnel ratings for key staffers, including his seventeen forest supervisors. Brandborg found himself downrated for general administrative abilities. Hanson based the rating partly on the comments of a review committee consisting of three assistant regional foresters, one of whom faulted "the rather strongly emotional approach which characterizes Brandy's earnest defense of what he believes in. As the committee sees it, the largest problem is to get Brandy to give balanced attention to the 'doing' jobs of national forest administration." Hanson concluded by saying that "frankly, Brandy, I believe that potentially you can turn in a top job providing you conscientiously try to curb your enthusiasms in some fields and stimulate yourself in others."[28]

Brandborg felt that he had long been engaged in precisely what his agency needed to be doing; in reply, he stated that several of his associates—men whose judgment he valued—had told him that his efforts "have resulted in better public understanding and support in the Bitterroot Valley of the complexities of wildland management than in any other national forest community that they know."[29] But neither Hanson nor Brandy's other critics in the regional office faulted his outreach programs, which were known to be outstanding; they objected primarily to his refusal to sell more timber from more acres of his forest. Brandborg's use of the term *wildland management* was telling. To him this meant the compatible integration of many uses on the national forest—including watershed protection, wildlife habitat, and backcountry recreation—while producing a modest amount of timber in a manner that would not detract from those uses. But to many in the agency, timber production on the Bitterroot could be greatly increased while maintaining other values.

Much had changed in the Northern Region since the 1930s, when Evan Kelley drove down to Hamilton to tell the Chamber of Commerce that they needed a countywide forestry and land-use policy. The agency's new emphasis was clear: holdouts such as Guy Brandborg needed to get in step with the region's timber program. Brandy remained in his position for three more years, but he was already considering early retirement. "The old faces are gone," he told George Ring, a former colleague from the Nezperce, in late 1952. "Clyde [Blake] and I have about run our strength as far as the Forest Service career is concerned." The following year he confided in a letter to Bob Marshall's brother, George, that he was thinking of severing his connections to the agency "to assume the role of private citizen in the interest of achieving better public understanding of conservation ideals."[30] He had spent nearly twenty years in Hamilton attempting to further those ideals, only to see a new and, to him, dangerous preoccupation with resource production take over his agency.

CHAPTER 9

Holding the Line

1948–1958

For the first few decades following World War II, Montana's sportsmen, farmers, ranchers, hikers, and foresters could all find a chair under the spacious awning called the conservation movement. Its principles remained largely utilitarian despite the emergence of new ideas about wildland preservation and land ethics. Many individuals in the various natural resource agencies of the federal government wanted to extend the gains that had been made during the New Deal, which had introduced progressive farming methods such as strip contouring as well as improved forest-fire protection and watershed rehabilitation. In 1948 representatives of seventeen public and private organizations met in Missoula to form the Montana Conservation Council, which was intended to promote public education and action on conservation issues. The group was a successor to the Northwest Conservation League, which had formed in 1938 in the state of Washington.

According to Brandborg, the idea for the Montana group came from Professor Joseph Severy, with whom he had worked on educational outreach to sportsmen in Ravalli County. To set up the organization, Brandborg and a Bitterroot Valley farmer he knew met with Severy and Kenneth Davis, dean of the forestry school at MSU-Missoula, who agreed to serve as the group's first president. Brandborg served on the group's board of directors until 1962. One of its more visible efforts was an annual Conservation Caravan in which busloads of teachers, Forest Service staff, agriculturalists, reporters, and interested citizens toured the state to examine land-use practices on farm-, ranch, and forest lands.

Arnold Bolle, president of the council from 1959 to 1962, recalled that an additional goal was to foster cooperation among the many organizations devoted to wildlife, soil conservation, and even civic beauty. The council, he said, "seeks to reach agreement on those issues where there are many areas of agreement" and not, as he put it, "dissipate our strength in arguments with ourselves."[1] For a time the council maintained a lobbyist in Helena to promote nonpartisan legislation, including a water-pollution control act that was enacted in 1955 and an underground-aquifer protection act in 1961. It supported in-service training of agency personnel—long one of Brandy's interests—to encourage narrowly trained technicians to appreciate the broader implications of land conservation. Educational outreach, though, remained the group's main focus. It sponsored training workshops for teachers, published a brochure on conservation education, and supported funding for MSU's Wildlife Extension program.

Brandy took part in these efforts as chairman of the council's education committee, a position he held through most of the 1950s. One of his priorities was to awaken interest in conservation among the state's schoolchildren. With Dr. Severy's help he designed a program to require the teaching of a conservation curriculum in the public schools, beginning with the elementary years. A companion program to train teachers was to be made available through their college-level preparatory courses. To gain support from conservative legislators, they tied their proposal to economic progress. "Conservation of natural resources is fundamental to the prosperity of Montana," it read. "The welfare and wise use of our farms, our ranges, our forests, our rivers, our minerals, our wildlife is basic to our way of life."[2] Eventually, Brandborg and others in the Montana Conservation Council succeeded in establishing a Conservation Education Division within the Montana Fish and Game Department to carry on the work.

The Montana Conservation Council succeeded in raising awareness of conservation goals, but the need for consensus among its disparate groups left Brandy feeling impatient. He wanted the group to take more assertive stances on issues such as forest depletion and agricultural soil loss, as well as oppose the full-development policies of Department of Agriculture secretary Ezra Taft Benson. Many agency personnel, though, feared speaking out or being perceived as raising controversy—activities Brandy had learned were not without risk. By 1960 he had become disillusioned with the council's work and took less part in its activities.³ Consensus, it seemed, was as elusive in the 1950s as it is today.

Few aspects of public policy brought questions of land use into sharper focus than wildlife conservation, especially of the state's big-game herds. For decades the only means sportsmen had to aid the recovery of elk, deer, and mountain-sheep populations were the state's game laws, but by the 1940s it was clear that habitat loss—chiefly encroachments upon winter range and summer feeding areas and escape cover—was equally crucial. In 1953 members of the Ravalli County Fish and Wildlife Association registered objections to the expanding road network in the upper drainage of the Bitterroot River and on the Bitterroot mountain face. The Forest Service's emphasis on timber production—even under Brandborg's conservative methods—was leading to increased vehicular traffic and human use in the backcountry, driving off big game from its usual haunts and possibly reducing reproductive success. In response to the sportsmen's protests, Howard Lee of the supervisor's office urged the forest's district rangers to stress the need to manage resources productively. "I believe our responsibility lies in pointing out to interested people the basic policy of 'greatest good etc.' and the multiple use objective upon which we feel all of our decisions must be based," he wrote. "Our position should be purely factual. I think the value and contribution of the timber resource to the local communities should be stressed."⁴ Significantly, he did not advise that his agency hold back the road-building program in areas of key wildlife habitat.

Brandy was sympathetic to the sportsmen and often sided with them in disputes with ranchers. To minimize further conflicts, he had each of the Bitterroot's rangers draw up multiple-use management plans for their districts—among the first to be devised in the region. The plans laid out provisions designed to minimize the impact of timber cutting and road building on watersheds, wildlife habitat, and recreational areas. The plan for the Darby district, for example, called for employing patch cuts of not more than one acre to produce more forage for big game. These clearings, together with natural openings and road rights-of-way, were not to aggregate more than 10 percent of the area involved. Other limitations included waterfront zones around streams and lakes, which were to be cut lightly or not at all, and construction standards for logging roads to protect water quality.⁵ The plans were noteworthy for attempting to reconcile conflicting uses—an approach that, had it been fully implemented and left in place, might have forestalled some of the conflict that was to come.

An unusual element of these early multiple-use plans was an attempt to estimate the economic worth of various forest uses. According to the Darby district's analysis, its 5 mmbf sustained-yield cut of timber returned some $325,000 annually (more than $2 million in today's dollars) to the local economy in wages, expenses, and profit. Cattle grazing produced a gross annual income to ranchers of $157,000. More surprising were the benefits accruing from amenity uses. The district supported a major recreational resource, with hunting, fishing, camping, picnicking, and other categories such as resort guests contributing to more than twenty-seven thousand visitor-days of use each year. Big-game hunters were felt to return about $10 a day to the local economy, with other recreational uses valued at $5.50, for a total of $291,000 in annual economic benefits—nearly equal to the timber resource. Topping this, however, was the value of the forest watershed to downstream irrigators and other users, which was valued at $1.50 per acre. Thus, the Darby district was believed to bring in $543,000 in annual benefits—more than timber and cattle combined—simply by existing in an undisturbed condition. On the Stevensville district, where many mountain streams were developed for irrigation, watershed use was valued at $3.00 per acre, for a total value of $674,000—more than double the value produced by timber cutting.[6]

Only the Darby district's plan was completed before Brandborg left the forest in 1955, but all of them fitted his desire to promote long-term values on the forest, including clean water, huntable wildlife, and scenic beauty. The high dollar values attached to recreational and watershed uses in the Bitterroot's first multiple-use plans, inexact as they were, should have raised a warning flag to anyone taking a broad view of the forest. The agency's timber planners thought that new roads and logging units would enhance these uses, but many individuals in the Bitterroot Valley preferred them as they were—a lesson the Forest Service learned too late.

In the fall of 1954, shortly after announcing his intention to retire, Brandborg issued his final annual report for the Bitterroot National Forest. Instead of reciting statistics on timber harvests and forage utilization, he chose once again to relate his philosophy of public forest management—perhaps in the hope that his successor might carry on his practices. He observed that each American owned, in effect, a one-acre share in the national forest system—which, owing to the country's growing population, was half of what it was fifty years earlier when the Forest Service began its work. Because of this, he wrote, "the demand for foodstuffs, building materials, water, and just plain living space place emphasis on intelligent management of all lands."

The answer to these increasing demands, in his view, lay not in bold new techniques of forest management but in reaffirming the agency's founding principles—the same Progressive ideals that Dorr Skeels had drilled into him in 1915 and 1916. He went on to quote at length from a 1905 letter of policy that Secretary of Agriculture James Wilson sent to Gifford Pinchot, the new chief of the Forest Service. The letter, which was actually drafted by Pinchot, directed that "all land is to be devoted to its most productive use for the permanent good of the whole people; and not for the temporary benefit of individuals or companies."[7] Brandy took the Wilson letter and Pinchot's subsequent elaborations upon it as his personal instructions, which seemed to him to be clear enough: the claims of industrial giants such as the Anaconda Company were to be resisted in favor of policies that benefited small operators and local people.

Embedded in the Wilson letter was Pinchot's famous conundrum that the national forests would be managed to provide "the greatest good of the greatest number in the long run." This enigmatic requirement, which was difficult to pin down in most real-world circumstances, would nonetheless stand as the Forest Service's mission statement throughout the century. By 1955 many in the agency believed that the answer to Pinchot's riddle was to increase resource production on every front—undertaking what historian Paul Hirt called a "conspiracy of optimism" in favor of the most intensive forms of management. This unstated but deeply felt belief held that the competing demands of a growing nation could be accommodated only through more efficient production. Everything from sawlogs to recreational visitor-days could be increased to cover demand if the agency's programs were fully funded. Following World War II, Hirt wrote, "the agency adopted the ideology of intensive management to justify increasing the allowable cut, believing that its foresters could greatly enhance forest production on a permanent basis."[8]

Although Brandborg believed in coordinated resource production, he sought his answers not in technologically driven expansion but in the needs and responsibilities of the local community. Logging could be boosted to a degree, but landowners were responsible for growing trees on their holdings as well. To him, the success of the federal forestry program depended on cooperative programs to ensure that everyone—including the state's major corporations—was working from the same sustained-yield approach. In his 1955 report he listed six such initiatives that he had helped start, ranging from the MSU Wildlife Extension program to his latest idea, an intergovernmental coordinating body called the Ravalli County Agricultural Resource Conservation Program.

The latter was supposed to bring together the Bitterroot Valley's ranchers and farmers with representatives of the Soil Conservation Service, Forest Service, and other state and federal agencies to improve irrigation, farming, and forestry methods. The program's introductory statement reflected Brandy's commitment to "harmonious community action, starting at the grass-roots, to correct these physical, social, and economic problems." The program languished for lack of strong leadership, Brandy recalled later. He had hoped that the county extension agents would rise to the task, but he thought that they were too narrowly focused on increasing agricultural productivity—"making two blades of grass grow where one grew before," as he put it. His interests were broader, encompassing social concerns as well as conservation practices, and he found it difficult to generate enthusiasm among people who had rows of their own to hoe.[9]

None of these outreach programs furthered Region 1's get-out-the-cut program, yet Brandy gave them his highest priority. Each represented a chance to educate the public in better land-use practices, which he accorded as much importance as managing the Bitterroot's pine and fir stands. A consistent theme of these programs was to improve everyday living standards and the quality of life in the Bitterroot Valley. There were sawmills that depended upon a steady supply of big ponderosa pine logs, ranchers who needed fence posts and irrigation water, and townspeople who wanted their elk in the fall and a pleasant place to fish or picnic in the summer. They would have these resources, he told them, only if the pines were harvested at a conservative rate, the high mountain watersheds were protected from fire, and the winter ranges at the valley's edges supported good grass. They must think in the long term by planting trees on marginal agricultural land, ensure that their fields were free of weeds, and keep stock numbers within the range's capacity.

His interpretation of Gifford Pinchot's dictum looked at the greatest good over the long run, but not necessarily for the largest number of people. His fiercely local approach was growing increasingly out of step with the times. The old Progressive agenda, never quite certain where it stood on the question of efficiency versus local use, had by now resolved in favor of larger combinations of capital that could make use of new forms of power and resource production. While others in the region's forests were marching into this challenging new era, Brandy continued to practice forestry (and, indeed, landscape conservation on a valleywide scale) as it had been done for the past forty years. The gap that opened up between his vision and that of the rest of his agency would not be visible to the public for another decade, but the tensions were already beginning to build.

Brandborg retired in March 1955, closing a forty-year career with the Forest Service and two decades as supervisor of the Bitterroot National Forest. His impending departure prompted a group of Bitterroot Valley community leaders to write to Forest Service chief Richard McArdle, asking that Brandy's successor continue his policies regarding timber, range, and wildlife management. Their letter was a glowing endorsement of his efforts to promote the economic better-ment of the county and conservation of its land, forests, and waters. Surprisingly, it also asked McArdle to avoid a large increase in the timber cut from the forest:

> We believe the administrative policies of Mr. Brandborg during the past twenty years have resulted in a very high degree of resource management that has and is contributing vitally to the economy and general well being of this county and its communities. The forest cutting budget of 12 mil-lion board feet of ponderosa pine and 14 million board feet of Douglas fir annually we believe to be as high as it should be for a sustained yield of logs for our wood working industries. Any faster rate of cutting would result in early exhaustion of the resource and resultant disruption of the economy dependent on the wood-working plants. Mr. Brandborg has resisted pressure to increase this budget and we hope this pressure will continue to be resisted in the future.[10]

The letter was signed by representatives of the Hamilton Chamber of Com-merce, Ravalli County Farmers Union, Darby Lions Club, the local American Legion post, and several other civic and sportsmen's groups. It appears to have been written by Glenn White, manager of the Taber Mill Company of Hamil-ton, one of the Bitterroot's many small timber processors that benefited from the forest's provincial approach to timber sales. White, who was already getting competition from the larger mills in Missoula, realized that a more substantial cutting program would only encourage this trend.

The letter went on to recommend several possible replacements for Brandy, including C. K. "Lanky" Spaulding, a former West Fork district ranger who now headed a national forest in Arizona. But McArdle's choice the following year was Thurman Trosper, a native of Montana's Flathead Valley who had been the timber-sale officer on Idaho's Clearwater National Forest. In this capacity he had overseen a large increase in the cutting of white pine to control blister rust. Regional officials wanted him to conduct a similar expansion on the Bitterroot, but he seems to have found the situation there to be different and carried on many of Brandy's practices.[11] The two men struck up a friendship based on their shared outlook on forest management, often making field trips together to examine the forest. During the five years that Trosper was on the Bitterroot, he brought about a gradual increase in timber cutting while trying to maintain the agency's historical emphasis on preventing losses from fire, insects, and disease.

In 1957 several of Brandy's friends, including Lillian Hornick of the Northern Region office, who was active in the Montana Conservation Council, nominated Brandy for the American Motors Conservation Award, a prestigious recognition given to conservation leaders who did not otherwise stand out in the public spotlight. Hornick collected a thick file of endorsements from many of the state's conservation notables, including Joseph Severy, Les Pengelly, Thurman Trosper, Baker Brownell, Roland Renne, Vic Bottomly, and James Vessey. Ernest Melby paid tribute to Brandy's work in his own field: "In all my educational experience, I have never known a man who assumed his responsibility more fully, who had more education in whatever he undertook and who had finer insights and sensitivities in relation to conservation and human values. I consider G. M. Brandborg one of America's finest citizens."

Stanley Antrim, Brandy's friend from the Bitterroot Valley, gave his perspective as a working rancher. "His devotion, enthusiasm and practical suggestions gave me the desire and many of the ideas which have become a part of my ranching program," he wrote. "This has not only made my venture more profitable but added an interest and satisfaction which brings a deeper joy in the work." Brownell's comments, though, drove to the heart of Brandy's interests: "His enthusiasm is infectious; his persistence under difficulties unwavering; his devotion to the land and its resources and the human communities on the land is enlightened and prophetic," he said. "Brandy is a man dedicated to the principle of conservation as a self-sustaining pattern of soil and growth, of life and human values. He has devoted his life to it and the effect of his work is important and lasting. In this context he is, I think, Montana's first citizen."[12]

Brandy had been nominated for the award in 1953 and received a certificate of merit at that time, but the extraordinary tributes he received in 1957 made an impression on the selection committee. His award was shared with nine other outstanding conservationists across the country. Hornick presented Brandy with a plaque and American Motors' check for five hundred dollars at the annual banquet of the Montana Conservation Council in Butte. Brandy did not often mention this honor, but the recognition must have delighted him.

His travels and outdoor activities were limited following retirement, partly as a result of his bad knees, but also so that he could be close to Edna, whose heart condition was growing worse. Consultations with doctors in Missoula pinpointed her trouble as a defective valve, but they did not believe she could survive an operation. The long illness ended with her death on March 12, 1958, with Brandy, Stewart, and Becky at her side. Condolences came from many of the family's friends, including Howard Zahniser, the executive secretary of the Wilderness Society, on whose governing council Stewart served. Zahniser told the senior Brandy that "you can only sense how earnestly we all want you to feel the warmth of friendship we have for you, perhaps it will help as much as anything we can say or do. We are thinking of you."

To a sympathetic note from John Craighead, a noted wildlife biologist who was active in Montana's conservation circles, Brandy responded, "Thanks a million for your kind and thoughtful expressions. This experience really puts me deep adrift in the wilderness believe me—So deep it seems that I will never get my bearings again—to take up where I left off." For a man who did not typically bare his soul to others, this was an acknowledgment of the great role Edna had played in his life. Her interest in literature and education had widened Brandy's limited cultural background and deeply influenced his approach to conservation issues. Stewart recalled that she had been his "companion in thought and development of their own philosophies...measuring carefully his impulsive desire to make the world a better place."[13]

For several years after Edna's death, his friends recalled, Brandy did seem to be without anchor, although he kept up his work with the Montana Conservation Council and other organizations. He also took a more active role in the growing movement to preserve wilderness in Montana, which would occupy much of his time during the next decade. Through Stewart's work with the National Wildlife Federation and later the Wilderness Society, which hired him in 1960 as its special projects director, the senior Brandy enjoyed meeting many of the movement's leaders, including Olaus and Mardy Murie as well as Howard Zahniser. As Zahniser's chief assistant, Stewart traveled extensively in the West to build support for a national wilderness bill and testified at hearings on the Forest Service's reclassification of its primitive areas. His father accompanied him on some of these trips, working to develop local wilderness committees within the Montana Wildlife Federation—an idea that in 1958 sparked the creation of a new and influential grassroots organization.

Dams, logging, and road building made the most obvious intrusions into Montana's wild country, but the growing use of airplanes, motorboats, and motorized scooters to reach backcountry areas also bothered hikers and horse users who were used to a little privacy during their outings. In 1958 two Bozeman residents, Kenneth and Florence Baldwin, decided they had seen enough damage in the mountain basins of the Gallatin River drainage. The Baldwins had helped form a committee on wilderness protection for the Gallatin Sportsmen's Association, but they felt that a statewide organization was needed to oppose further inroads into the wilderness.

At their invitation, twenty sportsmen and outfitters gathered at the Baxter Hotel in Bozeman on March 28, 1958, to discuss how to coordinate their efforts. One option was to form a local adjunct to the Wilderness Society, as some Montana sportsmen had suggested a decade earlier to combat massive dam proposals in the Flathead and Sun River drainages. The Bozeman participants thought that an independent group was needed, and so formed the Montana Wilderness Association (MWA), which would take a leading role in many disputes over Forest Service land allocations. The following year the group held its first annual meeting at Lambkin's Restaurant in the small town of Lincoln, Montana, at which Winton Weydemeyer was elected president. Guy Brandborg attended as a charter member and would serve on the group's governing council from 1959 to 1965.

The idea of land preservation fitted somewhat unconformably atop existing notions of resource use and conservation; to counteract this, wilderness advocates sometimes billed their cause as an extension of multiple-use doctrine, which still held sway as the governing rationale of federal land agencies. As a price for its acquiescence to the federal wilderness law then under consideration in Congress, the Forest Service sought its own legislative mandate, the Multiple Use–Sustained

Yield Act of 1960. (Wilderness uses were included in the measure, along with recreation and wildlife, thanks to Howard Zahniser's efforts.) Sustained yield—
perhaps the most critical part of the act's definitions—was held to be "the
achievement and maintenance in perpetuity of a high-level annual or regular periodic output of the various renewable resources of the national forests without
impairment of the productivity of the land." This granted the Forest Service wide
leeway in its timber operations, so long as it could guarantee continuous crops.[14]

The Multiple Use–Sustained Yield Act, for all its generalities, validated policies
the Forest Service had introduced many years earlier and allowed the postwar
timber industry to wrap itself in the Pinchot flag just as the Progressives had in
Brandborg's day. This connection was made explicit by Hardin R. Glascock Jr. of
the Society of American Foresters at a conference of the American Forest Products Institute in Washington in 1961. In terms reminiscent of Brandborg's farewell
message of 1954, Glascock asked the same question that has both inspired and
daunted the Forest Service since its inception: "How then can Uncle Sam's lands
be administered for the greatest good of the greatest number in the long run?
What basic concept should underlie public land management activities?"

His answer diverged significantly from Brandborg's. Taking note (as Brandy
had) of the country's rapid population increase, Glascock alluded to the federal
wilderness areas then under consideration and asked whether the country could
afford to "further divide our resource pie and designate additional pieces for
limited resource use." He believed that "water and wildlife and timber and recreation can be compatible uses by nature," and that "westerners hope that Uncle
Sam will not withdraw additional millions of acres of land from such use.…
[T]hey do not relish [the] prospect of an unfolding West being made largely
a seasonal and limited playground of the nation, crippling the development of
thousands of western communities."[15]

Where Brandborg had looked to the wildlands of the Bitterroot and Sapphire ranges to provide superb outdoor recreation and steady flows of irrigation water, others such as Glascock saw limitations upon the full development
of the nation's resources. Where Brandy called on the current generation to
moderate its needs so that resources might be equitably shared with future generations, another point of view held that forests could be put to maximum use
today without impairing their value. Both sides believed in making the land productive—though by how much and by what means they would differ greatly
in the coming years. The banner of Progressive utilitarianism could shelter
incompatible agendas, each laying claim to the scientific wisdom and social conscience of the Forest Service's founding father.

CHAPTER 10

Redeeming the Forest

1955–1962

In February 1955 P. D. Hanson announced that the national forests of the Northern Rockies had sold a record 1.1 billion board feet of timber during the previous year. That year the timber industry harvested 741 mmbf from those forests, more than a third of which consisted of salvaged spruce that had been killed or damaged by bark beetles. Much of the finished lumber produced in Montana and Idaho sawmills wound up in the 1.3 million new homes being built across the country for former GIs and their families. The chief's office believed that even this prodigious timber output could be increased; it set the Northern Region's cutting goal for the following fiscal year at 920 mmbf. By the turn of the century, the agency's top foresters expected the region to be cutting an astounding 2.38 billion board feet per year.[1] The great postwar expansion was hitting its stride, and for most of the regional timber staff and many of Brandy's coworkers, the boom fulfilled the long-delayed promise of making the national forests truly productive.

The new emphasis on large sales and heavy production worried owners of the Bitterroot Valley's smaller mills, six of whom informally banded together as the Bitter Root Forest Associates. They retained former West Fork ranger Sam Billings to present their grievances over log-scaling procedures, appraisal methods, and road standards before a hearing on federal timber-sale policies in Spokane in November 1955. Billings also brought up the forest's 1941 timber-management plan and its local-milling rule, which had been laid aside at the regional office's insistence. "It used to be the policy of the Forest Service to assist the local saw-mills on or adjacent to the national forest in preference to inviting large outside interests in to compete for the timber," he said. "Now the policy seems to be to favor the large operator."[2] His group wanted a return to the local-milling prefer-ence, by legislation if necessary.

Billings admitted that the larger outfits used wood more efficiently, but noted that local payrolls depended on the valley's small mills. But agency pol-icy no longer allowed preferential treatment of local mills except through formal sustained-yield agreements, which were contemplated only for dominant play-ers such as J. Neils in Libby. Supporting the small outfits did little to boost over-all production; only well-capitalized firms could take on the larger contracts needed to place more of the region's forests under management.

As if to underscore the new direction, assistant regional forester Axel Lindh made an extensive inspection tour of the Bitterroot National Forest that fall and sent Thurman Trosper, Brandborg's successor, a detailed list of suggestions for improvement. He applauded the forest's training program—a Brandborg hold-over—and granted that the Bitterroot's timber-management staff was more experienced than most in the region. The forest's timber sales, Lindh observed, showed evidence of coordination with other uses such as recreation and wild-life, a concern for protecting the soil, and good efforts at slash disposal. Public outreach, long one of Brandy's priorities, was also successful. "The Bitterroot has been blessed with a good reputation for I & E [the agency's information and education program]," Lindh offered. But in a backhanded critique of Brand-borg's policies, he suggested that "the first job here is to do a good job of man-agement and then show the public and community leaders the results of the good work."[3]

Lindh thought that the forest needed to offer larger sales in order to reduce administrative costs and meet the regional office's harvesting goals. Only 16.9 mmbf of what was then an allowable cut of 26 mmbf was taken off the forest during the preceding fiscal year. Lindh noted that "the Bitterroot during the past ten years has been on a deliberate small sale basis—apparently chiefly to avoid regional office supervision, but also because local industry appears to fear longer sales." Larger sales appealed to better-capitalized firms that needed to repay investments in new plants with specialized saws and log-handling equipment. These firms could also process the smaller trees that would other-wise be left as waste, which was an issue if the forest was to begin harvesting its extensive areas of uneven-aged, mistletoe-infected Douglas fir. These stands presented the most serious silvicultural problem on the Bitterroot, according to Lindh, and did not respond well to selection cutting.[4] He advised Trosper to try patch cutting (usually defined as openings of a few acres in size) followed by machine scarification of the ground surface to prepare a new seedbed, and also to begin clearcutting more substantial areas in the forest's extensive lodgepole pine stands. Brandy had brought up this idea as early as 1944, and several district rangers, including Charles McDonald, had experimented with small patch cuts to improve wildlife habitat, but clearcutting had yet to be implemented on a large scale. Until 1957, when the procedure came into greater use, only eleven cutting units on the Bitterroot had employed the method, none larger than twenty-six acres.[5]

Pressure for a radically expanded timber program was also coming from the Washington office, which had its eyes on nationwide housing goals. In 1956, in response to a request from chief Richard McArdle, Pete Hanson asked each of his forest supervisors to make a "quick revision" of their timber plans and give him a list of new roads needed to access uncut stands in the backcountry. These stands were already included in allowable-cut calculations, so opening them to logging would avoid cutting too much timber within already accessible areas. "The aim is to reach stands of timber that can be sold to mills or customers existing now or sure to be available within five years," Hanson wrote.[6]

Trosper's staff was already busy trying to accelerate production. "Timber sales have been increased in size, marking policies have been changed in relation to travel time, objectives and production," reported Carl Wetterstrom, Trosper's assistant in charge of timber management, early in 1957. "During the fiscal year 1956 the Bitterroot Forest for the first time in its history harvested the allowable cut in the Ponderosa Pine and Douglas-fir." Before the end of the fiscal year he hoped to offer the first sale of *Elytroderma*-infected fir in the Blue Joint drainage. The forest also planned to put up for sale a "considerable volume" of lodgepole pine that year.[7]

Meeting their silvicultural goals, however, would require more than salvage sales. Timber cutting would remain well below the forest's potential until more money was available to build roads and prepare dozens of new sales. "The maximum efficiency cannot be reached," Wetterstrom continued, "until such time that sufficient finances are secured to prepare for sale approximately twice the 26 million [board feet] allowable cut in one fiscal year for the Ponderosa Pine and Douglas-fir. Additional finances are needed to prepare in advance one large Lodgepole Pine timber sale." The forest, he was saying, would need to double its cut to begin addressing the problem of older, diseased, and decaying timber stands.

There was hope that this could be done; for the first time in the Bitterroot's history, the valley's lumber mills were beginning to demand significant volumes of timber from the forest. The Intermountain Company, in particular, was bidding aggressively on sales and sawing timber at a rapid rate. Wetterstrom assured Trosper in 1957 that the Darby district had nearly reached its objective for timber cutting and would "continue to make progress and fully redeem the responsibility which has been assigned to this unit on the Bitterroot Forest."[8]

The infected Douglas fir stands often were in areas where ponderosa pine had previously been cut, including lands in the Rye Creek drainage that had been acquired through exchange from the Anaconda Company and the Northern Pacific Railroad. High-grading the ponderosa pine had left many Douglas fir of good size but lesser value to mill operators. Wetterstrom suggested offering these stands at rock-bottom prices of one dollar per thousand board feet. "These areas are in urgent need of being cleaned up," Wetterstrom told the regional office.[9] Few of these stands were actually disposed of in this way, but his suggestion shows that foresters were as interested in improving stand health as in meeting industry's needs. For many agency men, the timber industry served primarily as a means to accomplish their silvicultural goals.

The regional office staff shared Wetterstrom's views on forest stand improvement. Charles Tebbe, who replaced P. D. Hanson as regional forester in 1956, left no doubt as to the new emphasis. In May 1957 he and his staff issued a new set of guidelines for preparing timber-management plans, making a clean break with the former policy of conservative, locally oriented forestry. "The greatest value of the national forests is not as a reservoir of old timber," the guidelines stated, "but as land which is or will be growing wood on every acre chiefly valuable for that purpose." This required growing "the best and largest crop possible" and getting "mature or deteriorating timber put into use before it spoils." Perhaps thinking of Brandborg's 1941 plan, its authors counseled that "a Forest Service Management Plan is not a means to develop policies; rather it is a device to interpret policies for a specific set of conditions." Brandborg's more limited version of sustained-yield forestry was also cast out: the guidelines stated that the "sustained yield capacity of a working circle is the ultimate cut which can be reached only when the working circle contains the desired growing stock of permanent forest types and normal distribution of age classes"—in other words, a completely regulated forest. This stood in sharp contrast to the Bitterroot's heavily managed ponderosa pine stands, which were surrounded by vast areas of protection forest in which the agency had historically made only nominal attempts at management.[10]

Shortly before he retired in 1954, Brandborg initiated a revision of the forest's timber-management plan, with timber staff officer Corland James conducting the review. The new plan, which was not approved until 1957, placed some 581,000 acres in the commercial-forest category, far more than the 1941 plan's 119,000 acres of commercial ponderosa pine. Increases in the ponderosa pine and Douglas fir components were already factored into the allowable cut, but some 300,000 acres of lodgepole pine formerly considered uneconomic to log now appeared suitable for pulp production—nearly six million cords worth. Although the plan no longer required local milling of sawtimber, it still envisioned that virtually all of the commercial ponderosa pine available from the forest would proceed to mills in the Bitterroot Valley.[11]

Thurman Trosper insisted that logging and road building must not damage watersheds, so the plan included provisions to keep tractors and road debris out of streams, size culverts large enough to handle peak flows, and design roads so that they would not shed sediment into streams. In a holdover of the protection-forest concept, and seemingly in defiance of the regional office's goals, the plan stated that "there will be instances where watershed considerations will dictate that marginal stands on upper slopes or poor sites are better left as protection cover than cut on the unlikely possibility of getting an improved stand." Each of these requirements would become major issues during the later controversy on the forest; had they been scrupulously followed, much of the criticism that occurred might have been averted.[12]

The most significant departure from the 1941 plan came in its treatment of Douglas fir and lodgepole pine, where for the first time clearcutting was to be employed, ordinarily in blocks of fifty acres or less. This, the foresters believed, would permit better reproduction and stocking control as well as the use of "cheaper and more efficient modern methods of logging."[13] In 1957, following adoption of the new plan, Trosper offered the first timber sales on the Bitterroot based primarily on clearcutting rather than selective harvest. That fall the forest sold 13 mmbf of ponderosa pine and Douglas fir in the Blue Joint drainage of the West Fork district, of which 383 acres, principally Douglas fir, were to be clear-cut in order to regenerate stands infected with the *Elytroderma* fungus. The foresters also specified clearcutting for a 114-acre block of timber in Rye Creek. The following year they offered another half-dozen such sales, aggregating just over 200 acres. Sales continued in this vein through 1961, after which another revision in the timber-management plan permitted a decisive increase in clearcutting.[14]

The forest continued to slowly expand its road network, especially in the West Fork, where it was trying to control the *Elytroderma* problem and gain access to other insect-ridden stands. But with limited appropriated funds, it was able to construct only 5 miles of road in the drainage in 1956. Logging contractors built more than 50 miles of road throughout the forest that year, using a portion of the money they bid on timber sales. By 1959 the Bitterroot estimated that it would need 2,500 miles of new timber access roads to manage such outbreaks and to begin cutting in previously inaccessible stands—an unprecedented expansion of the road network that was already drawing opposition from sportsmen.[15]

For years the Northern Region's timber experts had been trying to find money to build access roads throughout the backcountry of Montana and Idaho, thereby loosening the principal bottleneck to their development program. At a field hearing before a subcommittee of the Senate Committee on Public Works, held in Missoula in December 1957, Charles Tebbe laid out the region's goals in unmistakable terms. His engineers and road crews had built 420 miles of mainline timber haul roads during the previous five years, principally to salvage beetle-killed spruce, but during the next five years they needed to build another 1,900 miles of such roads, supplemented by 6,000 miles of purchaser-built logging roads. Eventually, he said, the region needed a total of *100,000 miles* of timber access roads throughout its seventeen national forests, one-fourth of which were main line. "We have the timber here, plenty of it, to sustain an allowable cut two-thirds larger than it is at present," Tebbe told the committee. "This is back-country timber, much of it in the smaller size classes, suitable for pulp and other forest products. But it cannot move without roads," he warned.[16]

Tebbe's plans called for nothing less than the transformation of Montana's and Idaho's backcountry into regulated timber-producing zones, at least outside of designated wilderness areas. To accomplish this, the demand side of the equation required attention. The Northern Rockies still lacked an integrated wood-products economy that could process many different types of trees on a long-term basis. Axel Lindh was thinking ahead to the day when the great bulk of the region's virgin timber would be put into production, not just through emergency salvage sales such as had boosted harvests during the late 1940s and early 1950s but also through regular sales of green timber. Tebbe, Lindh, John Castles, and University of Montana forestry professor Arnold Bolle met with Montana's congressional delegation to outline the problem. Tebbe could not directly ask for road and sale-preparation funds, Bolle recalled, but Mike Mansfield, who had considerable influence on the Senate Appropriations Committee, understood what was needed. He told the foresters to prepare a detailed report on timber supplies and potential demand within the region. He would see what he could do to line up support in the Agriculture Department and in Congress.[17]

Castles and Lindh welcomed the request and set to work on a remarkable study of the state's timber stands and wood-processing capabilities, titled *Full Use and Development of Montana's Timber Resources.* Tebbe prefaced the report, which was released as a Senate committee print in 1958, by laying out the new direction his agency was taking. "The overall picture...is one of great, unrealized opportunity. Montana's forests are very extensive. In large part they are not served by roads, which is the principal reason this great resource remains on tap. But on tap it is, and on the threshold of development to supply the needs of the State and Nation."[18]

The title of the report was telling: *full use* suggested that Castles and Lindh were just as concerned about bringing more forest land into production as with supplying the region's existing mills. Their ultimate goal was a thoroughly managed forest in which mortality, decadence, and crowding played less of a role. Reaching this silvicultural apotheosis required new mills that could utilize all age classes of trees—not just the large-diameter, mature sawlogs of the previous decades. The small-scale, localized timber management long practiced on the Bitterroot would have to go. There would naturally be dislocations: "Because of an excess of requirements over supply of the large-size quality timber that has traditionally been cut in a few places in western Montana," they wrote, "it is expected that some plants will be in supply difficulty. A very few closures have already occurred." Lindh and Castles noted that "what finally happens and to whom depends on a number of factors, such as the alertness of management to changing conditions, company resources, timber ownership, and the development of access to timber, and perhaps more importantly, the extent to which there is willingness and ability to shift dependence to the sizes and species and quality of timber that is available."[19]

Large-size quality trees were exactly what Guy Brandborg had been trying to grow on the Bitterroot for twenty years, with some success. The regional office now wanted to extend timber management into higher elevations and remote

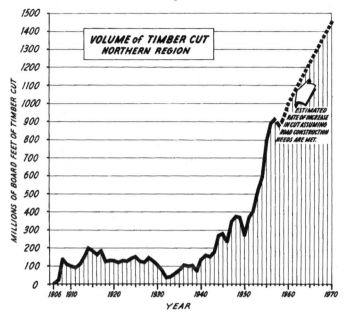

FIGURE 2. Chart of Region 1 timber production. Following World War II the Northern Region of the Forest Service greatly accelerated its timber production yet anticipated even higher yields in the future. Courtesy of USDA Forest Service, Northern Region Archives.

drainage basins, where there stood vast stands of lodgepole pine that heretofore had little economic use. The wood-products industry, Castles and Lindh were saying, would need to adjust to this new reality or face mill closures. The era of the big trees was drawing to a close—the result of the application of Forest Service doctrine as much as pressure from industry. After the long hiatus of the Depression years, the agency saw a chance to at last fulfill the promise of modern silviculture.

The *Full Use and Development* report devoted considerable attention to the problem of diversifying Montana's wood-products industry. A variety of mills could better utilize a wide range of forest materials, from sawlogs (the traditional product on which most mills depended) to peeler logs for plywood, and even mill waste for particleboard and fuel plants. The authors observed that "the sawmill which has pioneered here, which had made such incalculable contributions to the economy of Montana, and which has strained to develop and use one of the State's greatest resources, is simply not the medium on which the whole burden of development and use can or should be placed."[20]

A key component of this revamped industry would be new pulp and paper plants that could utilize so-called roundwood—trees that were too small to saw into dimension lumber. Lindh approached the Stanford Research Institute, a California think tank, to outline the possibilities for pulpwood development in the region. They identified five working circles, one of which centered on Missoula, in which long-term sales of up to 70 mmbf could be made. Lindh even arranged to take industry representatives from the West Coast on a two-week tour of advanced pulp, plywood, and veneer mills in Sweden, where industry had already adapted to using smaller trees.[21]

Shipments of sawmill waste had been traveling the rails to pulp mills in the Great Lakes states for several years, but a plant in western Montana would better serve the foresters' needs. When two midwestern firms, Hoerner Boxes and Waldorf Paper Products, teamed up to build a pulp mill outside of Missoula in 1957, the region at last had a means of using such waste, as well as the lodgepole pine that blanketed the upper slopes of the Lolo and Bitterroot forests. In response to this new development, the Bitterroot undertook an emergency inventory of its lodgepole pine stands and began designing sales that could remove substantial quantities from crowded, poorly growing stands at higher elevations.

The *Full Use and Development* report pointed the way toward achieving the maximum sustained yield from the region's national forests. Memo after memo during this period reveal the foresters' underlying thinking, which had little to do with aggrandizing their budgets or placating timber-industry lobbyists. Instead, they took a keen, almost overriding, interest in freeing the forest from the agents of loss and destruction—fire, insects, disease, and old age. Stoking industrial demand would allow federal foresters to practice the kind of silviculture they believed was best for the woods and lead the national forests into a promised land of biological productivity. Improving forests, not increasing the bureaucracy or serving as industry's handmaid, lay at the center of the Forest Service psyche.

The timber industry had its agenda, certainly, and was eager to see timber cutting expanded on the national forests. Many of its executives were trained in the same forestry schools as the agency's staff; they had listened to the same lectures and read from the same gospel of forest productivity. To industry men, the Forest Service had too long delayed active management of the public timberlands, and the results were apparent in stagnating stands of overmature timber that were prone to catastrophic destruction. Their mission, though it involved making a profit, dovetailed neatly with the Forest Service's.

In 1960, following Thurman Trosper's promotion to a position with the Division of Program Planning in Washington, Harold Andersen assumed the supervisorship of the Bitterroot National Forest. Andersen brought with him a get-it-done attitude toward timber management. He had served as a timber staff officer on the Kaniksu National Forest in the Idaho panhandle, where logging took a much higher profile than it had thus far on the Bitterroot. He had also conducted timber surveys in Alaska's Tongass National Forest, the nation's last virgin timber frontier. The Northern Region now had someone in charge who would focus the Bitterroot's staff and budgets on the paramount objective of forest regulation.

Almost immediately, however, Andersen had to deal with the first of two major forest fires on the Bitterroot—the largest blazes on the Montana side of the forest since the turn of the century. In July 1960, in the middle of a dry summer marked by large fires throughout the West, lightning ignited a blaze in beetle-killed lodgepole pine on Saddle Mountain, west of Lost Trail Pass at the southern end of the forest. In six days it burned more than 3,000 acres in steep, difficult-to-reach terrain. Sixteen hundred men worked to slow its spread; dozer operators plowed firelines straight up and down the mountainsides, but still the fire raged to the east and jumped Highway 93 before the control lines held.[22]

The summer of 1961 also was dry, and on July 16 a fire ignited in an area of lodgepole pine deadfall in the Skalkaho Creek drainage. Firefighters held this blaze to 300 acres, but adverse conditions persisted. Much of the Sapphire Range had been hard hit by mountain pine beetles in the 1920s and 1930s, leaving lodgepole pines in jackstrawed piles ten feet high or more and choked with thick new growth. Neither men nor machines could make much headway in such a forest.

At four o'clock on the afternoon of August 4, 1961, the lookout on Deer Mountain reported a lighting strike on a ridge below Crystal Point, fifteen miles east of Darby. Eight minutes later he observed smoke rising and reported the fire to the Darby Ranger Station. The dispatcher sent 36 men to fight the fire, but by six thirty, with wind spreading the flames, he requested 250 more men along with bulldozers to begin clearing a line. Less than three hours after it had started, firefighters estimated that the blaze had covered between 250 and 300 acres.[23]

A nearby fluorspar mine offered the only road access to the spreading fire, which was located in the undeveloped upper drainage of Sleeping Child Creek. The Mine fire, later renamed Sleeping Child, burned out of control for weeks in thick stands of lodgepole pine. By August 14 the forest had more than 1,700 men working the lines, with air support from planes and helicopters. Forty-one bulldozers pushed thirty miles of new road along rugged, wild ridges and cleared lines at the fire's northern and eastern edges. In places the dozers had to gouge their way through rock outcrops, damaging so many of the machines that a graveyard area was established in a nearby clearing. Ranchers in the East Fork were forced to move their cattle out of the mountains and watch nervously as successive firelines were overrun.[24]

In all, 28,000 acres burned before rains fell and the fire was brought under control on August 24. The episode came as a shock to the Bitterroot's staff and to many valley residents who watched the smoke plume rise far above the Sapphire's crest. There had been large burns in the remote mountains of the Selway-Bitterroot wilderness within the past thirty years, and in 1889 a fire burned 20,000 acres on Shook Mountain in the West Fork, but not in recent memory had there been a large blaze so close to the valley. Everett Miller, chief forester for Montana Forest Products, a mill located across the Sapphire divide in Philipsburg, told a reporter of the fire's frightening spread. "If we'd had roads, we could have stopped it—certainly held the damage down in spite of wind," he said. "That country up there has never been logged. There's dead timber all over it. When the heat got to those old snags, they just exploded. Some of the old boys thought they were being bombed."[25]

Harold Andersen wasted no time beginning salvage operations on both the Saddle Mountain and Sleeping Child burns. By the time the latter erupted, bulldozers had already scraped haul roads across the slopes below Saddle Mountain, and jammer yarders were winching ashen-barked trees up to a network of collector roads. Salvage operations began on the Sleeping Child burn that fall, which over a period of four years removed 90 mmbf of the estimated 110 mmbf of burned timber, mostly lodgepole pine. The pine was placed in the forest's unregulated category, meaning it did not count toward the allowable cut. The logs brought an unexpected windfall to sawmills in the Darby area, boosting the forest's total harvest to a peak of 76 mmbf in calendar year 1962.

The Sleeping Child fire drove home the point that many in the Forest Service had long been making—that the so-called protection forest in the headwaters of the Bitterroot River was not necessarily safe. Better access and improved management were needed to prevent further conflagrations and waste of timber, according to the agency. The Bitterroot constructed 102 miles of new roads in 1961, mostly for salvage operations, and from 37 to 77 miles annually during the following six years. By comparison, it had managed to build only 17 miles of new road during Brandborg's last year on the forest.

To ensure a healthy new stand in the burned area, Andersen had workers kill off the surviving patches of lodgepole by girdling individual trees and spraying brush with the herbicide 2,4-D. This raised concerns among some of the scientists working at the Rocky Mountain Laboratory in Hamilton, who feared consequences to fish and wildlife from the spraying. Lee Metcalf, now Montana's junior senator, also expressed concern over the forest's use of herbicides and especially the aerial spraying of the pesticide DDT to combat the spruce bark beetle and other forest pests. In 1962 Andersen took Metcalf and his wife, Donna, to view the Sleeping Child burn. Following the tour Andersen told Charles Tebbe, "I pointed out that any spray program would be carried on only after a careful weighing of the possible loss of timber values against the possible side effects of DDT, and then with every possible safeguard. The Senator stated he felt that the Forest Service has always exercised good judgment and care in this matter."[26]

To prevent more debacles like Sleeping Child, the Bitterroot's staff drew up a hazard-management plan to begin dealing with some 200,000 acres of crowded, slow-growing lodgepole stands in other drainages of the Sapphires. A test cut of 160 acres removed the overmature pine and leftover snags, but reproduction proved spotty even after leaving seed trees and broadcast burning the ground cover to open the pine's resin-bound, or serotinous, cones. Burning after harvest, in fact, promoted the regrowth of deep-rooted pinegrass, which competed with the seedlings for water and sunlight.[27]

Wholesale logging proved to be too expensive in the spindly masses of lodgepole, so in 1966 Mick DeZell, Andersen's chief of fire operations, proposed clearing a series of firebreaks to halt wildfires on the ridgetops. Each strip would be one-quarter to three-eighths of a mile wide and 7 or 8 miles long. The first breaks were planned for the Meadow–Tolan Creek divide in the East Fork of the Bitterroot River and the Sleeping Child–Skalkaho divide in the Sapphire Range. After logging the strips, the remaining slash would be burned and the next season's growth sprayed with 2,4-D. The program, dubbed "Operation Firebreak," began with a 300-acre controlled burn at the head of Two Bear Creek on the Sleeping Child–Skalkaho divide. Orville "Okie" Grossarth, the Darby district ranger, commented to Hamilton's *Ravalli Republican* that the plan would keep wildfires from burning through 70,000 acres of "worthless" lodgepole pine.

Reporter Bob Gilluly noted that "the cleared area will, of course, grow back to timber eventually. But it's liable to look like a long immense zipper for several years."[28]

Cutting firebreaks depended upon finding markets for small-diameter lodgepole pine, but with plenty of pulpwood available closer to Missoula, the program stalled out after clearing only a half-dozen miles of ridgetop. With the Sleeping Child salvage program also winding down, the Darby sawmills now depended on continuous sale offerings of Douglas fir and ponderosa pine, which the agency's foresters sought to supply from midelevation slopes that were now being opened to road access. For the first time installed mill capacity in the Bitterroot Valley enabled the foresters to extend silvicultural regulation well beyond Brandy's lovingly tended groves of ponderosa pine.

To put these stands into full production, supervisor Harold Andersen initiated a revision of the forest's timber-management plan, which, when implemented in 1962, raised the allowable sawtimber cut to 44 mmbf. Overall standing volume was calculated to be nearly three times as great as in previous plans. "There is a preponderance of overmature timber in all types and a void in young age classes," the plan stated. "The condition in each type can be improved by clear cutting older stands as rapidly as possible (within allowable cut limitations) and restocking understocked and nonstocked stands as rapidly as possible."[29]

With these words the Bitterroot let the genie out of the bottle—thenceforth clearcutting would be the means by which the forest would regulate the bulk of its timber stands, including the ponderosa pine type in which reproduction from Douglas fir was such a problem. All of these innovations—the salvage and firebreak programs, the new roads being built throughout the forest, and the adoption of modern harvesting techniques—spelled the end of Guy Brandborg's conservative timber program. They would also, as it turned out, bring an end to the widespread support the agency had long enjoyed among the residents of the Bitterroot Valley.

CHAPTER 11

Staking Out the Selway

1939–1967

With the timber side of its multiple-use program reaching fulfillment, Forest Service leaders in Missoula and Washington wanted to show that they respected other forest users as well, many of whom were agitating for a federal law that would set up a system of permanently protected wilderness areas. An opportunity to take the lead on this issue—and perhaps prevent Congress from usurping the agency's authority—lay with the Selway-Bitterroot Primitive Area, which at nearly 1,875,300 acres was the largest in the national forest system. The Northern Region had been examining the Selway since the 1940s for administrative reclassification as a wilderness area under regulation U-1, which Bob Marshall had written shortly before he died in 1939. This classification, along with the companion U-2 regulation establishing smaller "wild" areas, prohibited logging and road building and established a more uniform wilderness policy for the national forests.

But reclassification would not prove simple. Truck trails and irrigation dams had frayed the edges of the original primitive area, compromising the limitless wild country that had once thrilled explorers such as Marshall. Brandborg himself had supervised the completion of roads through Lost Horse Canyon and the Magruder Corridor, both of which intruded deep into the primitive area.

These projects were well under way by the time he arrived on the forest and had the strong backing of Major Kelley.[1]

Brandy felt a close connection to the Selway country, having helped build and supply its lookouts, fought its frightening wildfires, and ridden trails into its remote interior. Following the war he became increasingly worried as aggressive timbering replaced Region 1's historical emphasis on selective cutting. In 1947 he joined the Wilderness Society, then a relatively small group of enthusiasts that Bob Marshall had helped organize in 1935. In the summer of 1955 Brandy helped arrange for the society's governing council to visit the Selway on an eight-day auto tour and horse-packing trip. Thurman Trosper and other agency officials accompanied the group, which examined possible boundaries for a reclassified wilderness. Brandy joined them for the auto tour over the Magruder road, making the acquaintance of some of the nation's leading thinkers and writers on the subject of wilderness conservation, including Howard Zahniser, the society's executive director, and six of the society's council members, including Bob Marshall's brothers George and James.[2]

In April 1956 the regional office proposed that the boundaries of the new wilderness area be moved back to the ridgetops away from the existing road network, excluding lands such as the mountain face south of the Lochsa River. Also omitted was a remote 310,000-acre block of forested land along the Magruder road that the Forest Service designated, with a characteristic lack of flourish, as Area E. Zahniser responded in June by asking the agency to retain the Lochsa River and Magruder areas and set the boundaries closer to roads. But the lands on either side of the Magruder road contained almost 1 billion board feet of fir, spruce, and pine that the agency did not want to relinquish. It finally settled on a proposal to include 1,163,555 acres in a new Selway-Bitterroot Wilderness Area, leaving out more than 700,000 acres of the original primitive area, including 230,000 acres in Area E. This plan made its way to Washington and was formally released in August 1960. At a public hearing held in Missoula the following March, Guy Brandborg testified alongside Stewart, who had joined the staff of the Wilderness Society as Zahniser's assistant. Indulging in a little name-dropping, the senior Brandy recalled his work with Bob Marshall in drawing the primitive area's original boundaries. "I have traveled [this area] many times," he said, "and it is my firm opinion that the area affords exceptional opportunities for wilderness living that are unequalled anywhere else in the National Forest or National Park systems."[3] During the Wilderness Society's tour in 1955 he had discussed with Harvey Broome how the younger generation was taking less part in rugged wilderness adventures, and growing soft as a result. To Brandy, life in the backcountry was more than a tonic or a release from the workaday world; it was an essential part of manhood and citizenship.

When Secretary of Agriculture Orville Freeman released the final Selway-Bitterroot proposal on January 11, 1963, conservationists were disappointed to find most of Area E still missing. Other significant deletions were proposed for the Bitterroot Range's eastern front and above the Lochsa River, labeled as Areas D and F, respectively.[4] Disappointment would turn to alarm once they discovered that the Bitterroot National Forest, which had been making timber surveys in the Magruder Corridor since 1958, had active plans to begin logging in that area. Ten days after the secretary's decision, the regional office asked supervisor Harold Andersen to amend the forest's timber-management plan to include the Magruder Ranger District, which lay entirely in Idaho and had seen no appreciable logging. Andersen laid out the prospects for regional forester Boyd Rasmussen: "There are some excellent sawtimber stands, as well as extensive pole-timber stands on the district. On the average, the site quality is considerably higher than on the Montana portion of the working circle. Preliminary calculations indicate the area may support an annual allowable cut of twenty million board feet. This will increase the present allowable cut of the working circle by nearly fifty percent."[5]

In June 1964 the foresters completed their multiple-use plan for the Magruder district.[6] It called for reconstructing the Magruder road to accommodate logging truck traffic, with spur roads branching out across the benchlands above the major streams where most of the timber lay. About half of Area E supported commercial stands that could reasonably be accessed by logging roads, comprising an estimated 924 mmbf of sawtimber. That translated to 12.7 mmbf that could be cut annually at roughly a seventy-year rotation age—less than initial projections, but a significant addition to the 54 mmbf that was being cut from other parts of the forest in 1964. Anticipating controversy, Andersen delayed any timber sales for the time being, even though his cruisers had laid out an initial offering in the Slow Gulch area.[7]

In this era of limited public involvement, the agency's management plans were essentially in-house documents and not given wide distribution. If the Bitterroot foresters envisioned some opposition to their logging plans for the Magruder Corridor, they were wholly unprepared for the intense public reaction that ensued. The battle proved to be the training ground for a key group of

activists in the Bitterroot Valley and in Montana, most of whom would go on to
raise hell over the clearcutting issue a few years later.

To many travelers who were discovering the Mountain West in the years following World War II, the Bitterroot Valley seemed like an ideal location in which to
indulge one's outdoor interests. Among these migrants was the family of Doris
and Kelsey Milner, who had moved to Hamilton in 1951 when Kelsey, a micro-
biologist, took a position at the Rocky Mountain Laboratory. The summer after
their arrival they loaded tent and sleeping bags into their DeSoto station wagon,
headed up the narrow road over Nez Perce Pass (making three-point turns on its
switchbacks), and set up camp along the Selway River—a vacation they repeated
each summer in leisurely weeklong breaks. In the shelter of the streamside forest their four children delighted in sightings of bear and moose and the chance
to fish, swim, and jump off of rocks in the cold streams. The Selway became so
much a part of the family that one of their children was baptized in the river.[8]

Neither Doris nor Kelsey took a major role in the debate over the reclassification of the Selway-Bitterroot Primitive Area in the early 1960s; they were
simply among those who enjoyed its environs for a low-key vacation. So when
they encountered a bulldozer parked by the Magruder road near their camp on
Indian Creek one August day in 1964, they did not foresee the long struggle that
would engulf their spare time—especially Doris's. She related a decade later that
she was simply upset to think that the forests and waters they had known for
years were about to change drastically. "We had enjoyed the Magruder Corridor
as our place, we had learned [about] wilderness, we had taken our kids there, we
had had probably the best time we ever had in our lives. All of a sudden this was
going to change for reasons which we didn't think were right."[9]

Doris's first move upon returning to Hamilton was to contact Guy Brandborg, who was well known around town for his conservationist views. He apparently already knew of the logging plans from his agency contacts and had been
in touch with Clifton Merritt, a fellow Montanan whom Stewart Brandborg had
recently hired as the Wilderness Society's western field representative. Merritt
initially worked in the society's headquarters in Washington, D.C., and later in
Denver, but he took a keen interest in his native state, having organized opposition to Forest Service logging plans in the wild headwaters of the Flathead River
before coming to the Wilderness Society. He and Stewart advised the elder
Brandborg to set up a grassroots organization to fight the Forest Service's plans

for the Magruder Corridor. Brandy, in turn, saw the qualities of a natural leader in Milner: she got along well with people, yet she was determined to stop the logging in her beloved Selway. Brandy told Merritt that she had the "fire in the belly" to take on the agency, and he quickly helped her assemble an ad hoc committee to tackle the problem.[10]

What became known as the Save the Upper Selway Committee held its first meeting at the rustic Lochsa Lodge on the northern edge of the Selway wilderness on September 20, 1964, with twelve conservationists, mostly from Montana and the Bitterroot Valley, present. Milner was elected chairman of the group, with Ruth Brandborg (Brandy's second wife) serving as secretary. Their first move was to distribute a brochure publicizing the case against logging in the Magruder Corridor.[11] It depicted the upper Selway as "one of the most spectacular whitewater streams and scenic mountain canyons in the United States" and claimed that logging in this headwaters would threaten the sea-run steelhead trout that spawned in its clear streams. "The Upper Selway is one of the last, free-flowing streams of the Columbia River system," it said, and was "subject to active proposals for road construction, logging, and destruction!"[12]

Brandy drew on his extensive contacts in the conservation community to gain endorsements from the Ravalli County Fish and Wildlife Association and the Federation of Western Outdoor Clubs (FWOC), for which he served as regional vice president. Milner went so far as to copy names from the visitor logbook at Nez Perce Pass and send them appeals for help. A personal meeting with Senator Lee Metcalf laid the groundwork for his later support. As she reported to Clif Merritt, "I realize that we haven't moved mountains yet, but we have a steady pry on one."[13]

Miles Romney of Hamilton's *Western News* took up the cause early in 1965 with a long editorial titled "Save the Upper Selway Wilderness." Romney tied the fight to the larger issue of forest management, on which he had written in past issues. "As time progressed," he wrote, "it became evident to a large number of Americans that national forests were not just embryonic sawdust but in many cases constituted values which had little or no relation to lumber," he wrote. "If the industry is in such shape that it must depend upon a 12 million feet cut, we are indeed facing a terrible future."[14]

The county's daily newspaper, the *Ravalli Republican*, took no such stand, but it did print excerpts of an interview that Milner had sought with its editor,

Bob Gilluly. She said the upper Selway country was "a legacy for our children and future generations, [which would] far outweigh the few logs which could be cut from it." She charged that the Forest Service was simply trying to subsidize the sawmills in Darby. Harvesting all the timber in the Magruder Corridor, she said, "would require more than $4-¼ million worth of roads built at government expense.... If every cent paid for stumpage were applied to the cost of the roads needed to log the Selway it would take 40 years to pay for the roads."[15]

In the hard-edged world of conservation politics, wilderness advocates had to demonstrate that more than beautiful roadside groves were at stake. With Brandborg's coaching, Milner pressed supervisor Harold Andersen for facts on soil types, precipitation, and growing rates for stands in the Magruder Corridor, as well as the added cost of constructing roads to standards that would prevent erosion. Brandy was delighted with her growing dedication to the effort, but he and Merritt continued to orchestrate the action. "You really hit the 'jackpot' in your call to Doris last nite," Brandy wrote to Merritt in January 1965. "I had spent part of yesterday P.M. with her charting [a] course of action & going over rough drafts of attached letters—immediately following your call she came to our house to relate success—She really felt good—This indicates what people can & will do to preserve wilderness—if encouraged, guided etc.—A real gleam in her eye."[16] Brandy continued to work from behind the scenes, drafting letters for her to sign and laying out goals, but before long Milner would find her own feet and emerge as one of Montana's most active and knowledgeable conservation leaders.

The committee also benefited from the expertise of a Lewiston, Idaho, sportsman and conservation activist named Mort Brigham, who made his living traveling around the country designing sawmills. For decades he and his fellow anglers and hunters had been a force to contend with in the Gem State's very active politics of wildlife management. They had recently taken on the state's powerful mining industry in support of better care for streams and the valuable trout and salmon fisheries they supported. The prospect of extensive road construction and logging in the Selway's headwaters left him aghast. "When I think of roads along a river," he wrote to regional forester Neal Rahm in 1966, "the case of the North Fork of the Clearwater comes to mind. In the reach of the stream below Bungalow and Canyon Ranger Stations there were once some very fine cutthroat holes. In camping and fishing this country over the years, I had the holes named and knew just how to approach each hole to keep out of sight of the fish. In the 31 miles of this reach of the river, every single one of my old holes have been blown full of rocks."

The damage he had seen done to other river corridors in Idaho, each of which he had known intimately, portended ill for the Selway. "The excellent trout holes just above Sherman Creek and the several good holes at Five Island were also filled with rock when the road was built up the Lochsa," he told Rahm. "Skull Creek, on the North Fork, either was or will soon be all but obliterated by road construction. This was once the best cutthroat stream in the whole country. Lower Quartz Creek is a similar example, if others are needed. Now we are asked to believe that the whole Upper Selway can be logged without stream damage, and without erosion."[17]

With the Forest Service unwilling to budge, Milner asked her supporters to send letters to the Montana and Idaho congressional delegations, hoping to pressure Secretary of Agriculture Orville Freeman into issuing a stop order against the road building and timbering in Area E. Milner could be humorously direct: she told Arnold Olsen, who represented western Montana's House district, that "our committee has been hacking away for some action from Mr. Freeman on a stay for the Selway Area E. We don't want logging, or roads, or cows, or dancing girls in Area E, just wilderness....All the yak about Montana's growth—it's going to be largely in recreation."[18]

Miles Romney entreated Olsen more formally: "Let us go up the Selway from Magruder to its very source, beyond Thompson Flat, to Wood Hump, just under the Montana-Idaho border, all the way up you have unusual mountain scenery; you are alone in the wilderness. If it is not wilderness there is no such thing. Take out the trees and cart them to the Bitter Root. What is there left for the recreationist, for the outdoor lover? What pray tell is there left for the citizens of Idaho who have lost their timber, their watershed, their wilderness, their outdoor wonderland so that for a very brief interval the saws will hum in mills in the Bitter Root?"[19]

Other valley residents rushed to the agency's support. Vic Hollingsworth, the head of Citizens State Bank in Hamilton, told Forest Service chief Edward Cliff that the agency was on the right track in managing more of the forest for timber. Sam Billings, the former West Fork district ranger, pointed out in a letter to Lee Metcalf that forests needed active management to prevent fires and insect attacks. "We cannot preserve these areas the way nature made them," he said. Harold Andersen urged his employees to talk up the issue in the valley and get supporters to speak out. A classic public-lands fight was shaping up: as Milner reported to Bruce Bowler, a Boise activist, "We feel sort of like popcorn in a pan in the hot grease just before it 'blows.'" Timber interests, she said, had been "Almighty God in the past. But this has to change."[20]

By June 1965, with the Forest Service determined to press ahead in the Magruder Corridor, Brandy confided to Thurman Trosper that he feared the battle was lost. Trosper, from his perspective in the agency's Washington office, reassured him that it was far from over and advised him to take an indirect approach instead of his usual blunt expressiveness. "Beating them on the head too much and for too long will only tend to harden their position," he counseled. "But heavy pressure is needed in the first place to get [the] FS in proper frame of mind to reconsider decisions." He advised Brandy to find a way for the agency to save face and gradually back away from its timber plans. This might be done, he suggested, through an independent study team of the sort that Secretary Freeman had recently appointed to examine conflicts over Minnesota's Boundary Waters Canoe Area. A study committee, Trosper said, "would spook the F.S. into action to reconsider their decision. They will do just about anything to keep the politicians from moving in and taking the decision making."[21]

Trosper accurately foretold the course of events in the Magruder Corridor. Brandborg likely passed along his advice to Stewart and Clif Merritt who, with help from Frank Church, persuaded Freeman to agree to a two-year delay in logging plans for Area E. The Forest Service intended to offer timber sales after that period and continued with the reconstruction of the Magruder road from Nez Perce Pass to the Kit Carson campground on Deep Creek. Each side believed that major principles were at stake; no easy resolution seemed handy.

Brandborg and the Milners joined Harold Andersen and members of his staff on a two-day show-me trip into the Magruder Corridor during the last weekend of July 1965—the first of many tours the Bitterroot foresters would organize in the coming years to try to answer concerns about their timber program. The trip altered no viewpoints, but afterward Brandy urged Milner and Brigham to collect detailed statements from the preservationists in attendance for distribution to the Montana and Idaho congressional delegations. Copies also went to participants in the annual meetings of the Montana Wilderness Association and the Montana and Idaho wildlife federations. This was typical of Brandborg's tactics; by widely disseminating letters, fact sheets, newspaper articles, and editorials to anyone he thought might read them, he helped keep the issue on the front burner.

In the spring of 1966, to his great alarm, Brandy heard from his Forest Service contacts that the agency was moving ahead with logging plans despite the agreement with the secretary's office. He urged his friends to lean harder on the Montana delegation for support and informed Roger Pegues, the FWOC's conservation director, that "we have positively learned that F.S. is now actually surveying logging roads in Area E for three different lumber sales. One sale proposed for 8 million ft—.... We badly need you & Clif M[erritt] in Mont & Ida to organize efforts to stop F.S. in their tracks." Stewart Brandborg, who was getting regular updates from his father and from Milner, advised them that only legislative action would stop the timber sales. That May he drafted a bill to have the land north of the Magruder road added to the Selway-Bitterroot Wilderness and soon obtained Metcalf's agreement to introduce it.[22] The grassroots efforts were paying off for the Selway committee members. Their coalition of hikers, wildlife interests, agency insiders such as Brandborg and Trosper, and friends in the news media—backed by staffers for national environmental groups who cultivated relationships with key allies in Congress—would prove effective in Montana's environmental politics for years to come.

Brandy, in fact, had larger plans than saving the Selway; he regarded the fight as a means of developing the grassroots conservation leadership he had long hoped to establish in the Bitterroot Valley and throughout Montana. His efforts to direct Milner's committee from behind the curtain appear rather heavy-handed, yet he framed the issue in terms of the ongoing struggle he had been involved with for many years. He reflected on this campaign in a letter to Clif Merritt and Stewart in late 1966: "As you both know it takes a tremendous amount of organizing, pushing, bludgeoning, gabbing, consoling etc. to get people at grassroots to realize their place & responsibilities in the scheme of our democratic society—keeping them steered and functioning effectively is a real challenge," he wrote. "The Selway issue has caused more than one individual to cut their eyeteeth and [as a result] they are better prepared to tackle other conservation issues."[23]

Metcalf did not introduce his Selway bill until 1971, but, as Trosper predicted, the prospect of legislation prodded the Department of Agriculture into action. Metcalf had breakfast with Secretary Freeman on May 24, 1966, to press the notion of a review committee. Freeman, wanting to avoid a legislative fight, agreed. To head the study he appointed George Selke, a fellow Minnesotan who had been his legal adviser while he was governor of that state, and had chaired the Boundary Waters study Trosper referred to. Selke had strong ties to Montana, where he had served as the chancellor of its university system from 1946 to 1951 and had been a major supporter of the Montana Study. Guy Brandborg knew and liked him and would have approved of the choice, if indeed he had not suggested it.[24] Brandy wasted no time sending his old friend all the information he could amass on the Magruder Corridor issue.

Joining Selke on the review panel were five men with professional interests in forestry and wildlife management: Kenneth Davis, former dean of the MSU Forestry School and now at Yale; James Meiman of Colorado State University; Donald Obee of Boise College; Daniel Poole of the Wildlife Management Institute; and William Reavley of Salt Lake City, representing the National Wildlife Federation. The panel made field visits to the Selway and held public meetings in Missoula, Grangeville, and Boise to collect additional information. At the Missoula meeting on December 9, 1966, Guy Brandborg reviewed his involvement in the designation of the original primitive area in 1935–1936 and his trips into the Magruder Corridor with Howard Zahniser and the Wilderness Society council in the 1950s. "I agreed with them then," he said, "and I agree with them now: that the proposed use of this area for logging and the resultant opening of it through road construction poses a most serious threat to the fisheries, wildlife, and many other wilderness values of the wild Selway River." A network of logging roads in the upper Selway would eliminate what he called "one of the greatest big game wilderness hunting experiences to be found anywhere in the nation," reducing it "to the same low quality of road hunting chance that can be found in hundreds of areas in Idaho and Montana."[25]

Modern-day foresters, he said, had little opportunity to acquire "a working knowledge of basic wilderness philosophies and ecological concepts." He acknowledged that the new corps of rangers and administrators had better technical and academic training than in his day, but the result was that today's ranger did "most of his field work from the seat of an automobile, truck, helicopter, or airplane.... [We] rarely see a Forest Service Officer with a pack on his back— and very seldom astraddle a horse." This was a critical matter to Brandy, who had acquired his knowledge of the wilderness under the tutelage of trapper Griff Jones and various backwoods-savvy forest rangers. He asked how often the Bitterroot's staffers "have slept in a tent or under the stars away from the electric lights, the refrigerators, the gas stoves, and other comforts and contrivances of modern civilization.... [Y]ou will find that the boys in green jackets, because of other demands, are not sleeping out in the woods and living out of the pack sack." This, he felt, explained their lack of understanding for the views of those who treasured this wild country. His sentiments were shared by many of the thousand or so people who submitted statements to the Selke committee, but Brandborg's long connection to the Selway, his former position as a Forest Service official responsible for much of the area, and his friendship with Dr. Selke gave his views additional weight.

The timber industry did all it could to influence the Selke committee; one handbill distributed in the Bitterroot Valley urged supporters to "Act Now! Jobs and Businesses are Being Lost—You Can Help Keep Our Economy Strong—Increase Recreation." It stated that closing the Magruder Corridor to logging would throw a hundred sawmill and woods workers out of work and would "result in an economic decline equivalent to shutdown of all logging and sawmilling in the Bitter Root for 3 MONTHS each and every year." Timber access roads, its authors observed, would improve recreation for "you and I (the average citizen)."[26] With logging proceeding rapidly in the upper forks of the Bitterroot River, the owners of the four mills in the Darby area were looking across the state line for the next big cuts to sustain their operations—exactly as Miles Romney had foretold two decades earlier. Their handbill sounded the principal theme of the wildland debates that would continue in western Montana for the remainder of the century and beyond.

The Selke committee deliberated through the winter and forwarded its recommendations to Secretary Freeman in April 1967. Their findings, released that June and guardedly endorsed by Freeman, vindicated the conservationists' concerns. Although their report carefully avoided attacks on the Forest Service's motives or competence, Selke's panel believed that logging could indeed harm the area's soils and fisheries. Access roads were the main issue. "The combination of coarse texture and very weak formation of secondary structural units," they wrote, gave soils in the area "very high susceptibility to erosion. Thus the problem of logging impact on the soils of the Magruder Corridor is largely one of getting to the areas to be logged."

The corridor, the committee noted, served as "an avenue of access to two great wilderness and primitive areas of national significance." The Forest Service, it believed, should manage the area so as to "reflect and maintain wildland conditions consonant with these primary values." Although the committee did not propose returning Area E to protected wilderness status, it opposed extending the Magruder road up the Selway River from the Magruder Ranger Station and asked that logging in other parts of Area E proceed only under strict assurances that erosion and sedimentation would not occur. The agency's current state of knowledge about the area, it found, gave no such guarantee.

After reviewing the report, Secretary Freeman directed the Forest Service to come up with a new management plan that would better protect the upper Selway's watershed. Forced to shelve their logging plans for the time being, the Bitterroot's foresters still had room to maneuver if they could show that road construction would not damage streams and salmon spawning beds. Freeman also authorized them to proceed with improvements to the main Magruder Corridor road over Nez Perce Pass, including paving an eight-mile section.[27] Nothing was settled permanently, but the Selke committee's report and the secretary's decision enormously cheered the members of the Save the Upper Selway Committee. Their assertions about the high wilderness values found in the area and the potential for resource damage gained new credence.

Brandborg sent a letter of thanks to George Selke, which was received with evident appreciation. "Yes Brandy," he wrote in return, "we have stood shoulder to shoulder in many battles, always on the side of democracy with a small 'd,' for the rights of the people as a whole, realizing that the Creator intended that the resources of our world are to be used for the good of the many rather than for the few over the decades of time. Both you and I believe that as people are educated and learn tolerance what you and I stand for will triumph."[28] Like Brandy, Selke framed the issue not as a technical matter for foresters to decide but as a struggle to overcome an entrenched bureaucracy and its industrial clients. No polls had been taken to determine what the citizens of Ravalli County or western Montana wanted done in the Magruder Corridor, yet wilderness advocates were certain that their actions would benefit the citizens of the nation far into the future. To them it was not an issue of use versus nonuse; the Selway had long been performing its ideal function as a source of clear water, native fish populations, and magnificent, unmarred horizons.

The Forest Service's studies in the Magruder area would not be completed for several years and would resurface at a time when its personnel faced an even more glaring spotlight over their clearcutting practices on the Montana side of the forest. All of the major conservationist players in the issue, including Guy Brandborg and Doris Milner, now understood what was needed to derail Forest Service plans and rally public support. They would soon apply the same tactics to astonishing effect in the broader arena of forest management.

CHAPTER 12

A Fighting Democratic Faith

1964–1969

The Magruder Corridor fight allowed Guy Brandborg to do what he did best: feed inside dope about agency plans to his fellow conservationists, help them round up support from other organizations, and make sure they missed no opportunity to hold politicians' feet to the fire. The issue marked Brandy's return to active participation in conservation affairs and put him in touch with activists who were increasingly concerned about the direction public land management was taking. He enjoyed the camaraderie of his fellow leaders, who helped him weather occasional bouts of despair over the slow progress of conservation work. Doris Milner recalled that during the height of the Selway battle, when it appeared that the Forest Service was about to unleash the bulldozers, she drove up to his house to find him sitting alone in his yard, brooding over the difficulties they faced. That battle was won for now, but to many conservation leaders the movement was making little headway against mankind's propensity to despoil its nest. Brandy would sometimes take his friends to visit the old cemetery at Grantsdale, outside of Hamilton, to view what one acquaintance described as "waving timothy...knee-high among the pioneer graves," in contrast to the weeds outside the fence. Brandy commented that "the dead take better care of the land than the living do."[1]

He confided to Bruce Bowler, a fellow activist from Boise, that "I often wonder at my age why I should still be spending time on the social purpose of conservation—I suppose this is attributable to Gifford Pinchot's influence & contacts with him during the early days of the F.S."[2] He was referring to his evening with Pinchot and Evan Kelley in 1937, when the former chief gave him his marching orders to protect the public's interest in its forests. Three decades later it was not clear to him that Americans had grasped Pinchot's message and were ready to implement a comprehensive conservation program for their forests and fields. But soon he would get on the phone or sit down to write another batch of letters to make certain that conservationists presented a united front. As he told one friend, "I came from a family of fighters and it was not for ourselves. The earth is not a resting place for any Brandborg. Man was elected to fight for the emotional, intellectual, and ethical growth that goes on forward."[3]

By now nearly every activist and policy maker in the state was getting regular missives from Brandy, some scratched out on a yellow notepad in his sloping, crabbed hand, others edited and neatly typed by Ruth, calling for greater effort on behalf of conservation ideals. During 1967 he took pains to get his friends involved in the work of the Public Land Law Review Commission, Congressman Wayne Aspinall's attempt to overhaul and modernize the laws governing America's national parks, forests, wildlife refuges, and rangelands. As chairman of the House Interior Committee, Aspinall was one of the most powerful overseers of the nation's public lands and was inclined to listen to industry executives who wanted fewer encumbrances on the minerals, forage, water, and timber found therein. Brandborg hoped that the commission could be persuaded otherwise and circulated among his close friends a fifteen-page statement on the role that public lands could play in improving the lives of Americans, reprising his ideas of how to put men to work restoring abused land. After adding some of his friends' suggestions, he submitted the statement to Aspinall's commission and sent copies to nearly a hundred conservation leaders in Montana and throughout the nation, most of whom he knew personally. The statement summarized his land-management philosophy developed over a half century of working for forest, rangeland, and agricultural conservation and announced the themes to which he would devote the remaining decade of his life.[4]

The riots that were taking place in America's cities that year and the plight of citizens in its ghettos, Brandborg told the commission, were symptomatic of a lost relationship to the earth. "As man gets further removed from land and the things of the land," he wrote, "our troubles will be compounded. Man was not meant to live in a filthy tenement like a rat and in company with rats. For a man has a soul, a spirit that continues to cry inside him, demanding release from sordidness, filth and despair." This was an emotional statement coming from a former government employee—certainly not the careful, calculated language of a career bureaucrat. But those who knew Brandy understood his long concern with social issues. In dozens of talks, seminars, and public appearances over the decades he had propounded the theme of good forestry and good farming as a necessity for a functioning society. "If we continue only to treat the symptoms of social disease today," he went on, "and do not strike at the cause of this decay, then we are doomed as a Nation and as a people. We shall vanish as so many civilizations have vanished before us, and in fact our tenure as a civilization will have been much shorter than many."

The government could start, he suggested, by reviving one of his favorite New Deal programs. "The CCC was a work program, primarily, but from personal experience I can tell you it was more than that," he wrote. "It was a healthy return of young men to the land, and it was the making of these young men in more cases than not." It was not a far-fetched idea; the Bitterroot's old CCC camp at Trapper Creek had recently been reincarnated as a Job Corps center under President Johnson's Great Society agenda. "This program needs to be greatly expanded," Brandborg wrote. "There is work to do!" But the Job Corps, with its modern dorms and its focus on real-world job training, lacked the emphasis on backwoods living that characterized the older program. Brandy wanted more young men to learn how to heft an ax, pack a horse, fight fires, and breathe wood smoke by the campfire. "I have known many fine woodsmen in my day," he said. "There are still a few of these men left. They could provide the nucleus of a corps of trainers, who would once more teach basic skills to men who have too long been removed from the elements, and too long cooped up in the ghettos of our cities. Woodsmanship develops character, and character is the essential ingredient of good citizenship."[5]

Such job-training programs were often regarded as make-work efforts, a temporary expedient during hard times. Brandy, however, had seen federal conservation programs achieve real results, from Progressive Era forest land acquisition to the New Deal's shelterbelts, trails, and tree plantations. He saw no contradiction between government involvement in land-use issues and the grassroots populism he had grown up with and long advocated in the Bitterroot Valley. Such advice may have struck Aspinall's committee as overly idealistic— an old woodsman's reminiscences with little bearing on public land laws. But Brandborg took the commission's work seriously. In personal notes attached to copies of his statement, he asked his friends to submit their own views, arrange meetings with a particular congressman, or submit an op-ed piece to their local newspaper. Many of them sent cordial replies, including Sigurd Olson of Ely, Minnesota, who agreed that "modern man's divorcement from the soil" gave rise to the social unrest gripping the nation. "The Ecologic Crisis is exactly that," wrote Olson, whose own writings reminded thousands of readers of the importance of close contact with nature. "The issue is far more than wilderness, it is the total environment." He promised to use Brandy's ideas wherever he could. "They give me strength," he wrote.[6]

Brandborg, now in his seventies, owed his return to activism in part to a vigorous, dedicated woman named Ruth Melendy, whom he had met in the early 1960s while she was a professor in the Department of Public Administration at San Francisco State College. Ruth had grown up on a farm outside Portland, Oregon, and had studied English literature and the Greek and Roman classics at the University of Oregon. After further course work at Columbia University and Stanford, she launched into a career as an educator, eventually becoming superintendent of schools in San Carlos, California, where she had overseen the construction of six new schools during the state's population boom. She lived in Palo Alto, across the street from Brandy's daughter, Becky, who introduced them during one of his visits. They found they had much in common, from the enjoyment of books to a love of dancing, and were married in 1962. Brandy persuaded her to leave the Bay Area's cultural scene for Hamilton. A family story has it that upon reaching Lost Trail Pass during their move to Montana, Brandy stopped the car and got out to breathe in the mountain air. "D'ya smell that?" he told Ruth. "That's horseshit. We're in Montana now."[7]

Brandy may have played up his rural roots, but Ruth had kicked around pastures before, and she settled into an active life in Hamilton. She took leadership roles with the Hamilton Women's Club and the League of Women Voters, helped found a senior services program, and was a member of the local planning board and human resources council. Theirs would prove a fruitful collaboration. Her support and encouragement gave Brandy a renewed sense of mission, according to his family. Ruth spent countless hours accompanying him on field trips and attending meetings, afterward editing and typing his voluminous correspondence and hearing statements. She served as a kind of governing wheel to his dizzying energy. According to Stewart, she was "a great source of assistance, support, encouragement, and inspired ideas on her own." In taking on the duties of homemaking as well as serving as his personal secretary, she made it possible for Brandy to devote his time to the causes of wilderness and forest management.

The Northern Region's campaign to step up cutting was yielding results, both in timber volumes produced and in visible changes to the west-side forests. In 1963 the region's division of timber management directed each forest supervisor to "fill and keep full our timber sales pipeline." Sales were to be prepared at least one year in advance to ensure there were no breaks in supply, with the goal of having under contract at least twice the allowable cut in sawtimber. If mill capacity within a working circle was insufficient to handle the full allowable cut, the division would encourage new mills to locate there and would assist in developing economic methods of harvesting smaller low-value trees such as lodgepole pine.[8] Thus, on some forests, the agency's high allowable cuts were driving mill expansion, not vice versa.

To fully utilize its inventory of 3.5 billion board feet of sawtimber, the Bitterroot National Forest in 1965 again revised its timber-management plan. For this purpose Harold Andersen brought in Ray Karr, an assistant supervisor on the Tongass National Forest, who made use of new stand inventories that showed that 892,000 acres of the forest met the criterion for commercial forest land (CFL) and were available for logging—an increase of more than 300,000 acres from the last inventory.

Karr's chief concern was the advanced age of most of these stands; a well-regulated forest would have a full distribution of age classes, with new reproduction in some areas balancing the slower growth of old trees in others. Regulation of timber stands was a kind of Holy Grail for foresters, difficult to achieve outside of accessible lowland plantations and requiring aggressive cutting to bring about in the first place. This the Bitterroot forthrightly set out to do. Karr calculated that the forest could provide an annual cut of 66.3 mmbf by removing timber from 6,910 acres—nearly eleven square miles—annually. Of this total, 44 mmbf would be harvested by clearcutting some 6,430 acres annually; the remainder would be obtained by other methods such as shelterwood, thinning, and salvage harvesting. The harvest of ponderosa pine was increased to 17 mmbf, more than twice the amount Brandborg's foresters had envisioned in 1941. The increase partly reflected greater access to uncut stands brought about by the expanded network of logging roads built since World War II. The plan anticipated that roads would be extended still farther into the backcountry—including a substantial part of the upper drainage of the Selway River in Idaho.[9]

Karr based the overall cutting level on what was called the Kemp formula, a method of calculating sustained yield that the Washington office's timber branch had mandated as a means of quickly harvesting overmature stands, capturing their high volume, and replacing them with faster-growing young trees. Harvests would then be reduced at intervals in future years as the supply of old growth dwindled. This method replaced the area control that the Bitterroot had formerly practiced, whereby the total commercial forest land base was divided by a rotation age, yielding a corresponding annual cut. The goal was to reach a more balanced distribution of young and old trees under which a relatively even flow of timber products would eventually be realized. The immediate effect, however, was a onetime bounty as the old growth was hauled off—exactly what Brandborg had feared would lead to overbuilt capacity among the area's mills.

The top priority was to begin cutting in the middle elevations of the forest, where a parasite called dwarf mistletoe was reducing the vigor of Douglas fir and lodgepole pine. Mistletoe affected 70 percent of these stands and reduced growth by an average of 40 percent, according to Karr's estimates. Clearcutting these stands ran less risk of reinfection from trees left in a selection cut. To achieve the greatest efficiency, cutting would be done in large blocks with as few indentations or irregularities as possible. After logging slash was burned, bulldozers would mechanically strip off the remaining plant cover, removing six to ten inches of the soil. New seedlings would be planted by machine for maximum efficiency.[10] This was an attempt to correct a stubborn difficulty the Bitterroot foresters had been experiencing in earlier clearcuts, where moisture competition from grasses and shrubs was preventing reestablishment of a new stand. Herein lay one of the roots of the Bitterroot clearcutting crisis.

Forestry is anything but an exact science; the success of silvicultural treatments depends on a complex array of factors that are only partly subject to human control. Slope angle, orientation toward the sun, soil characteristics, moisture availability, browsing by rodents and deer, and competition from other plants all influence the success of young plantations. Of these, the latter gave the Bitterroot foresters the most trouble; the problem was worst on steep slopes where it was difficult to mechanically scarify the soil surface. After experiencing repeated plantation failures in such areas (in some cases only 5 to 10 percent of the seedlings were surviving), they decided that more drastic measures were needed.

Once again it was Axel Lindh who suggested a possible solution—an old one, in this case. In the 1920s and 1930s foresters on Utah's Wasatch National Forest had experimented with terracing severely overgrazed hillsides to prevent catastrophic runoff events. The method had also been employed on semiarid forest slopes in central Oregon and Idaho in the 1950s to regenerate burned-over areas. Lindh thought it might work on the Bitterroot, and after its foresters visited experimental terracing sites on the Boise National Forest in the early 1960s, they began employing the practice on both the Sula and West Fork districts.

Terracing was a machine operator's dream. After logging was completed, a medium-size bulldozer worked its way along the contour of the hillside, cutting level benches at intervals of eight to twelve feet down the slope. A tree-planting dozer would follow, usually the next spring or summer when soil conditions were favorable. The dozer towed a unique device called the Rocky Mountain Tree Planter, a smaller machine with a cab on the back housing a second person who faced toward the rear. Two metal blades on the dozer cut a furrow into which the operator would place the seedlings. A six- or eight-foot rope trailed behind the planting machine; when the end of the rope came even with the last planted seedling, in would go another. A second pair of blades on the machine pressed the soil back together around the seedlings. Because the trench was deeper than could be dug by hand, they could use planting stock with roots as long as eighteen inches—giving the seedlings a head start against competing pinegrass and animals. Sonny LaSalle, who headed one of the planting crews, recalls how his three-man team could set out as many as ten thousand seedlings in a single day, more than a much larger crew could put in by hand. With four thousand acres of cutover land to cover each year, the crews needed all the efficiency they could muster.[11]

The terracing method, first used extensively on the forest in 1964, yielded amazing results. First-year seedling survival averaged 85 percent, compared to under 50 percent with hand planting.[12] Although the Bitterroot was using local seed sources for its ponderosa pine, it had not selected them according to habitat type or elevation—an apparent disadvantage, yet the terraces still yielded growth rates nearly a third greater that would be expected for the site, according to LaSalle. This came about largely because they captured rainfall and retained snowpack longer into the spring. They also reduced the angle of incidence of the sun, a critical matter on south-facing slopes where seedlings could quickly desiccate in the summer heat.

Although terracing was a forest-regeneration technique, not a logging method, its use enabled harvesting on steep hillsides that might not otherwise have been cut—allowing the Forest Service to squeeze the greatest possible harvest out of a limited land base. In the mid- to late 1960s it was still trying to develop a market for the Bitterroot's high-elevation lodgepole pine, and considerable acreage across the state line in the Magruder Corridor was still inaccessible. The result was a heavy concentration of clearcuts and associated "jammer" logging roads in the readily accessible parts of the West Fork and East Fork drainages, and to a lesser extent along the Bitterroot mountain face. No longer was the Bitterroot's timber program limited to marking the big ponderosa pines in the foothills and supplying fine logs to the valley's small mills. The forest was now a full participant in the regionwide industrial expansion that Axel Lindh had foreseen in 1946.

Except for terracing, the Bitterroot's program matched in most respects the timber plans being developed for the rest of the Northern Region's forests. Road access was the key: once the main haul roads were punched in and a network of spur roads was developed, vast undeveloped stands could be harvested. The roads permitted better fire control and administrative access, as well as dispersing hunters and other recreationists. Campgrounds could be built along streamside corridors where timber harvesting was limited, helping to fulfill the agency's pledge to maintain multiple-use values. The clearcuts, while admittedly unattractive, refreshed browse for big game, temporarily increased streamflows for irrigators, and (as was sometimes argued) opened up scenic vistas along roads that were clogged with trees.

The foresters tended to discount the usefulness of undeveloped timber stands for purposes such as trail hiking or big-game cover. In most cases the trees were hundreds of years old and had passed the point of highest growth. Aesthetically, they lacked the conventional beauty of the well-spaced ponderosa pine stands closer to the valley floor or the picturesque snags clinging to alpine crags. Forest regulation meant that such amenities would be confined to designated wilderness areas, of which the Bitterroot already had some of the finest examples in the nation. The forest's annual reports for this period touted the benefits of its timber-management activities for all users, featuring photographs of beautifully thinned ponderosa pine stands and discussing the forest's work in slash cleanup, tree planting, and salvage of burned areas. Images of recently clearcut and terraced areas, if they were shown at all, were relegated to the background.

The agency was aware that there could be concern over the appearance of clearcutting; in a booklet issued in 1965 chief Edward Cliff defended the practice as meeting Mrs. Lyndon Johnson's call for a national beautification campaign. Timber cutting was nothing more than "landscape gardening on a massive scale," he noted. "Our toolsheds bulge with equipment ranging from the usual rakes and shovels to large modern machines....[I]nstead of a flit gun we use back pumps and spray-planes to control forest pests....Instead of garden paths, we have almost 200,000 miles of travel ways, ranging from rough access roads to modern forest highways." The pamphlet displayed a photo of a recent clearcut with the explanation that "when we harvest overmature, defective timber that would otherwise be wasted, there is bound to be a temporary loss of natural beauty."[13]

Some of the Bitterroot's personnel, however, grew uneasy with the intense timber management they were practicing. "It was harsh," recalls Sonny LaSalle. "I believe that we were cutting more than we could sustainably maintain over a long time." He and some of his colleagues felt that the local timber industry was unduly influencing affairs on the forest. "The big clearcuts were kind of a scary thing," recalls Ray Abbott, a forester on the Sula District during the 1960s. He anticipated criticism of the practice, yet forest officials in Hamilton and Missoula were calling for maximum production. "You gotta march to the driver, and that was the money coming in from timber," he observed recently.[14]

Former West Fork ranger Sam Billings expressed an older forester's concern, recounting how a timber sale he had laid out in the ponderosa pine type fell prey to the new high-utilization approach. "I selectively logged, marked it, and it was a fine looking stand," he said in a 1982 interview. "I thought that in probably another 30 years they could make another selective cut. But it was no good. They clearcut all the rest of it, and planted fast-growing trees and everything. Took 'em all out." He also had reservations about terracing, which he said "looked like the very devil." Later inspection convinced him that regrowth was thriving in the terraced units, but like Champ Hannon, it was difficult for his generation of foresters to see their hard fieldwork obliterated.[15]

Yet many former Bitterroot foresters, including LaSalle and Abbott, also spoke of the pride they felt in making new forests grow back under difficult conditions. More than three times the volume of sawlogs was coming off the forest than in Brandborg's day, supplying newly built and renovated mills in the Darby area as well as larger facilities near Missoula. Timber haul roads were being pushed into uncut stands in Blue Joint Creek, Mud Creek, and many other remote drainages in the headwaters of the Bitterroot River, which now echoed to the sound of jake brakes as logging trucks descended the grades. Full log decks kept the headrigs humming in the valley's major mills; smoke rising from teepee burners signified full employment. The wild growth of the mountain forests was at last yielding to more productive stands.

With prominent conservationists such as Interior Secretary Stewart Udall playing major roles in Washington, citizen activists believed the federal government could take significant steps to slow the degradation of the nation's land, air, soil, and water. Now was the time, many believed, to reverse the not so benign neglect of the Eisenhower years, when dams, highways, mines, and logging were the order of the day. This, to Brandy's thinking, could not be accomplished without struggle. He had been reading, as part of one of the local study groups he liked to organize, J. Leonard Bates's 1957 monograph, *Fulfilling American Democracy,* which examined the Progressive movement's ties to social activism. Bates believed that Progressivism was more than a scientific or managerial movement designed to ensure efficient resource production; it had its roots in populist claims for self-government. Brandy appropriated Bates's phrase for this activist view of conservation: "not a loose, vague theory, nor a matter of efficiency as such, but a fighting democratic faith."[16]

In company with Pinchot and activist foresters such as Kelley and Silcox, Brandborg saw no reason government agents could not promote the public welfare instead of the interests of corporations. As Bates wrote, "Most leaders of progressivism believed in a positive state. Some came to believe in the sort of factory and social legislation, welfare action, and limited government ownership that is associated with the New Deal. A few wished to go farther than the New Deal ever went."[17] It was time, Brandborg believed, to bring Progressive principles to fruition after a half century of lip service and political appeasement. This did not necessarily mean abandoning science or sound management—he felt that his agency's earlier silvicultural studies made the case for selective cutting and watershed protection. Rather, he focused on one of the Progressive movement's neglected facets: a concern for the welfare of workers and rural families.

Rehabilitating private forest lands, he believed, would directly help Bitterroot Valley residents. Early in 1967 he proposed to his friend Arnold Bolle, now dean of the forestry school at the University of Montana, a cooperative government effort to plant trees on understocked sites and thin overstocked stands, as well as undertake educational efforts to "acquaint the public with the economic and social implications that will accrue from proper forestry and other land use practices." Such a program, he told Bolle, would provide welcome work for valley residents and serve as a model for improved land use. "It would also help to establish in the mind of the public," he said, "that man's future does not rest upon economic expediency alone, but rests also upon the need to define and practice better land ethics."[18]

Bolle saw merit in the idea and had been discussing federal legislation along such lines with Lee Metcalf. Private lands in western Montana had been "going downhill for years," he told Brandy. But unless small landowners found markets for woodlot products, he said, it would be almost impossible to interest them in improved management.[19] Metcalf would introduce legislation in the Ninety-second Congress to regulate timber cutting on private lands, but the bill would languish. By then the controversy over clearcutting on the national forests would overshadow the situation on private lands.

Much of the concern over timber management in western Montana came from the increasingly vocal wilderness preservation movement, whose members objected to the extension of logging roads and clearcuts into formerly pristine mountains. Through much of the 1960s a battle similar to the Selway fight ran concurrently on the Lolo and Helena national forests, where preservationists were opposed to logging a wild mountain stronghold called the Lincoln Back Country. There, too, local citizens had gained the ear of Montana's congressional delegation and were pressing for wilderness legislation—a campaign that would meet with success in 1972 when Congress set aside the Scapegoat Wilderness, the first expansion of the nation's wilderness system made in direct response to a citizen initiative.

A hearing held in Great Falls in September 1969 on an early version of this bill, introduced by Lee Metcalf and Congressman James Battin, turned into a referendum on the Forest Service's practices in other parts of the state, notably the Bitterroot. Doris Milner brought with her sixty-seven letters from valley residents who had angry words for the timber harvesting that was often visible from their homes. "Great clearcut scabs are growing in number on the slopes facing the valley," Milner asserted. "Long strings of logging roads lace back and forth in ever growing ugly gashes. And out of sight, but not out of mind of those who care about watershed, are huge mountaintops skinned out, burned, a real desert: this is the headwaters of both forks of the Bitterroot River."[20]

Neal Rahm, the regional forester in Missoula, saw the Metcalf-Battin bill as a direct challenge to his agency's autonomy—which indeed it was. He took the Magruder and Lincoln Back Country battles as an incentive for change—to look for a way to take public opposition into account before it became a matter for Congress to decide. In 1967 he convened an in-house committee headed by Ken Keeney, his director of information and education, to examine the Northern Region's dealings with its constituents. The committee identified eighty instances, spanning virtually every forest in the region, where it felt a better job could have been done. Why had things gone wrong in so many places? "The problem was us," recalls Ray Karr, who served on the panel. He believes that his agency was locked into what he calls an "attitude of ownership" toward forest lands that led its leaders and staff to assume that they knew what was best for the land. Keeney's panel observed that true communication between the affected parties was lacking. Rahm used the opportunity to introduce more public outreach, beginning with a pilot program to study land-management options in the Pryor Mountains on the Bighorn National Forest. Forest officers contacted conservation groups, other government agencies, and local citizens to inform them of the agency's plans for the area and seek their advice. By 1970 similar efforts were under way to discuss potential conflicts over wilderness lands in the Idaho panhandle and in Montana's Mission Mountains.[21]

An informed public was not necessarily a satisfied public. Many people wanted their favorite parts of the forest segregated from incompatible uses, and they would continue to press the agency to zone areas such as the Magruder Corridor and the Lincoln Back Country off-limits to logging. Their success in halting timber sales in their favorite roadless areas had effects that rippled across the Northern Region. Because the agency had already included these areas in its allowable-cut calculations in anticipation of later harvests, it now faced the choice of reducing the overall cut or increasing the pressure on already developed areas. The Flathead and Lolo national forests still had large volumes of timber in other parts of their forests and were able to adjust without much dislocation. But when the Bitterroot was forced to delay sales in the Magruder Corridor, it lost the land base for nearly a fourth of its projected annual cut. Not wanting to reduce the sales program, its foresters elected to make up the loss from the Montana side, all the while hoping to one day gain access to the Selway.

The decision proved fateful. The forest's total sales volume during the high-production years of 1966–1968 averaged 64 mmbf. Conservationists may have won a reprieve for the wild interior of the Selway River, but they could now see the effects closer to home, as logging roads were pushed into many other road-less drainages on the Montana side of the Bitterroot. Formerly wild valleys such as Piquett, Blue Joint, and Overwhich creeks in the West Fork and Bugle, Meadow, and Tepee creeks in the East Fork hosted an expanding lacework of timber haul roads, logging spurs, and clearcut units. Richard Schloemer, a for-ester working for the Conner Lumber Company in Darby, recalled a conversa-tion with the forest's timber staff officer in 1968 in which he was told that within four years there would be a road into every drainage in the Bitterroot outside of its two designated wilderness areas.[22]

Brandborg recognized that logging would go on in the Montana portion of the Bitterroot forest; in his 1966 statement to the Selke committee he pointed out that lodgepole stands in the upper forks of the Bitterroot River could be har-vested with shorter haul distances than from the Selway. But he differed with his successors in three important respects: he now opposed development within the boundaries of the former Selway-Bitterroot Primitive Area (a change from his position as supervisor), he objected to the degree of land disturbance pre-sented by large-scale clearcutting, and, more fundamentally, he believed that the overall cutting level was not sustainable.

Forest sustainability had been an ongoing topic of debate since the agency's founding and would continue to prove highly contentious. Brandborg wanted the Bitterroot to set a relatively unvarying harvest level that would smooth out fluctuations in cutting from private lands, ensuring continued sawmill employ-ment in the Bitterroot Valley. The agency's current program envisioned a fall-off in cutting after most of the older stands were converted to young growth. Brandborg feared that with private supplies also dwindling, the result would be an unacceptable decline in local employment.

Most forest economists disparaged the even-flow formulation of sustained yield; trees should be treated as a capital resource, they argued, harvesting more when demand was high and letting them stand in times of slack markets. Mod-ern timber companies had to respond to shifting prices for wood products of all types, which required expansion in boom times and retrenchment during reces-sions. No less an authority than Arnold Bolle agreed with this assessment. In a 1966 survey of the Montana forest-products sector, he and his coauthors wrote that the even-flow doctrine could work against the viability of industry. "The development of products with a strong market potential may be inhibited by the continued production of others for which the projected demand is low," they maintained. "Stability in the sense of sustained yield of the resource may not be as important as the industry's capacity to adjust to new production and marketing conditions."[23]

Brandy could not abide this approach, although he did not criticize Bolle in public. Elasticity of demand translated in his mind to out-of-work loggers and sawmill employees; it was the government's business to modulate the ups and downs of the business cycle so as to minimize layoffs. His ideal of forestry envisioned local men cruising the woods, marking trees, and supervising sales that local contractors would harvest and haul down to nearby mills. By the late 1960s this formula appeared somewhat archaic; the Bitterroot National Forest was no longer a local timbershed that supplied fence posts, barn lumber, and a modest supply of select pine boards and sash material to the valley's economy. New transportation and financial networks ensured that the forest's resources would travel to distant markets and be subject to their demands. Workers and their families in Darby and Conner would ride the crest of this boom, only to find that conditions could change quickly in their volatile industry.

Sustained yield was often thought to be a precondition for community stability, but the connection could be tenuous, as Bolle and various forest economists argued. Harold Kaufman, who studied the timber industry in Lincoln County as part of the Montana Study, suggested that a stable community was not static, but was "one in which there is orderly change toward given goals: those goals embracing 'the good life' in whatever way it is defined."[24] Brandborg often used the term *community welfare* to denote these broader criteria. As he noted in his work on the Montana Study, such communities would offer not just employment in the woods, farms, ranches, and sawmills but also opportunities in adult education, the arts, and recreation. Their homes and buildings would be attractive and well maintained, suggesting that people wanted to stay there. There would be engagement with the issues of the day through community meetings and discussion groups. Woods and sawmill employment contributed to community welfare but were far from its sole determinant.

As always, Brandborg looked to the social effects of forest management. Directives from Washington to increase cuts usurped the relationship of the land manager to his immediate constituency. Too often, he said, agency officials "rest their decisions on dollar and cents values instead of the values that contribute to a more contented and satisfying life." So long as the politicians overseeing the Forest Service were beholden to industry's campaign donations, neither conservation nor other social needs would be served. To counteract such influence he called for "a re-birth of government for and by the people, with conservationists actively participating in politics from the courthouse to the White House."[25]

Unlike many of his colleagues in the preservation and environmental-protection fields, he believed that national forests still had a strong role to play in promoting the good of the community. As historian Curt Meine has noted, the notion of what constituted conservation was always in flux. In the transition to the environmental movement of the late 1960s and 1970s, he wrote, "we gained perspective on the full dimensions of humankind's environmental dilemma, as well as a broader base of support for actions to address it. But we also lost much in the transition to environmentalism, including the attitude of stewardship that formerly bound conservationists, hunters, farmers, ranchers, and other landowners more closely together."[26] Guy Brandborg was determined to keep that powerful coalition intact, for new forces were threatening to undo the gains of a half century of conservation work. Runaway clearcutting was, to him, a symptom of a larger failing of modern forestry, severing the enduring connection between rural communities and the land in all its variety.

CHAPTER 13

Collision Course

1965–1969

The four sawmills clustered around Darby drew most of their log supply from stands in the upper forks of the Bitterroot River, out of which streamed "a never-ending parade of trucks," according to Forest and Agnes Cooper, who owned a farm at Conner, close by the juncture of the West Fork road and Highway 93. The log trucks, as they reported to Lee Metcalf in February 1965, were "loaded as if every stick must be hauled out at the utmost speed." Agnes Cooper was superintendent of schools for Ravalli County and was the sister of Champ Hannon; both she and her husband had taken an active role in the Montana Study and continued to push for the broader development of their historically logging-dependent valley.

Most of the trucks off-loaded a few miles down the road at the three main Darby sawmills; a fourth, the S&W operation on the West Fork at Conner, had just reopened following a fire that destroyed the plant the previous March. It featured a double band-saw headrig that could produce 100,000 board feet of lumber in an eight-hour shift, using smaller-diameter logs than before. The firm was named for longtime lumbermen Dee Shook and Milo Wilson, who had opened the first modern mill in the Darby area in 1954. The current operation employed 150 men, including logging crews.[1] The Coopers acknowledged that these mills contributed to the local economy, but they felt that their owners' dominant motive was to harvest timber as fast as possible. They claimed that heavy logging in Rye Creek, a favorite fishing stream to the east of where they lived, was hastening the spring runoff. "The water is loaded with silt, soil coming down in tremendous quantity," they told Metcalf. "After the high water is over, the stream amounts to almost nothing."[2]

Two of Brandborg's former employees, rangers Champ Hannon and Charles McDonald, were also growing concerned about the forest's shift to intensive timbering. In the fall of 1966 they each took Brandy on separate trips into the Skalkaho Creek drainage to view the aftermath of the Sleeping Child burn, where the Bitterroot's foresters were completing extensive salvage logging operations. Don Aldrich, who had recently begun work as the executive director of the Montana Wildlife Federation, joined Hannon and Brandborg on their trip. Afterward Brandy fired off a missive to Miles Romney, publisher of the *Western News* in Hamilton. "I am well aware that no one but you writes your editorials," he offered, then proceeded to give his take on the Bitterroot's policies. "There is a growing public concern among people in the Bitter Root as to the effects of mountain sides blackened by forest fires, stripped by clear-cutting and burning.... Many feel that the judgment of other scientists should be solicited: ecologists, biologists, watershed managers, and other experts, before giving the forester a free hand in denuding the proposed ten-mile strip and engaging in other clear-cut and burning practices."[3] He was calling, in effect, for a multidisciplinary review of timber sales—an augury of things to come.

These comments could be dismissed as the griping of disgruntled retirees who had the habit of sticking their noses into the forest's business. Brandy was not exactly welcome in the supervisor's office, and serious antagonism had already developed between him and supervisor Harold Andersen over the Magruder Corridor affair. Now, with salvage operations pushing roads into formerly undeveloped mountain drainages, Brandy joined Aldrich in raising concerns about erosion and excessive hunter access. The proposed fuel breaks on the Skalkaho and East Fork divides would exacerbate the problem, they believed, as well as encourage local mills to overbuild their capacity.

The Sleeping Child salvage program had already drawn objections from a group of ranchers who ran cattle in the Sapphire Range. Beginning in 1962 they complained to district ranger Okie Grossarth that the agency's efforts to replant lodgepole pine in the burned area had reduced summer forage for their herds.

The Darby and Sula districts had seeded orchard grass in the burned area to prevent erosion and had allowed ranchers to temporarily graze the area, but long-range plans called for establishing a timber cover. Steep side cuts on many of the timber haul roads impeded cattle movement, already difficult in this mountainous terrain.[4]

The ranchers also maintained that erosion from clearcut and scarified logging units was sending sediment into their irrigation ditches. In late 1966 Grossarth and supervisor Merrill Tester, who replaced Harold Andersen that year, met with the group to explain their rationale for the roads and reforestation efforts. Scarifying the ground surface, they said, was necessary to prevent the growth of grasses that competed with the lodgepole seedlings. They doubted that the clearcut areas were shedding significant sediment into streams. In any event, Tester maintained, it made little sense to manage these high forested mountains for forage production.

This did not satisfy the ranchers, who took their concerns to Senator Mike Mansfield. Stanton Cooper, a member of the group, worried that the next spring's runoff "could cost private property owners in the Sleeping Child drainage many valuable irrigation diversions, well systems and even improved meadows." Cooper, along with fellow ranchers Jack Evans and Marvin Bell, asked Mansfield to arrange for an unbiased investigation through the Army Corps of Engineers or another agency. "One has only to drive a short distance in most any direction from Hamilton to see big scars on the surrounding mountains," they said. "If you drive to a mountain pass to enjoy the scenery about all you look at is the ugliness of terracing and clear cutting. This practice has spread so far now that this is about all that meets the eye wherever you turn."[5]

Mansfield usually let Lee Metcalf take the lead in conservation disputes, but his staff relayed the ranchers' concerns to chief Edward Cliff, prompting a flurry of memos to explain the situation. No supervisor enjoys getting inquiries from higher-ups about problems on their forest; Tester advised Grossarth to arrange further meetings and field trips with the ranchers to assuage their worries. In May 1968 Darby district staff met with the group at the Sleeping Child schoolhouse to discuss an eighteen-acre clearcut they were planning below the Skalkaho–Sleeping Child divide—part of the new hazard reduction program being tested in the Sapphires. They assured the ranchers, now organized as the Sleeping Child Water Users Association, that they planned no other timber sales in the drainage for the next five years. "The discussions were generally frank and open," Grossarth reported to Tester. The group gave its approval to the proposed cutting block, although they reserved judgment on the relatively new practice of terracing.[6]

Despite repeated meetings and field trips, some of the ranchers remained unconvinced about the agency's intentions. They aired their concerns at meetings of the Bitterroot Resource Conservation and Development program, whose participants usually discussed noncontroversial projects ranging from repairing irrigation ditches and stabilizing stream banks to building community playgrounds. One of the Sleeping Child ranchers, Gerald Bergh, chaired the RC&D's Recreation Committee, on which Guy Brandborg, Charles McDonald, and Doris Milner also served. Brandy's conservation leadership was well known within the ranching community, and Bergh, Evans, and Bell asked him to help make their case with the Forest Service. The committee's meetings quickly turned into an ongoing forum on forest management issues.

Proposals that advanced through the RC&D's subcommittees had to pass muster before a central program committee. Its chairman, a soil conservation district supervisor named Clarence Popham, was willing to discuss the logging issue and see if some action could be taken. At an earlier meeting Popham delivered a rousing call for civic betterment in Ravalli County—touching pointedly on forest management concerns. "I wonder what it would be like if we all sat back, if we didn't even try—except as individuals—to influence the future?" he said. "For one thing, we already have more sawmills in this area than can be supported by the annual yield available from our forests. What might happen? It could be still more mills. A gradual yielding to the political and economic pressures, our hills denuded, and our streams dried up and silted. Would you still like to live here?" These were exactly Brandborg's sentiments. He saw the RC&D group as a means of finally bringing about the grassroots action on forestry problems he had been seeking for decades. He told Miles Romney that he was heartened to see citizens taking on these issues, and hoped that the RC&D would "revive democratic processes and put them to work to improve economic, social, cultural and other aspects of life" in the valley.[7]

A few of the scientists working at the Rocky Mountain Laboratory, notably Dr. J. Frederick "Fritz" Bell, expressed their own concerns to the committee, including fears about the Forest Service's aerial spraying of DDT and other persistent insecticides to control the spruce budworm. But Brandy's strongest allies at the RC&D meetings were Milner and McDonald, who both brought unique perspectives to the issue. Doris and her husband, Kelsey, like many valley residents, could see the new clearcuts extending along the Bitterroot mountain face. "The continued clearcutting is becoming a source of unrest and apprehension among citizens," she reported to Metcalf in June 1967. "I was up on the east side mountains last week looking at areas that have been clear cut. I was looking for evidence of reforestation. There is very little in evidence. The overall picture is rather sad." She suggested that with the Selke committee's work finished, it was time to take a closer look at the rest of the forest. "No one disputes the importance of husbanding good watersheds and yet I wonder if the Bitterroot management plan, if there is such a thing, considers anything but the board footage sold?"[8]

Milner may not have been aware that the Forest Service often deferred replanting on cutover areas for up to a year until crews were available and soil conditions were optimal. But Charles McDonald's observations were more difficult to set aside. For years "Ranger Mac" had been taking civic and conservation groups on field trips throughout the Bitterroot Valley and adjoining forest lands to point out examples of good and poor land uses. During his last few years on the forest he had come into conflict with Harold Andersen and the regional office over the step-up in cutting, which he felt had outpaced reforestation work. Following his retirement in 1964, he continued to inspect cutting units on his old district, often noticing problems with replanting and erosion. His stature as a Forest Service veteran added credibility to the valley residents' complaints.

Such issues did not lend themselves to consensus before the RC&D committees, especially with a growing number of valley residents deriving their incomes from logging and sawmill work. But to Brandborg, the timber program was simply not sustainable. As he told Miles Romney, "An expanding economy can never be built on a rapidly declining natural resource base."[9] He would continue to speak at RC&D meetings and privately urge his friends to take action. As a result, the clearcutting controversy in Montana would catch flame not from an environmentalist lawsuit or a congressional hearing but through a grassroots forum of the type that Brandborg had been promoting for most of his career.

In the fall of 1968 Champ Hannon invited Brandy to take a closer look at what was happening in the headwaters of the Bitterroot. Hannon knew the West Fork country intimately, having worked there as a district ranger when only a rough track led up the river to the mining camp of Alta. He had hand-marked many of Brandy's timber sales, expecting that they would yield another selective harvest in the 1990s. Now, as they drove a hundred miles of back roads and logging spurs above Darby, Hannon was disturbed to see some of his work subsumed into closely spaced clearcuts of forty, sixty, or a hundred acres each. His concept of the sustained-yield principle, he told an interviewer in 1970, meant that "you cut the timber in such a way that you can cut without reducing the cut for all time to come." To him, "the 15 years work that I did for the Forest Service was just thrown away."[10]

The tour opened Brandy's eyes to the extent of changes on the forest, which in many places no longer resembled the green-cloaked hills he had known. That evening he told Ruth that he was determined to take the forest management issue to the people of Montana. As Ruth recalled years later, Brandy stood in their kitchen doorway and recounted what he had seen that day. "I'll never give it up," he told her. "I'll say it as it is."[11]

He began by outlining his concerns in a letter to Lee Metcalf. "What I saw yesterday was shocking and sad," he wrote. "The experience disclosed twenty years of scientific foresters' and other employees' hard work, long hours, working in hot, cold, and wet weather, climbing hills even on snow shoes, as well as the expenditure of tens of thousands of dollars gathering information, planning and executing a program on the public's behalf. All this has come to naught at the hands of present-day foresters." He noted that with the exception of his field trips to view the Saddle Mountain and Sleeping Child salvage work, he had viewed forest practices in recent years only at a distance—from his home or from the valley floor. His tour with Hannon, he told Metcalf, "provided positive proof that present-day foresters have not only betrayed their profession but the public trust by not adhering to sustained yield policies prescribed in well documented management plans."[12]

The letter to Metcalf signaled the beginning of a singular obsession with the issue. Drawing on his years of experience organizing citizen efforts, he urged his friends and acquaintances in the valley to write to their congressional delegation and speak out in other forums. As he told Ruth, "when Champ & I get on a stump the woods will be ringin'!"[13]

He redoubled his efforts to get the RC&D organization to take a stand on the issue. Brandy, Milner, and McDonald were present at a meeting of the group's Recreation Committee on October 1, 1968—a date that serves as the launching point of the Bitterroot clearcutting controversy. The committee briefly considered a proposal to obtain access easements to the Bitterroot River, after which Ranger Mac presented his idea of a wilderness skyline trail reaching from Lolo Peak to Blodgett Canyon. Then, according to the minutes that Milner was keeping, "several members of the committee expressed opinions regarding the way the multiple use practices are being carried out in the valley at the present time and voiced deep concern that the natural resources of the valley were going to suffer in the long run if they continue."[14]

The Sleeping Child ranchers had been raising similar questions for years, but they had yet to create sufficient concern among the RC&D members. Brandborg, McDonald, and Milner proved to be the necessary catalysts. At their instigation, the group decided to present a resolution to the full committee calling for Montana's congressional delegation to "select and assign a scientific study team to evaluate forest practices in the Bitterroot National Forest." In support of such a study, they cited the need to supply clean water for irrigation, fisheries, recreation, and domestic uses; preserve the natural beauty of the Bitterroot Valley for residents' enjoyment and to maintain real estate values; and maintain the valley's abundant fish and wildlife resources. They also addressed the issue closest to Brandy's heart, calling on the Forest Service and other landholders to "adhere strictly to practices that will assure a sustained yield in perpetuity. This probably will require a new and realistic appraisal of the timber that will be feasible to harvest without irreparable damage to other at least equally valuable resources."[15]

Milner did not record any debate on the resolution, which was adopted as Study Proposal No. 168, nor did she indicate who drafted it. Carefully worded to require only an impartial evaluation of the issue, it reflected Brandborg's long interest in bringing outside expertise to bear on local questions. But news quickly circulated that the conservationist lobby was up to something. Merrill Tester learned of the resolution on October 4 while he was on vacation. The following Monday he obtained a copy and got on the phone to Clarence Popham to ask him to delay action. Popham demurred, saying he would bring it up for discussion at the next meeting of the Program Committee.

Thirty-three people attended the Program Committee meeting on October 8. Merrill Tester asked for the floor and read for the audience's benefit the provisions of the Multiple Use–Sustained Yield Act of 1960, which directed the Forest Service to manage its holdings for a variety of uses, including timber production. He asked those present for greater understanding of his agency's mission, explaining that the Forest Service "cannot satisfy all the proponents of a given resource." He pointed out how the clearcut units at Guide Saddle—among the first substantial ones on the forest—were showing excellent regrowth ten years after harvesting. Discussion ensued, with Brandborg stating his belief that the increase in cutting in the ponderosa pine stands exceeded sustained yield, to which Tester responded that most of the clearcutting was being done in mistletoe-infected Douglas fir stands. Others in the audience asked about the effect of clearcutting on stream flows; Tester said that the openings collected more snow, but admitted that it tended to melt faster. Clarence Popham closed the meeting by referring the resolution to five subcommittees for study and written recommendations. "If the desires of the people are in favor of the request for a study," he concluded, "we will do everything in our power to carry out their wishes."[16]

Thus were the battle lines drawn. The next day Tester dispatched a personal memo to Neal Rahm explaining this alarming development. "It soon became evident at the meeting that the resolution is another move by the 'Save-the-Selway' group," he reported. "Doris Milner, Brandborg, Charles McDonald, Miles Romney, et al were there enmasse. In essence, the meeting was stacked by preservationists."[17] Tester's predecessor, Harold Andersen, had been badly stung on the Selway issue, and he did not intend to be ambushed by another panel of outside academics. But forces were loose that would quickly overwhelm his efforts to reason with a skeptical public and put a damper on the controversy.

Tester pointed out that he was conducting "natural beauty seminars" with his employees to lay out roads to scenic overlooks in the valley, but for many of the participants in the RC&D meetings, concerns about the appearance of the Bitterroot's clearcuts were secondary to watershed, wildlife, and sustained-yield issues. Tester may have misjudged the depth of his opponents' feelings—especially those of traditional forest users such as the Sleeping Child ranchers. Their complaints, along with Brandy's long concern with sustained yield, would give the clearcutting issue form and substance—going well beyond the raw appearance of the cutting units.

Lumber mill owners and their employees reacted angrily as word of the conservationists' latest move spread through the Bitterroot Valley. Although the resolution called for nothing more than an independent study of the clearcutting issue, they understood its intent—to halt the very practices that had given them nearly a decade of continuous employment. To air their side of the issue, they called a public meeting in Darby on October 17 that drew 140 people. Merrill Tester attended along with two of his staff, and noted that "a considerable amount of heated opposition and concern was expressed" toward the conservationists' resolution. The industry spokesmen pointed out that withholding timber sales in the Magruder Corridor had already taken 12 mmbf out of the forest's annual cut and that further reductions would endanger the area's mills. The *Ravalli Republican* reported that "Mrs. Kelsey Milner explained the point of view of the Recreation Committee, but was not well received, as most felt that persons whose 'bread and butter' does not depend on timber should not say whether the industry lives or dies." Tester noted that the crowd "gave her a pretty rough time."[18] Grassroots involvement cut both ways on the Bitterroot, Brandy's idealism notwithstanding.

Supervisor Tester continued to monitor the issue and send updates to Rahm. He was encouraged to find that not all of the subcommittees of the RC&D were friendly toward the study resolution. A meeting of the Cultural Improvement Committee on October 17 drew a hundred people, most of whom were opposed to the resolution, and similar comment surfaced in the Industry-Forestry Committee. The Agriculture Committee, on the other hand, supported it. Brandborg "made his usual strong accusations" at the latter, according to Tester. The Stevensville Grange and the Ravalli County Farm Bureau joined with the conservationists, while in Darby the mill owners, their workers, and various independent loggers formed the Bitterroot Multiple Use Association to defend the Forest Service's cutting program. They circulated petitions opposed to the Recreation Committee's study proposal and sent angry commentaries to the *Ravalli Republican*. Myron Alteneder of Darby, a leader of the multiple-use group, called on the agency to increase its harvest levels to 80 mmbf per year, noting that area mills were trucking timber in from four adjacent national forests. He criticized the earlier timber policies developed by Brandborg as outdated, pointing out that modern mills now utilized fir and spruce species that formerly were wasted.[19]

Supporters of the study resolution defended their right and duty to question the government's actions. "None of these groups are asking that the timber industry be shut down," wrote Jack Evans from his perspective in the Sleeping Child. "They are asking the Forest Service to do their timber harvesting in a different manner." He said that "the destruction of nearly all the grass in clear-cut areas has already cut down calf weights for ranchers" and cited what he said were "floods and erosion in the spring and a definite decrease in the amount of water for late summer irrigation which is imperative for crops of all kinds."[20]

Brandborg and his friends continued to line up support for an independent review. The Ravalli County Fish and Wildlife Association brought up the idea of getting the University of Montana's forestry school involved in the issue. This was probably Brandy's notion, given his long involvement with the wildlifers and his friendship with the Forestry School's dean, Dr. Arnold Bolle.[21] Brandy and Ruth hosted Bolle for dinner the following January and almost certainly would have pressed the idea. Lee Metcalf was already pursuing this tack with Bolle, as it happened, which would lead to one of the controversy's most significant outcomes.

As in the Selway battle, Brandborg and Milner understood that support from national environmental groups was essential if they were to overcome opposition from the Forest Service and the timber industry. Following the October 1968 RC&D meetings they attended a gathering in Coeur d'Alene, Idaho, of the Federation of Western Outdoor Clubs, an umbrella organization of hiking clubs and conservation groups. Brandborg served as the group's Montana vice president and frequently prodded it to play a greater role in conservation issues. The federation had recently hired a young, articulate conservation lobbyist named Brock Evans, who split his duties with the Sierra Club and would play a key role in wilderness and forestry battles in the region. The Recreation Committee's study proposal, Brandy told Evans, was "a real grass roots effort," which "indicates that the public have had their fill of forest industry influence upon the Forest Service.... You could scare the hell out of the forest industry by suggesting citizens make like approaches in other areas."[22]

Following the day's session in Coeur d'Alene, Evans relaxed with Milner and Brandborg over drinks in a hotel room, not quite believing their talk about how they were taking on the Forest Service and the powerful timber industry. "Brandy, you can't do that," Evans recalled telling him. "It's all we can do to snatch wilderness places away from their grasp. I see no way we can win these larger things too." But Brandborg replied that what the Forest Service was doing to the Bitterroot was "wrong, just wrong. And we're gonna take 'em on." Evans took an immediate liking to Brandy, describing him as "a great good natured bear of a man," but he had his own battles to attend to in the Pacific Northwest, where he advised small bands of citizens on how to deal with the steady approach of logging roads and clearcuts into their favorite hiking areas. But Evans was a key conduit to the Sierra Club, which could marshal thousands of activists nationwide. Brandy would go to some lengths during the next year to get Evans out to the Bitterroot for a firsthand look.[23]

The debate over Study Proposal No. 168 split the RC&D organization into rival camps. After the Darby multiple use association presented a proindustry petition signed by five hundred valley residents, Clarence Popham realized that the group could take no action favoring one side. This did not deter Milner, who asked Joseph Pechanec, director of the Forest Service's Intermountain Research Station in Ogden, Utah, to form a study committee to investigate the issue. This research group had an office on the campus of the University of Montana and consisted mostly of scientists who had not been directly involved in laying out timber sales or meeting cutting quotas. Milner had attended a public workshop Pechanec and his staff had presented the previous year in the Kalispell area, at which his colleagues' comments on the importance of conservation in American life struck her as "a sudden breath of fresh air in a closed room."[24]

Pechanec ran the idea of a special Bitterroot study past Neal Rahm, who agreed to cooperate, provided that some of his staff also participate. "What I have discussed with Mr. Rahm as the first step," Pechanec replied to Milner, "is the formation of a joint task force composed of two or three of the best men we have at the Station and at least a similar number of top men from the Regional Office in Missoula." Popham met with Rahm in early December to voice support for the idea, and Rahm obtained approval from Washington to launch the study.[25]

The Bitterroot Task Force, as it was known, consisted of three of Rahm's own division heads as well as three senior members of the Intermountain Research Station, including Blair Hutchison, who had coauthored the 1944 report on the timber situation in the Bitterroot Valley. Bill Worf, head of the Northern Region's recreation and lands division, chaired the panel, and Rahm gave him wide discretion to investigate and make recommendations. "As you can see from their responsibilities," Rahm assured Popham, "we have selected men with a broad array of talents and experience. Their charter is to make a thorough and penetrating analysis of resource management on the Bitterroot National Forest."[26]

Over the next six months, by Worf's estimate, the task force members spent half their time on the investigation. "We spent a lot of hours in the field and a lot of hours going over data, a lot of hours in motel rooms and conference rooms debating [the] writing," Worf recalled in a 1990 interview. In October 1969 they joined Brandborg, Milner, McDonald, and Miles Romney for a field trip and discussion of forestry issues. Brandy handed Worf hundreds of pages of documents dating to his days as supervisor, when less intensive methods of forestry were still favored. The task force examined many of the terraced areas in the West Fork that Champ Hannon alleged were eroding and not growing back, as well as clearcuts and roads in the Sleeping Child drainage. Worf had obtained assurances from Neal Rahm that he and his investigators would be allowed to dig deep and uncover any problems on the Bitterroot—essentially carte blanche to determine why this forest, of the sixteen in the Northern Region, was turning into a battleground.[27]

In his previous conservation battles Brandborg had paid little attention to cultivating the press, other than sending an occasional editorial comment to Miles Romney at the *Western News.* This he set out to change. In early December 1968, as the RC&D group was debating what to do with the timber issue, he invited an outdoor reporter with the *Missoulian* to have a look at the Bitterroot. Just as Champ Hannon had enlisted Brandborg in the fray that September, Brandy would bring in a new ally who, more than anyone else, would propel the controversy out of its beginnings in the Bitterroot Valley.

Dale Burk had joined the *Missoulian's* staff that year as the paper's state news editor, which involved rewriting contributions from dozens of correspondents in the small communities of western Montana. He had grown up in several of those towns, including the logging hubs of Trego and Eureka in the state's tall-timber country, where his father worked as an independent "gyppo" logger. Like many Montanans he enjoyed hunting and fishing, and soon after arriving at the *Missoulian* was offered the chance to write its outdoor column. Burk had already written a number of articles for national outdoor magazines and was eager to express his views on conservation matters. One of the issues he took on was a Forest Service plan to log along the border of the Bob Marshall Wilderness in the Bunker Creek drainage. This caught Guy Brandborg's eye, so he sent Burk a copy of the RC&D Recreation Committee's resolution on forest management practices. He suggested that Burk "delve into an issue that involves managing land and resources to assure the best protection of all outdoor assets for perpetuity.... I believe you will find the subject is basic in the maintenance of Montana's outdoor environment."[28]

Early in 1969 Burk attended a talk Brandborg gave at an environmental seminar at the University of Montana, after which Brandy introduced himself and again urged the reporter to look into the growing controversy on the Bitterroot. That summer Burk drove down to Hamilton to have dinner with Brandy and Ruth, and soon thereafter joined them on the first of dozens of tours of the forest he made with agency officials and environmentalists. He recalled his anxiety while riding in Brandy's battered Ford Falcon, peering over the edge of steep mountainsides as his guide steered with one hand and pointed out the window at some egregious clearcut. But Brandy's passion for the issue was contagious. Burk realized that this story could break open the larger issue of forest management in Montana, and with Brandy's help he laid out a strategy to gain the widest exposure for his articles.[29]

Burk interviewed other members of the RC&D Recreation Committee, several of the Sleeping Child ranchers, independent loggers, and forest supervisor Merrill Tester. Finally, he approached Ed Coyle, the paper's editor, with a proposal for an in-depth investigative series. "I was overwhelmed with the vehemence with which these fellows were after an inquiry," he recalled in 1988. "I was equally impressed with the Forest Service's attempts to get us not to do the articles....My feeling at that time was, and is, 'These were public resources, what have we got to worry about?' And that was my advice to my editor."[30]

Montana's newspapers had long had a reputation for subservient journalism under the ownership of the Anaconda Company. By 1959, when the company unexpectedly sold its newspapers to Lee Enterprises, a midwestern syndicate, the state's "copper dailies" were no longer company mouthpieces; they had simply become editorially dull—afraid even to take a stand on the weather, according to a Lee official. To make its Montana acquisitions profitable, Lee looked for editors who could present community issues in a lively, credible manner. The new owners made it clear that each of its papers would set its own editorial policy and be free to follow stories wherever they led.[31] Coyle, Burk recalled, was looking for a breakout issue to distinguish the *Missoulian* from its Anaconda-owned days, and so gave him the go-ahead. Burk's first Bitterroot series, which ran in nine parts from November 2–18, 1969, gave Coyle the controversy he wanted.

Burk led off the series by interviewing a third-generation logger from Darby named Ernie Townsend, who had thus far taken a low profile in the controversy. Townsend shared Brandborg's and Champ Hannon's concerns about heavy cutting in the upper Bitterroot River drainage. "They're ruining our timber stands for the next three generations," he told Burk. "They're taking out all the timber and pretty soon there won't be any more to log." Burk could not have found a more arresting lead for his series. Townsend was no Missoula environmentalist, but a local with long ties to the Darby timber economy. "Some of us love these mountains and wild areas," the logger continued. "They're part of us. We've enjoyed these areas for years and I want my kids and grandchildren to enjoy the same thing, and they're not going to be able to. Why do people want to take these things away from us?"[32]

The *Missoulian* encouraged its writers to do their own photography, which in Burk's hands attracted as much attention as his interviews. His shots of enormous clearcuts and terraced hillsides, some with piles of logging slash strewn about, made stark contrast to the thick regrowth in the Bitterroot's old selective-cutting areas. A caption in the Townsend article identified the latter as "sustained yield logging," implying that the clearcuts met no such criterion. This comparison alone would have vexed Forest Service staff, but the next article, which appeared two days later, contained equally harsh accusations from environmental lobbyist Brock Evans, who had recently visited the Bitterroot at Brandy's behest.

Burk enlisted rancher Jack Evans (no relation) to fly Evans and his wife over clearcuts in the Sapphire Range, the West Fork, and on into the Magruder Corridor, where the Forest Service was conducting further resource inventories that could lead to renewed logging plans. Afterward they examined clearcuts on the ground in the lower West Fork, Robbins Gulch, and Rye Creek. Evans compared the terraced hillsides he saw to strip-mined land, telling Burk that the Forest Service was "extracting a resource in a way that essentially destroys the resource." Evans, then thirty-two years old, was a charismatic speaker who could frame issues in stark terms. "Logging like you see in the Bitter Root, particularly in the Sleeping Child area, isn't logging, it's mining," he said. He cited the shallow soils, steep slopes, and fast-moving streams of the forest as indicative of fragile country that was all too easy to devastate through harsh logging practices.[33]

Evans now believed that the small band of activists in the Bitterroot could indeed drive the Forest Service to the wall with their protests. He raised the possibility of legal action through the organizations he represented—the ultimate red flag to the agency's leadership, which was already on a state of high alert. (Burk recalled that the day his first article appeared, a Forest Service staffer purchased five hundred copies of the *Missoulian* to send to the chief's office. The agency's attention was now transfixed on the series.) Evans's comments were the clearest indication yet that the Bitterroot was blowing up in their faces. No issue affecting the Northern Region, not even the Magruder Corridor or the Lincoln Back Country, posed such a direct threat to their operating assumptions. Conflicts over wilderness allocations were serious enough, but those could be categorized as multiple-use disputes pitting recreationists against the timber industry. Townsend, Brandborg, Evans, and their allies were throwing knives that struck dangerously close to the agency's heart—its gospel of forest redemption through scientific silviculture. These men were questioning not just where the Forest Service ought to log, but whether it knew how to manage timber at all.

CHAPTER 14

Engineering the Resistance

1969–1970

As Dale Burk's series unfolded in the pages of the *Missoulian,* surprised staffers in Forest Service offices from Hamilton to Washington examined the newspaper for signs and portents. Some felt that the series was part of a preservationist agenda to gain wilderness designation in the Magruder Corridor, as well as to defeat national legislation establishing a high-yield timber-management fund— Oregon senator Mark Hatfield's National Timber Supply Act. To many in the agency, it did not appear possible that the controversy on the Bitterroot could have grown solely out of local concerns, but had to have been orchestrated by national environmental groups such as the Sierra Club. Brock Evans's visit to the Bitterroot appeared to confirm this; they were not aware of Brandborg's entreaties to get him involved in the fray.[1]

Evans and Brandborg, although they were almost a half century apart in age, had shared a pivotal experience in their youth: both of them first set eyes on the Rocky Mountains at East Glacier Station, each of them riding west on the Great Northern Railroad to take summer jobs in Glacier National Park. Both felt a deep love of wild places, but Evans had major tree fights on his hands in the Pacific Northwest, where the Forest Service was assiduously converting roadless mountain drainages into managed forests. Brandy never made allowances for an activist's other commitments, however, and while meeting at the Milners' home following their forest tour with Dale Burk, he pressed Evans to direct the Sierra Club's resources to the Montana battle. Ruth Brandborg recorded her husband's words: "What I'm trying to convey to you, Brock, is that the Bitter Root could be a launching pad to make this a model effort for the nation." He employed stronger words, too, in trying to win Evans over—to him, there was no greater priority than what was happening in his home hills.

Conservationists often strategized in the comfort of the Milners' rustic, congenial home, located on a pine-studded glacial moraine west of Hamilton that gave sublime views of the high peaks of the Bitterroot Range. But Evans wasn't sure that the Bitterroot was the place to make a stand. "I thought to myself that this was a risky thing to do," he recalled, "since we had never really attacked the timber industry on its home ground before, but rather simply concentrated on trying to defend *de facto* wilderness areas. But grizzled old tough Brandy—a fantastic and vigorous man of some 75 years of age or more—persisted, and so did Doris; and almost single-handedly in those dark early days they took on the timber industry, and exposed some pretty terrible timber cutting practices."[2]

The leadership in Region 1 seemed unprepared to deal with a public relations crisis of this magnitude. Burk recalled that the day after his first article appeared, a deputy regional forester pressed publisher Lloyd Schermer to halt the series. "At first I felt intimidated," Burk said. "Then I was angry." Both Schermer and Ed Coyle continued to support him, and Coyle eventually took him off the state desk so he could concentrate on the new story. Still, Burk may not have realized how much controversy his series would generate. Visiting the Brandborgs at their home, he expressed doubts about what might happen to his career. Ruth gave him, he recalled, "a very gentle lecture on the need to stand firm." Brandy's reaction was more succinct. Observing that Burk had plunged the *Missoulian* into swift current, he told Ruth, "They can't back up now—the tail has to go with the hide from now on."[3]

Burk would need a thick skin in the years ahead as both he and the *Missoulian* came under heavy fire for appearing to be too cozy with environmentalists. He began to receive threatening telephone calls, and in what he found even more disturbing, his father had trouble obtaining logging contracts.[4] Montana had made progress since the days of Anaconda's heavy-handed political domination, but the timber industry still held sway in its forested regions.

Local affiliates of the Sierra Club, National Wildlife Federation, and Izaak

Walton League were already involved in campaigns against clearcutting in Wyoming, West Virginia, and Alaska. Earlier in 1969 Brock Evans visited Wyoming's Bridger National Forest, where sportsmen, outfitters, and hikers objected to logging high-elevation lodgepole pine and spruce stands in the Wind River Mountains. Wyoming senator Gale McGee was pressing the Forest Service for answers, and as in Montana, the Wyoming controversy would lead to another Forest Service task force study.[5] These, too, were grassroots campaigns in which local activists turned to the larger organizations for help—and in so doing brought the issue to national prominence.

Brandborg had a knack for drawing in well-connected activists. While attending an environmentalist meeting in Missoula around this time, he listened to the remarks of Otto Teller, a wealthy winegrower from California's Sonoma Valley who owned a summer cabin on the Bitterroot River south of Hamilton. An avid angler and a founding member of Trout Unlimited, Teller feared for the health of the river as clearcuts spread throughout its headwaters. Brandy, characteristically, asked him to approach the directors of the Sierra Club to try to get them involved in the issue.[6] Although this did not produce immediate results, Teller's contacts with the national media would pay off in future publicity. The two men became close collaborators in the Bitterroot campaign, Teller underwriting Brandy's considerable telephone, postage, and copying expenses. His help and encouragement would permit Brandy to broadcast his message widely, reaching activists in other states who were beginning to take notice of the emerging controversy.

During his trips into the backcountry, Teller noted which tributary streams were carrying sediment and afterward fired off detailed questions to the Forest Service. In response, Merrill Tester tried to explain the rationale for clearcutting, observing that there was often no alternative when mistletoe-infected Douglas fir were present. "In these situations it is usually the best silvicultural practice to clearcut and regenerate the stand," he told Teller. "Removal of the mature overstory trees accomplishes three important goals. First, it releases the understory so that accelerated growth may take place; second, it removes a source of disease infection; third, it utilizes potential mortality."[7]

Tester also faced questions from the RC&D's Recreation Committee. In answer to a query from its chairman, Gerald Bergh, he defended the relogging of older selectively cut areas as necessary to improve growth in the understory and curtail insect and disease problems. Some of the selective cuts also were not reproducing successfully, he said, owing to an insufficient seed source or a poorly prepared seedbed. They were not destroying the older cutting units, in his view, but simply correcting problems that had arisen in them. Clarence Popham, as chair of the RC&D's Program Committee, continued to reach out to the Bitterroot Forest's staff in an attempt to find areas of agreement, but Tester and his colleagues did not appreciate the criticism coming from Brandborg, McDonald, Milner, and their allies. Before long it was considered anathema for agency staffers to even be seen talking with Brandy or to park their car in front of his home. One of the RC&D's goals was to foster communication, but discussion was quickly turning into confrontation.[8]

Tester's critics, moreover, had more on their mind than silvicultural issues. Forest users from the Milners to the Sleeping Child ranchers viewed the nearby national forest as a reliable provisioner of things they valued, whether it was cattle forage, clean water, huntable game, or simply a wild forest landscape in which to camp and hike. The scale and pace of the forest's transformation deeply upset many Bitter Rooters who assumed that their favorite fishing holes, camping spots, and grazing grounds would remain unaltered. The multiple-use plans prepared years ago under Brandborg and Trosper had taken note of these constituencies and tried to coordinate uses so that each would trample as little as possible on the others. But the timber-management plans developed under Harold Andersen led to a virtual redefinition of multiple use: forest management now meant sawlogs and seedlings, with other uses such as watershed, wildlife, wilderness, and recreation fitting in only where they dovetailed with the timber plan. Tester and his staff continued to explain their management rationale, but they were offering answers to the wrong questions. The intricacies of forest regrowth were far from the minds of most Bitterroot Valley citizens; they simply saw what was happening on the mountainsides and wanted it stopped.

The *Missoulian*'s series on the Bitterroot had thus far featured few specifics; Burk's sources alleged mainly that the Forest Service was cutting timber too fast, creating landscape eyesores, and disturbing fragile soils. In the third installment Burk brought forth the claims of Sleeping Child ranchers Marvin Bell and W. O. Lovely, who along with their fellow ranchers had been claiming for years that clearcutting in that stream's headwaters was harming forage and interrupting irrigation supplies. "That watershed is part of our farms," Bell said. He showed Burk where a water hole he had long used had dried up, which he attributed to diminished late-season runoff. Lovely said that destructive floods had eroded stream banks, washed out irrigation diversions, and deposited silt in ditches. "If .

they [the Forest Service] keep it up we might as well forget about farming," he said. "If we haven't got the water we haven't got a damned thing." They called for a return to selective cutting, which they believed avoided such damage.[9]

Burk had persuaded Ed Coyle to run his articles as a series rather than as a single large feature, hoping that would generate more interest in the story. This it did, but it also delayed the Forest Service's chance to respond. When their turn came in the fourth through sixth articles of the series, they did not directly answer their critics' charges. To avoid any appearance of bias, Burk decided to submit a list of questions to the Forest Service and print their answers verbatim. Their responses were fact filled and nuanced, explaining the many silvicultural and ecological factors they had to account for in their timber-sale program. Supervisor Tester and his timber staff officer, Robert Feilzer, asserted that they had not abandoned sustained yield as a principle and that selective cutting generally did not meet the silvicultural requirements of pine, spruce, and fir on the Bitterroot.

Few public figures have the luxury of three consecutive newspaper articles in which to present their views, but the Bitterroot foresters seemed unable to take advantage of their time in the spotlight. Reciting statistics and forestry principles did little to counteract the agency's critics. Their most effective moment came when Tester, while touring the Sleeping Child drainage with Burk, pointed out a recent logging unit and said, "Any forestry is a long-term investment and you've got to look at it from this perspective or you get the wrong picture."[10] The foresters, unfortunately, did not have a decade or more to let their clearcuts regrow.

That became clear as Burk's series concluded with what was perhaps the harshest criticism of all—a challenge from one of their own. Guy Brandborg was allowed to bat cleanup in the last three installments of the nine-part series. Burk introduced him as one who "speaks with the authority of an experienced forester" and had a "life-long record of forestry management and conservation in the Forest Service." He depicted Brandy walking among the ponderosa pines in one of his old selective-cutting units in Chaffin Creek, where "the evidence of earlier logging was barely noticeable as only a random stump stood here and there while up around them a new forest had grown."[11] Brandborg contrasted his generation's approach to forestry with the wide swaths that were now being cut: "Now they have to knock everything down and destroy all the accumulated growth of a forest in one horrible swoop. It's disheartening, disgusting."

Brandborg's critique diverged from Evans's and other environmentalists in his pairing of conservative forest management with the continued prosperity of the Bitterroot Valley. "I am deeply concerned over how these practices affect the environment and economic stability of the residents of Ravalli County," he wrote in response to one of Burk's questions. "There are many people in the area directly dependent upon logging, lumbering and allied pursuits. This is the basic issue. Forestry practices today are entirely different from those applied when I was associated with the Forest Service. In fact, I am positively astounded over the scarring, tearing up of the landscape, destruction of reproduction and young trees well on their way to provide the next crop of timber. Erosion, destructive effects of burning, undisposed slash are very much in evidence. Seemingly, foresters have lost feeling for the good earth."

Burk's photo of a white-haired Brandy examining a young ponderosa pine, printed in a later series in the *Missoulian,* probably expressed matters most clearly. Here was a symbol of a bygone approach to forestry—one that was closer to most Americans' image of a uniformed ranger corps tending the trees with careful hand labor and a woodsman's affection. It mattered little that contemporary agency staffers also enjoyed seeing the pines grow tall. Their reputation was mired in the loose gravel of the West Fork terraces, a battleground they would have great difficulty escaping.

Two days after Burk's last article appeared, Ed Cliff offered his take on the controversy in a letter to Mike Mansfield. The chief's greatest worry was that environmental groups such as the Sierra Club would persuade Congress to get involved in the issue. Calls for special committee investigations, he said, "raise again the issue of administrative discretion in exercising the authority and redeeming the responsibilities assigned or delegated to us.... [F]ew management decisions can be made that will not be questioned by someone and often quite a few people. Should we get in a posture of submitting all such controversial decisions to congressional or *ad hoc* investigation or review, efficient and proper management of our National Forests could grind to a halt."[12]

If the chief was worried about the actions of environmental groups headquartered in Washington, he might well have taken notice of changing attitudes in Ravalli County. In late November 1969, just as Burk's last articles appeared, the *Ravalli Republican* polled its readers about the clearcutting issue. The sampling was certainly unscientific: readers could mail in a response form indicating greater or lesser approval for the Forest Service's use of clearcutting on the Bitterroot. The 259 responses came chiefly from the Darby and Hamilton areas, of which 88 agreed with the statement that "clearcutting should be used only in extreme cases of potential fire damage, disease and/or blighted stands." Surprisingly, the statement "I feel clearcutting should never be used" ran a close second, with 77 responses. Only 52 people agreed that the Forest Service's current policy on clearcutting was "about right," while 42 believed that "clearcutting has its place in forest management, but the Bitter Root National Forest is overdoing it."[13]

In the face of such adverse opinion, the forestry profession could hardly claim that the opposition consisted only of a few malcontents or that it was being directed from the Sierra Club's offices in Washington and Seattle. It was not so much that the public opposed forestry; the agency men, in their zeal to redeem the forest through intensive management, had simply sprinted ahead too far and too fast. This became clear as new controversy arose over a timber sale the forest advertised and sold that summer—a portion of the so-called Missoula Roundwood Sale, a gigantic multiforest project meant to salvage lodgepole pine in high-elevation lands in western Montana. Over a ten-year period the agency hoped to remove 364,000 cords of spindly, close-growing trees from eighty-four hundred acres along the Continental Divide from Gibbons Pass far to the north along the Sapphire crest.[14] The enormous clearcuts would be accessed by ridgetop roads, creating what Dale Burk called a "Sunday drive" extending for miles along formerly wild ridgetops.

The Roundwood sale was intended to supply pulpwood for the Hoerner-Waldorf mill in Missoula, as well as to create a continuous firebreak along the mountain crest—something the foresters had been contemplating ever since the Saddle Mountain and Sleeping Child burns. Only a portion of the sale was carried out, as the expense of cutting small trees and transporting them nearly a hundred miles to be processed proved too great. Nevertheless, it aroused the ire of some sportsmen who feared that easy road access would decimate elk herds, as well as hikers and horse users who wanted to keep the roadless backcountry intact. The foresters had good silvicultural reasons to want to regenerate the miles of stagnant lodgepole stands, which often grew so thick they were referred to as doghair, but once again they had outrun a skeptical public that saw the project as another abrogation of multiple-use values.

The national Sierra Club, fully cognizant now of the uproar on the Bitterroot, dispatched its consulting forester that August to have a look. Gordon Robinson had worked during the 1950s as the chief forester of the Southern Pacific Land Company, which had extensive timber holdings in California, western

Nevada, and southern Oregon. In that capacity he had persuaded the company to conduct a conservative program of uneven-age timber management, primarily through selective cutting of ponderosa pine. He also held to the traditional method of growing trees on long rotations in order to produce the highest-quality dimension lumber. Robinson had little use for the Forest Service's recent attempts to redefine commercial forest land to take in less productive higher-elevation stands, shorten timber-stand rotations, and employ new marking and scaling methods that emphasized fast growth from smaller trees.[15]

Robinson was already at work in Montana examining timber-cutting practices on the Flathead National Forest and at Brock Evans's behest made two trips to the Bitterroot in 1969. Brandy found in him a kindred spirit who enjoyed walking the forest and discussing the old methods they once practiced. In December he arranged for Robinson to present his views before a meeting of the Hamilton Lions Club. Robinson was not opposed to all clearcutting, but felt that openings should be kept as small as possible for the biological requirements of the species. Forests, he said, should retain a full complement of animal and plant habitats, and foresters must take, in his words, "extreme care to avoid damage to the soil, the all-important resource."[16] He also shared these views in meetings with Bill Worf and his agency task force, which was conducting its investigations at the same time.

Robinson's professional experience (both he and Neal Rahm were graduated in 1937 from the forestry school of the University of California at Berkeley) allowed him to go beyond the anecdotal observations of other conservationists. He took particular exception to the use of the Kemp formula to determine allowable cuts, believing it was weighted too heavily toward accelerating the harvest of mature sawtimber. He regarded this as a violation of the Multiple Use–Sustained Yield Act, which he said "does not say that they are to establish a cutting rate that can be sustained merely through the rotation."[17] This was the central point of Brandborg's critique, although he did not state it in technical terms. Sustained yield, to both men, meant avoiding falloffs in harvest levels, even if they were postponed for several decades.

The Hamilton Lions heard the timber industry's side of the story at their next meeting in January 1970. Craig Smith of the Intermountain Company faulted the Forest Service for not responding forcefully to its critics. "When the agency is accused of incompetence and fails to defend its practices, the lay public has no alternative but to be suspicious of the agency's programs," he said. "This reluctance to respond is a real concern in our industry." Smith explained why clearcutting was the method of choice in the Bitterroot's Douglas fir and lodgepole pine sites. The susceptibility of partially cut stands to windthrow was one reason, but the method was used primarily to reduce levels of parasites such as dwarf mistletoe and insects such as the spruce budworm and mountain pine beetle. He described one lodgepole stand they were currently harvesting, in which "only about one-third of the original forest is living, another third is comprised of dead naked snags standing and the remaining one-third has fallen and is piled up to 6 to 8 feet deep." Logging such stands, he said, would increase their productive capacity for timber crops and game habitat. Brandborg and Robinson's selective-cutting paradigm, he said, amounted to high-grading—an old and discredited industry practice.

Smith also disputed the ranchers' contention that clearcutting had dried up late-season stream flows, citing data gathered by the Forest Service at a gauging station on the East Fork of the Bitterroot River that showed only a three-day advance in the timing of peak runoff. The data, he said, showed an average 12 percent increase in total discharge from April to August and a 24 percent increase during the critical month of August. "If our sole interest was in short term gains or if we were operating on a 'cut-out and get-out' policy, we would probably subscribe to total use of selective harvest," he concluded. "But our industry has invested heavily for long term stability, and we are concerned about sustained production of timber beyond tomorrow or next year but into the future beyond our own lifetimes."[18]

The timber industry's need for a steady log supply was underscored several months later when the Intermountain Company announced that it would close its pine mill in Darby and lay off its fifty workers. The mill had been designed to use the larger ponderosa pine logs that had been coming off the forest for years, but the Forest Service, according to the company, had unduly restricted the supply of such trees. The mill closure led to angry charges and countercharges at local meetings and in the op-ed pages of western Montana's newspapers. Brandborg observed that while serving as supervisor he had discouraged Intermountain from locating in the Bitterroot Valley, where the allowable cut of ponderosa pine was already spoken for by local mills. He repeated his accusation that the Forest Service had exceeded the sustained-yield level of 10 mmbf of ponderosa pine set in the 1940s. To him, Intermountain was engaging in the same cut-and-get-out operations that had characterized the Anaconda Company in its earlier days.[19]

Robert Stermitz, manager of Intermountain's operations in the Bitterroot, quickly countered that in 1965 the agency had set the allowable cut for ponderosa at 22.5 mmbf, but with the Magruder Corridor out of consideration, this figure had been reduced to 18.3 mmbf. Since then, he said, Brandborg's and Burk's attacks on the forest's management policy had resulted in a further drop to about 10 mmbf—close to Brandy's original figure, but too low to sustain Intermountain's operations. He called the mill closure a "tragedy" and laid responsibility on the agency's critics. The clash continued into the summer, when Dr. Horace Koessler, the company's president, blasted Brandborg at a Forest Service meeting on the Magruder Corridor. He called the reductions "an absurdity" and said that it was "simply not fair to suck people into an area on this issue and have our federal people change the rules." He accused Brandborg of falsely maligning the Bitterroot's current leadership, saying it was "almost beyond my belief that a retired Forest Service officer would accuse the Forest Service in print of being incompetent liars." Several others at the meeting, including Fritz Bell and Stanton Cooper, came to Brandy's defense.[20]

The attack prompted an angry retort from Brandborg. In a *Missoulian* commentary, he said that "while I was forest supervisor many people, including Dr. Koessler, made repeated visits to my office to discuss the economic feasibility of installing another sawmill in the valley to cut ponderosa pine. Every individual, including Dr. Koessler, who sought these opportunities was discouraged from making such an investment.... [T]he capacity of the already existing sawmills was more than adequate to consume the allowable cut of ponderosa pine available on the Bitterroot Forest." He doubted that the high level of cutting could be sustained over the long term without damage to soils, wildlife, and watershed conditions. "A refusal to face facts will not bring back the timber cut in great quantities in too short a space of time," he warned. "If the remnants of the Bitterroot forests in the canyons of the mountain ranges and in the Magruder Corridor are surrendered to the industry, in a few short years the job will have been completed, and the long wait of a century and more for a new forest will begin."[21]

Koessler replied that in the 1950s his company had simply acquired an interest in the Jess Edens mill at Darby and had rebuilt the mill after it later burned down. "At no time was the Intermountain Company, or myself, involved in the construction of a new facility in the Bitterroot Valley," he said. "Mr. Brandborg's allegation concerning my and Intermountain's power to influence the Forest Service to exceed proper allowable cuts infers power and a goal which we have never had."[22]

The mill closure and its rehashing in the newspaper's op-ed pages highlighted the deep divisions in the Bitterroot Valley. The timber industry felt that it was operating under a legitimate, professionally prepared timber-harvesting plan that would ensure a continuous log supply for decades—but only if it was fully implemented, including within the Selway drainage. The ranchers, sportsmen, and conservationists allied with Brandborg had grievances over the scope and intensity of logging, while old-time foresters of Brandy's generation lamented the passing of the great pine stands that once ringed the Bitterroot Valley. The dialogue that was occurring in western Montana—and it could be still called that, despite the heat generated—was tackling substantive issues ranging from Douglas fir silvics to regional economic policy. This was not a debate over aesthetics. But unless the disputants could agree on what constituted a sustained yield of forest resources, there could be little peace on the Bitterroot.

In May 1970 the Northern Region's Bitterroot Task Force concluded its work and called a public meeting in Hamilton to explain its findings. Neal Rahm opened the meeting with a plea for understanding. For the past fifty years, he said, his agency had been a leader in environmental issues and was well respected by most of the public. Rahm acknowledged that those days were past. "As one of the targets on the firing line I find this post-honeymoon period trying and sometimes discouraging and irritating," he offered. "However, I am not here to turn back the clock. On the contrary, I believe the Forest Service is moving into a truly productive relationship with the American people—productive in terms of achieving the kind of resource management this Nation needs. We need to get out on the edge of the knife again. We have the public's interest—now we need its support."[23]

Blair Hutchison then presented a slide show depicting the main areas of controversy and addressed the Bitterroot's most glaring problem. "Terracing has been done on the Bitterroot National Forest, not because foresters like to construct stadiums," he said. "It has been done as a last resort because it is so difficult to establish young trees on that big part of the forest where pine grass and elk sedge grow." Other treatments, such as burning following logging, had not worked, and in fact seemed to encourage grass growth. "There is no argument that terracing is unnatural and unattractive at best," he admitted. "The raw scars all heal in time but hillsides with the stair-step look are not really a natural environment."[24]

The task force recommended that terracing be avoided on slopes steeper than 30 percent and that the forest employ new site-preparation and planting equipment that could operate on moderate slopes without danger to the operator. But the committee refused to issue a wholesale condemnation of clearcutting. As Bill Worf stated to the audience in Hamilton, "If we forego clearcutting we will have to forego timber growing on a large part of the Bitterroot National Forest. There is a large area of species that don't grow well under shaded, over-age, disease-ridden, and insect-ridden stands in this locality." The task force believed that the chief problem on the Bitterroot was the adverse aesthetic impact of clearcutting and terracing, which could be worked around with careful design of logging units. As Worf summed up: "In the opinion of the task force a substantial timber production can be maintained without impairing streams and watersheds and without any serious sacrifice of beauty."[25]

Despite their defense of Forest Service timber-management policies, the task force's published report (which was released soon after the Hamilton meeting) identified numerous problems in the Bitterroot's overall multiple-use program. They discovered that from 1966 to 1969 the forest had mistakenly overcut its ponderosa pine stands some 15 percent beyond the allowable harvest level for that species. In 1967 harvesting of ponderosa reached a high of 25.6 mmbf, which had come about because the forest had not broken down the overall cut by species, and additional ponderosa stumpage was being removed in timber sales where Douglas fir predominated.[26] This was a fairly easy technical fix that did not in itself validate Brandborg's assertion that the allowable cut of 18.3 mmbf of ponderosa pine was too high.

More generally, Worf's group acknowledged that there had been a misplaced emphasis on harvesting trees at the expense of other values, and as a result their agency had a real problem on its hands. "Any lingering thought that production goals hold priority over quality of environment must be erased," they emphasized. "Multiple use planning must be developed into a definitive, specific, and current decisionmaking process that it is not today. Quality control must be emphasized and reemphasized until it becomes the byword of management." In addition, the public "must be involved more deeply than ever before in developing goals and criteria for management."[27]

The task force members lay the blame for the problems on the Bitterroot not on Merrill Tester or his predecessors but on the Service-wide emphasis on timber production, which they felt had skewed perceptions among the Bitterroot's foresters. In a key finding, they stated that "there is an implicit attitude among many people on the staff of the Bitterroot National Forest that resource production goals come first and that land management considerations take second place." The pressure to meet timber production targets was "the result of rather subtle pressures and attitudes coming from above." The agency's field offices, they noted, were required to file weekly reports with Washington on their progress in meeting timber-sale objectives. The result was that sound management of other resources was sometimes neglected.[28]

This was the first public acknowledgment of the kind of pressures that field foresters such as Ray Abbott had felt in their work. But production quotas had not been created out of thin air in Washington; to a great extent they reflected data compiled by personnel in the field and the expectations of the silvicultural staff in the supervisors' and regional offices.[29] The agency's underlying goal—to improve forests through intensive management—remained in place at all levels. Most field personnel retained a heartfelt desire to carry this program to success. This amounted to mission drive, not pressure from above. The Washington office needed no crowbar to get its field staff moving in the desired direction.

Worf and his committee challenged the Sleeping Child ranchers' contention that cutting in the Sapphire mountain headwaters had eroded streams feeding into irrigation ditches. They found localized sedimentation where roads had been built too close to streams, but no serious damage. They pointed instead to the ranchers' own practices, observing that the worst damage occurred below the forest boundary where the stream channel had been "severely abused" by cattle. As for late-summer runoff, they compared stream flows in the East Fork of the Bitterroot River—the only nearby drainage for which detailed records were available—before and after the recent Sleeping Child fire and the clearcutting in other parts of the drainage. For the period 1957–1961, before significant clearing had been done in the drainage, August runoff in the East Fork had averaged 5,752 acre-feet. This had increased to 8,893 acre-feet during the period 1962–1968, after major clearcutting had begun and the Sleeping Child fire denuded significant acreage. Precipitation was slightly greater during the latter period, but it appeared that the loss of forest cover from about 10 percent of the drainage had freed considerable water that would otherwise have been taken up by transpiring trees.[30]

Much of the Bitterroot Task Force's report dealt with questions that had broader application within the agency, such as the need for better communication with the public, more effective multiple-use planning, adequate budgets and staffing in all specialties, and research appropriate to the needs of on-the-ground managers. A telling analysis showed that while the Bitterroot had received 95 percent of its requested funding for timber-sale administration and management over the fiscal years 1963–1970, it had received only 40 percent of the funds needed to reforest those acres. This deeply worried officials in the timber-management branch in Missoula, who understood the foolishness of economizing on replanting and thinning. Programs for recreation, wildlife habitat, and soil and water management were also grossly underfunded.[31]

These figures prompted some unproductive finger-pointing after the committee released its findings. Worf thought that conservation groups should use their political muscle to back up his agency's requests for balanced funding, particularly for silvicultural improvements such as thinning and reforestation. Conservationists, however, saw the funding imbalance as another indication of the agency's pronounced lean toward timber production. Brock Evans told Neal Rahm that he objected to the implication that the American people had not been willing to finance adequate management programs. "Neal, I know better," Evans wrote following the report's release. "I go back to Washington, D.C. a lot. You must surely know that the Forest Service has quite a large staff of people who do nothing but 'congressional liaison,' (i.e. lobbying). The Forest Service knows what it wants, and it goes out and lobbies for these things— just as do all federal agencies." The Forest Service was willing to promise high levels of cutting in exchange for flush timber budgets, which Evans called "the truest indication that the Forest Service is far more timber oriented than anything else."[32]

The task force report fell short of the broad indictment of clearcutting that the Bitterroot Valley activists had hoped for, but it was nevertheless the first official acknowledgment that the Northern Region's multiple-use program was out of balance. Don Aldrich expressed a degree of frustration in a letter to Lee Metcalf: "There was no I-told-you-so satisfaction in reading the many admissions of mismanagement—just a question. How can we stop it?" He felt that the task force report gave the Forest Service "all the justification they need to refuse to meet demands for logs unless the total impact of the harvest is understood."[33]

Brandy called the Bitterroot Task Force report a "breakthrough," although he was not optimistic that the agency would make the needed changes on its own. "It's becoming obvious that the on-the-ground forester can no longer defend or explain away existing practices," he told Metcalf. "Consequently, you can look to more and more public protests and appeals."[34] This was hardly what Metcalf or Rahm hoped would result from their efforts, but Brandy's prediction proved accurate.

Even with its carefully worded support for the overall mission of the Forest Service, including the paradigm of intensive timber management, the Bitterroot Task Force report stands as a landmark of bureaucratic self-analysis. Its language was unusually direct, and it prompted immediate changes on the forest. Bill Worf, stung by criticism of his committee's credibility, insisted they were getting orders from no one to shade their conclusions. "Regional Forester Rahm and [Intermountain Station] Director Pechanec left no doubt that they wanted an uninhibited appraisal of the facts," he assured his readers. "Their instructions were to make a complete and impartial analysis of the situation without regard to whose toes were stepped on."[35]

Their work was overshadowed by the much more controversial findings that Arnold Bolle's committee filed later that year, and in the end it came too late to head off the controversy. Had these insights been available to the agency five or ten years earlier, the Northern Region might have been able to adjust its timber program and logging practices in time. But by 1970 the environmental lobby had become deeply mistrustful of the Forest Service. One report, no matter how forthright, could not erase the legacy of years of heavy cutting. Neal Rahm and his staff would undertake heroic efforts to change direction, but the public's attention was now focused on the increasingly visible dissidents from the Bitterroot Valley.

CHAPTER 15

Under the Microscope

1970

As part of the Northern Region's damage-control efforts in the wake of Dale Burk's articles, Ray Karr, now head of the region's Information and Education (I&E) branch, got the *Missoulian* to agree to run another series in early April 1970 explaining his agency's approach to timber management. Authored again by Burk, but consisting mostly of excerpts from material that Karr had prepared, it outlined the agency's attempts to make timber cutting compatible with recreation, aesthetics, wildlife, and watersheds. Neal Rahm noted that stream gauges were being installed to monitor siltation and that cutting units were being shaped to resemble natural openings. The region's foresters, Rahm said, were instructed to consider all multiple-use values in designing sales.

To signal his desire to restructure affairs on the Bitterroot, Rahm appointed a new man to head the forest on the same day the Bitterroot Task Force presented its report in Hamilton. Orville Daniels had been the deputy supervisor of the Lolo National Forest, headquartered in Missoula, and had been watching the crisis envelop his neighbor to the south. His charge from Rahm, he recalled in a recent interview, was to "fix that mess on the Bitterroot." He began by speaking with as many Ravalli County residents as he could; to his surprise, he learned that anger and concern about Forest Service management practices were widespread in the valley. He was particularly struck when the president of a Hamilton bank, a longtime Forest Service supporter, told him that a proposed road along the Bitterroot mountain face near Hamilton would be a public relations disaster and should be dropped.[1]

Daniels set about reorienting the Bitterroot on less production-driven lines, taking heed of many of the recommendations of the Bitterroot Task Force. He eliminated the practice of terracing and began hiring nontimber specialists to balance the program (until that time the forest had not had a landscape architect, soil scientist, hydrologist, or wildlife biologist on its staff). Numerous planned timber sales were delayed while the specialists went to work; in his first six months Daniels was able to offer only 10 mmbf for bidding.[2] This was a considerable drop from the average annual sales of more than 50 mmbf during the preceding decade. Daniels cut his sales volume not for any technical or ecological reason, he says, but more out of the feeling that people just did not want to see that much cutting done. "It seemed to me that the agency was missing where the people were," he recalled. Eventually, and not without difficulty, he reduced the annual allowable harvest to around 30 mmbf. The reduction did not please residents of the timber-dependent southern part of the Bitterroot Valley, who were already dealing with the closure of the Intermountain Company's pine mill at Darby.

Daniels tightened controls on new sales and significantly reduced the proportion of clearcutting, but he could not rewrite timber-sale contracts already in the pipeline, which might allow the bidder four or five years to complete logging and cleanup work. Some valley residents wanted quicker results. In the fall of 1970 the ranchers in the Sleeping Child drainage contacted Dale Burk about the Skalkaho-Branch timber sale, a fuel-break project that involved the removal of lodgepole pine from the high country of the Sapphire Range. The sale had been made four years previously and would not be completed until the following summer. Stanton Cooper argued that logging it would further decrease late-season runoff, which had been particularly poor that year. He took strong exception to the task force's claim that logging in headwater areas increased rather than decreased such flows. His group had recently formed a legal defense fund to pursue litigation against the Forest Service, although no suit had yet been filed.[3]

Rancher Bill Lovely, whom Burk had featured in his first series of articles in the *Missoulian*, offered harsher criticism. He told Burk that the Bitterroot's staff had avoided taking the task force members to problem sites in the drainage. "We'll get the same old pacifier," he insisted. "They'll take us on another tour to show us what good guys they are or send a VIP to the little white schoolhouse to tell us that we don't know what we're talking about."[4] Daniels bristled at the allegation. He told Burk that he had made no additional sales in the drainage since coming to the Bitterroot and that the Forest Service was actively implementing the task force's recommendations. But Cooper claimed that previous salvage sales were causing serious damage by removing water-holding duff and exposing the ground to sun and wind. Little accommodation was possible given such wildly disparate views. The ranchers relied on the evidence of their eyes, while the agency men cited stream-flow data that contradicted these anecdotal observations. The runoff question would emerge again after flooding in the Bitterroot River in the mid-1970s convinced many of the valley's activists that clearcutting was indeed interfering with the hydrologic cycle.

A larger obstacle to lasting reform lay in the agency's unremitting drive to produce timber, which was institutionalized in Forest Service doctrine and intensified by political demands originating in the White House. The Great Society programs of the Johnson administration were partly to blame. The Housing and Urban Development Act of 1968, a centerpiece of the president's agenda, set a goal of twenty-six million new housing starts over the next decade to improve living conditions for poor and moderate-income families. This helped precipitate a sharp rise in lumber and plywood prices, exacerbated by reduced mill output owing to bad weather and a railcar shortage. In March 1969 President Nixon ordered the Forest Service to prepare 1.1 billion board feet of additional timber sales over the next fifteen months in order to bring down lumber prices. Ed Cliff, acknowledging "heavy pressure" to increase cuts, told a Senate panel that his agency could meet the target if it received more funds to build roads, reforest cutover lands, and conduct needed timber-stand improvement.[5] Rather than heed the rumbles coming from the Bitterroot, Bridger, Monongahela, and other forests, Cliff tried to keep afloat the agency's decades-long infatuation with full resource production. He hoped that the current crisis would spur Congress to balance his budget without having to curtail the timber program. But the Nixon White House, like preceding administrations, was concerned less with reforesting clearcuts than with increasing the supply of sawlogs and peelers.

The drumbeat increased in volume in June 1970 when Nixon endorsed the findings of the cabinet-level Task Force on Softwood Lumber and Plywood, which he had convened to investigate the price and supply problem. The task force recommended that the national forests increase their timber cut by 60 percent by 1980, or 7 billion board feet. Greater funding for replanting and timber-stand improvement, the group asserted, would keep the increase within sustained-yield parameters and not harm the environment. Unwilling to buck the administration, Ed Cliff stuck to this line, assuring his regional foresters in a July 1970 memo that the increased cut could be met. The administration's demands, however, only tightened the vise on the Northern Region's overworked forests.

The Forest Service took its orders from the executive branch, but Congress held the purse to pay for the needed roads and silvicultural improvements. For more than a year conservationists had worried about Mark Hatfield's Senate Bill 1832, the National Timber Supply Act, which proposed to channel Forest Service timber-sale receipts into a dedicated fund to pay for reforestation, sale preparation, and stand-improvement work. The Sierra Club's Gordon Robinson was particularly exercised about the measure, which he saw as dominant use in disguise, an unwelcome reprise of the federal highway trust fund that had spurred the postwar spree of interstate road construction. He and Brock Evans persuaded the club's leaders to take on the measure, even though it had already won approval from the House Agriculture Committee. Evans moved to Washington to coordinate the campaign, working with fellow lobbyists from the National Audubon Society, Wilderness Society, and Izaak Walton League.[6] It was the first major effort conservationists would make to derail the comfortable relationship among the congressional natural resource committees, the Forest Service, and the timber industry.

The environmentalist coalition managed to defeat the measure in early 1970 following additional hearings. At one of these, Representative John Saylor of Pennsylvania, a longtime ally in the fight for the Wilderness Act, brandished a letter signed by four retired foresters that called the bill "the antithesis of good conservation." Guy Brandborg was one of the four who put his name to the letter; also signing it were Gordon Robinson (its probable author), a former congressman and onetime professional forester from Vermont named William H. Meyer, and former Bureau of Land Management director Charles Stoddard. The foresters claimed that the Forest Service was "now selling timber at a rate about 50 percent in excess of that which can be sustained.... The result is that the principles of good forestry have been rationalized away."[7] Such opposition from the professional side of forestry helped Saylor and others defeat the bill. It would emerge again in the Ninety-second Congress, only to run into even fiercer opposition from a newly mobilized environmental movement.

Mike Mansfield's cosponsorship of Senate Bill 1832 drew a protest from Brandborg, who saw the measure as a giveaway to timber interests that had already overcut their own lands. "The history of private forest management in Ravalli County, as elsewhere in Montana and with few exceptions throughout the Nation, provides a sad story," he told Mansfield. "The private forest industry throughout its history has followed a cut out and get out policy, leaving behind idle men, idle lands and stranded communities. The ACM and NP [Anaconda Copper and Northern Pacific] companies as well as the small timber land owners made no attempt whatsoever to adhere to sustained yield cutting programs in harvesting the timber crops on the 127,000 acres of privately owned forest lands in Ravalli County." As a consequence, he wrote, it would be decades before these lands again contributed to Ravalli County's economy. Mansfield was not among the bill's active promoters, but replied that he had no intention of letting the timber industry "run rough shod over our national forest resources."[8]

Brandy's concerns were based as much on his fear of economic dislocation in the Bitterroot Valley as on the effects of clearcutting itself. This was the same horse he had been riding for more than three decades, dating back to his 1941 timber-management plan and before. The national environmental groups, in contrast, framed their arguments in terms of the intrinsic values found in the forest landscape. They were concerned primarily with soil erosion, disruption of wildlife habitat, visual impacts, and the loss of wild places for hiking and recreation. The difference was significant. Brandborg viewed properly managed forests as continuous producers of wealth, not just as recreational and aesthetic amenities or even as undisturbed biotic reservoirs. His comments to Mansfield betray his old-school orientation as a socially concerned conservationist. Sustained yield could mean many things, but to Brandy it signified local jobs that got passed down through generations of Bitterroot Valley families. That topic tended not to show up in the Sierra Club's action alerts.

With the Bitterroot becoming a flash point in the nationwide crisis over timber management, Neal Rahm made it clear to each of his forest supervisors and division heads that a better overall job of management was required. "He really wanted to provide the leadership to get a handle on the problems on the Bitterroot," Ray Karr recalled recently. At the same time, there was unmistakable pressure from the Nixon administration to increase cutting. "It came right from the Secretary of Agriculture," Karr said. "Careers depended on it—we couldn't break that." Across the Northern Region, rangers were feeling the heat, and field staff was cutting corners in laying out timber sales and logging roads. Rahm's predecessor, P. D. Hanson, had anticipated as much in 1946 when he ordered his timber staff to "short-cut on methods…without lowering standards." What had begun as an emergency effort to meet postwar housing needs had been built up to a permanent operation. Forest Service doctrine had countenanced a greatly expanded timber industry to aid its quest for forest redemption; now a mature industry expected its needs to be served.

Rahm outlined the dilemma in a March 3, 1970, memo to the head of the agency's timber-management division in Washington. The memo found its way to Dale Burk, who promptly published most of it. Rahm acknowledged that some of his staff were expressing doubts about the agency's timber-heavy orientation. As a result, he wrote, "a great deal of time is spent telling the users what competent managers we are." He listed specific problems with timber-sale administration, including road location and design, reforestation problems, visual impacts, and damage to streams. "Unfortunately, I do know the public— the anti-timber cutting public—can point to and take pictures of some of our mistakes," he wrote. "This doesn't help sell our capabilities as land managers."[9]

Rahm's memo came in response to an inquiry from the chief's office wondering what support he needed to head off the crisis. Rahm insisted that more money, by itself, would not solve the problem; what was urgently required was "expertise on the ground to perform an acceptable job." Federal hiring ceilings had made it difficult to find and retain staff with the field experience to lay out well-designed timber sales and monitor the performance of logging operators, he said. In recent years the agency had focused on other contract stipulations, such as scaling and valuation of timber, which were important for boosting Treasury receipts but left less attention for environmental stipulations.

An even more crucial question hung over the entire timber-sale program, Rahm maintained. For years the Northern Region had been heavily cutting its most accessible areas in anticipation of eventually entering roadless lands such as the Lincoln Back Country and the Magruder Corridor. Now, with these and other areas off-limits, they were left with too many shorn-off mountainsides in the front country. The region's staff hydrologists cautioned that to avoid watershed damage, no more than 10 to 20 percent of any given drainage should be cut during a fifteen- to twenty-year period. At the same time, his silvicultural staff was warning that adopting alternative harvesting methods to reduce the impact of clearcutting would further reduce yields. Something had to give, Rahm was saying, and more appropriations would not fix the problem. The American public could no longer expect constantly increasing harvests and at the same time maintain its woods as a pleasant place to camp, hunt, and fish. Multiple use, it was becoming clear, had its limits.

Rahm felt he had to do something to accommodate the increasingly vocal environmental lobby without backing too far off his timber targets. His answer was to tighten quality control within the timber program, hoping to avoid the kind of mistakes in sale design and road layout that had so inflamed the public. As a start, he sought to broaden the investigation he had begun on the Bitterroot. Even before Bill Worf's task force issued its report, Rahm convened another panel to review timber-harvesting practices on the other forests in his region. It consisted of the chiefs of his timber-sale and landscape-architecture branches, two staffers from individual forests, and a management analyst from the region's Division of Operations. This was to be an in-house review, with none of the publicity the Bitterroot had received; Rahm wanted specific problems identified and quietly corrected. The study team visited eight national forests, which were not named in the final report, and examined thirteen individual timber sales. The investigators presented their report to Rahm in July 1970. Titled *Quality in Timber Management: A Current Evaluation,* the report was not publicly released until the following year, after reporter James Risser of the *Des Moines Register* obtained a copy and excerpted it in a series he was writing on the clearcutting controversy.[10]

The study team identified numerous problems throughout the region, ranging from inadequate overall planning to the need for better wood utilization, slash cleanup, and reforestation. The panel cited instances of bulldozers working in streambeds, improper road design and location, and poorly located and installed culverts. They listened to rangers complain about excessive workloads that kept them from closely monitoring timber sales. Field personnel understood that a better job was needed, but pressures to produce timber forced shortcuts and lax oversight. "The external pressure is fairly obvious to most of us," the study team wrote, citing the timber industry's success in getting the Johnson and Nixon administrations to increase allowable cuts. "The internal pressure may be somewhat more subtle.... Often in the past, through inspection, or perhaps by innuendo, we have 'rated' a man or a unit by his or its execution of 'sell' goals. While our inspection process at various times pointed out isolated examples of poor quality in the sale job, few times did these inspection reports or followup action truly hold people accountable for quality."[11]

The study team called for setting more realistic timber targets based on the dollars and manpower that were likely to be available. Quality controls needed to be factored in from the beginning, they argued, and staff should be held accountable not just for meeting the sales quota but for doing a careful job on the ground. They offered a generic illustration of how bad results were often tolerated:

> A timber sale is planned in a given drainage. Specialist advice was sought and obtained regarding soil stability. The advice was not to build the road on the proposed location, or at least not without costly modification of "normal" methods. The sale *was* sold, the road *was* built in a "normal" manner, and sure enough, it fell off the hill. What happened then? Did anybody say, "How did this happen?" Or, "Who's responsible for this decision?" The answer is probably no. It was accepted as "just one of those things." Efforts were made to try to correct the situation, but little thought was given to who was responsible.

The study team did not advocate that personnel be harshly punished for such failures, but it asked whether they could not be "expected to act in a professional manner and be held accountable for their actions. If not, perhaps they are in the wrong position."[12]

The Northern Region's leadership was coming to realize the price it had paid for decades of obeisance to the agency's full production goals. In 1952 the regional office had downrated Guy Brandborg for focusing on staff training and public relations to the detriment of timber; now Neal Rahm had to play catch-up in those fields. To Rahm's credit, the two major staff reports he had ordered—those of the Bitterroot Task Force and his *Quality in Timber Management* panel—would not gather dust, and he would insist that every forest officer in the region get in line with his new emphasis on better timber management.

Before he could fully implement the needed changes, however, a third report would land on his desk—this one prepared by a group of professors at the university across the river from Rahm's downtown Missoula office. The School of Forestry at the University of Montana had enjoyed a long and cordial relationship with Region 1 of the Forest Service and had trained many of its staff and line officers. Now Dean Arnold Bolle and six of his colleagues would weigh in on the Bitterroot controversy, with results that seemed calculated to upset Rahm's plans for gradual reform.

For several years both Lee Metcalf and Mike Mansfield had been receiving a steady stream of letters from Bitterroot Valley constituents expressing concern about the effects of widespread clearcutting on soils, watersheds, and the valley's natural beauty. A longtime valley resident from Victor told Metcalf that "it will take at least three to six generations to overcome the damage. I have talked to dozens of our local citizens and they are 99% of the same opinion that I have. We all feel that clearing ground that has slope of 30 to 70 percent is strictly prohibitive. The duff works away leaving nothing but a hard packed surface that will grow nothing." Clearcutting whole hillsides drove home the scale of change to many old-timers in the valley, who in some cases saw their favorite hunting and fishing grounds drastically altered. As one Hamilton resident told Metcalf, "The impression that one gets is that mad men have gone berserk with giant machines."[13]

Adding weight to these assertions were the comments of former Stevensville district ranger Charles McDonald. "I hope my persistent efforts in directing your attention to the destruction of our Bitterroot timber is not regarded as an impertinence," he wrote in November 1969. "No doubt you have received numerous complaints and similar clippings to those I am enclosing. I have accompanied Mr. Wm. Worf of the Regional Office, and others on field study trips, all of which has not allayed my concern." McDonald cited a timber sale on the flanks of St. Mary's Peak, a prominent landmark west of Stevensville, which originated when he was ranger and was continued by his successor. He had recently observed that of the 185 acres that were clearcut, only two small areas of a few acres each had been replanted. "A large majority of people here are truly alarmed," he said, "and hope for a more unbiased study than is occurring by Forest Service appointed personnel."[14]

The correspondence to Metcalf and Mansfield does not appear to have been closely orchestrated, although Brandborg clearly was pressing his friends to write letters.[15] To most of these critics, including those in the RC&D group, the findings of the Northern Region's task force remained suspect. The real issues would not be dealt with, they believed, until a group of independent resource professionals on a par with the Selke committee could examine the forest. Brandborg, Milner, McDonald, and others on the Recreation Committee continued to press the Montana congressional delegation for such a study; Metcalf, especially, felt he needed to make a genuine response to constituents in his native Bitterroot Valley. Unbeknownst to them, he was discussing the possibility of a study with Arnold Bolle, with whom he was already working on a possible alternative to the National Timber Supply Act. Metcalf had discussed the Bitterroot citizens' concerns during Bolle's visits to Washington in 1967 and early 1968; these talks (as Bolle later recalled) "grew more serious as the problem became more serious. When the RC&D group came to the point of asking for a full scale congressional investigation, Lee thought of something on a lesser and more personal level—us."[16]

Bolle had visited the Bitterroot with several fellow faculty in the fall of 1968 to become more familiar with the issue. He envisioned a low-key approach in which he would advise Metcalf of his options without a great deal of publicity. "The faculty group was formed incrementally and tentatively," he recalled. "We were not sure that we really could have a constructive part in this. We needed to...understand just what the problem was and that a positive solution might be conceivable." His colleagues were reluctant to take on the task, not wanting to fan the flames of controversy, Bolle said.[17] But after the regional office's Bitterroot Task Force released its report, Metcalf believed that an independent analysis was still needed and urged him to proceed.

Bolle picked for his committee six professors affiliated with the School for Administrative Leadership, the university's short course for agency personnel that Guy Brandborg had helped found nearly thirty years ago. Four came from the School of Forestry: Richard Shannon and Robert Wambach were forest economists, while Richard Behan focused on policy questions such as the Lincoln Back Country issue. Les Pengelly, a leading figure in Montana's wildlife conservation circles, had long been interested in the effects of logging on the forest biota. Gordon Browder and Thomas Payne represented the Departments of Sociology and Political Science, respectively. All were familiar with Montana's public lands. Metcalf formalized his request in a December 2, 1969, letter to Bolle, and the Select Committee of the University of Montana launched itself into the troubled waters of the Bitterroot controversy.[18]

Metcalf asked the committee members to examine broader questions of national forest management as well as look at the Bitterroot. They were happy to comply. During the first half of 1970 they talked to everyone they could find with a stake in the controversy, including supervisor Orville Daniels, his staff, Bill Worf of the regional office, and Joseph Pechanec of the Intermountain Experiment Station. They met with Brandborg (who handed Bolle copies of his favorite social-forestry studies from the 1940s), other Bitterroot Valley conservation activists, the Sleeping Child ranchers, Bitterroot Valley real estate agents, timber-industry representatives, and reporter Dale Burk. By the end of the summer they felt they could make a real contribution to the debate and proceeded to write their report. They mailed it to Metcalf after the November election to avoid any appearance of political influence, even though Metcalf was not up for reelection for two more years.

Brandy encouraged Bolle and his colleagues to make a bold statement on the Bitterroot question. "Like most other issues, forestry has been studied threadbare," he wrote. "As you well know, studies have become a device that political, economic and other forces use freely to postpone meeting issues of public concern. Considering the practices that professionally trained foresters have condoned and defended since 1962, admittedly I am dubious that another segment of the scientific community will risk carrying the issue through to an ultimate legislative solution." Still, he believed that the Bitterroot offered the opportunity to make a worthy contribution—"if," he said, "the issues involved are carried to the 'finish line.'" Bolle was willing to risk moving beyond the typical academic study and told Brandy that his group had the full support of University of Montana president Robert Pantzer. Bolle related later that the president was rather startled when shown a draft of the report. "He said 'Oh, my gosh!' and after a pause added 'Just make sure you're right.'"[19]

Newspapers across the country jumped on the story after Metcalf released the report in Missoula on November 18, 1970. And no wonder: the members of the Select Committee had chosen their words for maximum impact, distilling their views into fifteen concise statements that faulted the Bitterroot's timber-cutting practices and the agency's overall approach to forest land management. The first three hit with hammer force:

1. Multiple use management, in fact, does not exist as the governing principle on the Bitterroot National Forest.
2. Quality timber management and harvest practices are missing. Consideration of recreation, watershed, wildlife and grazing appear as afterthoughts.
3. The management sequence of clearcutting-terracing-planting cannot be justified as an investment for producing timber on the BNF. We doubt that the Bitterroot National Forest can continue to produce timber at the present harvest level.[20]

The rest of the committee's findings were as applicable to the entire national forest system as to the Bitterroot. Integrated multiple-use planning was lacking, they found, and the public was effectively excluded from real participation in management decisions. Manpower and budget constraints meant that critical staffing needs were not addressed. Research was inadequate; the agency's bureaucratic structure favored top-down directives over on-the-ground experience. "High-quality, professional management of the timber resource is all too rare," they stated. Pressure to get out the cut was distorting management on forests such as the Bitterroot, but such pressure came from both Congress and the administration, not just local industry, according to the committee.[21]

By itself, such criticism was hardly new; the Bitterroot Task Force had come to many of the same conclusions. Bolle's committee took issue with the task force's focus on timber-management questions, saying it had given short shrift to the effect of clearcutting on wildlife, recreation, range conditions, and aesthetics. The professors minced no words: in discussing the task force's recommendation to have a landscape architect review timber sales, they wrote that "it is not clear whether such a person would have veto power over the sale and specifications, or whether he would be called upon, after the fact, to apply his skills toward a cosmetic treatment of an existing, or an about to be produced, eyesore."[22]

One of the most compelling analyses in the report, prepared by economist Robert Wambach, examined the economics of timber management as practiced on the Bitterroot.[23] "Clear-cutting and planting is an expensive operation," he wrote. "Its use should bear some relationship to the capability of the site to return the cost involved." To illustrate, he sketched out a simple economic discount calculation for site preparation and regeneration costs, including bulldozer terracing, which he assumed to be $50 per acre. "If we invest the $50 in stand establishment and charge no other costs throughout the 120-year [rotation] period, the stand at harvest would have to be worth $17,445 per acre, in order to return 5 percent on the initial public investment in regeneration. If the actual yield were 20 MBF per acre, the stumpage value would have to be $872 per thousand board feet." In 1970 pine or fir stumpage was fetching perhaps $25 per thousand.

The application of economic discounting to forest practices is subject to much controversy, and Forest Service and industry analysts would take a much different view of the question in their response to the Select Committee's report. Given the century or more it might take to grow new timber crops, interest rates have a way of ballooning costs. Wambach admitted that this was a cursory analysis, but his point was that there were less expensive ways to supply the nation's timber than plowing benches into the hillsides of the Northern Rockies.

The Select Committee expanded this thumbnail analysis into a broad indictment of Forest Service policies and operating assumptions. Chief among these was the agency's formulation of sustained yield, which they called "the core of forestry professionalism, the central tenet of professional dogma." Early-day foresters from Bernhard Fernow to Gifford Pinchot, they said, imported from Europe the idea of maximum production of sawlogs to meet an implied resource scarcity. American forestry sought to intensively manage land through heavy applications of labor and capital (terracing and machine planting being two examples), and in so doing it outran any rational economic justification and impinged on many other forest uses. "A major element in the Bitterroot Controversy was just this professional dogma," the committee asserted. "'Productivity,' we learned time and again, meant maximum physical production of sawlogs. Much timberland was being harvested ostensibly to 'get it into production.' The idea that a scraggly stand of overmature timber could and does provide other values was alien and largely absent from the thinking of most professional foresters we encountered: this in spite of their lip service to 'multiple use.'"[24]

To Bolle and his fellow academics, runaway clearcutting was a symptom of deeper problems within the agency. As he recalled in a 1989 retrospective, "The real problem was timber primacy, which now dominated and controlled Forest Service activity. This marked a clear departure from the broader congressional policy of multiple use as earlier conceived." The committee made this point in the context of the Bitterroot's terraced clearcuts, saying that all cutting methods "should protect or enhance the other values *on the site*. We heard many times that clear-cutting and terracing enhanced such other values on the adjacent hillside, or downstream, or over the ridge, and this is specifically what we do *not* mean."[25] They challenged the Forest Service to find an alternative to the cycle of clearcutting, terracing, and planting that required less capital input. The agency could rely on natural regeneration, they said, even if it lengthened the rotation period and led to irregular stocking. It could also defer or avoid cutting on poor-quality sites. Foresters could even pursue a version of the old practice of high-grading, in which the best mature trees were removed and nature was left to restock the stand. The committee called this approach "timber mining," a term that led to immense confusion in the news media.

By carefully logging certain old-growth stands as a gift of nature, they said, and not trying to reestablish a thrifty young forest, other forest values would not suffer. "We believe that on-site, co-existing, simultaneous values need not be sacrificed. Sensitive, careful timber mining would avoid doing so. We recommend cutting on a single-tree selection basis. We would minimize the permanent road system, building low-standard, single-lane, one-time roads that could be seeded to grass and closed at the end of timber mining activities. We would not terrace. We would not strip. We would not plant."[26]

More than any other statement in the Bolle Report, the notion of mining timber—without replanting or making other silvicultural treatment—stuck in the Forest Service's craw. The report's authors may have chosen the term with that intent, for it countermanded the entire corpus of agency thought and praxis. The Forest Service's silvicultural staff believed they were in the business of making forest land productive, much as the settlers of the nineteenth century had tried to make the Bitterroot Valley produce something more than grass for Salish horses. Mining, they felt, was what the timber barons had done to the eastern and midwestern forests and the Anaconda Company was doing to the pine stands of Rye Creek and Burnt Fork. It was the antithesis of forestry. The university folks probably could not have found a more irritating term.

Of all the criticism and rebuttals that followed publication of the Select Committee's report, the comments of two Northern Region retirees stood well for the disbelief and dismay that many in the agency felt. Clarence Strong, a former assistant regional forester, and G. M. DeJarnette, a silvicultural researcher, found the Select Committee's analysis deficient in practical value. "As foresters of long and broad experience," they wrote to Bolle, "we are greatly concerned because your report denies some of the basic facts involved in forest land management as we believe them to be." They took particular exception to selectively cutting lower-quality stands, especially if this meant accepting mistletoe-infected regrowth. Previous attempts, they warned, "are well known and well documented failures. There is not one but many cases where the residual trees and the regeneration coming up under them are infected to the degree that renders them useless encumbrances on the site. There are also many examples on natural burns where infected survivors of the fire have infected almost 100% of the regeneration coming up under them.... Where is the multiple use value," they asked, in "a closed canopy of low quality Douglas fir, often stagnated, and diseased stands which have no habitat value for big game, no recreational value except possibly as long distance viewing areas, and very doubtful watershed value?"[27]

Their criticism was sound but missed the point. The Select Committee was saying that there was more at stake in forest management than establishing thrifty young timber stands. Costs, aesthetics, and uses other than timber needed to be factored in. Foresters could plausibly argue that a well-spaced stand of healthy Douglas fir or ponderosa pine was pretty close to what the public expected in a forest, but they would have difficulty persuading economists such as Wambach that it was worth all the effort and disruption to the landscape. Redeeming the forest, the Select Committee was saying, was not an ultimate end, and the rest of society had a say in what those ends might be. Their argument recalls an analogy that Bob Marshall used in his 1933 book *The People's Forests,* in which he asked the reader to imagine a kingdom where people were made to labor fifteen hours a day to coax the maximum production from a woodland. The forest would thus be improved, but at the cost of everyone's welfare. "It is possible," Marshall wrote, "for a forest program to place too much emphasis on the forest itself and to consider insufficiently the related social values."[28] His fanciful example was not too far from reality on the Bitterroot—its foresters had achieved an efficiently run landscape, only to find that many people had very different purposes in mind for their woods.

CHAPTER 16

A Function of the University

1971

For the first two decades following World War II, the Forest Service stood as a model agency in the federal bureaucracy—a respected guardian of the nation's forests and caretaker of many of its most scenic mountainscapes. For most Americans the agency's public image framed a montage of Smokey the Bear, fearless firefighters, and the dedicated rangers who sometimes appeared in episodes of the *Lassie* show. Its employees felt secure in the principles that had guided their work for a half century, as codified in hundreds of directives bound into the Forest Service Manual. Foremost among them were:

- protecting forests from fire, misuse, and private appropriation
- finding new ways to make forests and rangelands more productive
- providing economic and social benefits to the nation through the multiple streams of timber, water, wildlife, forage, and recreation
- maintaining a high degree of professionalism based upon scientific management and personal incorruptibility

These principles held up the Forest Service's operations like the stout poles of an L-4 lookout tower. From its rangers and supervisors down to the seasonals on the fire lines, the agency's mission was virtually unquestionable. Some might grumble about the bureaucracy and the endless paperwork that kept them too much indoors, but few saw reason to question its central goals and purpose. Even fewer realized what chaos would ensue as they applied the doctrines of modern forestry in full view of the public.

Within the context of the agency's proud sixty-five-year-old traditions, the dissent of Guy Brandborg, Charles McDonald, and Champ Hannon was often dismissed as the griping of disaffected former employees who had failed to keep up with the times. The University of Montana's critique was harder to ignore. Where the three retired Bitter Rooters might be taking saw bites out of the agency's towering public image, Arnold Bolle's committee was cheerfully strapping dynamite to the support posts. Asked to examine the specifics of management techniques on the Bitterroot, they called into question the entire direction the agency had been taking for the last quarter century. Was it wise to carry off most of the big old trees for the immediate benefit of western Montana's mills? Did it make sense to try to force high-elevation forest land to produce quantities of pulpwood and sawlogs, where before it had mostly sheltered elk herds, provided vistas for hikers, and held the watershed together? The old-timers on the Bitterroot had been raising these questions all along, but the Forestry School faculty gave them credence and made it imperative to find answers.

The Select Committee members, if one is to believe Arnold Bolle's protestations, saw their report as a collegial, if pointed, critique: one bunch of resource experts talking with another as if in a campus colloquium. The Bolle Report belonged to the academic tradition of peer review—the professorial ritual of bold criticism and equally spirited defense carried out in seminar rooms and in the pages of journals. Few in the Forest Service were used to such robust give-and-take. They operated under the guidance of received wisdom from the agency's founding fathers, augmented by more recent directives from Washington and the regional offices. Their instructions were clear. They had a job to carry out, and there was neither time nor much inclination to engage in lengthy debates over theory.

The world had changed, though. The Bolle Report put Montana at the epicenter of the national debate over forest management. Lee Metcalf arranged to have twenty thousand copies of the report made available to the press and interested citizens (the press run would eventually mount to more than one hundred thousand). Newspapers across the country took up the story, which ultimately spread to several continents. "UM Study Condemns Forest Service Practices," ran the headline over Dale Burk's *Missoulian* article announcing the report. Burk had not chosen the head, but it upset the committee members nonetheless. "We thought we were being constructive and straightforward and honest and we weren't condemning anybody," Bolle said. "We were just putting the facts down as we saw them."[1] Ironically, it was his university panel that shifted the discussion out of conference rooms and academic quarterlies. Thousands of individuals with no forestry training whatsoever would now register their views where it mattered most: in the news media and before Congress. G. M. Brandborg and Dale Burk had not set this blaze—that honor belongs to a handful of ranchers on the east side of the Bitterroot Valley—but they had successfully fanned it to where it would rage on its own.

Brandy congratulated Bolle in a personal note that began with "Hats off to your crew!" He predicted that the Select Committee's report would have a tremendous influence on the profession of forestry. Brandy's friend Michael Frome used his column in *American Forests* to praise the committee's work as "impressive and authoritative...an encouraging breakaway from the professional norm." But the credit for stirring up the issue in the first place, he said, belonged to Dale Burk, who deserved an "environmental Pulitzer award," and to Guy Brandborg, who "should be honored as the environmental forester of the decade." The only disturbing side to the controversy Frome could see was that it took such a concerted citizen effort to bring the Forest Service to heel, and meanwhile many other landscapes in Montana and other regions were being similarly manhandled.[2]

The report initiated a thorough airing of the issues in professional meetings and forestry journals. Bolle's panel participated in several stormy sessions in the first months of 1971, including what Bolle called "a wild overflow audience" at a Society of American Foresters gathering in Missoula in January. "Committee members had a great time responding to questions, attack, and vituperation," he recalled. They also took part in a university alumni meeting in March 1971, at which Horace Koessler of the Intermountain Company called the report "no more than political demagoguery" and said it was a "criminal waste" to let lodgepole pine forests fall down and rot. Ed Shults of Tree Farmers, Inc., an Intermountain subsidiary, said the report was a political accommodation to satisfy a group of "obstructionist preservationists" led by Guy Brandborg. He said he had opposed Bolle's appointment as dean and would just as soon see him fired. "You don't deny it then," Bolle shot back. "What is this, about the tenth time you've tried it?" The dean was known for his dignified demeanor, but he would brook no criticism of his colleagues' competence or good intentions. Richard Shannon, a panel member, told participants at a meeting of the Inland Empire Section of the Society of American Foresters in Spokane that "we yield to no one in our concern for the profession. We believe that its integrity is threatened by our own lack of courage to do the job that is needed."[3]

Bolle credited university president Robert Pantzer for withstanding what he called "a rather cowardly & unethical action" on the part of Intermountain officials. Pantzer expressed his support to Bolle the day after the report was released. "The fact that it may become controversial is of little consequence," he wrote. "I am confident that it is a well documented and professional report which is of service to the people of this state. This certainly is one of the functions of a good University."[4]

Many professional foresters welcomed the Select Committee's analysis. Typical were the comments of C. Allan Friedrich, a retired thirty-three-year veteran of the Forest Service. The report validated his experience as a range conservationist in Region 1 during the 1950s, when he had authored a study that pinpointed watershed damage from certain logging practices. For that, he said, he was transferred out of the regional office to an assistant ranger position, and later to a different region. As he wrote to Bolle:

> Some of you, at least, must have actually lived the experience of hearing a different drummer than the one who accompanies the cry of "TIMBER." I have known many fine young men who seemed to hear that "other drummer" for a few years. Many soon learn that it pays to get in step, so they do. A few hang on stubbornly and do what they can from the inside, and some of these eventually get to fairly high advisory positions, but seldom get to make any important decisions. Others have sense enough to get out while they are still young enough to build effective careers in conservation while they are still less "bark-bound."[5]

Others in the profession offered substantive critiques of the report. John Zivnuska, dean of the forestry school at the University of California at Berkeley, expressed concern about some of the "roundhouse swings" the committee took. He noted that the report's authors objected to a dominant-use philosophy with regard to timber, yet such was already the case with national parks, wilderness areas, and wild rivers. "Does it all simply boil down to the proposition," he asked Bolle, "that dominant use is a fine principle when applied to values you rate highly, but immediately becomes suspect if suggested for values which somebody else values highly?"[6]

Controversy was as common among foresters as in any profession—Elers Koch and Ferdinand Silcox both stirred up dust when they questioned established doctrines on fire control and private forest ownership. Never before, though, had the dissent been so public. What was particularly exasperating to the agency's timber staffers were the academic affiliations of the committee members: there was not a silviculturalist or forest mensurationist among them. Disciplines such as economics, sociology, and political science had an obvious bearing on public policy issues, but to some careerists in the agency, the Select Committee was poaching on neighboring territory. A common theme was that the committee's heavy-gauge attack would encourage Congress to cut Forest Service funding and set back the cause of forestry. "The report becomes a club which some people who are very strongly antigovernment or anti–Forest Service can turn right around and clobber us over the head with," one official said.[7]

Publicly, at least, Northern Region officials appeared to be reconciled to the thunderstorm of criticism. John Milodragovich, chief of the region's division of timber management, asked the foresters attending the alumni meeting to "see what we can do in order to move ahead in these changing times, and do the things that we as professional foresters should, could, and know how to do. If we look back, we're dead." Neal Rahm, perhaps sensing the winds, praised the Select Committee's report as a worthy addition to the internal studies he had commissioned. Early in 1971 he met with Bolle for several hours to discuss the matter, and suggested that if his committee were serious about reform, it would press Metcalf for help at the next appropriations hearing. "Quality has a price tag on it," he told the *Missoulian* afterward. Privately, however, he felt angry and betrayed after reading the report. "It shattered Neal," Ray Karr recalled. For the dean of a prominent forestry school to voice such thoroughgoing criticism of the Forest Service was virtually unimaginable. For most of the century the nation's forestry schools had served as training grounds for industry and the agency, not as sources of dissent and criticism. It was as if the commandant at West Point had announced that the U.S. Army no longer served America's needs and required drastic restructuring.[8]

Many news stories that followed the release of the Bolle Report assumed that the Select Committee used the term *timber mining* as an accusation of abuse, not as an alternative to the intensive forestry that the Bitterroot was practicing. Some agency personnel felt whipsawed: the academicians wanted them to draw back from the very practices they had developed to successfully restock difficult sites, while the public accused them of stripping the land with no thought for tomorrow. Some wondered if it was all a matter of better public relations, requiring nothing more than careful explanation of the goals of long-term forestry.

They soon got their chance; shortly after receiving the university's report, Rahm ordered his staff to prepare a detailed analysis and rebuttal. Each section of the report was assigned to a corresponding division in the regional office, with Ray Karr's I&E group coordinating the responses. John Milodragovich, in contrast to his conciliatory public comments, had the strongest words. "The halo of academic freedom shows up in many statements in the report that are not supported in fact or logic," he stated. "The report is quasi-professional, published in an academic atmosphere that almost defies criticism of seemly shoddy work.... They have no new facts in their report. In my opinion, their statements of finding do not follow principles of logic." He continued:

> The Forest Service cannot manage the Bitterroot Forest under the multiple use–sustained yield mandate of Congress without using timber cutting to accomplish vegetative manipulation for a number of uses.... Unmanaged forests of the Bitterroot have given us commercial timber but with that commercial timber, a large abundance of unmerchantable trash. It seems only reasonable that the commercial timber pay for the cost of the noncommercial trash and regeneration of a new stand. We have gone through the experience many, many, times of mining the commercial values and leaving the trash to occupy the sites indefinitely.[9]

The Select Committee clearly did not have trash in mind when it proposed leaving residual stands to nature's devices. Such statements exemplified the gulf between production-oriented foresters such as Milodragovich, who saw little value in slow-growing, disease-ridden stands, and academicians such as Wambach and Behan, who could see little utility in pouring money into relatively poor sites. During a panel discussion held at the University of Montana shortly after the release of the Bolle Report, Blair Hutchison of the Bitterroot Task Force pointed out that as an economist, he regarded reforestation as a current cost, chargeable to timber-sale receipts. "This is a point of almost complete difference" between the task force and the Select Committee, he said. "The root of our environmental problems, whether it be water or air or land, has been the tendency to postpone costs." Robert Cron, also of the Bitterroot Task Force and Milodragovich's predecessor in the regional office, pointed out that more expensive logging systems such as high-lead cable yarders could reduce ground disturbance and trim planting costs, but the extra investment in the use of such equipment must be borne at the time of harvest.[10]

The timber industry, predictably, took strong exception to the notion of timber mining. The National Forest Products Association (NFPA) said that the idea amounted to abandoning silvicultural and timber-growing objectives on poorer sites. It asked whether the Bitterroot ought merely to "provide a backdrop for the good life of escapists from smog and congestion" or, alternatively, "maintain a steady flow of raw material to support the local economy and to help meet national requirements for forest products." It offered an economic analysis based on paying for regeneration costs from timber-sale receipts, which showed a much better return for clearcut harvesting. When the higher growth rates of managed forests were factored in, timber mining looked even worse, the association said.[11] The Select Committee's provocative notion never took hold within the forestry profession, even though it offered a low-cost alternative to the kind of practices that had brought it so much public disapproval. No cleverly written report could dislodge the long-standing doctrine of achieving maximum productivity from the nation's forests.

Neal Rahm could have simply given his staff's critique of the Bolle Report to the press and tried to weather the storm; instead, he used the opportunity to institute significant reforms in the Northern Region's approach to timber management. Three weeks after Metcalf released the Select Committee's report, Rahm called a news conference to present a new set of environmental goals for the sixteen forests under his jurisdiction. Adding gravity to the event was John McGuire, the agency's deputy chief. The report, titled *Management Direction for Northern Region,* set a tone of urgency for responding to public concerns about timbering practices. Months of intense work had gone into the report's preparation, only to see it overshadowed by the media attention surrounding the

University of Montana study. Still, Rahm hoped that his office's effort would correct the problems that had placed the Bitterroot in such poor regard.[12]

The *Management Direction* report acknowledged that the region's timber program was out of balance. "In the last four years regeneration cuts have been made on 245,000 acres. According to our records we have failed to regenerate 24,000 of these acres," it acknowledged. Some 84,000 acres were in need of thinning, with the backlog for both activities growing each year. Equally disturbing was that many of the region's sawmills had a capacity to process more timber than the forests' allowable cuts could supply. The agency had set this table for itself by encouraging new mills to locate in the region, but this had led to overcutting the more accessible stands, the report admitted. Henceforth, new multiple-use plans would balance timber sales with the need to ensure regeneration and protect other uses. The region would now "emphasize quality over quantity" in its resource production efforts.[13]

The *Management Direction* report represented a notable about-face from the *Full Use and Development* report of twelve years earlier. This became clear as Rahm closed his presentation by reading from a poster he had asked each of his field offices to display, which bore a personal message to his staff in the wake of the Bitterroot controversy. "The need is for change and the time is short," it read. "To merit the respect of the people we must seek their counsel and truly listen. We must start crusading for quality land management as never before. I want a dynamic and bold leadership from everyone in the organization in this region to accomplish our objectives. In case of a conflict between quality and quantity, the decision will be made in favor of quality land management."[14] To all appearances, the days of timber dominance in Region 1 were over.

Rahm had already elaborated on this theme in a November 25 memo to each of his division chiefs and forest supervisors, in which he insisted that "these are not idle expressions about an impossible ethic." New directives coming from the chief's office, as well as protests from the public, he said, "demand that we meet the test of quality management."[15] Rahm assured his staff that the controversies bedeviling the agency could not be ignored, nor were they necessarily to be feared. "In newspapers, in speeches, and on radio and television we are portrayed as unresponsive and selfishly oriented toward one function or another. We should not expect to eliminate such expressions, nor should we try to eliminate them. They are normal, healthy products of our free society. They confirm a growing interest in resource management.... [T]hese public expressions give us significant insight into our serious failure to effectively explain our management operations."

Rahm's press conference gave him just such an opportunity to explain

matters; his audience represented a cross-section of interests from the Bitterroot Valley and western Montana. Fred Wetzsteon, an East Fork rancher and a
vocal opponent of Guy Brandborg's policies as supervisor, asked whether "forestry personnel are going to publicly and forcefully declare for the continuance
of the progressive land-use management of the sixties, or is resource development and land-use management going to regress to the do-nothing of the forties
and early fifties?" Doris Milner expressed her support for the new program but
wondered how the Forest Service could follow it, given President Nixon's recent
directive to increase the allowable cut. Could sustained yield be achieved under
such pressure? Rahm replied that the president emphasized that environmental values would be maintained: "I feel very strongly about this," he added. He
pointed out that the region's extensive lodgepole pine stands had no net growth
and that by increasing cultural treatments such as thinning, these could be made
much more productive.[16]

Rahm used the forum to take issue with parts of the Bolle Report, particularly its avowal of timber mining. "It would be a policy of desperation," he said,
"to say now we are going to cut this timber off and we are not going to assure
regeneration. This is a philosophy of despair, because we are charged with getting the new crop and if we have to plant, then we have to plant." Terming his
approach "total land management," he said he wanted each forest to consider all
land values before harvesting timber. Already he had pulled some timber sales
from the bidding calendar to work in needed environmental restrictions.

In February 1971 Rahm issued a second management direction document intended specifically for the Bitterroot. Consisting of twenty-three direct
instructions, it made permanent most of the revisions Orville Daniels had instituted and contained a point-by-point response to the findings of the agency's
Bitterroot Task Force. "The Task Force analysis, the consensus of public comments, and our staff review are conclusive," Rahm announced. "A definite and
visible change in approach to management on the Bitterroot National Forest
is required." The emphasis was on the word *visible:* the new statement declared
that the public was not accepting clearcutting because of its aesthetic impact. It
reaffirmed that clearcutting was "a silviculturally sound system and the only way
to manage some stands," but Rahm instructed Daniels that "your management
methods will have to take this public displeasure into account.... The method is
to be used only where other cutting methods will not provide for replacement
of harvested timber with healthy trees."[17]

The new policy required consultations with soil scientists and geologists
before building new roads or cutting on slopes over 35 percent. Logging would

not be allowed in places where regeneration was not ensured. Terracing, which had already been put on hold, would not be considered in future sales. The cut in ponderosa pine would be reduced, slash disposal improved, thinnings accelerated, and consultations begun with Montana Fish and Game Department biologists. Multiple-use plans would identify possible areas for "backcountry" management.

Notably absent was any call to significantly reduce the overall allowable cut, as the Bolle committee had recommended, or protect large areas for wilderness. The new requirements focused on improving the agency's logging and road-building operations without challenging the long-standing assumption that most of its commercial forest land base would be managed for sawtimber. This did not exactly resolve the dilemma that Daniels faced, which was to somehow produce wood fiber in a way that harmonized with (as Rahm's directive stated) "vegetative, hydrologic, geologic, natural beauty, solitude, history, recreation, and other environmental factors."

The Bitterroot was already feeling pressure from the Intermountain Company, which had a capacity to saw 50 mmbf of timber annually from its remaining Darby mill, as well as from smaller operations such as the Del Conner, S&W, and Waleswood mills in the Darby area and the Van Evans mill in Missoula, which was processing 12–15 million board feet annually from the forest. Smaller operators, in turn, feared losing bids to the larger concerns. At Rahm's Missoula press conference, a Philipsburg mill owner complained that he had not been able to obtain national forest stumpage for eight months and that he had only enough timber to operate until March. Industry had grown used to a steadily increasing supply of logs but now faced a painful retrenchment. An environmental impact statement accompanying the new Bitterroot directive presented the challenge in stark terms, saying that reduced funding for the coming fiscal year would mean a 10 mmbf reduction in the forest's timber sales. Most area sawmills had enough timber to last perhaps a year, after which there would be "major social and economic impacts" in communities such as Darby. Revenues to Ravalli and Missoula counties from the so-called 25 percent fund were expected to drop to one-half to one-quarter of their previous high levels—a serious loss of income for local governments.[18]

Timber targets remained in place elsewhere in the region, but Rahm asked his employees to see to it that shoddy practices did not slip through. He set his thoughts down in a remarkable statement he sent to his forest supervisors and division chiefs in March 1971 that called for an internal shift in values and focus. "More than ever before, it is imperative that we operate as true land managers," he insisted. "We must develop a feeling for the land in all activities, and recognize its inherent capacity to produce an array of spiritual, recreational, and commercial values. In short, each of us must cultivate such a deep feeling for the land that it becomes our point of reference for all decisions and actions. To keep harvest, use, and management activities in balance with land capabilities and environmental quality is our most fundamental job."[19] This was more than window dressing; Rahm genuinely believed that timber management could be conducted in a way that would not harm other forest values. He knew that his credibility was at stake, both with the public and, notably, with his field staff. He told the *Missoulian* that "time and again when I went into this quality over production [issue], they said, 'We're hearing you, but do you really mean it?' And I said, 'Sure I mean it.' But just saying it doesn't prove the credibility."[20]

Part of the problem lay with the vastly increased pace of timber sales and logging, which stretched his rangers' ability to monitor compliance with environmental stipulations. He told reporters about one timber sale he had visited that had particularly disturbed him. "I asked the young forester of the district how often he got out to this sale and he said he could get out only twice a month," Rahm said. "You know what happens when you turn gyppo loggers loose for a day, sometimes you end up in trouble. The big operators squeeze them, so they don't have much to go on."[21]

To ensure that his ideals were understood and carried out, Rahm listed specific goals for the region's forests for the coming fiscal year. He asked his employees to take extra care in road design and construction, closely monitor contractors' logging practices, and take "imaginative action" to handle the growing problem of slash disposal so that there was less need to burn logging waste. Public involvement was crucial: "We must demonstrate that we are willing, even eager, to share the opportunity of managing National Forest land," he said. "We must strive for a truly meaningful relationship with people, not only by asking for their help, but also by implementing the results of our joint efforts." These statements reflected the advice of his I&E chief, Ray Karr, who had made a study of public involvement issues and hoped to introduce a less confrontational approach than had characterized the Bitterroot dispute. With that forest in mind, Rahm described a "chain of disruptive forces that results from distrust, frustration, and insecurity. In their place we must build positive assisting forces based on credibility, respect, and confidence."[22] It was an idealistic stance—a serious self-examination that was unprecedented within Region 1, and perhaps anywhere in the agency. No approach short of this, he felt, would release the region's field staff from the grip of paralyzing conflict.

Rahm may have been putting on an optimistic face for the press, but he appeared intent on accomplishing more than damage control. In a much different era his predecessor, Evan Kelley, had rallied the troops to attack the scourge of wildfire; several decades later Pete Hanson sent his men out in the forests with flagging tape and marking paint to counter the spruce bark beetle. These were crusades that trained foresters could understand. Now the region's head was expecting his employees to embrace change of an altogether different order. It was asking a lot of men who were imbued with the get-it-done spirit of the postwar era.

Translating these ideals into practice, moreover, was far from easy. Orville Daniels not only had inherited the clearcutting issue but also had to deal with the recurring controversy over the Magruder Corridor, where logging and road building had been held in abeyance since the Selke committee's report in 1967. After reviewing watershed studies that were released in 1970 and 1971, Daniels cut the anticipated logging in the corridor by half and called for still more baseline fisheries data before proceeding.[23] This split-the-baby approach satisfied no one. Mills in the Bitterroot Valley wanted access to all of the area's timber, but the Save the Upper Selway Committee still stood in the way. Simply voicing a commitment to multiple-use principles and promising to do a careful job of logging would not solve the basic conflict over land allocation. The heart of the issue lay in the unresolved directives embodied in the Multiple Use–Sustained Yield Act. Should public forest land be zoned into areas of segregated uses, such as wilderness and commercial forest, in order to minimize conflicts? Or could many different uses be harmonized within a particular landscape? The activists on the Bitterroot made it clear they would not be satisfied with a logged-over middle landscape in trade for the high, inviolate peaks of the Bitterroot Range. The University of Montana's Select Committee had simply translated and extended those gut feelings into the language of forest policy.

The changes that Neal Rahm ordered on the Bitterroot and his other national forests constituted one of the most abrupt and comprehensive policy shifts the region had undergone and signaled the beginning of major changes nationwide as well. Guy Brandborg applauded Rahm's initiatives and hoped that they meant a return to more conservative forms of forest management. "In taking that position you demonstrated [a] quality of leadership that your subordinates, other scientists, the public and publicly oriented political forces will respect and praise," he offered. "You are in a key spot to make a most worthy contribution to the public by putting the cause of forestry on all forest land on a scientific management basis." Brandy regarded the citizen revolt he had helped orchestrate as a necessary counterbalance to political and economic pressures from above. "If the Forest Service in the '30s had had a 'people's lobby' backing its position, the necessary funding and legislative provisions would have become realities at that time," he said.[24]

Lee Metcalf, in a letter to chief Ed Cliff, commended Rahm's "encouraging receptivity" to the Bolle Report.[25] His goal all along had been to settle the controversy on the Bitterroot through something less than a full-fledged congressional investigation. The reforms inspired by Dean Bolle's committee and by the Bitterroot Task Force sufficed for his purposes. He further understood that the people of western Montana were not speaking with one voice. Timber interests regarded Rahm's reforms as a step backward from the silvicultural progress of the 1960s. Neither was the Forest Service about to return to the socially oriented, small-scale forestry that Guy Brandborg had fostered thirty years earlier.

The situation in the Selway drainage was instructive: there the Forest Service was conducting detailed studies to make sure that logging did not damage important environmental values, yet no such studies had ever been prepared for the rest of the forest. It was not clear whether comprehensive changes were even possible within the Bitterroot's general forest zone, for industry representatives were watching developments with acute interest. During the 1950s Axel Lindh and John Castles had invited Montana's timber industry to join in the great quest to make the forests of the Northern Rockies more productive. Now the agency's leaders seemed to be backing away from commitments to supply their mills. Such questions led many of the disputants to conclude that the issue could be resolved only at the national level. Despite Rahm's and Daniels's earnest efforts, it was to Washington that industry lobbyists and citizen activists now turned.

CHAPTER 17

Forestry on Trial

1970–1971

The grassroots uprising on the Bitterroot in the late 1960s paralleled a similar outcry on West Virginia's Monongahela National Forest, where sportsmen were taking strong exception to the clearcutting of mixed hardwood forests that formed ideal wild turkey habitat. Continued logging of such stands—despite promises from chief Ed Cliff to limit the practice—led West Virginia senator Jennings Randolph to take up the issue. Like Lee Metcalf, he expressed doubt that the Forest Service was being truly responsive to his constituents. In Wyoming, Senator Gale McGee added his voice to the uproar after outfitters and outdoor enthusiasts noticed huge clearcuts appearing in the high country of the Bridger, Shoshone, and other national forests. In 1970 he wrote an introduction to a locally produced Sierra Club booklet that was intended to spur creation of a national commission to investigate Forest Service timbering practices.[1]

The Sierra Club report included contributions by three Montanans close to the issue: Dale Burk, Clif Merritt, and Guy Brandborg. Burk let loose an emotional cry for reform, accusing the Forest Service of conducting a "masterfully calculated campaign to level this nation's present forests, leaving in their wake a vast public tree farm on which the forest values can be measured only in terms of the amount of wood fiber produced."[2] Merritt decried the pressure to meet allowable cuts, which had led to extensive timbering in roadless lands throughout the West. He cited recent congressional testimony by former deputy chief Edward Crafts, who said that under the leadership of Lyle Watts and earlier chiefs, allowable cuts were considered a ceiling, only later becoming "the floor below which the cut will not be allowed to fall."[3]

Brandborg amplified Crafts's contention by recounting how the agency had abandoned the New Deal's social forestry goals. Following the war, he said, "the forestry, scientific and academic professions have been more concerned with job security, advancement in rank and remaining peaceful until they could qualify for retirement. No attempt has been made by professional foresters to assume leadership to re-introduce legislation to solve the Nation's private and public land forestry problem."[4] He regarded the agency's current leaders as weak reeds, all too easily swayed by industry, in contrast to the visionary reformers he had known. The latter had included Senator Clinton Anderson of New Mexico, who in 1949 introduced legislation establishing federal guidelines for regulating private forest lands. The measure was a belated follow-up to President Roosevelt's 1938 message to Congress that established a joint congressional committee to study the forest-regulation issue, and as late as 1949 it had the Forest Service's backing. Now conservationists had another chance as Lee Metcalf threw his support behind the regulation effort. His Forest Lands Restoration and Production Act, Senate Bill 1734, set comprehensive standards for timber practices on the nation's public and private forest lands. Drafted largely by the Sierra Club's Brock Evans and Gordon Robinson, it emerged as the chief alternative to Mark Hatfield's National Timber Supply Act during the early 1970s.[5]

In June 1970, well before the Bolle Report surfaced, McGee asked the Council on Environmental Quality (CEQ) to look into the clearcutting issue. The council, which had been set up under the National Environmental Policy Act of 1969 as an advisory body to the White House, commissioned the deans of five forestry schools to report on the environmental consequences of, and economic justification for, clearcutting. Their report, which was not published until 1972, was far less critical of the Forest Service's practices than the University of Montana study. The deans did point out problems with the agency's blanket application of clearcutting on steep slopes, highly visible areas, and sites where regeneration was difficult. Working from these and other analyses, the CEQ drafted an executive order amounting to a ban on clearcutting except where regeneration was ensured and where it would not interfere with wildlife, watershed, or aesthetics.[6] Faced with solid opposition from the Forest Service, the timber industry, and the Nixon White House, the order went nowhere, but the implications were clear to agency personnel. Their cherished autonomy to practice forestry as they saw fit was in danger.

Chief Cliff tried to reassure his staff that their timber program was by no means out the window. In a January 1971 address to his regional foresters and division directors, he affirmed that the previous year had been challenging and that the agency would have to "adapt to the changing times, to the changing needs and the desires of the public, and to the new rules of the game being written by the Congress, the Executive, and the courts." He said that for the past ten years his office had been trying to obtain more appropriations from Congress to fully fund all of its programs. "We have consistently recommended increases in the non-commodity activities," he maintained, but while timber sale preparation received virtually all—97 percent—of the amounts requested, other programs that did not return dollars to the federal Treasury fared less well. "Even in the timber program we are out of balance," he said. "The activity that is at the very bottom in funding is timber stand improvement and reforestation—the activity that is needed for us to continue a strong timber harvesting program."[7]

From the regional offices to Washington, Forest Service leaders had to grapple with the question of how far to take reform. Would their critics be satisfied, as Ed Cliff hoped, with incremental changes in timber operations and promises to better fund other programs, all without lowering allowable cuts? Environmental groups, energized by their defeat of the National Timber Supply Act in the Ninety-first Congress, believed that more substantial reform was within reach. They now had mailing lists in place and local activists ready to mobilize their members. They would find the platform they needed in a series of dramatic hearings before Congress.

For several years Brandborg had been pressing Montana's congressional delegation to hold field hearings on timber-cutting practices, which he hoped would spur regulatory legislation of the sort Clinton Anderson had introduced. In January 1970 Mike Mansfield agreed that hearings would be useful, saying he would pursue the idea through Senator Metcalf. At first Metcalf demurred, informing Brandy in June that he was "continuing to analyze the Forest Service findings in the Bitterroot study and to explore the various possibilities for a review of policy in the public land management field"—his first indication of his talks with Arnold Bolle.[8]

Brandborg believed that only by seeing the Bitterroot firsthand would congressmen and senators with jurisdiction over the Forest Service fully grasp citizens' concerns about overcutting and other forest abuses. He asked Bruce Bowler of Boise, who was on friendly terms with Frank Church, to press the senator for hearings before his Public Lands Subcommittee, a key panel on which Metcalf also served. "As you know," he wrote to Bowler, "Pres. Nixon by directive told Interior & Agric[ulture] Secretaries to proceed as before—overcut, rape & raid public lands. The only solution I see is for us country boys and girls to insist upon a congressional investigation.... If you concur that is our last resort[,] appeal to Frank Church to set up the procedures.... On the ground look-see—I am making like appeal to Lee & Mike." Bowler agreed to lay the idea before Church, but no response was immediately forthcoming.[9]

Acting on his own, Brandborg lacked the political clout to spur Church and Metcalf into action, but he had the knack of sowing seeds in many places. With the Sierra Club now on board, and grassroots campaigns under way in several states, the senators finally relented. On August 24, 1970, Metcalf wrote to Church to suggest that "due to the high level of public and Congressional concern which has recently emerged in the area of forest management and clearcutting, the question has been raised whether informational hearings on these subjects might be useful at the present time." Ordinarily, the subcommittee did not oversee the internal workings of the Forest Service, which was part of the Agriculture Department, but Metcalf suggested that it could extend its jurisdiction in this case. "If you are presently considering the possibility of hearings, I would like to express my support for the idea."[10]

Continuing his mail bombardment, Brandy framed the issue as a matter of good governance—a means, he told Church, "to regain public confidence in Congress and in our political system." Senator Church was among the leading critics of the administration's continued involvement in Vietnam, and the previous year he had introduced a measure to block funding for the president's incursion into Cambodia. This attempt to reassert Congress's control over the war did not escape Brandborg's notice, who hoped that the senator would try to box in Nixon on public lands as well. Church was at first noncommittal, forwarding such letters to the Senate Agriculture and Forestry Committee. But with Metcalf, Mansfield, Gale McGee, and Jennings Randolph also pressing for hearings, Church announced on December 11 that his committee would convene hearings in Washington early the following year to examine the "vigorous controversy" over clearcutting practices. He invited Brandy to testify, citing his "fine background and knowledge as a forester," and saying he would "personally see to it that your name is on the witness list."[11]

The subcommittee's hearings were set for April 1971. Brock Evans and other conservation lobbyists scoured their ranks for effective witnesses, from grassroots activists such as Doris Milner to credentialed scientists who could take on the agency's experts. So many wished to testify that Evans requested two days of hearings—which in the end proved insufficient. The Forest Service and the timber industry were less than thrilled to have to defend their practices before the conservationists' allies in Congress. Kenneth Pomeroy of the American Forestry Association summarized the situation in a terse message to his member groups: "Forestry is on trial. Clear-cutting is the issue. Court will convene within a few weeks on a day not specified. The verdict may determine whether professional foresters or untrained laymen will decide how public forests will be managed."[12]

Thus far the national news media had paid little attention to the issue, but with McGee, Metcalf, and Randolph publicly asserting scandal, several reporters sensed a major story. Brock Evans and Otto Teller of Trout Unlimited helped steer them to grassroots activists such as Brandborg. James Risser of the *Des Moines Register* visited Montana early in 1971 and featured Brandy as part of a wide-ranging series on forestry reform. He called him "an almost legendary figure" in the Bitterroot Valley who represented the populist heritage of Gifford Pinchot and Theodore Roosevelt. "In my day," Brandborg told Risser, "the forester was imbued with a land ethic that no generation could be allowed to damage or reduce the future wealth by the way it uses natural resources. There was never any fear then in speaking out against the special interests and in making decisions that were for the good of the public."[13]

As an outspoken representative of an older era, Brandborg's weather-beaten visage was prominently featured in numerous articles. His pronouncements were grounded in history and in a deep regard for the land, making the rebutting comments of an industry official, Ed Shults of Intermountain-owned Tree Farmers, Inc., appear somewhat petty. "They're stinkers," Risser quoted him apropos of Brandborg and Burk. "They go down the line with the preservationists. They've been brainwashed."

That March CBS News sent veteran Vietnam War correspondent Richard Threlkeld to Montana to interview the main players in the Bitterroot battle. Brandy and Dale Burk accompanied Threlkeld, along with Merrill Tester and several timber-industry officials, on a tour of clearcut areas in Robbins Gulch, southeast of Darby. The program aired on Walter Cronkite's evening news program just as the Church subcommittee opened its hearings. The segment ended with Dale Burk asking, "Are we foresters or are we wood merchants?"—a comment that brought angry responses from industry supporters back in Montana, he recalled.

Threlkeld told Burk that White House counsel Charles Colson phoned CBS to try to get the segment dropped.

A shorter version of Risser's *Register* article appeared in the *Washington Post* the day before the Senate hearing, adding to the interest. In it Risser made a case, based on interviews with the Sierra Club's Gordon Robinson and several individuals in the timber industry and the Forest Service, that collusion in bidding on timber sales was commonplace. Risser had obtained an internal memo indicating that the agency was aware of the problem, but its officials hardly wanted this issue added to the pile of difficulties they faced.

More than two hundred people crowded into the Senate committee room on April 5 to hear a comprehensive lineup of environmental advocates and a smaller number of timber-industry lobbyists and mill owners. To accommodate the nearly one hundred witnesses, Senator Church postponed testimony from Forest Service officials until a later date. The hearings opened with a statement from Gale McGee detailing his staff's investigations of Wyoming's national forests, where clearcuts covering hundreds of acres sprawled across the high country. He spoke of finding "clouded streams that were once sparklingly clear, whole mountainsides laid bare." Some slopes showed little or no regrowth even after being planted several times. "The fact of the case to me simply said that at that altitude, in that area, with those particular conditions that were abiding, the clear cutting had been a sorry, sorry policy."[14]

Jennings Randolph laid out the long history of the controversy on the Monongahela, expressing indignation at what he believed was stonewalling from Forest Service officials. Closely spaced clearcuts continued to appear on steep slopes, he said, despite the agency's assurances that they would be more careful. He claimed that the Forest Service intended to clearcut every acre within the general forest zone over the next century, converting mature hardwood stands to plantations less desirable for certain wildlife species. His views were backed up by several fellow West Virginians, including Ralph Smoot, a former Forest Service ranger whose advocacy of selective cutting echoed the views of Charles McDonald and Champ Hannon. "We were taking out the trees that were ready to go and keeping a healthy forest growing," he said of his earlier efforts. "The national forest was a place where high quality, large timber could be grown on long rotations to insure the Nation a supply of fine veneer logs and high-grade lumber."

Guy Brandborg, the most senior of the conservationist witnesses and one of the instigators of the proceedings, led off a citizen panel during the afternoon session with an attack on chief Edward Cliff, who, he claimed, "has a long record of appeasing instead of regulating forest users." Cliff, in his view, had "prevented forest officers on the Bitterroot Forest from exercising their regulatory responsibility, and applying their competence in complying with the mandates of the Multiple Use–Sustained Yield Act." He called on Church's committee to remove Cliff and "reassign him, he and his close associates, from having anything whatsoever to do in prescribing policies for administering the National Forest System."[15]

Brandy cited a letter his former boss Evan Kelley had sent to a mutual friend concerning the changes in their former agency. "God, I wonder what has killed the fighting spirit of the Service," Kelley asked. He wrote of "the tearing down infringement of the influence seekers," saying "it hurts me beyond measure to be compelled to acknowledge that my life long fellow workers…have become, without realizing it, the victims of such influence."[16]

Brandy then resurrected the issue of regulating cutting on private forest lands, referring to a directive sent down during the Eisenhower administration. Chief Richard McArdle, he said, had ordered the field offices to destroy copies of the 1939 *National Forest Economy* report that had called for an active government role in the acquisition and regulation of private timberlands. Subsequently, his superiors adopted what he called a policy of appeasement toward timber companies and livestock operators. "Verbal instructions were given to avoid regulatory action if it would result in congressional appeal," he said. "I received a verbal reprimand from [the] Regional Forester for permitting a ranger under my supervision to exercise his regulatory responsibilities that led to an appeal. The ranger was threatened with a transfer if he caused another appeal." The case in question (for which he gave no details) involved Charles McDonald, who was known for keeping a close watch on grazing permittees and logging contractors.

The Senate panel had convened to hear an assessment of current Forest Service policy and practices, but Brandborg had longer experience in the field than any other witness, and he felt that the institutional and leadership changes that had occurred in his agency were responsible for the current dilemma. "The underlying cause of protests over forestry practices," he said in his prepared statement, "is the Forest Service's failure to harvest timber under long accepted silvicultural practices, based on a philosophy of a land ethic and perpetual yield.…Some foresters are saying that clear-cutting is the issue. This is not the issue. The basic issue is that the owners of forest land have been denied a voice in determining how their land shall be managed."

Comments such as these had raised hackles among his associates for years.

But to Brandborg, the chief and his staff had violated the sacred precepts of his agency—including those of maintaining a steady timber output and carefully monitoring forest users. Directives from the top had created a climate in which rangers no longer felt able to rein in bad practices. Worse, even, than the spread of clearcuts through the forest was his former agency's unwillingness to take the lead in social activism. But he was beating on a drum few others heard. After Brandy completed his statement, Lee Metcalf praised him as a "longtime conservationist and an expert on the Forest Service," and gently directed him back to the question at hand, asking if he could justify any of the clearcutting that was being done in the Bitterroot Valley. "Absolutely none," he replied.

Following a mild demurral in defense of the Forest Service from Arizona senator Paul Fannin, the committee heard from Brock Evans, the Northwest conservation representative for the Sierra Club and the Federation of Western Outdoor Clubs. He, too, challenged Cliff's approach to the forest crisis: "We wish to state emphatically that the problem is not as we see it simply the matter of getting more funds and more staff to supervise more timber sales," he stated. "We feel that timber is already grossly overfunded in comparison to all other multiple use values." Evans pulled no punches: "We think the problem goes much deeper than financing. We feel it goes to the very roots and the basic philosophy of the Forest Service itself…perhaps best characterized by a feeling that if there are big trees which can be economically cut they should be cut."[17]

Evans reiterated the Sierra Club's call for a full-scale congressional investigation into agency practices. He was rebuffed, however, by the conservationists' strongest ally on the committee:

> SENATOR METCALF. I want to ask a question. Do you think that there really is a need for any more study and survey committees?
>
> MR. EVANS. I do not believe, Senator—
>
> SENATOR METCALF. Haven't we studied this matter enough?
>
> MR. EVANS. We studied it on the Bitterroot National Forest, on the Monongahela—certainly in southeast Alaska there are terrible problems there, and I can name national forests in Washington and Oregon that certainly need attention. I think we need a study on a national basis.

SENATOR METCALF. We studied the Bitterroot National Forest largely because it was a representative national forest.... [T]his morning Senator McGee talked about a blue ribbon committee. And as far as I am concerned, the blue ribbon committee was the Bolle committee.[18]

For Metcalf, Arnold Bolle's Select Committee had given him the maneuvering room he needed, and he asked the Sierra Club representative whether it was not time to act. Evans, recovering quickly, politely agreed.

The parade of conservation advocates continued throughout the day and included Gordon Robinson, Idaho wildlife activist Ernie Day, and outdoor writer Michael Frome. Only James O'Donnell of the American Plywood Association spoke in favor of current clearcutting practices. Most industry witnesses were deferred until the following day, when Lowry Wyatt of the Weyerhaeuser Company and Robert Hansberger of Boise Cascade attempted to stem the tide. Wyatt said that "misinformation, misrepresentation of the facts of forest life cycles and misapprehensions about the relationship between growing trees and growing outdoor enjoyment have confused the public. As a consequence, people little understand the essence of forest management as a bulwark of this American resource heritage." He disparaged environmentalists who had "achieved comfortable levels of living" and wanted to "reserve forest use for their leisure activities and esthetic appreciation." W. D. Hagenstein of the Industrial Forestry Association, a trade group based in Portland, Oregon, took note of the president's call to increase harvests by 7–8 billion board feet to meet housing needs. His organization was among those supporting the National Timber Supply Act, which Oregon's senator Mark Hatfield had recently reintroduced. It would again run into heavy fire from conservation groups at field hearings later that year.

By the end of the second day the subcommittee had heard from fewer than half of the witnesses who had signed up. Dale Burk recalled his disappointment as the hearing ended before he and his Montana friends, including Arnold Bolle and wilderness activists Cecil Garland and Doris Milner, had a chance to testify. In a 1979 article for Living Wilderness, he described how "from behind the closed oak doors a voice boomed loud enough to be heard in the hearing room: 'No, dammit, we can't quit now. I can't go back in there and tell my people to go home. They haven't even had a chance to present their case.'" Lee Metcalf won an additional day to accommodate his fellow Montanans and others from both sides of the issue.[19]

The extension permitted the subcommittee to hear what was by far the most sensational testimony to date. It came from a University of Montana professor who until now had taken a low profile in forestry affairs. Robert Curry was an environmental geologist with a broad interest in land-use practices in the West. He claimed that clearcutting was far worse than an aesthetic nuisance. "Most hillslope forested lands," he said, "harvested by all but the most expensive, careful means, are physically losing their soil covers by erosion, despite all Forest Service claims to the contrary." He claimed that clearcutting and even some selective cutting exposed formerly shaded soils to sunlight, greatly increasing biological activity within them. This, he said, set off "a chain of events ultimately resulting in sterilization of the soil by leaching it of its stored chemical nutrients, with or without erosion."[20] Because the process happened within the soil, the streams draining the area might remain perfectly clear. He predicted that soils thus affected could become sterile in as few as twenty years and called for an immediate moratorium on clearcutting while scientists conducted a crash research program.

Frank Church called Curry's testimony "very alarming" and asked for his evidence. Curry was extrapolating from a controlled watershed study carried out in New Hampshire's Hubbard Brook Experimental Forest, where researchers Herbert Bormann and Gene Likens had cut over a thirty-eight-acre area and treated it with herbicides to prevent regrowth.[21] Runoff from the small watershed increased, as expected, and so did suspended particulate matter—an indication of the importance of standing trees and other vegetation in controlling erosion. But concentrations of dissolved solids in the runoff, especially nitrate, were much higher than expected, leading Bormann and Likens to theorize that quantities of nitrogen were being produced in the soil without the usual reuptake by plants.

Curry claimed that nitrification, as the process was called, would occur anywhere forest cover was removed and sunlight reached the ground, accelerating soil microbial processes that converted nutrients to soluble ions, which could then be washed away. He believed that this had happened historically throughout the Old World and had contributed to the loss of forests in Mediterranean countries. "Thus by erosion alone," Curry said, "we are rapidly and directly and surely turning our western states into Dalmatias. It took 500 years to strip the soils from the 250-cm rainfall areas of the Dalmatian coast with more like 1000 years to denude the soils from Israel, Turkey, Greece, Italy and Lebanon."

Dr. Curry's testimony was notable as one of the first incursions into the agency's presumed mastery of the technical side of forestry. Environmentalists often

pointed to denuded hillsides and silted streambeds as examples of poor practices, and even the Forest Service's experts sometimes agreed with them: it
was always possible to do a more careful job of logging. But the sustained-yield
approach rested on the presumption of continuous forest cropping over many
centuries, which Curry had pointedly called into question. The Forest Service
could hardly let these assertions go unchallenged, and its watershed experts
quickly assembled data to challenge Curry's broad-brush application of the
Hubbard Brook study. Their findings would be featured at the second round of
hearings held on May 7.

By now the agency's leaders must have felt like Cornwallis at Yorktown,
their status as defenders of the established order in doubt, their timber program beset by environmentalists in league with congressmen and the news
media. Chief Cliff had his staff prepare a report laying out his agency's rationale for timber management, which was circulated to the Senate committee
members on the morning of the first hearing. Titled *National Forest Management in a Quality Environment,* it was intended to show how the Forest Service
was taking an interdisciplinary approach to timber management. Responding to
critiques from the Bitterroot Task Force and other reviewers, the agency promised to "redefine the mission of timber-management functions, to strengthen
multiple-use aspects, and to reflect emerging concerns for environmental quality." Fifteen pages of photographs showed a variety of cutting practices representing the agency's best efforts, with no pictures of terraced hillsides or vast,
naked clearcuts. Further on, a photo of recent clearcut units showed how proper
design could make them "appear almost like parts of the natural landscape"—
suggesting that the agency still regarded visual aesthetics as the chief drawback
it must address.[22]

If there was any doubt that production concerns still drove national policy, the booklet emphasized that the Forest Service must respond to the Nixon
administration's call for increased logging from the national forests. Meeting
cutting goals, however, was "further complicated by challenges to plans to harvest timber in areas not yet roaded, or where some people feel that such cutting
is incompatible with other uses.... [I]t is possible that these impacts may importantly restrict the rate at which additional yields can be achieved." In this round-
about fashion, Cliff was warning Church's subcommittee that if it paid too much
attention to the demands of environmentalists, the president's housing program
would suffer. Hikers and horsemen, the brochure suggested, ought to be satisfied with the fourteen million acres already set aside as wilderness, plus additional reservations for wild and scenic rivers and other natural areas.

The chief's explanations did not make a strong impression on the subcommittee, whose members continued to listen to witnesses from university forestry schools, retired agency personnel, angry sportsmen and retirees, and others who made it clear that the Forest Service had become an empire unto itself. Church, Randolph, and Metcalf constituted a powerful bloc that would not be satisfied with mere assurances of reform. Following the hearings, they asked committee staff to devise specific guidelines that would require the Forest Service to bring its timber practices in line with what the public was demanding.

That April in Washington marked the end of an era for the Forest Service. The comfortable, assured world they had known was truly being turned upside down. The agency's longtime certainty of purpose, legendary among American bureaucracies, would be replaced with heartfelt questioning, internal discord, and a new search for direction that continues to this day. Thanks in large part to the actions of Guy Brandborg, Dale Burk, and Arnold Bolle, the Bitterroot controversy was now a national issue.

CHAPTER 18

Reporters to the Scene

1971–1973

Intensive timberland management dovetailed neatly with America's postwar reliance on industrial technology, but by the early 1970s such practices were undergoing the same critical appraisal as was given the supersonic transport, offshore oil drilling, and dams in national parks. Many members of Congress wanted to show that they were in tune with environmental concerns following the first Earth Day; reforming timber practices was one more task on the larger agenda. The first foray came two weeks after the initial round of hearings before the Senate Public Lands Subcommittee, when Wyoming's Gale McGee, who did not sit on the committee, introduced legislation to place a two-year moratorium on clearcutting while a blue-ribbon commission conducted a study of the practice. Fourteen senators signed on as cosponsors that spring, not including Frank Church or Lee Metcalf, who saw little need for further investigations. McGee urged Church to hold hearings on his bill, citing (among other research) the statements of Robert Curry regarding soil-nutrient loss. "It is not my intent to say that the case against clearcutting has been scientifically demonstrated," McGee said, only that "these studies and others should give us great pause." Church replied that he would wait until his own hearings concluded that June. Without his support, McGee's bill had little chance of passage, but it was a clear shot across the Forest Service's bow.[1]

The timber industry tried to stem the avalanche of adverse publicity arising from the hearings. W. D. Hagenstein of the Industrial Forestry Association, writing in the professional journal *Western Conservation,* said that environmentalists had used the prestige of Church's subcommittee to attack clearcutting "emotionally, pseudoscientifically and vociferously." Senator McGee and his friends, he said, "have planted a new Terror Tree (*Silvicultura castigata*)," he wrote. "The terror tree is a creation of the Devil, for it defies the laws of God. Its characteristics are complaining and its propagation political. It is a noxious weed in Nature's garden of plants useful to man." Hagenstein pointed out that selective harvesting could not maintain fire-adapted forests against cataclysmic change. "Nature has always perpetuated lodgepole pine by clearcutting," he said, "either by fire or the mountain pine beetle."[2] Such broadsides outlined the future course of the forest management controversy: a war in the news media for hearts and minds, and a somewhat more civil dialogue among scientists and resource experts over the particulars of forest management. As Oregon's junior senator, Bob Packwood, expressed to Frank Church following the April hearings, "You're stepping into a beartrap whichever way you go, and yet, it's a situation, as far as Westerners are concerned, which must be bared."[3] His mixed metaphor foretold the intense debate that would consume much of the national media's attention in the years ahead, in which reporters, politicians, and the public would try to make sense of the conflicting claims of scientists and advocates alike.

Forest Service and industry witnesses counterattacked as the Church subcommittee met in Washington on April 7 for its second round of testimony. Ed Cliff sought to defuse Robert Curry's alarming charges with a hastily assembled staff analysis of ten watershed studies across the country that showed much lower losses of nutrients. A recently completed study on the Flathead National Forest, in which clearcut units were strewn with slash and broadcast burned, showed nitrogen losses of 3.4 pounds per acre in comparison to 2.7 pounds on nearby unlogged areas. Its author, Norbert DeByle, stated that "in all cases, the amount of nutrients contained in the soil is very high compared to amounts lost in any type of cutting." Cliff chose not to cite another of DeByle's papers, which examined surface erosion from the same area. It showed rather high sediment loss following a severe summer storm—as much as 1,500 pounds per acre from one steeply sloped clearcut unit. Erosion fell significantly after three or four years of revegetation.[4]

Curry expanded on his thesis in an August 1972 symposium on even-age management at Oregon State University, in which he maintained that soil-nutrient losses "may be considerable for some limiting nutrients" in clearcut areas. When added to impacts from surface erosion and mass wasting, long-term reduction in site productivity could result, Curry believed.[5] Scientists on each side of the issue cited their version of the precautionary principle: Curry believed that clearcutting should be banned or at least severely curtailed until it could be shown that it was sustainable over the long term, while his critics, not wanting to throw the timber industry into a tailspin, saw little need to take such drastic action unless his hypothesis could be proven.

Guy Brandborg was no scientist, but as a student of W. C. Lowdermilk's theories about the collapse of civilizations due to topsoil loss, he took keen notice of erosion and sedimentation problems. His eyes and ears in the Bitterroot, including Champ Hannon, Fritz Bell, and Otto Teller, often reported instances of streams running turbid or roads unraveling after rainstorms. Later that spring Brandy advised Lee Metcalf that Hannon had just made a trip into the West Fork of the Bitterroot River and found streams below timber-sale areas "running black with mud and debris." He pointed out that although the Bitterroot Task Force had not found widespread erosion on the forest, thus far only a small percentage of its 750,000 acres of commercial forest land had been clearcut. Much worse awaited, he feared, if the cutting program continued unchecked.[6]

Otto Teller enlisted Trout Unlimited's executive director, R. P. Van Gytenbeek, to press the Environmental Protection Agency for a study of erosion and siltation in the Bitterroot River's headwaters. The EPA was trying to develop an approach to controlling nonpoint source pollution, including runoff from farming and forest practices, but as yet it had no formal regulations in place. In late June the agency sent two staffers to make an initial inspection of the Bitterroot. Teller and Brandborg joined them for a tour of logging units on the Trapper–Chaffin Creek divide, the Blue Joint area, and Bugle Creek on the East Fork. The latter two areas were the scene of some of the largest clearcuts on the forest.

The EPA visit produced no spectacular condemnations of the Forest Service. John Green, the agency's regional administrator in Denver, reported to Van Gytenbeek that although the clearcut and terraced areas were aesthetically unpleasing, his staff did not observe any extensive erosion. He did warn of "a definite potential for severe erosion" in many areas, however, and advised the Forest Service that his staff would be making additional investigations. Green approved of the forest's extensive changes to timber operations, which specified that clearcutting would be done under a multiple-use plan to protect wildlife and conserve soil and water resources. Orville Daniels felt vindicated upon reading Green's comments; he reported to Steve Yurich, who had replaced Neal Rahm as regional forester in July 1971, that "this is an excellent letter and one of the first that supports our change of management direction and the practices of clearcutting."[7] Brandborg's friends, however, felt that serious problems were still being overlooked.

Some agency scientists agreed. Around this time Arnold Bolle obtained a Forest Service staff analysis of the potential for erosion occurring in terraced areas. The author, who was unnamed, believed that the terraces' ability to hold moisture, while an advantage for growing trees, also made them susceptible to mass wasting. "Water should not be allowed to accumulate [on the terraces] as it not only adds to the weight of the soil mantle but severely reduces its internal cohesion," the paper stated. "Such an area is the Bluejoint–Muddy Creek–Tough Creek area on the Bitterroot." No major landslides or obvious surface erosion had been seen in these areas, but the author noted that insufficient time had elapsed to observe the effects of climatically severe storms.[8] Disastrous road failures and landslides had occurred in granitic soils following heavy rainstorms in 1964–1965 in the South Fork of the Salmon River drainage in Idaho, and some fisheries specialists in the agency were concerned that similar events might occur on the Bitterroot.

Officially, the agency continued to insist that erosion from the Bitterroot's logging activities was isolated and was not a serious concern. Clearcutting and road building would continue, albeit at a reduced rate, and without the in-depth scientific assessments that environmentalists believed were needed. To them, simply assigning a soil scientist to provide input into sale design was insufficient to deal with the mounting cumulative problems from decades of heavy cutting. Robert Curry's testimony was a harbinger of the crucial role that scientists would play in the forest debate as environmental groups added specialists to their staff who could directly challenge the agency's operating assumptions.

Publicity has a way of begetting itself; the Church subcommittee hearings allowed the Bitterroot activists to keep national attention focused on their forest. That summer Gale McGee, at Metcalf's request, took time from a family vacation to tour the West Fork drainage with Miles Romney, Brandborg, Champ Hannon, and Dale Burk. Brandy took the group first to a stand of ponderosa pine that had been selectively cut in 1947, then to an uncut research stand in Overwhich Creek, both of which he knew would give perspective to the scenes to follow. They returned downstream to the heavily roaded mountains above Painted Rocks Reservoir and drove the miles of switchbacks up to Took Creek Saddle, where they could witness the intensively managed landscape that was contemplated in the Bitterroot Forest's 1966 timber plan. Burk's photograph of McGee and Brandborg standing at the head of a terraced clearcut in Took Creek became one of the iconic images of the battle. It was perhaps the least-auspicious time to observe these clearcuts; many of them, like Took Creek, had been planted only within the last several years, and the inconspicuous seed-lings growing in neat rows did little to ease the appearance of terrifically worked-over hillsides. Terracing itself had been halted, but its legacy was all too obvious. McGee told Burk that the Forest Service "lacked the feeling of a land ethic" and had "flagrantly defied compliance with the Sustained Yield–Multiple Use Act." He brought up the possibility of bringing legal action against the responsible officials and promoted his idea for a two-year moratorium on clearcutting and a blue-ribbon study.[9]

Further damaging accounts followed in the national media. Otto Teller had been pursuing a story with Gladwin Hill, the *New York Times*'s Los Ange-les bureau chief, who ranged across the nation in search of environmental sto-ries. Hill spent nearly a week on the Bitterroot that summer in the company of Brandborg, Burk, and local Forest Service officials. His two-part article, which appeared in mid-November, covered the forest-policy issue from a nationwide perspective, but featured Burk's photo of Brandy and Gale McGee at Took Creek. Hill connected the dots on a wide range of issues, including pressures to open new wildlands to logging as well as Gordon Robinson's assertion that the agency had systematically overestimated its allowable cuts. On the Bitter-root, he depicted "whole mountainsides so skinned of centuries' growth of pon-derosa pine and Douglas fir that they look more like man-made pyramids for a weird science fiction film."[10]

Tours of the Bitterroot, Dale Burk recalls, were turning into a growth indus-try for the Missoula bus charter service that took reporters and agency offi-cials along the forest's narrow mountain roads. One trip with Gladwin Hill has become legend. The group had driven up the wide, peaceful East Fork val-ley past scattered ranch buildings and idyllic summer homes, then turned south to follow a timber haul road that switchbacked six miles up the mountain slope toward the Continental Divide. Along the way they stopped to inspect cutting units and admire the dense, uncut hillsides in between—all a normal part of a working forest. When the bus reached a convenient wide spot at a road junc-tion, an agency official asked the driver to turn around. Just then Brandborg's voice boomed out: "Son, there's a better turnaround up there," he said, point-ing on ahead. A Forest Service staffer was heard to say "Oh, my God"—he knew, as Brandy did, what lay around the bend. As the bus continued into the drain-age of Lodgepole Creek, a dramatic vista opened over a clearcut in excess of a thousand acres—part of the enormous firebreak that was planned to extend for miles along the Continental Divide. The unit was known thereafter as the Oh-My-God clearcut.[11]

In retrospect, the incident in the East Fork shows how complex forest management problems eluded full treatment in news articles—even those written by experienced environmental reporters such as Hill. People gasped at the Oh-My-God clearcut not only because of its size but because so much waste wood appeared to have been left behind—acres and acres of mature trees were strewn across the ground, their bark long since fallen off. These trees, it turns out, were remnants from the mountain pine beetle epidemic of the 1930s and had lain concealed for decades until the loggers arrived and took off the overstory. The fallen forest told its own tale of ecological change—of how high-elevation forests renew themselves either by fire or beetle, just as W. D. Hagenstein promised. Years ago this deadfall had defeated the sheep growers of the East Fork who tried to move their flocks through the jumbled logs. By the 1960s the regrowth had become crowded and stagnated; the foresters hoped to reestablish a new stand and keep it properly thinned so that it would grow faster. The oversize clearcut in Lodgepole Creek represented either the best or the worst of forest management, depending on what the viewer had come to see.

Earlier that year Brandborg had proposed a Bitterroot visit to James Nathan Miller, a muckraking author whose exposés of water-project boondoggles and other government-sponsored environmental abuses were often featured in *Reader's Digest*. Miller made the tour with Brandy that summer, his subsequent article giving the Bitterroot controversy its widest circulation in the news media. Like Brock Evans, he compared the clearcuts he had seen on the Bitterroot to a strip mine. "All around us, covering a square mile of mountainside, was nothing but bare brown earth," he wrote. "'Look over there,' said Guy Brandborg, my guide. He pointed to other slopes a mile, three miles, five miles away. All bore the same huge scars. The area looked like a battlefield." It was "'forestry gone mad,'" Brandborg said. But Brandy hardly fitted the picture of an environmental extremist. He told Miller that clearcuts should be "maybe 30 or 40 acres at most. Some of the cuts on the Bitterroot approach a thousand acres." He related how his former agency had abandoned the multiple-use approach and become sawlog foresters: "They're wiping out animal habitats. They're scraping logging roads out of steep slopes where the gashes in the soil pour mud in the streams. They're destroying some of the forest's most beautiful trails and campsites."[12]

For all the apparent devastation, though, Miller chose not to write a one-sided diatribe in the style of Bernard DeVoto. In his view, the Forest Service's timber-management policies did not represent a conspiracy to hand public lands over to the timber industry so much as "a sincere belief that what they were doing was in the public interest. America needed lumber. It wasn't until the late 1960s, when we all suddenly discovered ecological virginity, that we started yelling rape." Nevertheless, the article prompted the agency's Washington office to send a sharp rebuttal to the *Digest*. "The tone of Mr. Miller's article is set by a discussion of management of the Bitterroot National Forest—especially as seen through the eyes of one retired Forest Service employee," it said. "We respect the author's prerogative to seek personal views about natural resource matters and to report thereon. However, it seems somewhat less than objective to dwell so heavily on only one side of an issue."[13]

Similar rebuttals went to the editors of the *Washington Post* in regard to James Risser's article, as well as to the *New York Times* and the *Atlantic,* which had published an article by conservationist Paul Brooks on Alaska's Tongass National Forest titled "Warning: The Chain Saw Cometh." Dale Burk obtained copies of the letters from a Forest Service contact and wrote blistering counterrebuttals to the various editors, all of which served to keep the national press interested.

Among the many tours Brandy gave during these climactic years was a 1973 overflight of the Bitterroot with George Wilson of the *Washington Post.* As mile after mile of gaping clearcuts passed underneath Jack Evans's noisy Cessna, Brandy shouted to the reporter, "This is what we're fighting. There'll be nothing left of our forests if this keeps up."[14]

Most Montana newspapers presented milder takes on the story. In October 1971 the *Kalispell Daily Interlake* sent reporter Larry Stem on a two-day, five hundred–mile media tour of the Bitterroot, sponsored by the Western Wood Products Association and its Montana affiliates. The resulting nine-part series was written in a chatty, personal style, in contrast to Burk's hard-hitting features and editorials. "How well [the industry] fares is the main factor between a sick and healthy economy," Stem wrote. "There are those who say junk the timber industry and 'maintain the looks.' It takes little analysis to show how shortsighted a viewpoint this is, even for a person who lives and dies in a concrete megalopolis."[15] The *Daily Interlake* served Montana's timber-rich Flathead County and shunned the damn-the-torpedoes editorial approach of the *Missoulian.*

The severest editorial denunciations came from Miles Romney in Hamilton, who for decades had used his *Western News* as a personal forum to excoriate Forest Service excesses. In late 1971 he ran half-page aerial photographs of recent clearcuts showing huge slash piles and skid roads running in all directions. "No potato field was ever more thoroughly gouged," he wrote of one cut in the upper Sleeping Child drainage. "There you see the remnants of the forest, little, big, some good, some bad, some old and some young; trunks and boughs have been pushed into a semblance of windrows, ready for burning, like a sacrifice to the gods. One wonders when the forest will return to this once verdant landscape.... Attila would marvel at this scientific achievement of the experts."[16]

The *Ravalli Republican* (later the *Ravalli Republic*), the Bitterroot's largest-circulation paper and its only daily, took a more objective stance. Editor Bob Gilluly gave equal space to the claims of the timber industry, Forest Service, and environmentalists and felt that his balanced coverage helped build circulation over Romney's paper. Gilluly regarded Brandborg and Milner as effective advocates, but he reserved his greatest admiration for Orville Daniels and his district rangers, who he believed were trying to thread a course through the maze of conflicting interests. He recalled recently how thoroughly the Bitterroot Valley was polarized between the thousand or so people in the Darby area who drew their paychecks from the timber industry and citizens in Hamilton and points north who objected to excessive clearcutting.[17]

Guy Brandborg had always generated strong feelings in the Bitterroot Valley; he rarely made room for views that differed from his, and too often his critiques became needlessly personal. When Bud Moore published a heartfelt plea for understanding between the contestants in the timber conflict, Brandy sent him a critical note, saying essentially that he was giving in to the resource abusers. As a ranger on the Lolo National Forest, Moore had been responsible for introducing timber management and road building to the wild upper Lochsa drainage. "I made some good decisions, a few bad ones and the results of those bad ones still haunt my conscience," he wrote in a *Missoulian* op-ed piece. "In places the job done has been of far less quality than the balanced multiple use my service is committed to achieve." While shouldering some of the blame, Moore felt that the public had stood too long on the sidelines and failed to support the agency when it was faced with "single purpose pressures—especially those camouflaged as public need."[18]

Brandy seemed blind to his friend's soul-searching, missing a chance to reinforce relations with an important official in the agency. Moore was in charge of fire control and aviation for the Northern Region and was the most highly placed friend the conservation community had in the regional office. "I was possibly one of their biggest interior critics," he recalled recently. "I got listened to. But that was because I respected the opinion of people like Brandy." The way out of the impasse gripping the Northern Region, Moore told a meeting of the Society of American Foresters, was through what he called "intense multiple use planning," in which the agency would assess the capability of each forest ecosystem to "produce on a sustained yield basis recreational, spiritual, or commercial resources in order of priority." Only then, he believed, could forest officers "join the public effectively in the decision making process…long before rigor mortis sets in on the agency position."[19]

Moore, like Rahm, viewed the public as a potential ally in crafting better decisions that would stand up to outside scrutiny. Undaunted by Brandy's attacks, he continued to visit him in Hamilton to discuss the issues. "I bored into him and he bored into me," he recalled of these sessions. "He was seen as a great threat to the regional office. I tried to bridge that as best I could." His idealism matched Brandy's, yet he was confident that his agency could come up with good decisions in the face of timber-industry pressure.

Steve Yurich, who had worked under Neal Rahm as a district ranger in southwestern Colorado and was Rahm's personal choice to replace him, wanted to draw in the agency's critics to see if some accommodation was possible. He announced his intentions in a commentary for the *Missoulian* published in late 1971. "If we are going to try to sustain a life style and culture similar to our present sophisticated level, it's a cinch we're going to have to solve our problems, and the way to solve them is by working together and not rock throwing," he wrote. He placed high hopes on the region's new multiple-use plans as a way of determining the land's fitness for various uses. Simply splitting the difference between interest groups was not enough, he said; the current combatants did not necessarily represent all of the public's needs, either now or in the future. His actions seemed to back up his statements. In December 1971 Yurich issued a new "program emphasis" statement for the Northern Region that called for withholding road construction and timber harvest from roadless areas until the new plans were completed and the public had a chance to make its views known.[20]

Brandborg's intransigent stances and his ability to organize action had earned him considerable enmity within the Forest Service, but they also ensured him a place at the negotiating table. In early January 1972 Bud Moore arranged for Yurich to spend the better part of a day talking with Brandy and Ruth at their home in Hamilton. Brandy used the occasion to show Yurich the various documents that had guided management on the Bitterroot during the 1930s and 1940s. "Steve came clean [and] took his hair down and told it as it is," Brandy reported to Stewart. "It was like visiting with old Glenn Smith and the Major." Afterward Yurich thanked him warmly for "sharing the burdens, problems, and opportunities—it was like having a great weight lifted from my shoulders." He had his own agenda for the meeting; he wanted conservation groups to oppose an Agriculture Department proposal to close the regional office in Missoula under a Nixon administration plan to create a new superdepartment of energy and natural resources. Brandy asked Stewart to take this up in Washington to prevent what he called the "dismemberment" of the agency. "Steve is O.K.," he said. "All he needs is time and help to get Nixon etc. and industry off his back. Suggest we change our tactics. We have flogged them enuf. Industry is claiming reduction in cut will cause job loss etc. Steve says he could put 10,000 or more men to work tomorrow if Congress provides funds. Let's hammer on that to counteract industry's claims."[21]

Yurich needed the help; the ongoing timber sales in the region would not wait for his reform efforts to take hold. "How I wish we could stop the clock for two years and be able to get on top of the multiple-use planning job," he told a meeting of his forest supervisors in February 1972. "Somehow we will integrate management so that we can contribute to people's needs and still have harmony with [the] environment." He was proud of the steps his staff had taken thus far, yet the pressure to produce timber would not relent. Already Region 1 was offering for sale 95 percent of its allowable cut of nearly 1.2 billion board feet. To meet the administration's request to boost this still further, they had scraped together an additional 195 million board feet, mostly from salvage sales. There were opportunities to increase yields through precommercial thinning and restocking old nonproductive burned areas, but funds for this work would not show up. The region was already pushing timber as hard as it could, and Yurich had little room to maneuver.[22]

It did not help matters when the agency's research branch released a report that examined the timber-growing land base on a sample of five national forests in the West, including a portion of the Lolo in the Northern Region. The authors, which included Blair Hutchison of the Bitterroot Task Force, found that the agency's timber planners had not taken into account all of the constraints that would ordinarily limit logging within the commercial forest land base. These included areas that were too steep to reasonably log, did not produce the minimum twenty cubic feet of wood fiber per acre per year, consisted of unusable patches or stringers of trees in higher-elevation areas, or had to meet other multiple-use goals. On the Lolo 116,000 acres were believed to be unsuitable for logging—16 percent of the total timberland base. Subtracting the growing potential of these stands would require substantial reductions in allowable harvests, as Gordon Robinson (who kept track of such studies for the Sierra Club) was quick to point out.[23] The limitations varied on each forest, but the study strongly implied that the Northern Region's new multiple-use plans would likely yield lower cutting levels.

Equally alarming was the assessment of Yurich's timber management chief, John Milodragovich, who informed him in an internal memo that the region was now looking at a replanting backlog of nearly 33,000 acres and another 130,000 acres of cutting units that needed commercial thinning for optimal growth—figures that were substantially higher than in 1971. In addition, millions of acres of uncut, overly dense stands were in need of precommercial thinning. "This performance is inconsistent with our Management Direction for the Northern Region," Milodragovich warned. To balance the program, he said, "a major re-ordering of priorities must take place. We will have to realistically assess our Reforestation-TSI [timber stand improvement] capabilities, then schedule timber sales within that capacity." In other words, unless the pace of replanting and thinning was stepped up, allowable cuts would have to be lowered. It was a sobering analysis, and Yurich knew he needed to get on top of the situation. To address the growing backlog, he hoped to find funds to hire seasonal workers as part of federal job-training programs—creating, as he had told Brandy, ten thousand new jobs in Idaho and Montana.[24]

The meeting with Yurich spurred Brandborg to think about the next stage of the forest management battle. He confided to Dale Burk on several occasions that it was time to moderate their attacks on the Forest Service, lest the agency be dragged down to the point of ineffectiveness. He still felt a sense of loyalty to the organization and saw his criticism as a means of returning the Forest Service to its former role as a progressive conservation leader. Burk recalled how he and Brandy walked out of the Capitol at the conclusion of the 1971 Church subcommittee hearings, ready to celebrate their victory. "Brandy put his arm around my shoulder and said, 'We have to make sure they don't destroy the Forest Service.'" Brandborg still claimed a degree of ownership in the controversy, even as more of the heavy lifting was being done by lobbyists for the national environmental groups. After meeting with Yurich, he told Lee Metcalf that "Ruth and I are confident that Steve will do his best to reorient the thinking and action of employees under his jurisdiction." He supported Yurich's idea of employing timber-industry workers in reforestation, thinning, and other stand-improvement work. "Steve and other Regional Foresters must respond to the justifiable fears on the part of woods workers and their families," he said. "Industry, of course, capitalizes on this fear." A comprehensive employment program, he told Metcalf, would "pull the fangs of industry," as well as restore forests to a productive condition.[25]

Doris Milner, too, felt that Montana conservationists needed to have an answer to the threat of layoffs. She joined William Grasser, who owned a small ski area at Lost Trail Pass and was part owner of the Shook and Wilson saw-mill in Darby, in proposing a silvicultural work program through the Bitterroot RC&D organization in May 1972. It called for deploying a fifty-man summer workforce consisting of high school graduates and college students. Orville Daniels outlined the work that needed to be done on the forest, which included 10,000 man-days of reforestation, 93,000 man-days of thinning, as well as road-side erosion-control measures, slash cleanup, rehabilitating abandoned roads and trails, clearing stream channels, building trails, and creating openings for wildlife. In all, he anticipated that more than 150,000 man-days of work could be usefully accomplished, which was far in excess of what his own budget could support.[26]

Brandborg hoped that a forest rehabilitation program could be accomplished under Metcalf's Senate Bill 1734, which sought to improve both private and public forest land. Although the Forest Service officially opposed Metcalf's bill (as well as Senate Bill 350, Mark Hatfield's rival measure) at hearings in Washington in March 1972, associate chief John McGuire acknowledged (under Metcalf's questioning) that his agency faced a reforestation backlog nationally of five million acres. Brandborg saw this as an opportunity for the kind of federal work program he had been advocating for years. Restoring forests was more reward-ing than cutting trees, he told Dale Burk, and would help break the chain of loy-alty that workers felt toward the industry. "These are skilled and great people," he said, "the backbone of the timber industry. They are concerned about how lands and resources should be managed to serve the public instead of special interests. By and large conservationists, they have an understanding of a land ethic." He urged Dale to write another series for the *Missoulian* focusing on such workers, expanding upon his portrayal of Ernie Townsend in his first series on the Bitterroot. "The woods worker needs to know that he has friends," Brandy said. "That in a free society he doesn't have to be subservient to the grasping, politically influenced timber industry for the sake of a job."[27]

Attitudes in the Bitterroot seemed to be changing, Brandy exulted in another letter to Metcalf in April 1972. He and Ruth were encouraged by discussions at the RC&D meetings of the need to create more jobs locally. "The task is one of causing people to realize that forestry and agriculture are the foundation of the economy of western Montana," he said. "This is one battle that is taking shape for a win."[28] But his hopes did not account for the new realities in the industry. Its workforce had changed significantly during the timber boom of the 1960s, which had promoted unusually steady sawmill employment throughout west-ern Montana. Many mill workers and loggers were now raising families and paying mortgages, in contrast to the footloose lives their fathers and grandfathers had lived in the remote logging camps of western Montana and northern Idaho. They were now a more conservative lot who usually cast their allegiance with the mill owners rather than with labor organizations or social movements. When they opened their paycheck envelopes to find handbills calling on them to protest some new environmentalist initiative, they tended to comply.

Brandy's thinking was still rooted in the heyday of the CCC and ERA in the Northern Rockies, when Major Kelley's work crews fanned out into the woods to build trails, plant trees in burned areas, and remove shrubs that hosted the white pine blister rust. Nowadays this was considered work for college students and the unemployed, not family wage earners. Planting trees and clearing culverts would not solve the problems of mill workers in the Darby area who faced layoffs as the timber industry contracted after a decade of enormous harvests. Lacking federal funds, Milner's and Grasser's RC&D proposal never took shape, nor was the Northern Region able to undertake any major new work programs. The Montana timber economy remained yoked to cutting and processing sawlogs and veneer peelers, with only fitful attempts to diversify into secondary processing and manufacturing.

On a more personal level, the efforts of individuals such as Bud Moore and Ray Karr to broker a truce with the Bitterroot dissidents appeared to be bearing fruit. With Brandborg offering qualified support for Daniels's and Yurich's reforms, hope spread among the more progressive agency staffers that the controversy could yield useful results. Daniels touched on this in talks he gave to Forest Service and professional groups throughout the country. He described the Bitterroot as a "rather typical" national forest that had worked its way into the limelight largely owing to the heterogeneous population of the Bitterroot Valley, which was in some ways a weathervane for the Rocky Mountain states. "Valley residents were historically economically dependent on the land, but the population is rapidly shifting to a non-dependent, sophisticated, highly trained group," he observed. "They have, in many cases, immigrated to the valley because of its amenity values, its remoteness, the wild land character of the national forest, and the nearness of the wildernesses. In many ways, we have a representative sample of the middle class throughout the nation." Daniels saw this as a positive trend and advised those in his profession to pay close attention to true public involvement—first by informing citizens about the forest situation, then inviting them to play a real part in making decisions. "We must be open and candid. The time for secret strategy and game playing is past," he said.[29]

Difficulties remained, to be sure. Neither Yurich nor Daniels was inclined to toss aside the Forest Service's decades-old orientation toward significant timber production; both were gradualists who hoped that a modest reduction in cutting would gain breathing room to institute needed reforms. A typical case was a new management plan that Frank Salomonsen, Daniels's Stevensville district ranger, had devised for the highly visible west side of the forest along the Bitterroot mountain face. Salomonsen, newly arrived on the forest, worked with the Bitterroot's landscape architect to try to make logging less objectionable as seen from the valley floor. Cutting in some areas would be limited to selective and shelterwood harvest systems, with openings no more than five acres in size. Other areas would be closed to logging except for salvage of dead, dying, or hazardous trees.

Salomonsen made a similar effort to ameliorate visual impacts from a timber sale planned for the mountains east of Stevensville, modifying a clearcut block to instead employ selective harvesting, with logs skidded by crawler-tractor to a haul road at the edge of the unit. This avoided the use of unsightly and erosive jammer roads crisscrossing the sale area. Logging slash was to be hauled off and burned in a pit instead of left in place or piled along roadsides. It was expensive forestry, but the result was akin to what Charles McDonald had long practiced on the district. Clearcutting was still employed in areas less visible from the valley, but cutting units were no longer designed with sharp, unnatural edges. Such efforts led Doris Milner to remark to western Montana congressman John Melcher at a forum in Missoula that "I see a real intent in the Bitterroot on the part of the Forest Service to understand our problems, to involve the public in management. I am pleased with their attitudes and cooperation."[30]

Even with the Bitterroot and the Northern Region trying to embark on a new course, Brandy saw a need to keep up the pressure at all levels. He and his fellow dissidents—chiefly Milner, Hannon, McDonald, Burk, and Teller—continued to monitor the forest's timber-sale program and report instances of what they considered shoddy logging and road-building practices. An overstory-removal sale in the Trapper–Chaffin Creek area that was logged during the winter of 1971–1972 particularly disturbed them. It had been sold in 1968, before the new environmental restrictions came into play, but Brandborg and Hannon felt that the district ranger should have monitored the logging contractor's work more closely. Once again they took Dale Burk to view the damage. He reported examples of skid trails running down steep slopes and poor cleanup following logging. Hannon was disturbed that so many young ponderosa pines were harvested, knocked over, or damaged. "They have no business cutting trees that have not finished their growth," he said. Brandborg told Burk it was a "crime" that more control was not exercised over the sale. "It doesn't matter how good an attitude you have toward quality management if you don't apply it on the ground," he said.[31]

Generally, though, Brandy continued to be optimistic about Yurich's and Daniels's new direction. As he reported to Milner the following year upon visiting a timber-sale site with Charles McDonald and staff from the supervisor's office, "It was reassuring to realize that differences in timber marking and logging practices were easily reconciled" as a result of the visit. "In addition, the ranger stated that management practices on future sales would be of even higher quality. If our findings reflect Forest and Region-wide attitudes, the Forest Service is demonstrating that it is on its way to managing all resources in the public interest."[32]

The dramatic changes on the Bitterroot were the work of innovative leaders at the supervisory and regional levels, aided by citizen observers who made sure that the district staff did not slip up in the field. Was this situation unique to Montana, with its long heritage of grassroots citizen action? Or could such reforms be instituted Service-wide through legal and legislative mandates? In the wake of the Church subcommittee hearings, national environmental groups hoped to enact a strict regulatory framework that would ensure proper forestry practices and safeguard roadless wildlands. Their efforts would consume activists for the next several years in a campaign to institutionalize forest reform—an attempt to replicate, through new laws and policies, the locally informed and highly personal work of activists such as those on the Bitterroot.

CHAPTER 19

Maneuvers and Negotiations

1971–1974

In May 1971, while the members and staff of the Senate Public Lands Subcommittee digested testimony from the previous month's clearcutting hearings, twenty timber-industry executives gathered in Washington for a meeting of the president's Softwood Lumber and Plywood Industry Advisory Committee, an outgrowth of the previous year's Task Force on Softwood Lumber and Plywood. The group included major producers such as Weyerhaeuser, Boise Cascade, and Potlatch as well as a number of smaller independent mills; Horace Koessler of the Intermountain Lumber Company was the sole Montana representative. Individual statements were not noted, but the industry leaders advised the committee that "an adequate and continuous timber supply" was the most serious problem hindering the president's goal of twenty-six million housing starts over the next decade. It was essential, they said, to enact Senator Hatfield's American Forestry Act (Senate Bill 350, formerly the National Timber Supply Act) and increase timber harvests from the national forests by 7 billion board feet per year.[1] Such talks revealed the convenient pipeline that the timber industry had to Washington's power centers, in contrast to the environmental groups' mostly confrontational stance.

While Forest Service chief Ed Cliff was careful to distance his agency from the dominant-use themes espoused by industry, he continued to insist that allowable cuts on the national forests could be raised substantially if reforestation, wildlife, and environmental programs were funded up to par. Environmentalists, however, feared that simply handing the Forest Service more money would mean more timber roads reaching far into undeveloped "de facto" wilderness areas. Providing more funds for recreation could backfire, too, since the agency had a predilection for building large RV-friendly campgrounds and other developed facilities and using these as justification for still more roads. The game reached a point of absurdity when statements began showing up in Forest Service environmental analyses touting the benefits of "forest openings"—that is, clearcuts—as a means of improving the vistas from logging roads. To the grassroots activists in the Rockies and the Pacific Northwest, the timbermen still seemed to be calling the shots at the national level, blocking reforms of the type being instituted in the Northern Region.

Partly to counteract the adverse publicity generated by the Bolle Report and the Church subcommittee hearings, President Nixon announced the formation in September 1971 of a five-member panel that would examine the questions of timber supply and environmental protection on all national forests. The members of the President's Advisory Panel on Timber and the Environment (PAPTE) covered the spectrum of environmental concerns; its chairman, Fred Seaton, had served as secretary of the interior under President Eisenhower, while Ralph Hodges of the National Forest Products Association represented the timber industry and, as environmentalists would learn, had personal access to Nixon's staff. The panel made extensive tours of the western national forests during 1972, including a July visit to the Bitterroot, where agency officials showed them the infamous clearcuts at the head of Took Creek. Dale Burk learned from an undisclosed source that the panel had met privately with Steve Yurich and pressured him to back away from his commitment to restrict logging. According to Burk's source, Hodges and another panel member "accused the Forest Service of bowing to citizen pressure in reducing the region's allowable cut to allow for more balanced management." Yurich refused to budge, telling the panel that the reforms outlined in Neal Rahm's management direction document were "the only course an honest professional could take."[2]

The panel further riled affairs while in Montana when it canceled a public listening session, leading Brandborg to opine that its members did not want to discuss "gut issues" such as President Nixon's recent directives to increase timber cuts. He complained that the panel suffered from a "total timber orientation."[3] But Louise Townsend of the Del Conner mill in Darby also expressed disappointment that the region's smaller mills did not have the close access to the president that industry lobbyists seemed to have. Although the PAPTE group held no direct authority over the Forest Service, the meeting with Yurich was an ominous sign of where the administration stood on the reform issue.

That became clear early in 1972 when reporters discovered the fate of the CEQ's proposed executive order limiting clearcutting. On January 13 lobbyists for the NFPA met with top administration officials, including the CEQ's Russell Train, Agriculture Secretary Earl Butz, and Interior Secretary Rogers Morton, claiming that any restrictions on the practice would have a detrimental effect on lumber prices and make it harder to achieve the administration's housing goals. The CEQ was forced to back down. The *New York Times* called the CEQ's proposal "a laudable effort" and lamented its "swift extinction" at the hands of industry.[4] Whereas the Forest Service in the 1950s had courted the timber industry as a partner in its efforts to intensify national forest management, it now had on its hands a politically powerful interest group that depended upon a full-scale timber-development program. What had begun as a collegial relationship now appeared, to environmentalists at least, to be that of a privileged client demanding handouts.

A second gut issue also bothered Brandborg as the chess game between environmental and industry lobbyists continued. The discussions thus far presupposed a need for significant expansion of housing stocks across the nation and hence an ever-increasing allowable cut. Robert Wambach of the Bolle committee disputed the need to build or rebuild what amounted to half the country's homes and suggested that before long, alternative building materials would come into much greater play.[5] But Brandy had a more fundamental critique: he looked with disfavor at the homes being built on the outskirts of Hamilton and Missoula, many of which exhibited such shoddy construction that he thought the wind could blow through them. Such structures would not last more than fifty years, he believed, in contrast to his and Ruth's turn-of-the-century home that was likely to last for several lifetimes. Such construction methods contributed to what he called a "continuous draw on the forests to replace timber that should have lasted longer," he told Mavis McKelvey in 1975. As one who had taken an ax to raw logs in order to craft cabins and lookout buildings, he appreciated the value of careful construction—skills that in the long run would mean far less need for timber.

The wastefulness extended to public buildings, as well; in the mid-1970s he and Bill Jellison of the Rocky Mountain Laboratory tried to salvage some of the high-quality doors, flooring, and window sash from the Ravalli County Courthouse as it was being demolished but were told that nothing could be taken from the site. He called these materials "the best lumber that was ever put into any building" and noted that there were residents of the county that had to nail cardboard over their windows in the winter to keep the cold out. "The shortages in this country are all of our own doing," he told McKelvey.[6] But in the nation's headlong rush to build new subdivisions, old-timers who raised discomfiting questions about the squandering of resources were brushed aside. Raw materials were easily obtained from the woods, mines, and fields, and public policy dealt only with how to accelerate the process. Even the national environmental groups found it difficult to tackle this issue. The Sierra Club and its allies attempted to obtain federal restrictions on exports of raw logs, but the underlying factors that drove the demand for wood products were much more difficult to address.

By the fall of 1971 it was clear that Congress was going to place some limits on clearcutting, regardless of the administration's stance. While Gale McGee's bill calling for a moratorium and study was unlikely to pass, Iowa congressman John Culver had asked the General Accounting Office to make a comprehensive probe of Forest Service logging practices. Laurance Rockefeller Jr., representing the recently formed Natural Resources Defense Council (NRDC), had visited the Bitterroot and was talking legal action against the agency.[7] Frank Church and Lee Metcalf still hoped to spur reform without dragging out the issue in lengthy, high-profile investigations. Their staff had been quietly working with the Forest Service on a set of guidelines for timbering practices that would address public concerns while still allowing the agency to move forward with most of its sales.

Church retained former deputy chief Ed Crafts to advise his committee; shortly after the April hearings, Crafts outlined the committee's possible options, ranging from a redefinition of commercial forest land to omit vulnerable areas to an outright ban on clearcutting in the eastern hardwood forests. An additional option, which Crafts favored, was to direct the Forest Service to roll back the allowable cut by several billion board feet to allow the agency to catch up with the nationwide reforestation backlog. He suggested that if the agency did not show sufficient willingness to change its practices, the threat of new legislation might prove catalytic.[8]

The subcommittee's final report eschewed these measures, reflecting Church's and Metcalf's desire to allow the Forest Service considerable latitude in meeting environmental-quality goals. In March 1972 Church announced a set of guidelines called *Clearcutting on Federal Timberlands* that was developed with the help of the chief forester's office. They specified that allowable cuts could be increased only if intensive management practices were fully funded and could reasonably be expected to work—a provision Ed Cliff had publicly supported and one that gave him the leeway to respond to President Nixon's requests for more timber.[9] The guidelines further stated that clearcutting could be used only where it was "silviculturally essential" and must avoid areas where "soil, slope or other watershed conditions are fragile and subject to major injury." They also stressed the need to protect aesthetics and ensure prompt reforestation. Cutting units were to be kept to a minimum size and shaped to blend with the surrounding forest, and a multidisciplinary review was to be conducted to determine the impacts of a particular sale.

The subcommittee's guidelines, which Cliff agreed to follow, put into play nationwide many of the changes that Neal Rahm and Steve Yurich had already instituted in the Northern Region and were perhaps the most direct legacy of the Bitterroot controversy. In practice, they meant that the era of enormous clearcuts was over and that specialists other than foresters would have a say in the design and location of cutting units. But the guidelines said nothing about logging within roadless areas, protection of critical wildlife habitat, or safeguarding headwater regions, all of which were of supreme importance to the activists in the Bitterroot Valley. Making cutting units smaller, in fact, meant that more were needed to meet timber targets, and spacing requirements meant that more miles of road would have to be constructed in undeveloped watersheds. By leaving allowable cuts where they stood—and even countenancing further increases—the subcommittee failed to relieve the pressure on the field offices that led them to cut corners on so many sales.

By the summer of 1972 the Bitterroot controversy had been subsumed into the anti-clearcutting campaigns of the nation's major environmental groups. While this made it easier for the Montana activists to publicize their cause, it also greased the tracks toward significant confrontations in Congress and the courts—a far different course from the attempts at accommodation and reform that were beginning to take hold in the Bitterroot Valley. Both the Sierra Club and the NRDC made frequent use of the courts to spur federal agencies to adopt stricter environmental standards. John Adams, the NRDC's executive director, came to the Bitterroot in the fall of 1972 to follow up on Laurance Rockefeller's initial examination. Accompanying Adams was one of his group's cofounders, Gifford Bryce Pinchot, the only son of the Forest Service's first chief. Their visit gave Brandborg an opportunity to renew memories of the elder Pinchot, with whom he had visited the Lick Creek timber-sale area in 1937. The son, a retired professor of biology at Johns Hopkins, consulted with various environmental organizations and usually did not grab headlines, but Dale Burk would change that. Burk accompanied Pinchot and Adams on a tour of the Bitterroot's East Fork along with Brandy, Arnold Bolle, and several Forest Service staff, during which he recorded Pinchot's evident shock at seeing expanses of uprooted trees and bare earth. "At one point," Burk wrote, "Pinchot stood in the middle of a vast clearcut of several hundred acres on the Bugle Creek drainage on the Bitterroot, his hands resting on his hips and his head shaking from side to side. 'If my father could see this,' he said, shaking his head, and then his voice choked up. 'But I'm glad he can't,' he finished, almost in a whisper."[10]

It was high theater. "My reaction is that it's appalling, it's unbelievable," Pinchot was quoted as saying. "I think seeing this would have killed my father."[11] Brandborg had taken the group to Bugle Creek to view a clearcut that bordered the Anaconda-Pintler Wilderness Area. At one point, Burk recalls, Brandy walked over to the edge of the unit to locate a wilderness boundary sign, finding it hidden behind a pile of logging slash. A Forest Service staffer told Burk that Pinchot had looked only at older clearcuts and had not seen the results of the more stringent controls that Orville Daniels had instituted. Burk retorted that Pinchot viewed cuttings of "many vintages, including past and present. And, perhaps more damningly, that very response by the agency shows it is still caught in a thinking process that emphasizes timber concerns and not other resource values."

Afterward Brandborg reported to Pinchot that the publicity surrounding his visit was helping to force the agency back on the path that his father had laid out. "This was clearly brought home to me a few days ago when Regional Forester Steve Yurich called on me," he wrote. "During the course of our discussion he said, 'All I want for Christmas is time to orient the thinking of my subordinates to the Old Master's point of view.'" Brandy regarded his discussion with Yurich as a breakthrough. He told Pinchot, "There is nothing further to be gained by continuing a confrontation. While we were together in our back yard last month, we briefly talked about a different approach. A cooperative approach will provide encouragement and will garner strength from many sources."[12]

The clash of interests was far from over, however. The Pinchot tour received as much publicity as Senator McGee's visit to Took Creek and came to symbolize the wide gulf between clearcutting's proponents and opponents. The American Forestry Association ran several articles critical of the younger Pinchot in its magazine *American Forests*. "In the plethora of verbiage that has overloaded our communications media," wrote F. Bruce Lamb, a forester in private practice, "the realities of controlling ecological conditions in the Bitterroot area are almost entirely ignored, even in professionally prepared reports." He faulted Brandborg for neglecting his forest while he was supervisor, leaving it "in an almost completely stagnant condition, riddled with disease and insects, accumulating dangerous amounts of fuel on the ground that make uncontrollably intense and devastating fires an ever-present prospect." Unless these stands were harvested and regenerated, he said, renewal through extensive wildfires was the likely result.[13]

The clearcutting storm had originated in large part on the Bitterroot, so it was appropriate that this forest would serve as a test case for the Northern Region's attempts to reform its timber-management policies. Orville Daniels faced an enormous challenge in dealing with an already polarized constituency in the Bitterroot Valley. He had eliminated or scaled back the high-impact forestry practices that had drawn so much bad press, but the resulting drop in harvest levels threatened a new crisis as the Bitterroot Valley's sawmills ran low on log supplies. Daniels had considerable latitude in setting constraints on individual sales, but he faced insuperable conflicts in determining the land base for the forest's timber program. His timber staff wanted to take the pressure off of the front country close to the Bitterroot Valley, where many drainages had been cut so severely that further logging would risk unacceptable damage to watershed quality and wildlife habitat. Yet with harvesting in the Magruder Corridor stalled, there were few accessible timber stands in the backcountry to choose from. New sales would have to come from the remaining undeveloped drainages on the Montana side of the forest—places in which conservationists saw a panoply of other resource values.

Daniels hoped that his new multidisciplinary approach to planning would minimize conflicts and permit timber operations to go ahead in such areas. He asked John Lowell, his district ranger at Sula, to have another look at a development proposal for the drainage of Moose Creek, located in the headwaters of the East Fork of the Bitterroot River high up against the Sapphire Range's crest. As modified from the original 1967 proposal, Lowell envisioned more than twenty miles of road construction that would permit the initial harvest of 10 million feet of timber—all of which was sorely needed in Darby's mills. The plan met the forest's silvicultural goals, too; the Sleeping Child fire had burned up to the edge of the basin, and staff were concerned that Moose Creek could easily be next. The spruce bark beetle was also flaring up in the drainage, adding some urgency to their project.[14]

To reduce environmental conflicts, the planning team intended to make less use of clearcutting, pay special attention to road design and location, and get input from the forest's new landscape architect and wildlife biologist. All this was explained at a public meeting in Hamilton in June 1971 that drew more than five hundred people—part of the forest's effort to involve citizens early in the process. But none of the foresters' preparations changed the fact that trees would be cut and roads built in a relatively pristine landscape. Moose Creek was a natural extension of the Anaconda-Pintler Wilderness Area, just as Area E in the Magruder Corridor complemented the Selway-Bitterroot Wilderness. The area's meadows, bogs, and deep spruce forests gave ideal summertime cover for a substantial elk and moose herd. Doris Milner was concerned about the steady loss of roadless lands outside of designated wilderness areas; she served notice to Daniels that conservationists would oppose the plan. It was the Selway conflict in miniature: Conservationists wanted to hold on to the idea of a protection forest in the high country, preferably by designating a companion wilderness area to the Anaconda-Pintler along the Sapphire crest. But if the agency could not manage timber in such areas, it would mean yet another drop in the forest's allowable cut.

Guy Brandborg, Don Aldrich, and others joined the protests at the Hamilton meeting, while industry officials turned out a large number of mill workers, loggers, and their families. Milton Van Camp of the S&W mill at Darby, which Intermountain had recently acquired, recalled scouting the area while he was salvaging timber from the Sleeping Child burn in 1962. "I can remember thinking what a miserable place to fight fire Moose Creek would be and it looked like a cinch to burn someday.... The build-up of natural fuels is more impressive to me now than it was ten years ago. Fire danger above all makes managing the upper Moose Creek drainage as a completely roadless area a very poor risk." William Grasser made the same point. As the operator of the Lost Trail ski area, he noted that "I have a first hand view of the Saddle Mountain mess daily, and it's far from recreationally acceptable as a pretty area. It has no leave strips, no wildlife cover, no protection for streams or soils. Orville, instruct your people to do their jobs and harvest all the area suitable and not reserve any because they happen to be visible to a few people for a short time. We can easily press this pure wilderness or back country recreation idea right into forest land neglect."[15]

Concerns about wildfire among Bitter Rooters closely tracked their beliefs about the overall aims of forest land management. Mark Boesch, who had once worked under Charles McDonald on the Stevensville District, said that the Saddle Mountain fire "swept across Highway 93 as though it were not there" and that fuel breaks had only a temporary effect. "Anyone who has ever seen a wildfire whip through a patch of even-aged reproduction during a dry summer will testify to that." Van Camp, Grasser, and Boesch were among the early disputants in the second great controversy on the Bitterroot—one that would come to the fore a quarter century later when enormous wildfires swept through the very areas they were discussing that night.

Brandborg, like Milner, understood the significance of the Moose Creek plan in setting a new direction for the Bitterroot. In years past he had spent many hours with Ravalli County sportsmen trying to resolve conflicts over elk and livestock use in the East Fork. Now its headwaters' forest, which provided the best summer habitat for big game in the drainage, was at risk. "Take a look at Meadow Creek or any other logged area in the East Fork," he asked the Hamilton audience. "Then make up your own mind if that is the way you want the Forest Service to manage your land and your resources.... It will also be obvious that clearcutting and other destructive management practices have seriously altered recreational assets—fish and wildlife habitat, for example, to the extent of jeopardizing the future of the East Fork elk herd."[16]

In a letter to John Lowell the day after the meeting, Brandy pointed out that decades earlier he had examined the area with the region's silvicultural staff, which at that time still adhered to the protection-forest concept. "Regardless of how much dead and down timber there was on the higher elevations and on slow-growing sites, it was our opinion that these sites be reserved for watershed and wildland uses," he wrote. "Water is the life-blood of the Bitterroot, as elsewhere. As you well know, the nation's timber needs can be adequately provided for by growing timber on better sites than Moose Creek." Aiming for a constructive tone, he sympathized with agency staffers who faced pressures from the public. "Though we greatly respect what you are trying to do not only as a forester but as a public employee, this makes it even more important that your decision reflect a line of action that will protect the public interest. You are involved in a decision that incorporates a philosophy of the greatest good to the greatest number in the long run. I appreciate the fact that it is not an easy decision to make."

While Brandborg supported Milner's goal of keeping the Moose Creek area roadless, he saw possibilities for forest management in some drainages if the agency would revise its choice of silvicultural tools. "I believe the problem of managing the resources under your jurisdiction would vanish," he told Daniels, "if you announce that henceforth all future timber sales on the Bitterroot, regardless of species, are going to be disposed of under a selective marking system." He still hoped that the Bitterroot could return to the conservative practices he had employed while supervisor, which he believed would provide a modest flow of logs while retaining the beauty and usefulness of the forest. "Not too many years ago," he wrote, "local timber, business, civic and other organizations supported a program designed to maintain timber supplies on the Bitterroot Forest in perpetuity as a means of providing economic and social stability for the people in the area. The necessary forces are waiting 'in the wings' locally and elsewhere if they are mobilized and directed to secure proper management and full production of all resources on public as well as private lands. This is the basic challenge as I see it."[17]

Faced with what promised to be strong opposition, Daniels decided to delay the Moose Creek sale until the necessary resource studies were complete, which did nothing to aid the valley's mills in the short run. He finally advertised the sale in May 1974 and awarded it to the Intermountain Lumber Company, whereupon a coalition of Montana and national environmental groups blocked it through an administrative appeal. In 1977 Bob Bergland, the incoming secretary of agriculture, rejected all bids on the sale pending disposition of the roadless areas in the Sapphire Range.

The conflict over the Moose Creek sale was repeated in virtually every national forest in western Montana as the Forest Service sought new areas from which to produce wood fiber. Many of these were adjacent to designated wilderness areas and contained approach trails hikers used to reach the high country. As obscure roadless areas from Mount Henry on the Kootenai National Forest to the West Big Hole on the Beaverhead were flagged for logging roads and clearcuts, local activists followed Milner's example and filed administrative appeals demanding that the agency prepare environmental impact statements on the sales. The appeals amounted to little more than delaying actions, but environmental leaders used them to build a record of opposition to the sale program that would give weight to their legal and legislative campaigns. All this made it still harder for the Forest Service to meet its timber-production goals.

Both the agency and environmental groups wanted some way out of the impasse, which consumed tremendous effort on both sides with little resolution on the ground. In August 1971, at the urging of Stewart Brandborg, now the Wilderness Society's executive director, and Mike McCloskey, his counterpart at the Sierra Club, the CEQ prepared a second executive order to require the Forest Service to evaluate all roadless and undeveloped areas under its jurisdiction and determine which were suitable for classification as wilderness. Areas not selected would be released for timber development. The order was never signed, but the Forest Service's leadership agreed with its logic: by settling the undeveloped-lands issue it could get on with its timber program with less interference from environmentalists. Chief Cliff already had on hand a nation-wide list of such areas that he had requested from his regional offices in 1967, which he dusted off for a new round of analyses to be known, memorably, as the Roadless Area Review and Evaluation, or RARE.[18]

The RARE program produced thumbnail analyses of 1,449 individual road-less tracts comprising 56 million acres, setting off a long and contentious strug-gle over the disposition of potential national forest wilderness lands. By June 1972 the agency had narrowed the list of areas it thought should be studied fur-ther for wilderness, and in 1973 Secretary Butz released a list of 274 areas, com-prising 12.3 million acres, which were afforded interim protection pending further analysis. It would be up to the Congress to decide which areas to desig-nate as wilderness and thus settle the debate over their use.

The conservation community throughout the West expressed keen disap-pointment in Butz's decision, particularly for the way in which the Forest Ser-vice had set high hurdles in the path of any new wilderness recommendations. The Bitterroot National Forest proposed only two areas for wilderness study, both in the Magruder Corridor on the Idaho side of the forest, totaling 138,000 acres. The agency could find no areas on the Montana side that it thought were worthy of study, including the Sapphire Range and the drainage of Blue Joint Creek. The agency fragmented these areas along state or national forest boundaries and analyzed them as smaller units; they also faulted them for lack-ing spectacular mountain peaks and lake basins. The scant recommendations nationwide prompted environmental groups to bring suit against Secretary Butz; a settlement in that case required the agency to prepare environmen-tal impact statements on future proposals to build roads or sell timber within roadless areas studied under RARE. This gave further impetus to the agency's multiple-use plans, which now became the vehicles for "releasing" de facto wil-derness area to timber use.[19]

In Montana Milner and her fellow wilderness advocates asked Clif Merritt of the Wilderness Society to devise some kind of legislative surcease from the con-tinual assaults on roadless lands. Merritt assembled a list of ten roadless areas that he and his local cooperators believed were in critical danger. Once again Lee Metcalf was willing to help, and in 1974 he introduced Senate Bill 393, the Montana Wilderness Study Areas Act, which when enacted into law in 1977 required the Forest Service to protect the ten study areas while it conducted an in-depth evaluation of their suitability for wilderness designation. No develop-ment could take place within them until Congress gave the go-ahead—a criti-cal feature, as it turned out. Even before the measure passed, Milner used it to forestall further timber sales within the Sapphire and Blue Joint roadless areas—the two areas on the Bitterroot she and Merritt had picked as most in need of protection. Both areas remained unlogged, forcing Bitterroot Forest supervisor Robert Morgan, who inherited the issue from Orville Daniels, to look elsewhere for timber.

Brandborg and Milner both had close ties to the national environmental movement, but they brought strikingly different temperaments to their work. Milner saw real possibilities in working with the Bitterroot's rangers and supervisory staff on questions of individual timber sales. Her first experience in this regard had been with Harold Andersen, whom she described in a 2002 interview as a "tough old German....I knew I was never gonna get nowhere with him. And so, we just got along." Her approach was the mirror image of Brandborg's, which Andersen resented as meddlesome. Milner had never worked for the Forest Service and saw her role as a concerned outsider. "He was managing the forest, I wasn't," she said.

Later supervisors, especially Daniels and Morgan, appreciated her willingness to consider their positions and not automatically assume that they were in bed with the timber industry. This led Brandy to admonish her that she was spending too much time talking with the men in green. The two leaders recounted some stormy arguments over tactics. "Our relationship has not all been sweetness and light," Milner admitted. Brandy respected her abilities as a leader, though, and he seemed to relish his role as a burr under her saddle. "Doris gives me hell because I'm so rough and tough," he recalled with evident pleasure in 1975.[20] Despite their distinct personalities, they managed to remain friends and continue working together.

Brandy saw no need to back off of his own uncompromising stands, even when dealing with friends and neighbors in Hamilton whom he had known for decades. "The going is gonna be tough," he told Mavis McKelvey in 1975. "I appreciate it right here in this town. You know, my friends are few, because I've taken a position. And, maybe it's my fault, maybe I should have gone to them and said to them, here, you're wrong, but I haven't." As this statement suggests, the concept of active listening did not come easily to him. One forged ahead no matter the opposition. Or, as he told his friends, "to avoid criticism, say nothing, do nothing, be nothing." Still, he occasionally felt that he was not getting the full support of his allies. During a field trip with a group of Forest Service retirees in the summer of 1972 to examine some East Fork clearcuts, he turned to Charles McDonald following one particularly animated discussion. "Damn it!" he told his old friend and colleague. "A fella needs help when he's being skinned out!"[21]

For a time Brandborg offered his support to Neal Rahm and Steve Yurich, hoping they would buck the pressure coming from Washington, but he soon returned to his trenchant critiques, holding these men to a standard they could not reasonably achieve. This was a strategic error; both Rahm and Yurich had put their careers on the line to try to balance other resources with timber management in the Northern Region. Ray Karr, who worked closely with both men throughout the Bitterroot controversy, said that the Washington office remained uneasy with the situation in Montana and never fully accepted their insistence on taking a new direction. Most Montana conservationists, on the other hand, saw their role as applying continuous pressure in the face of one development proposal after another. In dealing with the crises of the moment, they may have missed an opportunity to advance the position of their friends within the agency.

Brandborg's newspaper commentaries and statements at public meetings led many people to believe that he was uncaring or unfeeling of others. Even his supporters in the Bitterroot Valley sometimes felt that he overdid his attacks on agency personnel. He could also deliver stinging rebukes to those in the conservation community whom he thought were not pulling their weight (Don Aldrich recalled Brandy once telling a fellow conservationist that the best thing he could do for the movement would be to leave it). Brandy deeply valued his friends, however. A particularly hard blow came in 1972 when he learned that Champ Hannon was dying of cancer. Hannon told Brandy how difficult it was for him not to live to see the end of their quest for better forest management—a battle for which he had recruited Brandborg four years earlier. In October, following one of their last visits together, Brandy returned home and tearfully shared with Ruth his grief at losing one of his closest friends. Following Hannon's death in December, Dale Burk memorialized him as "firm, resolute, honest, courageous and quietly outspoken" as well as "a gentle, happy man with great sensitivity and goodness of heart."[22]

In 1973 Doris Milner was elected president of the Montana Wilderness Association, a position she held for four years. Her duties expanded beyond the Bitterroot as she organized volunteer efforts to protect wild forest areas across the state. A gregarious and outgoing leader, Milner was able to draw in students attending Montana's two universities as well as old-line progressives who wanted to change the state's image as a friend to resource-extraction interests. Besides building support for Metcalf's Senate Bill 393, she spent much time assisting grassroots activists working to secure wilderness designation for the Middle Fork of the Flathead region and the lofty Absaroka-Beartooth mountains north of Yellowstone National Park. Dale Burk was closely involved in the Middle Fork campaign and authored a book, titled *Great Bear, Wild River,* that extolled the area. Burk joined Milner on trips to Washington to testify at hearings on Lee Metcalf's Great Bear Wilderness legislation, which was passed in 1978 following the senator's death.

As chairman of the MWA's forestry committee, Brandborg exhorted its members to not lose sight of the fundamental issue underlying the loss of Montana's wild areas. "We are very close to the end of a long, long struggle to come to grips with the consequences of decades of forest exploitation," he told the group at its 1973 annual meeting. "We cannot afford to digress until all forest land resources are scientifically managed and until that objective is adequately financed. This course of action will best assure protection of backcountry and wilderness values."[23] Although Brandy supported new wilderness designations, he believed that simply setting aside such areas would not cure the basic problem of forest land use. His concern with the fundamentals of land management—encompassing both land conservation and economic reform—was unusual among Montana's conservation leadership.

Milner's and Brandborg's divergent approaches presaged a deeper split within the Montana conservation community between its radical activists and its more accommodationist reformers. Many public lands activists who came of age during the 1960s believed that the federal government was inextricably entwined with large business interests and could offer little in the way of environmental leadership. To them, the Forest Service had been captured by the industry it was supposed to regulate. As one Sierra Club lobbyist remarked in 1974, "It is very hard these days to separate the profession of forestry from the profession of business management of a large industrial corporation."[24]

Brandborg enjoyed working with Montana's younger activists and shared their distrust of corporate America. He counseled them on tactics and in 1973 helped Helena environmental activists Phil and Robin Tawney establish a legislative lobbying group called the Environmental Information Center. But for all his populist leanings, he still believed that government could improve the lives of ordinary people, and he held a deep faith in the possibility of a satisfying and progressive agrarian life. Nor did his views always mesh with the most recent incarnations of Democratic Party liberalism during President Kennedy's New Frontier or President Johnson's Great Society. Despite the advances those programs made in civil rights and fighting poverty, their natural resource policies were wedded to the full-production imperative. Johnson, in fact, relied on national forest timber-sale receipts to help stanch the red ink from his social programs and war venture. Calling on the Forest Service to alleviate housing crises and budget shortfalls was well-established practice by the time Richard Nixon and Earl Butz took office.

More than any pronouncements from the White House, though, it was the profound shift in orientation among Forest Service leaders during the 1950s and 1960s that was hardest for old-timers such as Brandborg, Hannon, and McDonald to accept. These men had reached line-officer positions in the Forest Service at a time when chiefs Silcox, Clapp, and Watts were actively promoting federal acquisition and regulation of private lands. Brandy and his friends still believed in these kinds of strong government action to better people's lives and wondered what had changed from the days when their superiors stood up to industry lobbyists. To them, the agency had lost its essential integrity; its current leaders, Brandy wrote on the eve of the Bitterroot controversy, suffered from "a disease of bureaucratic autocracy, where one man too often calls the shots, and where there is more concern over status and image projection than there is over doing a needed job even at the expense of fighting special interests opposed to the end of abuse."

He particularly objected to how the Hatch Act, which enjoined federal employees from taking part in election campaigns, had been used to stifle dissent within the agency. He knew from personal experience that rocking the boat often brought swift disapproval and sometimes demotion or transfer, and, thinking of friends such as Earl Sandvig, he lamented the loss of "able administrators...cast into limbo because they are men with conscience and a sense of duty."[25] But when Forest Service leaders in Montana attempted to change direction, however tentatively, Brandy found it difficult to publicly support them. His demand that civil servants comprehensively challenge the status quo proved to be an unattainable ideal. In the end he could not abide the compromises that men like Rahm, Yurich, and Daniels had to make in the face of overwhelming pressure from above. These leaders would move the Northern Region marginally away from its heavy timber orientation, but they could not escape conflict with those who sought more fundamental changes in its forestry program.

PLATE 1. Guy M. Brandborg in 1969. *Courtesy of Dale A. Burk.*

PLATE 2. Guy Brandborg showed the terraced clearcuts of Took Creek to Wyoming senator Gale McGee in August 1971. McGee's reaction: "The worst I've seen." *Courtesy of Dale A. Burk.*

PLATE 3. Terraced clearcut in the Mud Creek drainage, West Fork Ranger District. Terracing was astonishingly successful in regenerating ponderosa pine—and equally effective in arousing adverse public opinion. *Courtesy of USDA Forest Service, BNF Archives.*

PLATE 4. Terraced clearcuts above Took Creek, West Fork District, Bitterroot National Forest, 1974. One newspaper account likened such scenes to "man-made pyramids for a weird science fiction film." *Courtesy of USDA Forest Service, BNF Archives.*

PLATE 5. Today the hillsides at Took Creek are clothed with young ponderosa pine. Douglas fir (*foreground*) have reseeded from the edge of the cutting unit in this 2008 photo. *Photo by author.*

PLATE 6. Springtime in the Bitterroot Valley, 1952. Como Peaks in background. *Photo by R. H. McKay, courtesy of Archives and Special Collections, University of Montana–Missoula.*

PLATE 7. Hauling logs from the East Fork of the Bitterroot River in the 1890s. *Photo by Bertie Lord, courtesy of the Ravalli County Museum.*

PLATE 8. The Anaconda Company's sawmill outside of Hamilton, Montana, closed in 1915, after which the company shipped logs by rail to its mill in Bonner, near Missoula. *Courtesy of Archives and Special Collections, University of Montana–Missoula.*

PLATE 9. An Anaconda Company official inspects part of the Lick Creek timber sale in 1909. Selective harvesting was well established as Forest Service doctrine in the agency's early days. *Photo by W. J. Lubken, courtesy of USDA Forest Service, Northern Region Archives.*

PLATE 10. The family of Charles and Betsy Brandborg (*seated, front row*), about 1905. Guy is to his father's right. *Courtesy of Stewart Brandborg.*

PLATE 11. Brandy (*center*) with coworker Frank Jefferson (*left*) and ranger Stanley Sanderson (*right*) on the Lewis and Clark National Forest, about 1916. *Courtesy of Stewart Brandborg.*

PLATE 12. Brandy (*disguised as cook*) and friends on the Lewis and Clark National Forest, about 1916. Note the extensive burned area. *Courtesy of Stewart Brandborg.*

PLATE 13. G. M. Brandborg during his ranger days on the Helena National Forest. *Courtesy of USDA Forest Service, Helena NF.*

PLATE 15. Edna Stevenson of Radersburg, Montana. She and Brandy were married in 1924. *Courtesy of Stewart Brandborg.*

PLATE 16. The Brandborg family in the early 1930s. *From left:* Guy, Edna, Stewart, and Becky. *Courtesy of Stewart Brandborg.*

Plate 17. Lookout construction, Nezperce National Forest, 1920s. Assistant forest supervisor Clyde Blake is perched on the roof, with the seasonal lookout inside. Note hand-hewn support timbers. The cabin appears to be a prefabricated D1 or D6 model, a twelve-by-twelve-foot design with an observation cupola, which was often erected without a support tower. *Courtesy of Stewart Brandborg.*

Plate 18. Guy Brandborg (*left*) and Clyde Blake hewed logs for the cabin of this R3-style lookout. The horse is Sage King, Brandy's favorite. *Courtesy of Stewart Brandborg.*

PLATE 19. Brandborg's duties on the Nezperce included monitoring sheep allotments such as this one on the scenic slopes below the Seven Devils Mountains in 1925. *Photo by K. D. Swan, courtesy of USDA Forest Service, Nezperce NF.*

PLATE 20. Three generations of Bitterroot National Forest personnel pause during a 1935 field trip to the Lick Creek timber-sale area. *Kneeling, from left:* former supervisor W. W. White, former ranger Than Wilkerson, and ranger Clyde Schockley. *Standing, from left:* Joe Hessel, Philip Neff, Kenneth Davis, Guy Brandborg, Leslie Eddy, Stan Lawson, I. V. Anderson, Russell Fitzgerald, Albert Cochrell, Harold Lewis, and Harley Hartson. *Courtesy of USDA Forest Service, BNF Archives.*

PLATE 21. Sawmill in the Burnt Fork drainage in the northern Bitterroot Valley, about 1935. Brandborg tried to offer small timber sales to support such outfits, which often were an adjunct to a family farm or ranch and supplied lumber for local use. *Courtesy of Ravalli County Museum.*

PLATE 22. Part of the "golden stream" of fine ponderosa pine sawlogs headed for the Anaconda Company's Bonner mill in 1940. *Photo by K. D. Swan, courtesy of USDA Forest Service, Northern Region Archives.*

PLATE 23. Evan W. Kelley, regional forester for the Northern Region, 1929–1944. *Courtesy of USDA Forest Service, Northern Region Archives.*

PLATE 24. G. M. Brandborg, Bitterroot National Forest supervisor from 1935 to 1955. *Courtesy of USDA Forest Service, BNF Archives.*

PLATE 25. Depleted range, Bitterroot National Forest, 1938. Forest Service personnel had to deal with the historical overuse of the public's land, shown above the fence. The private land below the fence displays better care. *Courtesy of USDA Forest Service, BNF Archives.*

PLATE 26. Headwaters of Fred Burr Creek in the Selway-Bitterroot Wilderness Area, 1964. *Photo by Charles McDonald, courtesy of USDA Forest Service, Northern Region Archives.*

PLATE 27. View north across the Magruder Corridor from Salmon Mountain on the Idaho side of the Bitterroot National Forest. The Forest Service's attempts to open this area to logging in the 1960s ignited the first major citizen protest on the Bitterroot. *Photo by K. D. Swan, courtesy of USDA Forest Service, Northern Region Archives.*

PLATE 28. Doris Milner of Hamilton, Montana, led protests over logging in the Magruder Corridor in the 1960s and joined Guy Brandborg in opposing large-scale clearcutting on the Bitterroot. *Courtesy of Doris Milner family.*

PLATE 29. Charles H. McDonald, Stevensville district ranger from 1944 to 1964 and a critic of the Bitterroot's timber-management policies. *Courtesy of USDA Forest Service, Northern Region Archives.*

PLATE 30. The Sleeping Child fire of August 1961 was the first major blaze on the Montana side of the Bitterroot National Forest since the Forest Service began fire-protection efforts. *Photo by E. A. Hanson, courtesy of USDA Forest Service, Northern Region Archives.*

PLATE 31. Timber-salvage operations from the Sleeping Child fire netted 90 million board feet of lodgepole pine and other species, sparking the growth of nearby sawmills and fueling the subsequent clearcutting controversy. *Photo by Richard Venable, courtesy of USDA Forest Service, BNF Archives.*

PLATE 32. Foresters on the Bitterroot began clearcutting stands such as this one in Guide Creek in 1957. Reforestation (shown here in 1965) was not always this successful and led to more drastic site-preparation methods. *Photo by Danny On, courtesy of USDA Forest Service, BNF Archives.*

Plate 33. A logging unit in ponderosa pine on lower Willow Mountain, Stevensville Ranger District. Seedling survival tended to be poor in such areas owing to competition from grasses. Terracing, the foresters found, was the answer. *Courtesy of USDA Forest Service, BNF Archives.*

Plate 34. Terracing as a site-preparation method came into widespread use on the Bitterroot National Forest in 1964. The lower drainage of Little Blue Joint Creek, shown here in 1967, was one of the most heavily cut. *Courtesy of USDA Forest Service, BNF Archives.*

PLATE 35. Yarding ponderosa pine in the Overwhich Creek drainage, West Fork district, 1964. *Courtesy of USDA Forest Service, BNF Archives.*

PLATE 36a. Reforesting a terraced clearcut using the Rocky Mountain Tree Planter, Blue Joint Creek, 1965. The operator faces to the rear and drops seedlings into a furrow carved by the bulldozer. *Photo by Ernst Peterson, courtesy of USDA Forest Service, BNF Archives.*

PLATE 36b. Rocky Mountain Tree Planter in operation, about 1965. The blades in front of the operator extend into the ground and close the furrow around the seedling. *Photo by Ernst Peterson, courtesy of USDA Forest Service, BNF Archives.*

PLATE 37. Terraced clearcut in Mud Creek awaits planting. *Courtesy of USDA Forest Service, BNF Archives.*

PLATE 38. Clearcuts in the Little Sleeping Child drainage. *Photo by Ernst Peterson, courtesy of USDA Forest Service, BNF Archives.*

PLATE 39. Key Forest Service officials in the Northern Region (*clockwise from top left*): Axel Lindh, chief of timber management during the 1940s; Neal Rahm, regional forester during the late 1960s; William R. "Bud" Moore, chief of fire and aviation during the same period; and Orville Daniels, Bitterroot National Forest supervisor from 1970 to 1974. *Courtesy of USDA Forest Service, Northern Region Archives.*

PLATE 40. The Del Conner sawmill south of Darby, Montana, in 1966, at the height of the logging boom on the Bitterroot. Note the extensive log decks. *Photo by Scott Brown, courtesy of Clarence Strong Collection, Special Collections and Archives, University of Montana–Missoula.*

PLATE 41. Arnold Bolle, dean of the School of Forestry at the University of Montana, 1970. *Courtesy of R. W. Behan.*

PLATE 42. *Missoulian* reporter Dale Burk broke the clearcutting story in western Montana in 1969. *Courtesy of Dale A. Burk.*

PLATE 43. G. M. Brandborg, *New York Times* reporter Gladwin Hill, and former ranger Champ Hannon in May 1971. *Courtesy of Dale A. Burk.*

PLATE 44. Sierra Club activist Brock Evans was at the center of public lands battles in the Northwest during the 1960s and early 1970s. He toured the Bitterroot with Guy Brandborg and Dale Burk in 1969 and likened the forest's terraced clearcuts to strip mines. *Courtesy of Dale A. Burk.*

PLATE 45. Senator Frank Church (*right*) confers with a Subcommittee on Public Lands staffer at hearings on clearcutting practices in April 1971. *Courtesy of Dale A. Burk.*

PLATE 46. Wine magnate and fishing enthusiast Otto Teller (*left*) provided material support to Brandy's campaign to reform forest practices. *Courtesy of Dale A. Burk.*

PLATE 47. CBS News reporter Richard Threlkeld interviewed Guy Brandborg in advance of the Senate hearings on clearcutting practices in April 1971. *Courtesy of Dale A. Burk.*

PLATE 48. Skid trail in the Bugle Creek drainage, East Fork Bitterroot River, July 1971. Such practices caused localized erosion and were among those the Northern Region wanted to prevent in future timber sales. *Courtesy of Dale A. Burk.*

PLATE 49. Roads typically are greater sources of stream sediment in forest landscapes than clearcuts. Critics of the Biterroot National Forest timber program pointed to instances such as this muddy logging spur in the Sleeping Child drainage. *Courtesy of Dale A. Burk.*

PLATE 50. The Northern Region's Bitterroot Task Force cited poor road construction and maintenance as a primary cause of stream sedimentation. *Courtesy of USDA Forest Service, BNF Archives.*

PLATE 51. In attempting to clear huge firebreaks along the Continental Divide, the Forest Service left itself open to charges of forest devastation. The "Oh-My-God" clearcut in the East Fork of the Bitterroot River became a poster child for environmentalists, including activists Otto Teller and Doris Milner, shown at far right on a 1973 forest tour. *Courtesy of Dale A. Burk.*

PLATE 52. Ponderosa seedlings in terrace, West Fork District. *Courtesy of USDA Forest Service, BNF Archives.*

PLATE 53. BNF personnel employed bulldozer scarification to prepare a new seedbed after clearcutting. Teepee Point, Sula District. *Courtesy of USDA Forest Service, BNF Archives.*

PLATE 54. Thinned ponderosa pine, lower West Fork drainage, 2007. The Forest Service is making more use of prescribed fire in an attempt to re-create presettlement conditions in such stands. *Photo by author.*

PLATE 55. To log or not to log? Bitterroot Valley activist Larry Campbell examines a live ponderosa pine damaged by adjacent timber felling in the Middle East Fork timber sale, 2007. *Photo by author.*

PLATE 56. Guy M. Brandborg, 1970. *Courtesy of R. W. Behan.*

PLATE 57. Lee Metcalf, Montana senator from 1960 to 1978. *Courtesy of Montana Wilderness Association.*

PLATE 58. Brandborg family, about 1970. *Standing, from left:* Stewart and Guy. *Sitting, from left:* Ruth Brandborg, Beki Brandborg (daughter of Stewart and Anna Vee Brandborg), Virginia Carney (friend of family), Alice Calhoun (neighbor child), and Becky Simons (sister of Stewart). *Courtesy of Stewart Brandborg.*

Charting a Workable Future

1971–1976

After suffering body blows at the Church hearings and in the national press, Forest Service leaders at all levels of the agency realized that they must show more concern for recreation, wildlife, wilderness, and watershed protection or face onerous restrictions from Congress. To better integrate long-neglected forest values into actual practice, chief Ed Cliff issued a directive in November 1971 that formalized the multiple-use planning process for all national forests.[1] Attempts of this sort had a long history within the Forest Service, dating at least to the Copeland Report of 1933, but with few exceptions (such as the Bitterroot's efforts of the early 1950s), the emphasis was on writing so-called functional plans for individual resources. These typically made little reference to each other and generally assumed that timbering would take precedence on west-side forests.

The Multiple Use–Sustained Yield Act of 1960 clearly required a more integrated planning effort, but it remained up to individual forests to decide how to proceed. In 1972 Orville Daniels brought in a planning officer to help create detailed management plans for major subdrainages of the Bitterroot River. The first of these covered the Burnt Fork drainage of the northern Sapphire Range, in which twenty-one thousand acres of higher-elevation lodgepole forests were to be managed as a backcountry area in which little logging would be done, while another twenty-nine thousand acres of roadless lands were allocated to some form of timber production.[2]

Daniels's major innovation was to create a forestwide multiple-use plan to elaborate upon the reform-minded directives issued in the wake of the Bitterroot controversy. Mostly a statement of planning principles, it left specifics such as timber-cutting levels to the unit plans. But unlike the resource-specific plans of the 1960s, timber management was expected to take its place alongside, and in many cases subordinate to, the Bitterroot's other resources. Some of its language would have astonished a production forester of the old school. "Though some good tree-growing sites are present," the plan stated, "recreation including esthetics and natural beauty, high quality water, and wildlife offer the greatest management opportunities, and both local and distant public demand for these values is strong. On the other hand, there is a high degree of economic demand and local dependency for timber from the National Forest. Thus, because logging has strong potential to adversely affect other values, the challenge is to manage most land for recreation, water, wilderness, and wildlife values while furnishing a reasonable supply of commercial wood products."[3]

The plan acknowledged that only 12 percent of the Bitterroot's commercial forest land was of good quality for growing timber crops. Up to half of the CFL, moreover, lay on slopes exceeding 60 percent, and thus was subject to excessive soil disturbance and visual scarring from roads. Wood volumes per acre were below the regional average, and regrowth of vegetation on many sites was slow. For the first time the Bitterroot was laying out the ecological and social limits to wood-fiber production—something no previous administrator, even Guy Brandborg, had explicitly quantified.

To deal with the new reality of forest management in a fishbowl, Daniels called for each employee to develop an ethic that respected the capabilities of the forest and the wishes of the public. "A land ethic is the result of an emotional and intellectual process," he wrote in a preface to the plan. "It is important to have a sensitivity to the ecological balance and unity of our ecosystems, realizing a change in one part will always affect another.... Only after the fullest possible understanding and an evaluation of gains and losses, should any change in the ecosystem be made."[4] Such statements, if put into practice, would close the door on a quarter century of what Arnold Bolle termed *timber primacy*—the root cause of the Forest Service's difficulties with the public.

The prominence given ecological values in the 1972 forest plan irritated proponents of the Bitterroot's timber industry, including William Grasser of the S&W firm. "I repeatedly find the plan to be over-intoxicated with recreation concerns," he told Daniels. Maintaining viewing areas would come at the cost of growing timber, all for the benefit of "a transient public that for a greater part are ignorant of land reform and timber needs of our local area."[5]

The individuals behind the Bitterroot controversy were hardly transients; most had lived in the valley for decades, if not their whole lives, and their concerns extended well beyond the amenity issues of recreation and aesthetics. Brandborg had been claiming since the 1930s that private forest lands in the Bitterroot were being overcut, which had led to excessive pressure to log the national forest. "Everything that will make a noise in a sawmill is now being cut," he told Lee Metcalf in March 1974. "A large part of these materials is from clearcuts on watershed lands."[6] Forest depletion was a difficult assertion to prove, however. The 1943 Zach and Hutchison report made similar assertions, but industry, as Brandborg noted, managed to utilize younger and younger stands, delaying their ultimate exhaustion.

Another Forest Service study issued in late 1974 through the Intermountain Forest and Range Experiment Station buttressed Brandborg's assertions of dwindling private timber stocks. Innocuously titled *The Rocky Mountain Timber Situation, 1970*, the report assessed timber supplies on public and private lands from Montana to Arizona. Its authors, Alan Green and Theodore Setzer, determined that decades of heavy logging on lands owned by the forest industry in the Rocky Mountains were due to end in the near future. In 1970 production from these lands reached a peak of 983 mmbf, but they projected this figure to fall by more than half as industry was forced to balance cutting with the rate of growth on its own lands. "The present level of sawtimber cut cannot be maintained except perhaps in Region 4," they warned (this was the Intermountain Region, which took in Wyoming, Colorado, Utah, and southern Idaho). Montana's forest industry, the report strongly implied, was in for a rough ride during the next several decades.[7]

Whereas the authors of Bolle Report zeroed in on one famously controversial area and then generalized to the entire national forest system, Green and Setzer looked at the overall timber-supply situation, which allowed their troubling conclusions to be largely ignored. This time, unlike in the 1930s and 1940s, the national forests could not be counted upon to relieve the situation. The heavy cutting on private lands was the massive unseen planet whose pull affected everything else in the system—including harvests on adjacent national forest lands, which in some cases had to be restricted in order to avoid further damage to watersheds. The leadoff began in 1972 when the Anaconda Company sold its timber holdings, along with its mill and plywood facilities in Bonner, to

U.S. Plywood–Champion (later Champion International). Instead of reducing its cutting to match growth, the new owners embarked on a plan of rapid liquidation to establish faster-growing young stands, increasing lumber production by 50 percent by 1979. The lumbering spree continued into the 1980s as the state's largest industrial owners—primarily Champion and the Plum Creek Timber Company, which acquired the extensive timberlands once owned by the Northern Pacific—converted standing trees to cash in order to pay off high-interest bonds.[8]

By this time several of the Bitterroot's mills were already shuttered—victims of a scenario that had played out earlier after the Anaconda Company logged most of its timber holdings in the valley. But there was little the agency could do to make up for the drawdown of private stocks, short of pursuing every last stick of timber in roadless areas. No matter how often Brandborg and others raised the alarm, the forces of the regional timber economy ground relentlessly toward their own end.

In the winter of 1974, after observing a heavy mountain snowpack that threatened to create high runoff early in the summer, Brandborg's thoughts again turned to W. C. Lowdermilk's thesis on the lasting impacts of poor land use on human societies. Two years earlier Ravalli County had suffered $1.5 million in flood damage to its roads, bridges, and private property—exacerbated, he believed, by higher peak flows coming off the clearcuts on the national forest. In February he shared his thoughts with Thurman Trosper and Don Aldrich. "I predict—and I hope I am wrong—that with the heavy snow pack and its high water content, especially if rains occur during the peak of the run-off, damage to stream habitat and property in western Montana will exceed anything heretofore experienced."[9]

His fears were justified. When the weather warmed in June, many streams in western Montana and northern Idaho spilled their banks. The lower Bitterroot River crested at 29,000 cubic feet per second (cfs)—a fifty-year flood event. Bank erosion tore out part of a main irrigation siphon across the river, which required $300,000 in repairs; more than $1 million of damage was done to irrigation canals in the valley. At Darby, in the river's upper basin, the river was carrying more than 11,000 cfs, virtually as high as in the flood years of 1947 and 1948. Brandborg commented in the *Missoulian* that "sandbagging, dike and other repairs are not abiding solutions to flood problems. Most floods in Montana are a direct result of mismanagement of forest and grasslands." Heavy snowpacks had occurred earlier in the century, he said, but without causing as much damage during the melt. He cited the experience of Forest and Agnes Cooper, who owned a ranch near the mouth of Rye Creek south of Darby. Neither they nor their parents had experienced damaging floods until 1948, following heavy cutting on private lands in the creek's headwaters.[10]

Whether clearcutting contributed to floods was a subject of long contention within forestry circles. The Forest Service was conducting controlled watershed experiments on the Fraser Experimental Forest in Colorado that showed significant increases in peak flows and total water discharge following strip clearcutting.[11] A study of a considerably larger forest watershed in Idaho, in which about one-fourth of the lodgepole pine cover was harvested, also showed definite increases in peak flows.[12] With much of the Bitterroot National Forest's high country still uncut, it was a considerable leap to assign blame for the floods to clearcutting, yet an increase in peak flows from logged areas could have marginally added to flood heights. Brandborg, however, saw in the floods of 1974 grim forebodings of landscape destruction and economic ruin. In the spring of 1975, another high-water year, he and Ruth made a long auto trip through north-central Montana, revisiting scenes from his days as a young ranger on the Lewis and Clark and Helena national forests. He reported his observations to Senator Metcalf:

> *Every* stream, large and small (Sun River, Teton, Milk, Musselshell, including the Missouri River) was flowing thick with the black soil which came from severely eroded farmlands, severely overgrazed public and private grasslands, clearcut and overcut private and public forest lands. In crossing the Divide, heading for Townsend in the Helena Forest, we found Deep Creek running black within about four miles of the Divide. There was increased silting as we proceeded down the canyon—all the result of misuse of public forest lands. When I left the Helena Forest in 1924 to serve a ten-year stint on the Nez Perce in Idaho, Deep Creek was a blue-ribbon trout stream, besides being an attractive, much used recreational area. Despite Montana's dependence on tourism, natural resource management is literally destroying these assets, statewide. In short, without question, Montana's very next generation is headed for a lower standard of living, thus suffering the hard experiences of hordes of people in foreign lands.[13]

Degradation of forests, farmlands, and rangelands brought poverty to rural areas, he believed, and ultimately to whole nations and civilizations. Yet these larger questions of land use proved harder to grapple with than the clearcuts he had long decried. Assessing land-use trends required a long perspective: he and his friends in the Bitterroot Valley had the experience but lacked the scientific training and credibility needed to make their accusations stick.

The Brandborgs' trip that spring included a visit with one of Montana's best-known students of the land. A. B. Guthrie Jr., author of the Pulitzer Prize–winning novel *The Big Sky*, had corresponded with Brandy since 1970 about mutual friends such as Bernard DeVoto and the battles over the stockmen's bills of an earlier era. In June 1974 Brandy, Ruth, and Dale Burk took Guthrie on a tour of the Bitterroot National Forest's clearcut areas. Afterward Guthrie sent Brandborg a copy of a script he had written for a documentary film being produced at Montana State University in Bozeman. It detailed various threats facing Montana's landscape—clearcuts, subdivisions, coal strip mines, factory pollution—and ended with a call for environmental redemption. "Where is the voice of Montana?" Guthrie wrote. "Whose is that voice? Where is the voice of fact, of prescience, of anger and thunder? Who can command heed? I listen for that voice."[14] He, like Brandborg, felt the anguish of prophecy ignored.

The Brandborgs invited Guthrie to return later that year to speak to Hamilton's League of Women Voters group, in which Ruth was active and Brandy had joined as its first male member. Guthrie urged its members to "fight past and present Forest Service policy down to the last ditch." Observing that he was often accused of being antiprogress, he retorted, "I can't stand against progress because I don't know what it is. Neither does anyone else. Better to call it change, and change, though it may jingle the cash register, is no good if it comes at the cost of old and real values."[15]

The Guthries owned a summer cabin on the Teton River at the edge of the Rocky Mountains, country Brandy knew well from his first years with the Forest Service. "Don't you ever get over that way?" Guthrie wrote the following May. "All trespass signs will be removed and all gates unlocked on word that you are coming. There may even be—no, there will be—a bottle to loosen tongues and sharpen ears."[16] Ruth and Brandy stopped by during their eastern Montana jaunt; their conversation is unfortunately not recorded, but both men shared a doubtful outlook on questions of human land use. Boone Caudill, the young antihero of *The Big Sky*, epitomized how the reckless waste of nature's bounty went hand-in-hand with ruined lives. Brandborg did not possess Guthrie's outstanding ability to invoke the sweep of the Montana plains, but his voice was no less prophetic.

The Bitterroot floods prompted Brandborg to once again ask Lee Metcalf to obtain an Environmental Protection Agency study of the Bitterroot.[17] Metcalf was reluctant to sponsor another round of investigations, but he used his influence out of respect for his friend. This time Brandborg left nothing to chance, assembling twelve local supporters at his home to present their concerns to a staffer from the EPA's Denver office. Ruth chaired the meeting and allotted time for each Bitter Rooter to detail his views. Forest Cooper related his observations of flooding in Rye Creek; George Holman, a retired teacher, told how the Bitterroot River had swept away a dozen large ponderosa pines from his land north of Hamilton. John Brennan, a retired air force officer who owned timberland in the West Fork drainage, remarked on excessive turbidity in the West Fork as a result of logging on steep slopes in Woods Creek, located above Painted Rocks Reservoir. He attributed changes in the river's channel to high peak flows coming off the forest. Stanton Cooper reiterated the views of ranchers in the Sleeping Child area regarding past damage to their irrigation works.[18]

Brandborg suggested that the EPA look at the Moose Creek sale area, as well as a proposed sale in upper Lick Creek, adjacent to the drainage's historical selective harvests. "Selling [this] volume of timber on the Upper Lick Creek, with the other sales scheduled for 1975, supports the conviction that the Bitterroot Forest, already cut beyond its sustained yield capacity, is fast exhausting its timber supplies," he wrote in a letter cosigned by nine others. "The issue is maintaining a forest economy in perpetuity."[19]

The EPA had no mandate to examine economic issues or calculate sustained yield, and the Army Corps of Engineers was the lead federal agency when it came to flood control, but EPA regional director John Green promised to look at the Lick Creek sale and take the allegations of erosion into account. The results greatly disappointed Brandborg's group. Judging the sale "to be proper, adequately safeguarded and not a potential hazard to water quality," Green determined that no further study would be undertaken. The staff report stated that "although the aesthetic impact of this practice is severe the resultant impact on water quality does not seem to have been excessive. The most severe impact on the water resource was undoubtedly the increased peak flows generated from cutover areas." Brandborg believed that the denial reflected pressure from above—what he termed "the long standing instruction that one federal agency should not criticize another federal agency."[20]

Most resource professionals who were familiar with the Northern Region gave the Forest Service credit for making a sincere effort to improve its work and were reluctant to second-guess the results. The close scrutiny that citizens gave timber sales on the Bitterroot National Forest also ensured that fewer mistakes were being made on the ground. Supervisors Daniels and Morgan, aware of this scrutiny, made sure that their staffs and contractors paid attention to the new guidelines. Their efforts did not satisfy the Bitterroot dissidents, who still felt that the overall timber cut was too high and depended too much on logging in road-less areas. But the criticism coming from Brandy and his friends was starting to appear overdone to many individuals who otherwise might have sided with the conservationists. The agency in Montana had responded to the public's concerns, if only halfway, and it was enough to relieve the worst of the pressure.

The turnaround on the Bitterroot, although incomplete in the eyes of local activists, may have saved it from becoming the legal test case that the Natural Resources Defense Council had considered in 1972. Instead, the group's lawyers targeted the Monongahela National Forest of West Virginia, where sportsmen and conservationists had been battling the Forest Service for nearly a decade. In 1973 the NRDC joined with the Sierra Club's legal defense fund to bring suit against the agency, working with a local chapter of the Izaak Walton League and the West Virginia Highlands Conservancy. The decision in *Izaak Walton League v. Butz,* as the case was known, hinged on a strict interpretation of the Forest Service's 1897 Organic Act, which limited timber harvesting to the removal of dead, mature, or large-growth trees that were individually marked for sale. In the mixed-hardwood forests of the Monongahela, clearcutting clearly violated the agency's original charter. The district court decision applied only to that forest, but following the government's unsuccessful appeal to the Fourth Circuit Court, which was finally resolved in August 1975, the clearcutting ban stood on firm legs throughout the eastern states.[21]

Forest Service leaders and the timber industry feared that environmental groups would try to extend the ruling nationwide, with devastating effects on the agency's timber-sale program. A return to selective logging, they argued, would mean reductions of up to 50 percent in sale volumes. The national environmental groups chose not to pursue an aggressive legal strategy, fearing that the political backlash would harm their chances of obtaining suitable timber-reform legislation.[22]

The Monongahela decision affirmed Champ Hannon's and Guy Brandborg's style of labor-intensive, boots-on-the-ground forestry that they had practiced during an earlier era. Brandy congratulated Gordon Robinson for his work in helping prepare the case and asked the NRDC staff whether a similar lawsuit might be initiated on the Bitterroot. But the case had such broad implications for the Forest Service that it could be resolved only in Congress—as the Fourth Circuit had suggested in its decision. What had begun as local, independently conceived struggles in several states had finally coalesced into a clash between the ascendant forces of environmentalism and the twenty-five-year-old alliance of convenience between the Forest Service and the timber industry.

Although Lee Metcalf had broken ranks with that alliance, he still hoped to find some accommodation that would permit logging to continue. In February 1976 he sent Brandborg a draft of a bill to be introduced by Senator Hubert Humphrey in an attempt to resolve the issues unleashed by the Fourth Circuit, whose decision still stood ready for application by the first environmental group that cared to use it. These groups were loath to let go of the 1897 Organic Act's evident prohibition of clearcutting, but they knew that the threat of litigation was a potent bargaining tool with which to obtain strong protective language in a new bill. Their congressional allies, however, including Metcalf, understood that they would have to replace the older language with something less restrictive.

Chief John McGuire had his staff working on language that would legalize even-age management simply by allowing forests to designate blocks of timber for cutting, as had always been done in laying out clearcutting sales, instead of marking individual trees. He also wanted the autonomy to choose management prescriptions that met varied silvicultural needs without setting stringent requirements on logging practices. The agency's proposal was not made public, but parts of it were incorporated into Senate Bill 3091, Senator Humphrey's amendment to the Resources Planning Act—legislation he had sponsored in 1974 to aid the Forest Service's budget-making process.[23]

A key part of the Humphrey bill required the Forest Service to produce comprehensive management plans for each national forest. These would be prepared according to Service-wide standards and would attempt to coordinate all uses of the forest, from wood-fiber production to wilderness. Public participation in the development of these plans, it was hoped, would help avoid the unremitting conflict of the past decade.[24] This did not satisfy environmental advocates who wanted a more prescriptive approach to regulating cutting practices. Jennings Randolph agreed to introduce their alternative to the Humphrey bill, which was drafted by four individuals who had taken prominent roles in the clearcutting debate: retired forester Ralph Smoot, forestry professor Leon Minckler, the Sierra Club's Gordon Robinson, and Arnold Bolle of the University of Montana. Randolph's Senate Bill 2926, introduced in February 1976, included limits on the size and spacing of clearcuts, required long growing rotations of two to three hundred years, and specified that timber-harvest levels from each ranger district must be maintained on a nondeclining, even-flow basis.[25]

Bolle provided Brandborg with an advance copy of the Randolph bill and asked for his comments. "Please be as frank and ruthless as you can be. This is urgent," he added. Brandy had no trouble with the stringent requirements in the bill, calling it "a superb accomplishment." His only suggestion was that it also regulate cutting on private lands, as Metcalf had proposed with Senate Bill 1734 during the Ninety-second Congress. "Thirty-seven years ago was the last time that any Administration, in cooperation with the Forest Service and too few members of Congress, assumed leadership to place *all* forest lands on a scientific management basis," he told Bolle. "Way back, the public wouldn't believe that the timber industry would rape the public lands after it had exhausted timber supplies on private lands. The public has been taught a sad lesson," he said. Bolle was not inclined to recommend draconian measures for either public or private timberlands. Like McGuire, he argued for less prescriptive language, believing that the Forest Service should have greater flexibility in adapting management to various situations. So did most of his colleagues in the forestry profession, who almost unanimously supported the Humphrey bill.[26] Without their support, Brandy's long efforts to reform practices on private forest lands would get no further.

Brandborg flew to Washington in March 1976 to appear before the joint congressional subcommittees that were considering the rival forestry bills. He was eighty-three years old and in poor health, suffering from metastatic prostate cancer that had been diagnosed several years earlier. But he refused to miss this chance to achieve meaningful and lasting reform within his former agency. Dale Burk joined him on the conservationists' panel. Burk was attending Harvard at the time as a Nieman Fellow, a prestigious journalism award granted largely on the basis of his work covering forestry issues for the *Missoulian* (Brandy had suggested he apply for the fellowship). Rather than detail the drawbacks to clearcutting or address the specifics of the proposed legislation, Brandy once again called attention to the close relationship between forest lands and the well-being of rural areas:

At one time forestry ranked next to agriculture in providing work opportunities for people of the Bitterroot and many other Montana communities. It no longer maintains that position because of the directive of ex-president Nixon who, reflecting the strong influence of the timber industry, increased the annual timber cut on national forests beyond their sustained yield capabilities.... Mills which could have continued in operation as long as cuts were limited to growth capabilities are now closed. One of the three remaining larger sawmills shut down within the last few months. People in Ravalli County and other forest communities of Montana are desperate to save what little timber remains in the National Forests.[27]

For Brandborg, the years of struggle and acrimony over the Bitterroot National Forest revolved principally around the issue of sustained yield. The torn-up hillsides, the incursions into roadless areas, the streams running dark with sediment—these failings of the modern forestry paradigm were secondary to his concern for the rural economy and to his vision of how forests could provide for human welfare. Few others in the environmental movement were directly addressing this issue. While their lobbyists were trying to get sustained-yield language added to the final bill, their primary motivation was to halt the Forest Service's program of road building and logging in roadless areas and secure better protection for the forest environment. Brandy certainly supported these goals, but he returned again and again to the question of maintaining jobs in a permanent forest economy.

By now there was little doubt that the Northern Rockies' forest industry was in serious trouble. Larry Blasing, a lobbyist from Missoula who represented a trade group of midsize lumber mills in Montana, Idaho, and eastern Washington, laid out the situation for the joint Senate-House panel. Eleven sawmills had closed in Montana and Idaho since 1970, the peak of the timber boom. Two were from the Bitterroot: Intermountain's pine plant had closed in 1970, while just two months before the hearing, as Brandborg had mentioned, the Waleswood plant, which had employed sixty workers in Darby, shuttered its doors. Across the Sapphire divide, Louisiana-Pacific had closed a mill in Philipsburg after the Deerlodge and Lolo national forests announced a moratorium on logging in the headwaters of Rock Creek, a nationally recognized trout stream. Western Montana sportsmen, including Don Aldrich of the Montana Wildlife Federation, led the effort to restrict logging in this drainage, fearing that sedimentation would fill in the stream's highly productive gravel spawning beds. Eighty mill workers were laid off in the closure.

Blasing blamed his industry's troubles on an overall 28 percent drop in timber-sale offerings in the Northern Region from fiscal years 1971–1975.[28] The decline was partly the result of the region's quality-management program instituted under Neal Rahm. Withdrawals of commercial forest land in places such as the Lincoln Back Country and Magruder Corridor added to the problem. The decrease in public timber offerings hit hardest in midsize and smaller producers that did not own large reserve stocks, including all of the Bitterroot mills, which now faced competition from mills located across the Continental Divide that were also feeling the pinch.

Montana's political leadership, from county commissioners to the governor, was acutely aware of the mill closures and wanted some means of ensuring predictability in log supplies, which to them meant minimizing withdrawals for wilderness and other environmental purposes. But Lee Metcalf, although he had long championed labor causes, took heed of warnings that the high cuts of the 1960s could not be sustained forever. Ignoring the theoretical justification for adjusting harvest levels to match demand (as Arnold Bolle had argued), Metcalf successfully retained language from the Randolph bill that would require the Forest Service to maintain harvests at or below the level that could be sustained indefinitely. This provision, known as nondeclining even flow, was one of the linchpins of what would become the National Forest Management Act (NFMA) of 1976—a landmark statute that effectively drew the curtain on the Bitterroot clearcutting controversy. Under its provisions, temporary departures from even flow were permitted so long as the ten-year average established in the forest management plan was not exceeded, or if multiple-use objectives required a contraction in sales.[29]

Metcalf, acutely aware of the potential for more mill closures, was noncommittal in his public statements on the Randolph and Humphrey bills, saying only that he saw good features in each proposal. But as the House and Senate subcommittees thrashed out the final provisions of the NFMA, he took a strong environmental stand, offering amendments that incorporated many of the Church subcommittee's 1972 guidelines on clearcutting. These included provisions to ensure public participation, promote diversity of forest types and species, prohibit logging on fragile or marginal lands, and protect wetlands and important wildlife habitat. Clearcuts were to be held within a maximum size limit (unlike in the Randolph bill, it was left to the agency to establish this criterion), cutting units were to be blended into the surrounding forest, and an interdisciplinary team would weigh in on each sale. Roads were to be put to bed within ten years unless made part of a permanent road system. These provisions still did not suffice for the environmental groups working on the bill; among other amendments, they proposed to allow clearcutting only where it was "silviculturally essential," instead of the less restrictive finding that it was the "optimum method."[30]

Metcalf's championing of the even-flow provision grew directly out of Guy Brandborg's concerns about overbuilt mill capacity. Metcalf informed him that the issue "dominated a good deal of our markup sessions" and would "undoubtedly draw a lot of fire from the industry." But he acknowledged that Brandborg was "absolutely right about the devastating effects" of excess capacity and said he would continue to fight for it.[31]

Robert Wolf, a staff member of the Congressional Research Service who played a key role in the deliberations on the NFMA, recalled that "there was simply no way that Lee Metcalf was going to stay supporting it unless there was sustained yield language in there." While Arnold Bolle understood the technical and economic criticisms of sustained yield, he also paid attention to the political climate in Montana. "For the Bitterroot," he said in a later conversation with Wolf, "these people wanted sustained yield right there, not cut out then go somewhere else."[32] He threw his support behind Metcalf and the even-flow language despite his earlier reservations.

The Forest Service tried at the last minute to gain a little wiggle room around the even-flow provision in the Humphrey bill; in a markup session on May 4 John McGuire asked the committee to allow his agency a 5 percent variance in the sustained-yield level over the long run, giving the agency some flexibility to liquidate more of its old-growth stands. Metcalf objected, telling McGuire that on the Bitterroot the agency "went into a ranger district and clearcut almost the entire district, even though in Region 1 you had a sustained yield operation." He told the committee, "I hate to again retreat from a position where I have already fallen back quite a bit." The committee rejected McGuire's proposal.[33]

Metcalf's amendments joined other provisions in the Humphrey bill that required prompt reforestation, the compilation of forestwide management plans, and the identification of lands unsuitable for timber harvest. Taken together, the NFMA was the most complete statement that Congress ever made on the subject of forest management. Although it did not ban clearcutting outright or force the Forest Service to protect natural values in all instances, it was widely seen as a victory for the environmental movement. The law owed its existence to the clearcutting controversies that began on national forests in

West Virginia, Wyoming, and Montana. Many of its provisions could be traced directly to the management directions that Neal Rahm issued for the Northern Region and the Bitterroot National Forest in 1970 and 1971. If the bill seemed to favor the environmental cause, it also incorporated much of the Forest Service's new approach to forest management—changes it had hammered out at great cost during the preceding six years. The agency had come a long distance from the 1960s, when its intransigent position in favor of maximum timber yields led a group of citizens in the Bitterroot Valley to propose Study Proposal No. 168 and ignite a nationwide controversy.

The art of political compromise as reflected in the NFMA did not appeal to Brandborg and his friend Charles McDonald, who said in a joint interview with the *Missoulian* that the provisions of the 1897 Organic Act requiring individual marking of trees should be left in place. They said that pressure to relax the old standard came from a timber industry that had expanded beyond the ability of the national forests to sustain. "Brandborg and I have pleaded with these mill owners not to increase their capacity," McDonald asserted. "People cannot honestly say they haven't been warned."[34]

In his testimony on the Humphrey and Randolph bills, Brandborg laid the blame for overcutting the national forests on chief John McGuire, asserting that he had failed to stand up to pressure from the Nixon administration to increase allowable cuts. McGuire was present at the final markup of the NFMA and was widely viewed as a moderate, hewing to neither environmentalist nor industry doctrine. But to Brandy he was a straw in the wind who bent to Secretary Butz's demands for increased cutting. With the Watergate scandal in mind, Brandy called for criminal prosecution of any agency official who acceded to the administration's pressure.

His bitterness toward his former agency became apparent in a commentary published in the *Missoulian* two months before the NFMA hearings. The Bitterroot National Forest had recently given small cash performance awards to two foresters working on the West Fork district for carrying out its timber-sale program. "In view of the existing unlawful forest land use practices," Brandborg wrote, "it is ludicrous that timber managers be given cash awards from public funds for contributing to the exhaustion of timber supplies." Instead, he said, such individuals should be charged with personal criminal liability. "It would take few convictions to convince other employees in the Forest Service that it is their obligation to enforce the laws of the land."[35] Whereas some of Brandy's colleagues in the environmental movement agreed that the Forest Service's actions verged on the criminal, his venting of such frustration, which he repeated in other contexts, erased any further chance of dialogue with Forest Service officials.

Dale Burk ascribed Brandy's rancorous public statements to the pain he was enduring from his advancing cancer and his feeling that he had little time left in which to effect change. Friends and family members said that at times he despaired of the course that the nation was taking, with less attention being paid to the ideals of community action and individual responsibility in caring for the land. For more than forty years he had promoted his vision of forest management in Ravalli County—one that depended on an informed, involved citizenry and a responsive, public-spirited bureaucracy. He was still not satisfied with the changes that he and his friends had secured in the operations of the Bitterroot National Forest, as well as in most of the Northern Region. Their work culminated in significant new legislation clarifying the Forest Service's mission; perhaps most important, his former agency now felt a responsibility to listen to public opinion as never before. For most activists it might have seemed a worthy harvest, but in the time he had left, Brandy would continue to seek deep-seated changes in the Forest Service's approach to timbering.

CHAPTER 21

Legacy of a Conflict
1976–2006

For four decades Guy Brandborg had been telling Bitterroot Valley residents that the health of their farms, ranches, and overall economy depended upon the care they took of the surrounding forest lands. He had lost hope, however, that his former agency would sponsor a comprehensive program of land stewardship reaching across all ownerships. In February 1976, in a last effort to promote this nearly lifelong vision, he joined his friends Bill Jellison of the Rocky Mountain Laboratory and K. Ross Toole of the University of Montana in proposing that Ravalli County take on the contentious issue of valleywide land-use planning. Speaking at a meeting of soil conservation district supervisors, Brandy noted that two hundred thousand acres of farmlands in Montana had been damaged the previous fall by wind erosion and that the Bitterroot River continued to wreak costly floods owing to forest mismanagement in its headwaters. "People in this valley are left with no alternative than to depend upon local constituted authorities to intercede in their behalf," he said.[1]

Toole, an outspoken professor of history who had studied the nineteenth-century denudation of forest lands in the Bitterroot, said that "if the forest had been used wisely, no mill would be closed now in the valley and no stream would dry to a trickle by July. It is probably too late to reverse this situation, but not now to try would be criminal." The three activists asked the district supervisors to implement comprehensive guidelines for land-use practices on private and public lands—an issue that would remain highly controversial in Ravalli County into the following century, when Stewart Brandborg would take a prominent role in support of a limited land-use planning and zoning program. This initiative would run into fierce opposition from those who wanted no restrictions on what they could do with their land—even if that meant a less livable valley for all.

Guy Brandborg lived to see only the beginning of the changes that he and his friends had helped instigate on the Bitterroot National Forest and within Region 1. By the time he traveled to Washington to testify at the NFMA hearings in the spring of 1976, his health was failing. With his body bent from increasing pain, he was carrying on the fight out of some deep reserve of strength—driven by the need to rally public support to his cause. In February 1977, after his doctor determined that cancer had spread throughout his body, he checked into St. Patrick Hospital in Missoula to begin chemotherapy. Not ready to relinquish the good fight over the fate of public lands, he set up an office in his hospital room, laid out his notes on hospital carts, and enlisted nurses to dial his phone calls. Arnold Bolle recalled visiting Brandy at the hospital and telling him of his decision to retire from the University of Montana. Brandy asked what his plans were, to which Bolle replied that he hoped to catch up on some fishing. "Do that for two weeks," Brandy said. "Then you have to get busy, 'cause there's still an awful lot to do."[2] Bolle remained active in Montana's conservation affairs, later becoming president of the Montana Wilderness Association.

The aggressive treatment quickly laid Brandy low and in the end could not arrest the disease. Ruth stayed in Missoula to be at his side. Dale Burk visited Brandy often during this ordeal and was with him and the Brandborg family when he passed away on March 11. Brandy had just turned eighty-four, a forest veteran who had lived half of his life at the foot of the Bitterroot Range.

He had kept his allegiance to the Bitterroot National Forest at a time when the agency routinely transferred its officers to new posts so that their ties were strongest to the organization, not to the land. A promotion to a staff position in Missoula or Washington probably could have been his, but he and Ruth had many friends in the Bitterroot Valley and his work lay there. He refused to be an interchangeable cog in the Forest Service apparatus, knowing that few others would carry on his unique program of tailoring national forest management to serve a local agriculturally based constituency. From Elers Koch to Orville Daniels, the Bitterroot had seen its share of visionary, activist supervisors, but none possessed the combination of passion, idealism, and single-minded staying power (others would call it stubbornness) that made Brandy a force to contend with.

He had known every chief of the Forest Service, beginning with its founder, Gifford Pinchot, whose charge to serve the greatest good of the greatest number over the longest time turned up once again in a tribute to Brandborg in the *Missoulian*. Sam Reynolds, who ran the newspaper's editorial page and had printed many of Brandy's commentaries over the years, called him "a giant of a man" who uttered a simple truth: that all parts of the forest economy must live in harmony. "The forest has to produce timber," Reynolds wrote. "Properly nurtured, it will produce more and more. That will give stability to the forest industry, and sustain the communities depending upon it. Jobs will be more secure. There will be no reason for deadly battles over the use of this resource. There would be harmony—perpetual harmony."[3]

Reynolds understood what drove Brandborg's uncompromising activism: a vision of how a public forest and its dependent communities could work in close attunement, producing and using resources in a constant, predictable exchange. That this vision was not terribly realistic in the America of the 1960s and 1970s did not seem to bother Brandy; he constantly strove to carry out the old Progressive ideals in the face of larger forces, just as his father had stood with the small landsman against the Northern Pacific Railroad in the 1880s. Both men believed, as did many Scandinavians of the Old World and the New, that government had a role to play in setting bounds to capitalism.

In the last month of his life Brandy gave interviews to Dale Burk and Don Schwennesen of the *Missoulian,* whose combined story appeared three days after his death and served, along with Reynolds's comments, as the newspaper's final tribute. Brandy chose not to reflect on his long Forest Service career or grow nostalgic about packing mules, building lookouts, or riding the range. Instead, he gave yet another pointed commentary on what he termed the "superficial understanding" of forestry issues among Montana's political leaders. Only Lee Metcalf, he said, recognized the importance of the state's national forests to its citizens and to its economy. He called upon President Carter, who had assumed office two months earlier, to ensure that new leadership in the

Department of Agriculture and Forest Service took decisive action to halt what he termed continuing forest destruction. The recently enacted NFMA was too severely compromised, he said, to offer much hope for reform. "Eminent scientists and conservationists presented abundant evidence of overcutting violations at both the 1971 and 1976 Senate hearings," he said, "but the laws were not enforced. Illegal cutting practices have continued."[4]

By this time Brandborg's influence within Montana's growing environmental community had waned, although its leaders respected his long record of organizing citizen action. Regional forester Steve Yurich, who had transferred to head the Eastern Region of the Forest Service the previous summer, paid Brandy an indirect compliment when he told Don Schwennesen that he had "never seen a public like that in Region One" in terms of its willingness to get involved in issues of land management.[5] Brandborg had played a dominant role in generating interest in forest management in Montana. Many of the activists he recruited, including Doris Milner and Dale Burk, would continue to play important roles in Montana's environmental movement. As a model of how citizen activists could alter a federal agency's course—not just block a specific project but institute meaningful and lasting reforms—the Bitterroot controversy will remain an enduring story.

The National Forest Management Act also bore Brandy's influence, chiefly through Metcalf's championing of its nondeclining even-flow provision. The law's long-term effect on Forest Service policy is less clear: the agency has invested hundreds of millions of dollars in preparing the forest plans mandated under the act, but many critics believe it remains wedded to timber production and subject to the shifting winds of Washington politics.[6] Nor have forest plans done much to resolve the controversy over timber harvesting and land allocation: by 1989, according to one industry executive's count, the plans devised for the Northern Region's forests had been met with 177 administrative appeals and lawsuits from industry and environmental groups. One environmental leader, bemoaning the lack of specificity in the new forest plans, believed them to be a step backward from the older unit plans devised for individual drainage basins, which at least told the reader what changes could be expected on the ground.[7]

What does seem clear is that the persistent involvement of a concerned local public—a hallmark of the Bitterroot controversy—is still the most effective way to reform land-management practices. It took the lobbying muscle of national environmental groups to bring many of these changes to fruition, but no national forestry standards or planning mandates can substitute for informed citizens who keep track of what is going on in their woods. That the Bitterroot activists accomplished what they did without recourse to the courts speaks volumes. The NFMA and the Endangered Species Act set legally enforceable standards that environmental attorneys have used to great effect, but these groups still rely on local citizens to monitor the public agencies—following the model that was originated and field-tested in Ravalli County and a handful of other localities in the late 1960s.

Doris Milner had tangled with Brandy on many occasions in their joint campaigns, but they maintained a warm regard for each other. After his death she sought to create a suitable memorial to his decades of effort on behalf of conservation in Montana. Brandy had willed his body to the University of Oregon's School of Medicine in Portland for use in cancer research, so no funeral was held. Milner thought that a mountain peak would be the most appropriate monument to his life. Working with a committee of the Montana Wilderness Association, she selected as the best candidate an unnamed crag between the forks of Lost Horse Creek south of Hamilton and asked Bitterroot National Forest supervisor Bob Morgan if he would support the idea. "Brandy was not a gentle or retiring person," she admitted. "He stood firm in his convictions that the nation's resources were to be managed for the welfare of the people." His legacy included conflict, she said, but he had also brought changes to the agency and better understanding of resource management by the public. The Lost Horse peak, 7,478 feet high, was easily visible from Highway 93 in the valley and was "rugged and craggy, quite in keeping with Brandy."[8]

The occasion called for yet another letter-writing campaign. Many of Brandy's friends and associates wrote to the Forest Service in support of Milner's plan, including Vic Reinemer, Lee Metcalf's staff director, who noted that he appreciated Brandborg's "awesome contribution to forest management and resurgent interest in the land ethic." He advised Morgan to "be sure the peak selected is large, craggy and snow-capped, with iron in its bowels, as befits a memorial to Brandy." Morgan may have sensed an opportunity to smooth some of the hard feelings left over from Brandy's days as an activist. He gave the proposal his support and passed it up the line to the agency's Domestic Names

Committee. The final decision rested with the Interior Department's Board on Geographic Names, which gave its approval to Brandy Peak in April 1978.

Milner set August 12, 1978, for a celebration to be held at the Como schoolhouse south of Darby, where the peak's sharp summit stood out on the Bitterroot skyline. District ranger Ted Ingersoll and his staff cleaned the grounds and make arrangements to host the crowd of 175 well-wishers. Morgan along with regional forester Bob Torheim and associate chief Rex Resler all spoke at the gathering, and on the Forest Service's behalf they presented Ruth, Stewart, and Becky Brandborg with framed photographs of Brandy from his days as supervisor of the Bitterroot, alongside a photo of his namesake mountain. Mavis McKelvey read from some of the letters that had poured in to Ruth. Scott Reed, an environmental attorney from Coeur d'Alene, Idaho, noted that in the next thunderstorm an electric bolt was likely to spike heavenward from Brandy Peak, accompanied by a booming voice saying, "Now God, this is what you do."

One of the most meaningful tributes came from a former subordinate. Vern Hamre, now the regional forester in Ogden, Utah, recalled in a letter to Ruth his days as a young ranger in the early 1950s on the Sula district. Calling those years a "high point in my Forest Service career," Hamre depicted how the Bitterroot under Brandborg's leadership "was taking tender loving care of the trees, grass, soil and water. Old timers working for Brandy, such as George Haynes, George Wright, and Champ Hannon, made certain that every foot of road was carefully located, every tree to be cut was carefully selected, and any disturbed soil was reseeded. The land ethic prevailing on the Forest at that time is the same as we, even now, are trying to achieve on all Forests."[9]

It was a fitting summation of Brandborg's accomplishments. Hamre was depicting a time when Brandy's rangers, field staff, and friends in the ranching business felt a close relationship to the land and a strong sense of community. When new Forest Service leaders seemed to abandon that connection in favor of an industrially based, intensive-use program—one that left less time and manpower for checking culverts or reseeding road cuts—these old-timers looked to Brandy as a bold advocate who could steer the agency back to its former ways. Hamre told Ruth that his boss had been "a generation ahead of the rest of the Forest Service in the areas of public involvement, environmental education, and land use planning. He firmly believed that those affected by a decision should be involved in making the decision."

Whether Brandy's friends espoused his Progressive social activism or a more traditional rural conservatism, all of them objected to the intrusion of modern management techniques and assumptions into their lives. The economic restructuring of their means of making a living threatened to turn their closely knit communities into mere suppliers of resources to far-off corporations. They had experienced this under the heavy hand of the Anaconda Company and were determined to prevent its return.

Where Brandy differed from most rural land users was in advocating a strong government role in protecting its citizens. The Forest Service that he knew guarded both trees and people. Properly constituted, the agency did more than mediate the flow of forest resources to the towns, farms, and ranches of the Bitterroot Valley; it also strove to lead local residents toward a harmonious relationship with their own land and with the public estate that surrounded them. Brandborg saw land use as an expression of a culture's deepest needs and beliefs. A democracy could not work, he believed, if it did not function at the local level, and for this to happen a significant number of its citizens must have a close, informed, and caring relationship to the land. People were not units of production, in his view; workers counted for more than the extraction of resources. Small towns had a greater role to play than assisting with the flow of wealth from the land to the centers of power.

This dream was never fully realized in Brandborg's time and became even harder to reach in the present age. Many of those gathered on the lawn of the Como schoolhouse on that warm August day brought with them new concepts of the utility of national forests such as the Bitterroot. To some the forest was a playground, albeit a lofty and challenging one. For others it was a last refuge for endangered species—possibly a future haven for the wolf and grizzly bear. Fewer of Brandy's successors in the environmental movement drew their living from the forest and valley, as had Champ Hannon, Marvin Bell, Jack Evans, Agnes and Forest Cooper, and Ernie Townsend. The old coalition of sportsmen, backcountry horsemen, hikers, biologists, maverick loggers, and progressive landowners, which had halted dams in the postwar years and in large part powered the state's wilderness preservation movement, was giving way to a new generation of environmental advocates who were rapidly colonizing the territory represented by the NFMA and the Endangered Species Act. Its leaders, who often worked for newer foundation-supported groups springing up throughout the country, were more intent on preserving the earth's natural biota than protecting hiking trails or fishing holes. Their goals overlapped with those of the older conservationists, but rarely did their leaders speak out about the welfare of rural communities or the value of woods work.

Where the old conservation ethos made room for responsible economic use of the forest, the new leaders promoted the preservation and restoration of primeval forest conditions throughout the entire public domain. While conservation pioneers such as Elers Koch and Guy Brandborg wanted to retain extensive areas of wilderness in the Selway, the Bitterroot Range, and the Sapphires, they believed that closer to the Bitterroot Valley the forest could provide modest quantities of logs and forage. Their vision of a working forest that is pleasing to the eye, is eminently sustainable, and is still possessed by mystery in its far corners would lie fallow until a later generation again took up the challenge.

In 1987 the Bitterroot National Forest issued its first forestwide multiple-use plan prepared under the provisions of the NFMA. In contrast to the heartfelt ecological manifesto Orville Daniels released in 1972, the new document took on the dry, professional language of the federally mandated planning process. A key change was a reduction in the total area of commercial forest land from 750,000 acres identified in 1972 to 586,332 acres now labeled "tentatively suitable" for timber management. Set-asides for roadless-area studies, including the Sapphires and Blue Joint areas from Metcalf's Senate Bill 393, were partly responsible for the reduction, but the NFMA also required the Forest Service to identify smaller areas in the forest landscape that were not capable of producing much timber, such as stringers of trees, rocky outcrops, streamside corridors, critical wildlife habitat, and excessively steep slopes.[10]

Watershed protection assumed higher importance than in previous timber-focused planning documents; in order to prevent excessive peak flows and damage to streams, no more than 25 to 40 percent of a single watershed could be cut over or be in early stages of regrowth at one time. Tellingly, the heavily cutover drainage of Took Creek was among those identified as exceeding the cutting limit; decades would be needed for this area to reach what was called full hydrologic recovery.[11]

After accounting for these restrictions, the forest planners projected an annual allowable cut (now called the allowable sale quantity) of 31 mmbf for the initial ten-year planning horizon, followed by a slight drop in the second and third decades, then an increase to 42 mmbf as regrowth from older cuttings became available.[12] These amounts were a significant reduction from the cuts of late 1970s, which averaged around 45 mmbf, but by 1987 sale volumes had already declined to around 30 mmbf per year. According to the Forest Service's economic analysis, the two remaining larger sawmills in the Darby area would receive sufficient log supplies to continue operating for another twenty years. These mills needed about 50 mmbf annually from the Bitterroot, the adjacent national forests, and privately owned lands. As private stocks dwindled after about 2010, the agency predicted that shortfalls could occur.[13]

Outside influences would accelerate this schedule. During the 1980s Montana environmental groups filed dozens of administrative appeals of timber sales and management plans based partly on the NFMA's requirements for thorough, ecologically based planning and protection of forest watersheds and other values. A new citizen organization called Friends of the Bitterroot (FOB) filed appeals of five proposed timber sales during the first two years of the new plan, citing violations of the NFMA, National Environmental Policy Act, and Endangered Species Act. The group's founders included Stewart Brandborg, who had retired from his advocacy work in the nation's capital to live near his childhood home, and John Grove, a retired Northern Region forester who had helped plan some of the early clearcuts on the Bitterroot. Grove took the lead in opposing several sales along the Continental Divide that would have compromised roadless areas and interfered with important elk summer range and migration routes. The sales were halted, and the group remains highly active in the Bitterroot Valley—continuing valley residents' tradition of volunteer conservation action into the new millennium.

Additional appeals, including one of the 1987 forest plan, came from the American Wildlands Alliance, a Denver-based group that Clif Merritt helped found in 1977. (The Wilderness Society had dismissed both Merritt and Stewart Brandborg in 1976 as part of a major reorganization.) These and other environmental groups wielded a new hammer against the Forest Service's timber-sale program: the poor economics of cutting remote high-elevation forests. Tom Barlow, an attorney with the NRDC who had led its campaign for the Randolph bill, now brought attention to what he termed "below-cost" timber sales. For years the Forest Service had justified its sale program to Congress partly by citing the benefits of road construction, which improved access for recreationists and firefighters. Barlow believed that the agency's accounting was skewed; logging roads incurred heavy environmental costs by dumping sediment in trout streams, reducing wildlife escape cover, and tearing up valuable wildlands. Even looking at the direct administrative costs of timber-sale administration, many sales in high-elevation lodgepole pine forests appeared to be money losers, the NRDC claimed.[14]

Forced to adhere to strict standards of environmental protection, the Bitterroot's district rangers and supervisory staff often had to reduce the size of their timber sales or withdraw them altogether. By 1990 sale volumes from the Bitterroot National Forest fell to their lowest levels since the Great Depression, averaging less than 10 mmbf throughout the decade. Private lands took up some of the slack but could not replace the shortfall for the Darby sawmills, which lacked large timber holdings of their own. The logging restrictions brought protests as dramatic as those staged by environmentalists in earlier years, including the May 1988 "Great Northwest Log Haul," which brought three hundred loaded log trucks from points throughout the West to Darby in symbolic support of the beleaguered Darby Lumber Company mill.[15]

Protests could not reverse declining lumber prices and reduced log supplies, and by 1998 the remaining two sawmills in the Darby area closed, leaving 145 workers to search for new jobs. Some of them found employment in the valley's burgeoning log-home industry, which by 2000 employed the equivalent of 405 full-time workers, compared to 157 working in small sawmills and related timber-processing businesses and 95 in logging work.[16] The sawmill closures, though highly distressing for those involved and a major shock to the town of Darby, did not lead to depressed economic conditions throughout Ravalli County. Its lumber and woods-products sector actually grew from the days of the Bitterroot controversy: in 1972 workers in this industry brought home about $11 million in income, whereas by 1998 the sector accounted for $27 million in the county, after adjusting for inflation. Timber's relative contribution to income and employment remained about the same, while retail and service sectors expanded in the wake of the growing popularity of the Bitterroot Valley as a place in which to live, retire, and vacation.[17]

Farming and ranching in the valley lost its once dominant position as a source of employment and income, reflecting nationwide trends and the replacement of much of the county's agricultural land by ranchettes and residential areas. These changes worried many longtime residents who feared the loss of traditional ways of earning a living, yet as Orville Daniels noted in 1971, the Bitterroot was in many ways a flagship for the social and economic changes that were sweeping the Intermountain West. Much of northern Ravalli County served as a bedroom community for Missoula, while expansion of service-related business, health care facilities, and government operations in the Hamilton area helped to diversify its economy. Retirees who were attracted to the valley's scenic location and abundant recreational amenities brought additional sources of income.

By the turn of the century, timber, beef, wool, and fruit crops no longer ruled Ravalli County. With little intention or forethought on the part of most of its residents, the Bitterroot Valley has emerged as a prototypical New West living space—part bedroom community, part recreational destination, with a mix of hopeful new entrepreneurs and diehard traditionalists attempting to coexist. What value, then, do national forest lands still have for those who call the valley home? Despite the roads and clearcuts in its headwaters, the forest remains a major source of clean water for irrigation and downstream fisheries. Recreational uses of the forest have exploded, including ATV and trail-bike riding, rock climbing, and mountain biking, all of which bring new challenges as more users crowd onto trails that were built to serve the firefighting needs of the 1930s. Still, many parts of the forest continue to function as a reservoir of ecological values and open space, providing habitat for fish and wildlife as well as a refuge from crowding, commercialism, and society's strictures.

The social and economic changes that swept Ravalli County into the twenty-first century have supplanted Guy Brandborg's vision of his forest as an anchor for community stability. No longer merely a supplier of resources to a bucolic rural area, the Bitterroot National Forest must now respond to outside economic forces that relegate small towns and agricultural areas to insignificant roles. Yet Brandy understood that if rural residents in places such as the Bitterroot were to achieve satisfying lives and create socially supportive, lasting communities, they must not passively accept the dictates of the global corporate system. The clearcutting controversy demonstrated that the full-development paradigm of modern forestry, which the Forest Service embraced in the 1950s partly as a means of integrating its operations into the larger economy, was simply too abusive of other forest uses. Timber's reign is over, probably for good, and the citizens of Ravalli County must decide whether to actively plan for their collective future or be content to bob and drift on waves generated outside of their valley.

The Bitterroot's 1987 forest plan remains in effect today while its planning staff prepares a revision, as mandated every fifteen years under the NFMA. A draft proposal was released for public comment in 2005, but a final decision is not expected until the fall of 2010—an indication of the difficulty the agency faces in responding to shifting public pressures and changes in administrations. The new plan will undoubtedly emphasize thinning and fuel reduction in the so-called wildland-urban interface—the web of towns, homes, cabins, and farms that lies on forested land all along the margins of the Bitterroot Valley and fingers far into the East and West Fork valleys.

Such projects assumed added urgency in the aftermath of the worst fire seasons the Bitterroot has experienced in modern times, including the enormous fires of the summer of 2000, which burned more than three hundred thousand acres of the national forest and destroyed seventy houses. (By comparison, the Saddle Mountain and Sleeping Child fires of 1960–1961 burned a total of about thirty-one thousand acres.) This conflagration caused more visible change on the Bitterroot National Forest in one month than most valley residents had experienced in a lifetime and left blackened stands visible from most points in the valley. Most Bitter Rooters saw the 2000 fires as an unmitigated disaster that destroyed live timber, displaced big game, and contributed to stream sedimentation, not to mention the aesthetic loss of mile after mile of green forest. They supported a Forest Service plan to salvage standing timber in some forty-six thousand acres of the burned area, which would have produced 181 mmbf of sawtimber and house logs—twice the amount that was hauled off following the fires of 1960 and 1961.[18]

The salvage program of the early 1960s helped build the modern timber industry in the Bitterroot Valley and, to critics such as Guy Brandborg, created an unsustainable appetite for further timber supplies. The new salvage effort, known as the Bitterroot Burned Area Recovery Plan, drew fire from Friends of the Bitterroot and other environmental activists whose concerns centered on the workings of the forest itself. They argued that the drastic changes wrought in the 2000 fires should be accepted as part of the natural cycle of forest ecosystems and pointed to the role that standing dead trees play as homes and food sources for cavity-nesting birds. As the trees fall to the ground they retain moisture, return nutrients to the soil, and create new stream habitats for fish. Postburn salvage logging would run logging equipment across already damaged soils, they argued, initiating erosion and giving weeds a toehold. Even the agency's traditional goal of reforesting burned areas as quickly as possible has come under question; recent research has highlighted the importance of so-called early-successional ecosystems in sustaining a broadly diverse assortment of plants and animals that may not thrive under a closed forest canopy.[19]

Environmentalists were also concerned that the Forest Service was targeting too many live green trees and old-growth stands to qualify as a salvage project and objected to how the Bush administration, through Undersecretary of Agriculture Mark Rey, exempted the salvage plan from administrative appeals. The Forest Service revised its plan to include fewer acres and stay out of roadless areas and old growth, but still wound up in court. By the time the injunction was lifted in early 2002, following negotiations between seven environmental groups and top administration officials, many trees had begun to check and decay and were less useful to industry. The plaintiffs agreed to allow salvage work to proceed on fourteen thousand acres of burned land but faulted the agency for delaying promised watershed-restoration work. Most of the funds earmarked for this work were siphoned off to pay for fire-control efforts on other national forests.[20]

Demonstrations were held in Hamilton and Missoula by supporters and opponents of the Burned Area Recovery Plan, carrying forward the long history of contention over the Bitterroot's commercial forest lands. Significant wildfires occurred again throughout the West in 2003, prompting Congress to pass the Healthy Forest Restoration Act to facilitate thinning and prescribed fire work within the wildland-urban interface. Environmental groups protested provisions in the law that sped up environmental reviews and, they say, subverted protections given to wildlife and other ecological values under the NFMA.

In recent years Bitterroot National Forest officials have convened consensus groups and tried to explain their agency's emphasis on so-called ecosystem management, in which achieving a desired stand condition takes precedence, in theory at least, over capturing the standing volume of timber. The agency faces many challenges in trying to restore stands to conditions like those found a century or more ago, when large ponderosa pines dominated dryer sites in the Bitterroot's lower elevations and Douglas fir and true firs made up less of the understory. Not only must foresters deal with the effects of a century of fire suppression, which has led to unnatural fuel buildup, crowded stands, and changes in species composition, but there is the added threat posed by anthropogenic climate change. Land managers are already dealing with drought, low stream flows, increased tree mortality, and widespread mountain pine beetle outbreaks exacerbated by milder winters. Thus far the Bitterroot National Forest is not among the hardest hit by the beetles, but as stands that grew back in the wake of the epidemic of the 1920s and 1930s mature, they will become more susceptible to attack. Climate change likely contributed to the recent severe wildfire seasons and may be responsible for a host of less visible ecological changes in the forest, ranging from increased weed infestations to high mortality in whitebark pine stands.[21]

The ecosystem-management approach has led to a curious reprise of old practices: today machines are once again crawling over some of the Bitterroot's terraced tree plantations, tearing apart green trees and ripping up the soil. Unlike the massive disturbances of the 1960s, this is part of an experimental forest-restoration project in the East Fork drainage during the summer of 2010, in which a backhoe equipped with a grapple hook is loosening subsoils compacted during logging and terracing in the mid-1960s. Another attachment literally chews up crowded ponderosa pines into various sizes of woody debris, which is left in place to replenish the soil. The remaining trees will grow better, the foresters hope, and the revitalized soil will support better elk forage (the Rocky Mountain Elk Foundation, a nonprofit hunters' organization, is helping pay for the project). Cole Mayn, the Bitterroot National Forest's soil scientist, hopes to apply this technique in the heavily cutover West Fork drainage as well.[22]

Such restoration projects reverse the flow of dollars from the federal Treasury back into the forest, repaying an environmental debt incurred four or five decades earlier. The nimble entrepreneurs behind these small-scale efforts understand the need for new forestry techniques, and they exhibit some of the same resourcefulness that the citizens of Darby displayed in the 1940s during the Montana Study, when the demise of the Anaconda Company's timber operations prompted its citizens to start various new business ventures. These projects, though expensive, may help Bitterroot Valley residents partially unyoke from the global corporate economy that has thus far failed to offer them lasting work and left a legacy of damaged land.

No public official in the valley is calling for a return to the days of massive clearcutting, but there is strong support for some combination of salvage logging, forest thinning, and restoration work that could resurrect some of the lost timber jobs. New businesses and government-supported initiatives have found ways to utilize small-diameter trees for biomass conversion, including a steam boiler that provides heat to public schools in Darby and Victor, replacing older oil-powered units.

Craig Thomas, a longtime industry forester from the Bitterroot Valley, believes that biomass projects are the energy source of the future in the western states, offering opportunities to thin crowded forests and displace expensive, environmentally damaging fossil fuels. The Forest Service estimates that the cost of collecting and delivering biomass from thinning projects on the Bitterroot is comparable to that of piling and burning it in place and would eliminate most of the smoke thus produced.[23]

Biomass gained additional interest in late 2009 with the closure (due to adverse market conditions) of Missoula's Smurfit-Stone linerboard plant, a key user of logging waste and small-diameter trees. Montana governor Brian Schweitzer responded to the closure by calling for more federal funds to set up biomass conversion plants of the sort Thomas advocates.[24] Environmentalists caution that emissions from such plants pose a hazard to air quality in mountain basins such as the one surrounding Missoula. They also insist on a careful accounting of the projects' carbon budgets and question whether large-scale thinning to produce biomass fuels would actually improve forest health. But for slash destined to be burned anyway, biomass conversion appears to offer real advantages.

Making use of smaller-diameter trees, chips, and wood waste in home and building construction offers some of the biggest opportunities in efficient forest utilization. Darby boasts a modern high-ceilinged new library whose interior features four- to six-inch roundwood that was locally harvested and processed. Many problems must be solved to make such projects economically self-sustaining; the Darby school district sometimes finds it cheaper to use wood waste from log-home plants than slash from forest-thinning projects. But the Bitterroot National Forest's timber-sale program has never been especially profitable; federal subsidies for public timber harvesting ought to support the most environmentally benign forms of logging and forest restoration.[25]

Forests evolve constantly, sometimes in unpredictable directions, and so too must the communities that depend upon them. As important as log supplies are in western Montana's economy, its human capital is most crucial. When Guy Brandborg came to the Bitterroot Valley in 1935 he recognized that it would take forward-looking citizens to meet the challenges of rural life in a forest setting. The Bitterroot Valley will find its future not in federal largesse or the leavings of the global economy but in the careful work of those who want to see its forests and rangelands sustained far into the future.

Afterword

Bare Cone Lookout, August 2007

On a still, smoke-filled afternoon in an overheated Montana summer, I leave behind the clearcuts of Took Creek and drive eight miles up a rocky forest road to Bare Cone, a high point on a ridge that leads westward into Idaho and a two million–acre expanse of wild mountains and river canyons. On its top stands a squat R-6 lookout tower that watches over the lodgepole forests of Blue Joint Creek, a roadless area set aside in 1977 as a potential addition to the Frank Church–River of No Return Wilderness. The forest guard steps out on the parapet and invites me up for a look. His Osborne firefinder stands useless in the center of the cabin as we peer through the smoke toward Rombo Mountain, ten miles to the east, where a fire is making its way through patches of forest and old clearcuts. All we see are occasional flare-ups when a tall pine or fir goes off. His watch over, we share dinner and conversation as the light dims. Afterward I bed down in the lush beargrass beneath his perch and stare at a handful of stars that penetrate the gloom.

Much has changed in these mountains since the days of the annual human migrations between the Clearwater River and the buffalo prairies, when Nez Perce parties at times must have camped under similar skies. In the 1920s Forest Service crews improved the old route into a pack trail to supply the lookout station; in the 1960s surveyors followed parts of it to stake P-line for logging roads. Clearcuts have replaced much of the ancient forest that once covered these hills, although patches survive along steep hillsides and in dark drainage bottoms. The new trees growing on the clearcut terrace rows are a hopeful sign, but less encouraging are the blossoms of spotted knapweed growing on old jammer roads. The lookout points out other trails that have become favored routes for motorcyclists—a sound rarely heard when I first visited these mountains thirty-three years ago.

For a time the fires that shaped these forests grew scarce under the Forest Service's watchful eye. Then they returned—first as a handful of small, carefully monitored blazes in the Selway-Bitterroot Wilderness during the 1970s, part of the innovative White Cap Fire Management Area established under supervisor Orville Daniels. Then came an enormous unwilled explosion in the summer of 2000 that burned through a third of the entire national forest, roaring through wilderness and timberlands alike and igniting a new round of controversy over salvage logging.

From Bare Cone this evening it is clear that nature cannot stay its hand forever. This tower stands between two landscapes—one to the east that is nominally controlled by man, another to the west and north where primeval forces are largely unrestrained. This becomes evident the following morning as I wake to an atmosphere partially cleared of smoke. Close by are the clearcut drainages of Mud Creek, Tough Creek, Took Creek, and lower Blue Joint. The big machines got this far, then were halted. To the north of the Magruder road stand the peaks of the Selway-Bitterroot, while to the west lie mile upon mile of unbroken wild country in the Frank Church Wilderness, the legacy of an epic conservation battle that set the stage for the Bitterroot clearcutting controversy.

The demarcation between human influence and wildness that appears so striking from my mountaintop is partly an illusion. Wildfire has leaped over the line and now burns in the managed forests to the east. Motorbikes roar up Razorback Ridge and probe the wilderness to the west. Smoke blows out of the Selway into the Bitterroot Valley even as exotic weeds creep into the mountains. As humans we try to mediate this exchange of energy, but our labors seem ineffectual. The Bitterroot Range no longer neatly divides a wilderness world from a settled landscape. Every acre is now subject to man's pervasive influence, even as natural forces extend their power into lands we thought were ours. An uneasy coexistence between the warring entities now appears mandatory.

Despite these unsettling thoughts, it is a lovely, hopeful morning as I gather my bedding, say good-bye to the lookout, and drive back down the road that encircles Bare Cone, stopping at a tiny spring partway down the mountain for a cool drink. Then the road descends through the clearcuts and emerges at the West Fork of the Bitterroot River, which still retains some of its freshness in the middle of this difficult summer.

Jennings Camp Creek, October 2007

Autumn rains finally took care of the multiple fires that burned for months on the Bitterroot and adjacent national forests. The gray blanket that lay over the Bitterroot Valley has given way to a brilliant oblique light that highlights the pyramidal peaks of the Anaconda Range to the east. Scattered around my camp in an old clearcut are piles of young Douglas fir branches that have been laboriously chopped and stacked for later burning—part of the Forest Service's attempt to reduce fuels and promote the growth of the remaining trees. Early this morning the throaty buzz of chain saws rose out of the East Fork valley, where the thinning work continues. Clearing saplings is the most benign aspect of the Middle East Fork fuel-reduction project, an example of the new face of timber management on the Bitterroot. The sale, authorized and funded under the Healthy Forest Restoration Act, comprises commercial and precommercial thinning of overcrowded stands as well as regeneration harvests to control the Douglas fir bark beetle.

From my vantage point above the East Fork, the legacy of past logging is clear; as much as one-third of the surrounding forest was cut over in the 1960s, with more than five miles of logging roads lacing through every square mile of these hills. Compared to the enormous clearcuts in places like Bugle Creek and Lodgepole Creek, the Middle East Fork sale appears pretty low-key—an attempt to produce some sawlogs while enhancing the forest's resistance to fire. Most of the owners of cabins and summer homes down in the East Fork welcome this project—especially those who have chosen to let trees grow on their property practically up to their eaves.

This view is not universally held. I am here to meet with a representative of Friends of the Bitterroot, the environmental watchdog organization established in 1988 by Stewart Brandborg and other Bitterroot Valley activists, including Larry Campbell, who is my guide today. Accompanying us is Matthew Koehler of the WildWest Institute, a regional action group that favors protecting forest biodiversity over what it views as excessive, ill-considered logging.

Koehler steers his VW van up the switchbacks above the East Fork, stopping to let us admire a small band of bighorn sheep that roves along the dry, grassy slopes. We pile out at the top of a logging unit from which most of the overstory has been removed. Cleanup is nearly complete, but Koehler and Campbell are upset with the results. Too many green trees were cut, they say, for this to qualify as a forest-restoration and fire-control project. Quality control also appears deficient: they point to a fire line running straight down the slope, where it could channel erosive runoff. Some of the "leave" trees bear sizable scars from removing their neighbors. Mostly the two environmentalists dispute the rationale for such logging. Thinning the forest, Koehler insists, will not stop a large wildfire in a year such as 2000. "Imagine this forest before it was logged," he tells me. "Now it's hotter, drier, windier." Ground disturbance also brings increased risk of invasive weeds and compacting of already damaged soils.

Campbell offers reasons for letting such fires have their way. "The element that's hard to replace is a big standing dead tree," he says. He would prefer to see a burned old-growth forest than one supposedly restored through logging. Dead beetle-infested trees make ecological offerings to woodpeckers and flycatchers. Thinning the forest next to towns and summer-home areas makes more sense, he says, than trying to prevent fire at miles' remove.[1] The FOB says that it spent many hours in discussions with BNF supervisor Dave Bull and his staff in an attempt to resolve their differences, but the group was overruled in September 2005. Court action followed, but the environmental groups lost their case before the Ninth Circuit Court of Appeals, allowing the project to continue.

In a strange twist to the Bitterroot's long history of public contention, Larry Campbell, FOB president Jim Miller, and Stewart Brandborg (then eighty-one years old) were more or less forcibly excluded from a Forest Service press conference called to announce the final decision on the sale. Supervisor Bull, fearing that a confrontation might occur with a half-dozen supporters of the sale who were invited to attend the meeting, directed armed Forest Service officers to escort the three men from the building. Brandborg, whose father's portrait hangs on the wall of the supervisor's office, described his group as "three old geezers with pieces of paper and pencils."[2] This curious sideshow suggests that the Forest Service has undergone some sort of retrograde motion since the days of Neal Rahm, Steve Yurich, and Orville Daniels.

As we return down a different road we stop to examine rills that have formed on the road surface during last week's rainstorm. We are in the granitic layers that weather to a consistency between sand and gravel—soil that is easily swept away by moving water. I am reminded of the controversies of decades past: the complaints of the Sleeping Child ranchers, the response of the Bitterroot Task Force, the field trips with reporters. For all its attempts at reform, the Forest

Service has yet to escape conflict. The environmentalists of today have moved the goalposts a good distance, it is true, asserting standards for ecosystem health that will admit very little new logging.[3] In the remaining roadless areas they watch over, Guy Brandborg's protection forest lives on.

The Bitterroot Valley, August 2008

If Matthew Koehler represents the modern face of the environmental movement in Montana, John Grove speaks for its origins. An avid fly-fisher, he believes that the past, present, and future of the Bitterroot Valley are found in its streams. "The main resource on the Bitterroot isn't the timber—it's the water," he tells me as we sit in his modern home located a short walk from the Bitterroot River. "It's the most valuable resource there is." A fly rod lies on his kitchen table; he has postponed a date with a Bitterroot trout to tell me about his years working with the Forest Service, here and elsewhere. Watershed protection, he believes, should be the Bitterroot National Forest's highest priority. Sedimentation from logging roads continues to be a problem; erosion from the fires of 2000 added to this, but he believes the Forest Service could have focused on remediating burned areas instead of on salvage logging.

I ask him what level of timber harvest he thinks the Bitterroot could sustain and still protect watersheds, wildlife, fisheries, and roadless lands. After reflecting, he points out that the Bitterroot is currently harvesting about 8–9 mmbf of timber per year. He would prefer to see tighter controls on many sales and a stronger commitment to slash cleanup and road restoration, but after accounting for these needs, he believes that the forest could continue to offer a sale volume a little under that amount. I immediately think of G. M. Brandborg's 1941 timber-management plan, which called for an annual harvest of 7.5 mmbf of pine plus a limited harvest of other species. The trees are smaller today and the species mix has changed, but it appears that the Bitterroot has come close to full circle.

The environmental groups' opposition to the salvage program and subsequent timber sales gave rise in 2007 to a new advocacy group in the Bitterroot Valley. The Big Sky Coalition drew support from residents throughout the valley who support salvage and thinning projects as a means of reducing wildfires. Sonny LaSalle, the group's director, worked on the Bitterroot during the height of its clearcutting program and was later the supervisor of several national forests in Idaho and Colorado. He sees a great need for forest-restoration projects that make use of thinning, some commercial logging, and judicious use of prescribed fire. "Without active fuel management we are going to lose more and more 400- to 500-year-old trees—legacy trees," he said in a recent conversation. He believes that it is possible to gradually return the valley's ponderosa pine forests to their older open, savanna-like condition that was once maintained through frequent ground-burning fires. This state can be reached only with some biomass removal, he says, since in most cases the fuel loads underneath the trees (including thick blankets of needles) are so high that any use of fire would scorch and kill mature specimens.[4]

Is common ground possible between such disparate interest groups? LaSalle offers the example of the recently approved Trapper-Bunkhouse sale south of Darby, which, like the Middle East Fork, represents the agency's attempts to answer the daunting challenge of forest management in the wildland-urban interface zone. In an effort to reduce fuels in this popular mountain-home area, the Forest Service plans to thin trees on fifty-eight hundred acres while removing some commercial timber to help pay for the operation. The sale was offered without an environmental group appealing it, but as of the end of 2009 it had not attracted a qualified bidder—an indication of the marginal economics of the new approach.[5] Restoration projects cannot take place in an economic vacuum; the Forest Service still needs buyers who are willing to use small-diameter trees and comply with new, and often intricate, logging and road-construction requirements.

Projects such as the Middle East Fork and Trapper-Bunkhouse are a far cry from the massive clearcuts of former years. Once market conditions rebound, it seems reasonable to expect the Bitterroot National Forest to provide a modest supply of sawlogs to local firms and—if it can stick to its promises—begin to reverse decades of human-induced ecological changes. Restoration work of many kinds is urgently needed on this and other forests in the Northern Region, including careful reintroduction of wildfire, closing and regrading many unnecessary and eroding timber roads, and slowing the spread of invasive weeds.

This workload adds to the backlog of thinning and planting that agency leaders have long espoused but never seem to catch up with. It is time to get serious about putting people to work improving stand conditions in commercial forest areas as well as undoing widespread environmental damage throughout the national forests. These programs will not be moneymakers, but timber sales on the Bitterroot have lost money for many years, if one factors in costs for administration, road building, and environmental protection work.

Much of Guy Brandborg's work can be seen as an attempt to reunite the frayed strands of Progressive thought, bringing together the goals of long-term forest sustainability, active management to produce useful forest products and services, and satisfying work for men and women who could raise their families in one place. These goals could still form the basis of a renewed agency mission. The Forest Service desperately needs a long-term mandate that will encourage bold action to address the legacy of past environmental damage. The leadership in Washington must allow its mavericks and experimenters some room to maneuver, or the agency will succumb to the dull inertia of most other federal bureaucracies—where the talk is of change, but no one can seem to implement it.

Some of the needed changes will draw upon the conservation leadership the agency demonstrated in the 1930s and 1940s, when men such as Silcox, Kelley, and Brandborg fought for true reform of forest practices on all ownerships. Their ideas seem radical today, but the nation cannot afford to split its forest estate between a tightly protected public sector and a badly overexploited private one. The lessons of the new science of conservation biology are clear: a biotic heritage that is limited to alpine wilderness areas ultimately cannot survive, even in remote strongholds.

The Bitterroot was once known for producing high-quality ponderosa pine sawlogs that fetched higher bids than any other forest in the region. Lumber from the mature pines such as those Elers Koch and Champ Hannon marked for cutting is far scarcer today. National forest lands may be the only place where trees can be grown on the long rotations needed to produce high-value products. Managing some old-growth stands in this way would benefit watersheds and wildlife, compared to more intensive alternatives, and will leave pleasant places for recreation.[6] We must also find a way to reintegrate fire with the landscape on a much larger scale, both in working forests and in wilderness. This will be a lengthy, difficult, and expensive process that will require consistent support from the public.

One other factor, perhaps the most difficult of all, must be taken into account. Guy Brandborg envisioned that most of the products of his national forest would go to local farms, ranches, and small-scale sawmills, not to giant absentee corporations with little interest in long-term land husbandry. There would be exports of lumber and agricultural commodities, to be sure, but his focus was on maintaining lasting communities over the long haul. In these days of near-catastrophic fluctuations in national and worldwide financial markets, with corresponding disruption of employment and income, there is renewed interest in capitalism on a small scale. The Bitterroot Valley, with its intimate relationship to its surrounding forest lands, is an ideal place to cultivate new ways of doing business—from high-value wood-products manufacturing to high-quality guided recreation—all with an eye toward creating long-lasting employment opportunities in nearby communities.

Environmentalists rightly insist that federal lands belong to all Americans, and they are wary of the heavy influence that local interests exert over resource management. Consensus groups and collaborative efforts come with this built-in drawback. The Forest Service must remember that in its earlier days its leaders tried to uphold the interests of people who did not have a large economic stake in resource production. But the green groups need to flesh out their vision of how local communities could prosper next to, and indeed within, a well-managed and well-protected ecosystem. They have made attempts in this direction, but not as clearly and consistently as they might.[7]

At the height of his career in government, Guy Brandborg demonstrated an exceptional ability to engage people in productive conversations about the need for sound land-use practices. He did not always convert his listeners to his way of thinking, and his enthusiasm often turned to impatience, but many longtime Bitter Rooters attested to the power of his ideas. The question he asked in those years—can we both manage and conserve our forests?—remains unanswered. It will take a great deal of good thinking and careful experimentation to find the answers. People who love the woods will always have conflicting ideas of how to take care of them, but conservation will happen only if we pay attention to the land—and to each other.

Toward Lost Trail Pass, October 2008

Stevensville, Corvallis, Hamilton, Darby—the towns of the Bitterroot Valley pass behind as I drive down the still rural east-side highway and join the traffic on U.S. 93 for the drive home. Just beyond Darby and the site of one of its former lumber mills, I grab a last look at cloud-ringed North Trapper Peak, then head past Rye Creek and the pleasant fishing access site on the Bitterroot River that Champ Hannon and his family donated to the Montana Fish and Game Department. The record of many individuals' impact upon the land is here to read for those who are inclined to understand it. I have made only a beginning, but it has nonetheless been a fascinating and inspiring exercise.

As I climb out of the Bitterroot Valley amid a gathering autumn snowstorm, one last stop beckons. A few miles below Lost Trail Pass, the Forest Service has resurrected an old Nez Perce travel route that leads up to the Continental Divide. The trail climbs through a forest of ponderosa pine and Douglas fir that survived the fires of 1960 and 2000, then enters an old clearcut unit. I leave the trail and seek out a windswept ridge where the giant pines still grow. Most of them show scars from old burns and stand as a reminder of the forest's former grandeur. Memories flood in as the daylight fades. I think back to 1974, when I first met Ruth and Guy Brandborg at their home in Hamilton and listened to the old supervisor expound on the principles that govern the management of our national forests.

Doris Milner's idea of naming a mountain peak after old Brandy is an honor reserved for few women or men, but the grove of pines I stand beneath is an equally fitting memorial for both of these individuals. Perhaps it will also serve for Champ Hannon, Charles McDonald, and others still living who cared deeply about the future of the Bitterroot National Forest. Reserve a place of honor for them underneath these magnificent limbs, for they stood for a unique idea: that in our democracy we can find a way to use the bounty of this forest in a manner that leaves the land unimpaired for all who follow.

Notes

Introduction: Took Creek Saddle, Southwestern Montana, August 1971

1.   Dale A. Burk, "Sen. McGee Views Bare Bitterroot and Says: 'This Is the Worst I've Seen," *Missoulian*, August 26, 1971.

2.   Gladwin Hill, "National Forests: Physical Abuse and Policy Conflicts," *New York Times*, November 14, 1971. Burk included excerpts from many of his Bitterroot articles in his book *The Clearcut Crisis: Controversy in the Bitterroot*.

3.   Quotation is from Brandborg's last interview (Dale A. Burk and Don Schwennesen, "New Forestry Leaders Needed, Says Brandborg," *Missoulian*, March 14, 1977).

4.   Several former Bitterroot foresters recalled their experiences with clearcutting at Took Creek and Guide Saddle: John E. "Jack" Bennett, oral history interview by Ray Karr, KRTA OH-318, January 12, 1994; Ray Abbott, telephone interview by author, October 17, 2007; and Sonny LaSalle, telephone interview by author, July 23, 2008.

5.   Axel G. Lindh, memo to Northern Region forest supervisors and rangers, November 15, 1946, GBP 10/2. Lindh was the Northern Region's chief timber specialist in the years following World War II. The Northern Region, or Region 1, is today one of nine in the country's national forest system and encompasses national forests and grasslands chiefly in northern Idaho, Montana, and North Dakota.

6.   Figures on terraced and clearcut acres are from BNF Archives, Bitterroot Task Force data.

7.   Bitterroot National Forest 1966–1967 activity report, BNF Archives. A board foot is a one-foot-square section of wood that is one inch thick, used for measuring the quantity of raw timber or finished lumber. Nearly half of the cut that year was from salvage sales in recently burned areas.

8.   Richard Behan, e-mail to author, September 9, 2009. Guy Brandborg could also be highly abrasive toward public officials and others with whom he disagreed. In 1971 Montana conservation activist Cecil Garland asked Stewart Brandborg (Guy's son who was then executive director of the Wilderness Society) whether he was responsible for a reported tirade aimed at Ed Zaidlicz, the state director of the Bureau of Land Management. "My guess," Stewart replied, "is that you have confused me with some other Brandborg within your wide circle of acquaintances.... If it turns out to be the other character in the state of Montana by the same name, you would observe as I do that he runs his own course and that when in his judgment he decides to dispense a little hell he dispenses it with great courage and effectiveness" (Brandborg to Garland, October 22, 1971, TWS, series 2, 6/23).

9.   Outdoor author and columnist Michael Frome, in his book *Promised Land: Adventures and Encounters in Wild America,* described Guy Brandborg as a "two-fisted populist" who "helped me to evoke protest against squandering the heritage of our forests for greed and gain" (277–78). Luke Popovich recounted the Bitterroot clearcutting controversy from the forestry profession's viewpoint in his two-part retrospective, "The Bitterroot: Remembrances of Things Past" and "The Bitterroot: A Fading Polemic." Arnold Bolle, one of the key players in the controversy, remembered it in "The Bitterroot Revisited: A University [Re]View of the Forest Service." Richard Behan, a member of Bolle's well-known faculty review committee, recalled their work in *Plundered Province: Capitalism, Politics, and the Fate of the National Forests,* 151–58. Each of these narratives mentions Brandborg's involvement in general terms.

10. Typical are the comments of Bill Worf, who played a leading role in the Bitterroot controversy as head of a Region 1 investigative team during 1969–1970: "In the Forest Service a district ranger's [pay] grade was linked to how much timber he cut," he recalled recently. "Grade depended on job load, and timber was the job." While serving as supervisor of Wyoming's Bridger National Forest in the mid-1960s, he took the side of his district rangers who were expressing strong reservations over the magnitude of cutting they were expected to carry out.

Chapter 1. The Forests of the Bitterroot: 1878–1930

1.   Among many works on the ponderosa pine is Stephen F. Arno, Carl E. Fiedler, and Matthew Arno, "Giant Pines and Grassy Glades: The Historic Ponderosa

Ecosystem, Disappearing Icon of the American West." Not all of the presettlement ponderosa stands in the Northern Rockies formed open savannas; some had considerable undergrowth of trees or shrubs, depending on slope, aspect, and the severity of recent fires (Michele R. Crist et al., *Restoration of Low-Elevation Dry Forests of the Northern Rocky Mountains: A Holistic Approach*, 6).

2.   Donald J. Pisani traces the rocky courtship between forest conservationists and irrigation interests, who found reason to make common cause in establishing forest reserves despite the somewhat tenuous science behind the "forest influences" argument ("Forests and Reclamation, 1891–1911").

3.   Samuel P. Hays, *Conservation and the Gospel of Efficiency: The Progressive Conservation Movement, 1890–1920*, 265. Char Miller discusses Pinchot's advocacy of public forestry as a corrective to the Gilded Age's concentrations of wealth and power in "Back to the Garden: The Redemptive Promise of Sustainable Forestry, 1893–2000." The 1897 act is also known as the Forest Service Organic Act.

4.   The creation of the reserves is discussed in Harold K. Steen and Christine Guth, *The U.S. Forest Service: A History*, 26–28.

5.   Gerald W. Williams and Char Miller, "At the Creation: The National Forest Commission of 1896–97."

6.   Carole Simon Smolinski and Don Biddison, *Moose Creek Ranger District Historical Information Inventory and Review, Nez Perce National Forest*; O. F. Shumaker, "Bitterroot National Forest Administrative History" (typescript, BNF Archives); Lawrence Rakestraw, "Forestry Missionary: George Patrick Ahern, 1894–1899."

7.   The Bitterroot National Forest's chronology is drawn from USDA Forest Service, Northern Region, *The Bitterroot National Forest: In Celebration of a Century of Conservation*, 2–4, and from appendix 1 of "Region One Forest Chronology," USFS-NR. The disposition of the original reserve is shown on a helpful map in Albert N. Cochrell, *The Nezperce Story: A History of the Nezperce National Forest*, 127. Initially spelled as one word, it is now the Nez Perce National Forest. The Selway National Forest was created in 1911 out of the Clearwater NF.

8.   Richard U. Goode, "Bitter Root Forest Reserve," 388.

9.   Ibid., 398; John B. Leiberg, "Bitterroot Forest Reserve," 270. The report included a map depicting areas burned within the past thirty-five years.

10. Goode, "Bitter Root Forest Reserve," 398–99; Leiberg, "Bitterroot Forest Reserve," 260.

11. There are various ways of scaling, or calculating, the number of board feet in a tree. Some version of the Scribner scale was in common use in the western national forests through most of the twentieth century. Variance in actual scale is minor for the purposes of this book.

12. K. Ross Toole and Edward Butcher, "Timber Depredations on the Montana Public Domain."

13. Leiberg, "Bitterroot Forest Reserve," 274–75.

14. The company underwent a number of name changes since its incorporation in 1881 as the Anaconda Mining Company. *Copper* was added to the title in 1895; after Marcus Daly sold the company to Standard Oil in 1899, it was renamed the Amalgamated Copper Mining Company; it reverted to the previous title after its holding company was dissolved in 1915. Following common usage, I refer to it as the Anaconda Company.

15. *Western News* (Hamilton, Mont.), February 15, 1899, cited in Edward Bernie Butcher, "An Analysis of Timber Depredations in Montana to 1900," 85, 87. Anaconda operated in the valley under a subsidiary, the Bitter Root Development Company.

16. Michael P. Malone, Richard B. Roeder, and William B. Lang, *Montana: A History of Two Centuries*, 332; Robert D. Baker et al., *National Forests of the Northern Region: Living Legacy*, 43. The Montana Improvement Company was a consortium of the principal timber companies in western Montana, including Anaconda, the Northern Pacific Railroad, and several Missoula capitalists.

17. Clarence Strong to William Worf, February 6, 1970, GBP 2/6.

18. Les Joslin, *Uncle Sam's Cabins: A Visitor's Guide to Historic U.S. Forest Service Ranger Stations of the West*, 16.

19. Gifford Pinchot, *The Fight for Conservation*, 43.

20. Henry S. Graves to Secretary of Agriculture, March 24, 1910, NAS 95-63A209, box 9, folder "S—Plans—Bitterroot—Timber Management, 1908–1926."

21. Mallory N. Stickney, Acting Forest Supervisor, to District Forester, April 4, 1912, ibid.

22. BNF historical timber records, folder "Info on Timber in Bitterroot."

23. The Lick Creek sale is well described in Helen Y. Smith and Stephen F. Arno, eds., *Eighty-eight Years of Change in a Managed Ponderosa Pine Forest*. Anaconda obtained the rights to the stumpage from an Idaho partnership that had underbid the company. The BNF's FACTS timber-sale database lists five clearcutting units in the Lick Creek area from that period, aggregating 178 acres; I could find no mention of these sales in the historical record.

24. Michael G. Hartwell, Paul Alaback, and Stephen F. Arno, "Comparing Historic and Modern Forests on the Bitterroot Front." The researchers also found significant increases in the proportion of Douglas fir, as well as a serious decline in whitebark pine in the upper-middle elevations of the Bitterroot mountain front.

25. Figures for the Shannon-Bunkhouse and Lost Horse timber sales are from contractual records in the Bitterroot National Forest's permanent files, box "Lick Creek Experimental Area," and from "Summary of Bitterroot National Forest Timber Management Plan, FY 1966 to FY 1972," BNF historical timber records.

26. John W. Lowell to District Forester, April 8, 1925, NAS 95-63A209, box 9, folder "S—Sales—Bitterroot—1906–1923."

27.   Harvest levels are from regional fact sheets from 1926 and 1956, NAS 95-60A70, box 3.

Chapter 2. Pinchot's Corps: 1881–1924

1.   The July 4 incident is described in Steven J. Keillor, *Cooperative Commonwealth: Co-ops in Rural Minnesota, 1859–1939*, 147–48. Keillor drew his account from news clippings and other materials in the Charles W. Brandborg Family Papers at the Minnesota Historical Society.

2.   Brandborg's recollections are from an oral history interview with Mavis McKelvey, May 6, 1975, Hamilton, Montana (KRTA OH-413-02, side A).

3.   Historian Don Lago, writing of the values that many Swedish immigrants brought to the United States, observed that "in Scandinavia, nature was a force far stronger than humans. The best humans could do was to obey nature's rules. There was little conception of humans totally subduing nature" (*On the Viking Trail: Travels in Scandinavian America*, 43–44). Yet Axel Lindh, Brandy's nemesis in the timber branch in Missoula who pressed him to increase wood-fiber production, was also a Swede. Natural law, it seems, is open to interpretation.

4.   The Brandborg family's remembrances include a genealogy written by Guy's brother Warner in 1959; additional recollections by brother Ralph in a March 3, 1964, letter to the Minnesota Historical Society (both in the possession of Stewart Brandborg); and Guy's brief recollections of his upbringing and career, dated March 7, 1975 (copy in Mavis McKelvey Papers, KRTA).

5.   Donald H. Robinson, *Through the Years in Glacier National Park: An Administrative History*.

6.   Brandborg discussed his first summers in Montana in his March 1975 account (see note 2), with additional details in his Forest Service ranger notebooks (collection of Stewart Brandborg) and in McKelvey's unpublished 1977 manuscript (in author's possession), "Brandy Peak Dedication," which she prepared for a memorial service held on August 12, 1978.

7.   H. B. Ayers, *The Lewis and Clarke Forest Reserve*. The Flathead reserve was subsumed into the Lewis and Clarke in 1903, then split out again when each was designated as a national forest in 1908. The *e* in *Clarke* was dropped at that time.

8.   Stewart Brandborg, telephone interview by author, May 18, 2008.

9.   The State University of Montana at Missoula was known for a time as Montana State University. In 1965 it became the University of Montana, and Montana State College in Bozeman became Montana State University—today's MSU.

10.   GB, McKelvey interview, May 6, 1975, side A; *Forestry Kaimin* (Montana State University) 13 (March 1915): 47.

11.   In his biography *Gifford Pinchot and the Making of Modern Environmentalism*, Char Miller describes how the chief inculcated a missionary zeal in his corps of

supervisors, rangers, and foresters (see esp. 279, 332). Miller writes that Pinchot brought to his administration "a keen awareness of and rapid political responses to a degrading and exploitative economic system" (358–59).

12. GB, McKelvey interview, May 21, 1975, side A.

13. Dupuyer Centennial Committee, *By Gone Days and Modern Ways.*

14. American Forestry Association, *Proceedings of the American Forest Conference,* 56.

15. The history of mining at Radersburg is described on the Montana Department of Environmental Quality's Abandoned Mine Reclamation Web site, http://www. deq.mt.gov/AbandonedMines/linkdocs/techdocs/36tech.asp.

16. A key figure in the agency's efforts to regulate grazing in Crow Creek was Thomas Lommasson, a range examiner for the Northern Region office, with whom Brandborg continued to work in later assignments.

17. GB notebook entries, 1917–1918, collection of Stewart Brandborg.

Chapter 3. From the Snake to the Selway: 1924–1935

1. John B. Leiberg, *The Bitter Root Forest Reserve,* cited in Cochrell, *Nezperce Story,* 99–100.

2. L. C. Hurtt, "Forests Are Great Asset to Residents," *Idaho County Free Press* (Grangeville, Idaho), February 5, 1925; "Demand for Grazing Land Indicates Livestock Gain," *Idaho County Free Press* (Grangeville, Idaho), February 16, 1928; Stewart Brandborg, interview by author, August 6, 2007.

3. GB to Regional Forester, November 27, 1951, GBP 14/12; Roy A. Phillips, "Recollections," in *Early Days in the Forest Service,* by USDA Forest Service, Northern Region, 2:20.

4. "Problems of Rangers on Nezperce Forest," *Idaho County Free Press* (Grangeville, Idaho), January 21, 1932; McKelvey, "Brandy Peak Dedication," 13–14 (see chap. 2, n. 6).

5. Stewart Brandborg, interview by author, August 6, 2007, Hamilton, Montana.

6. Log drives: Charles McCollister and Sandra McCollister, "The Clearwater River Log Drives: A Photo Essay." Nezperce timber: USDA Forest Service, "Estimates of National Forest Timber, District 1, March 1926," personal collection of Stewart Brandborg.

7. "Progress Made in Developing Nezperce Forest," *Idaho County Free Press* (Grangeville, Idaho), December 10, 1925.

8. Forest fire data: "Nezperce Fire Data 1921 to Date [1930]"; lookout towers: "Nezperce Forest, Fire Control Improvement Needs, 1932"; both from GB's notebooks in the possession of Stewart Brandborg.

9. The Forest Service's district offices were renamed regional offices in 1933, with their heads known as regional foresters.

10. Amelia Fry, "The Making of a Regional Forester," KRTA, oral history OH-240, October 10, 1964 (sound recording).

11.   Bud Moore, *The Lochsa Story: Land Ethics in the Bitterroot Mountains,* 181; Moore, interview by author, September 29, 2007, Condon, Montana.

12.   John W. Lowell, "Report on Addition to Forest Road System," November 28, 1927, NAS 95-60A70, box 7A, folder E—"Roads & Trails—Bitterroot—General—Over Three Years Old." Construction of the Magruder road is drawn from Shumaker, "Bitterroot National Forest Administrative History" (see chap. 1, n. 6).

13.   Clarence Sutliff, "Selway Forest Fires of 1934," in vol. 4 of *Early Days in the Forest Service,* by USDA Forest Service, Northern Region.

14.   B. A. Anderson, "Mushrooms," 11.

15.   Headley to Silcox, September 17, 1934, cited in Smolinski and Biddison, *Moose Creek Ranger District,* 106–7.

16.   "Board of Review Report, Selway Fires—1934," Northern Region history files, 5100 Fire Management.

17.   The role of the 1934 Selway fires in formulating the ten o'clock policy is discussed in Stephen J. Pyne, *Year of the Fires: The Story of the Great Fires of 1910,* 266–67. Burned acreage figure is from Baker et al., *National Forests of the Northern Region,* 151.

Chapter 4. Protection Forest: 1935–1939

1.   Joseph Kinsey Howard, *Montana: High, Wide, and Handsome,* 285. Cattle rustling and arson: E. Duke Richey, "Subdividing Eden: Land Use and Change in the Bitterroot Valley, 1930–1998," 40–45.

2.   GB, McKelvey interview, May 21, 1975, KRTA OH-413-01a, side B.

3.   Mary C. Horstman and Kristi Whisennand, *The History of Sheep Grazing on the Lolo and Bitterroot National Forests, 1907–1960,* 9.

4.   Ibid.; GB, McKelvey interview, May 21, 1975, KRTA OH-413-01b, side A.

5.   John McClintic, interview by Dave Filius, February 1977, box "History of Bitterroot Forest & Valley," folder "Sula Area History," 26, BNF Archives; Earl Sandvig to Clayton Weaver, October 10, 1970, TWS, series 4, 30/2.

6.   Paul H. Roberts, Memorandum to Region 1, October 11, 1949, grazing files, NAS 95-60A70, box 8A, folder "G—Inspection—General."

7.   Leon C. Hurtt, "Bitterroot Range Inspection Report, 10/22/20," NAS 95-60A70, box 8A, folder "G—Grazing."

8.   Bitterroot National Forest, "Elk Management Plan," March 28, 1933, NAS 95-60A70, box 14, folder "W—Plans—General—Permanent Folder"; Fred Wetzsteon and Edgar Wetzsteon, interview by Richard Walker, December 20, 1976, Sula, Montana, box "History of the Bitterroot Forest & Valley," folder "Sula Area History," 24, BNF Archives.

9.   GB to District Ranger, Sula, Montana, May 28, 1941, NAS 95-60A70, box 8A, folder "G—Cooperation—Sula Stock Association."

10. Map titled "Rangers' Proposed Road Plan, 11/13/35," NAS 95-60A70, box 7A, folder "E—Roads & Trails—Bitterroot—General—Over Three Years Old."

11. USDA Forest Service, Northern Region, "The Bitterroot National Forest: In Celebration of a Century of Conservation," 6; "Nez Perce Trail Is Replaced by Modern Highway," *Western News* (Hamilton, Mont.), October 12, 1933; unsigned memo to District Forester, March 27, 1934, NAS 95-60A70, box 3, folder "E—Roads & Trails—Bitterroot—General"; *Magruder Road Corridor* (brochure), USDA Forest Service, Nezperce and Bitterroot National Forests.

12. Carl A. Weholt, "They Pioneered the Bitterroots," in *Early Days in the Forest Service,* by USDA Forest Service, Northern Region, 4:116–17.

13. Region 1 engineering records, NAS 95-60A70, box 7.

14. GB to Regional Forester, October 16, 1937, ibid.

15. Ernst C. Peterson, "A Thousand Miles of Backpacking," 12.

16. Marshall described his grizzly encounter in "Impressions from the Wilderness," 12.

17. In 1936 Bob Marshall was employed by the Interior Department's Bureau of Indian Affairs, but he still consulted extensively with Forest Service chief Ferdinand Silcox and other agency officials. See James M. Glover, *Robert Marshall: A Wilderness Original,* 67–97; and AnneMarie Moore and Dennis Baird, *Wild Places Preserved: The Story of Bob Marshall in Idaho.*

18. Stewart Brandborg, interview by author, October 12, 2007.

19. Stewart Brandborg, transcript of interview with Joanna Tenny, July 12, 2002, Missoula (Wilderness Institute, School of Forestry, University of Montana, tape 1, side B). Also Stewart Brandborg, interview by author, August 6, 2007, Hamilton, Montana. Marshall's hike is described in the *Northern Region News* 9 (July 6, 1937) and is cited in A. Moore and Baird, *Wild Places Preserved,* 141–42.

20. Stewart Brandborg heard this from George Marshall, Bob's brother, who served with Stewart on the governing council of the Wilderness Society (Tenny interview, tape 1, side B).

Chapter 5. Forests for the People: 1937–1941

1. Warren Pollinger, "Lands of Ravalli County, Montana, and Some Problems in Their Use and Development," 1057–63. His report was sponsored by the Hamilton Chamber of Commerce and the Ravalli County Improvement Association. The Copeland Report was formally known as *A National Plan for American Forestry* (Senate Doc. 12, 73rd Cong., 1st sess., 1933).

2. Pollinger, "Lands of Ravalli County," 396, 401.

3. F. A. Silcox, "A Challenge."

4. Roosevelt's message was reprinted in USDA Forest Service, *A National Forest Economy: One Means to Social and Economic Rehabilitation, Preliminary Draft,*

copy in Northern Region history files (file 4800, Forest Resources Economics Research) and in GBP 1/2.

5.   Ibid., 15, 63, 89. Silcox discussed his controversial program in his article "A Federal Plan for Forest Regulation within the Democratic Pattern."

6.   *Northern Region Notes* (December 1939): 24; Stewart Brandborg, interview by Joanna Tenny, July 12, 2002, Missoula; quotation is from GB to Wayne Aspinall, November 5, 1967, GBP 10/6.

7.   USDA Forest Service, *National Forest Economy*, 175–76.

8.   F. A. Silcox, "Foresters Must Choose." The role of the National Industrial Recovery Act is discussed in Richard A. Rajala, *Clearcutting the Pacific Rainforest: Production, Science, and Regulation*, 123–24.

9.   Evan W. Kelley, March 11, 1938, speech to Ravalli County Chambers of Commerce, USFS-NR series 1680-1, folder "Evan Kelley—Speeches & Writings."

10. Ibid.

11. Brandborg, interview by Tenny, July 12, 2002.

12. "Management Plan for Bitterroot Working Circle, Bitterroot National Forest, Bitterroot Valley, Mont., 1941," GBP 2/2, 12.

13. The Rye Creek agreement was reached on February 28, 1941. In exchange for its land and timber, the Anaconda Company received an equal value of national forest timber on 122 acres in sections 3 and 4, T.2 N., R.19 W., valued at $4,223.40. Negotiations on the exchange were initiated in 1937. This and Brandborg's correspondence with Major Kelley regarding the exchange, dated May 3 and May 15, 1940, are in NAS 95-60A70, box 18.

14. "Acquisition Progress 1922 to June 30, 1945," R1 mimeo, GBP 8/4.

15. M. H. Wolff to GB, July 31, 1943, and GB to Wolff, August 3, 1943, ibid.

16. K. Ross Toole, *Montana: An Uncommon Land*, 195, 195.

17. Regional timber-cutting figures are from David Calkin, *Historic Resource Production from USDA Forest Service Northern and Intermountain Region Lands*, table 5. Figures for the Bitterroot's cut were recorded only informally; the most complete record is titled "Summary of Bitterroot National Forest Timber Management Plan, FY 1966 to FY 1972" (BNF historical timber records).

18. GB to Koch, November 20, 1936, NAS 95-60A70, box 10A, folder "Timber Management—thru 1943"; Koch to GB, February 2, 1939, ibid.

19. Edward Morris to K. Matthews, June 4, 1987, BNF historical timber files.

20. "Management Plan for Bitterroot Working Circle, Bitterroot National Forest, Bitterroot Valley, Mont., 1941," GBP 2/2. The cutting limit in ponderosa pine had previously been set as high as 20 mmbf. Elers Koch endorsed the fifty-year cutting cycle based on yield tables developed by Walter H. Meyer in *Growth in Selectively Cut Ponderosa Pine Forests of the Pacific Northwest*. Koch acknowledged that the period was arbitrary, but he advised Brandborg that "a variation of 10 or 15

percent in the predicted growth rate after cutting would probably not change that set-up. In other words, we will follow that plan and take what growth we get" (Koch to GB, March 16, 1940, NAS 95-60A70, box 10A, folder "S—Plans—Bitterroot—Timber Management—through 1943").

21. Mill production data are from individual rangers' reports to GB, all dated March 26, 1940 (NAS 95-60A70, box 10A, folder "S—Plans—Timber Management—through 1943."

22. Samuel T. Billings to Brandborg, ibid. "Select" includes the highest grades of pine, while "shop" contains more defects.

23. Philip Neff, "Data Re Labor, Utilization, Taxes, Etc. for Timber, Logging, and Manufacturing in Ravalli County, Montana," Division of Timber Management, Northern Region, February 14, 1941, NAS 95-63A209, box 9, folder "S—Sales—Bitterroot—1938–1943." Mine stulls are support posts and timbers.

24. Elers Koch to GB, April 4, 1941, ibid.; E. E. Carter to files, June 24, 1941, ibid.

25. Historian David A. Clary notes that District 1 tried to disallow timber sales to large companies with their own holdings, but was overruled by chief forester W. B. Greeley (*Timber and the Forest Service*, 33).

26. GB, McKelvey interview, May 6, 1975 (KRTA OH-413-02, side B).

Chapter 6. To Manage and Conserve: 1941–1954

1. GB, "Can We Manage and Conserve Our Forests?" (typescript, n.d.), GBP 4/11.

2. Brandborg to Regional Forester, April 28, 1948, NAS 95-60A70, box 10A, folder "Timber Management 1948–50."

3. GB, "Can We Manage and Conserve Our Forests?"

4. Ibid.

5. Ibid.

6. In 1951 Leon Hurtt, a range conservationist in the regional office and Brandy's former boss on the Nezperce, noted that Brandy was then being considered for a position in the Washington office to train agency staff in the art of good public relations. Hurtt called him "probably one of the best qualified men in the Service for the kind of work needed to get rangers, supervisors and others to see the whole range management program in proper perspective with public relations." Either the position was not created, or Brandy declined the move (Leon C. Hurtt to Walt L. Dutton, December 29, 1951, GBP 6/15).

7. Sandberg's remarks were made as part of Brandborg's nomination for the 1956 American Motors Conservation Award (Victor O. Sandberg to Ed Zern, August 17, 1957, AMC Award Collection, Denver Public Library, 2/29).

8. Quoted in Jo Rainbolt, "An Elephant in Every Yard," *Missoulian*, April 17, 1978.

9. Sandberg to Zern, August 17, 1957.

10. Ray Karr, e-mail to author, January 28, 2007.

11. W. C. Lowdermilk, *Conquest of the Land through 7,000 Years*. Lowdermilk worked

in the research arm of the District 1 office of the Forest Service (now Region 1) from 1919 to 1922. Soil-erosion data are from a 1934 Soil Erosion Service survey, cited in a December 14, 1939, memo by H. H. Bennett, http://www.law.yale.edu/documents/pdf/tables_figures.pdf.

12. Range inspection report by C. A. Joy and E. D. Sandvig, December 23, 1941, NAS 95-60A70, box 8A, folder "Grazing."

13. GB, "Organizing to Accomplish the Conservation Land-Use Objectives in Ravalli County" (typescript, n.d.), GBP 14/3.

14. Ibid.

15. "Better Use of Resources Planned for Ravalli County," *Great Falls Tribune,* September 16, 1945.

16. GB, notes for a talk given in the late 1940s, GBP 8/10; John Coleman and Edward McKay, "An Interview with Champ Hannon," MHS OH-2, January 21, 1970.

17. Ibid. Entomologist F. P. Keen identified four stages of maturity and vigor in ponderosa pine as a means of evaluating the risk of bark beetle attack ("Relative Susceptibility of Ponderosa Pines to Bark Beetle Attack"). His classification of maturity in ponderosa pine is described in Philip A. Briegleb, *Growth of Ponderosa Pine by Keen Tree Class.* The Bitterroot foresters used the Keen system as a proxy for culmination of annual increment.

18. Alfred Runte, *Public Lands, Public Heritage: The National Forest Idea,* 80–81.

19. Annual growth rates following thinning at Lick Creek ranged from negligible to a high of 126 board feet per acre per year, depending on the residual stand volume, with growth greater in stands that were cut heavier. The Lick Creek sale is one of the best documented of the Forest Service's early timber sales. The various studies conducted in the sale area are reviewed in Smith and Arno, *Eighty-eight Years of Change;* and Stephen F. Arno and Carl E. Fiedler, *Mimicking Nature's Fire: Restoring Fire-Prone Forests in the West,* 65–73.

20. Ruth Brandborg recalled Brandy's account of the Pinchot visit for reporter Jo Rainbolt in 1978 ("An Elephant in Every Yard").

21. George Hollibaugh, "Grizzly Bear, Mountain Goat, and Moose Study—1942," NAS 95-60A70, box 14, folder "W—Plans—General—Permanent Folder"; Wetzsteon and Wetzsteon, interview by Walker, 31–32 (see chap. 4, n. 8).

22. Hollibaugh, "Grizzly Bear, Mountain Goat, and Moose Study"; B. Moore, *Lochsa Story,* 277–78.

23. "A Report on the Educational Program, 1951–52" [mimeo, no author given], GBP 18/7; J. W. Severy and W. L. Pengelly, "Montana's Venture in Wildlife Education."

24. Vern Hamre, notes of meeting, January 27–28, 1954, NAS 95-60A70, box 9, folder "G—Management—General—C. Y. 1954."

25. Bernard DeVoto, "Sacred Cows and Public Lands," 268.

26. Wallace Stegner, *The Uneasy Chair: A Biography of Bernard DeVoto,* 297, 310.

27. Brandy's meeting with DeVoto is mentioned in a letter from Baker Brownell to

Joseph K. Howard, June 29, 1946 (Joseph K. Howard Papers, MHS 5/3). Avis DeVoto, Bernard's widow, acting upon Chet Olsen's advice, burned much of the correspondence between DeVoto and his Forest Service contacts after her husband's death to forestall retribution against those still working in the agency. According to Avis, Olsen described the letters as "dynamite" (Avis DeVoto to Thatcher Allred, March 17, 1969, Chester Olsen Collection, Stewart Library, Weber State University, Ogden, Utah, 1/1).

28. Charles H. McDonald, "The 'Battle' on Bass Creek," in vol. 4 of *Early Days in the Forest Service,* by USDA Forest Service, Northern Region. McDonald also described the incident in a 1972 oral history interview with John Coleman (MHS OH-4, side A).

Chapter 7. Timber Boom: 1941–1955

1. George S. Haynes to GB, April 29, 1944, NAS 95-60A70, box 10A, folder "S—Plans—Bitterroot—Timber Management—1946."

2. GB to Regional Forester [Evan W. Kelley], January 10, 1944, NAS 95-60A70, box 10A, folder "S—Plans—Bitterroot—Timber Management—1946."

3. The 1944 sale is listed in the Bitterroot's timber sale (FACTS) database. A patch cut is a small clearcut, generally no more than a few acres in size.

4. Fred Stell, "Annual Cut Work Sheet," June 25, 1946, NAS 95-63A209, box 9, folder "S—Sales—Bitterroot—Policy—1939–46."

5. "Summary of Cutting Budget: Bitterroot Working Circle, February 1947," NAS 95-60A70, box 10A, folder "S—Plans—Bitterroot—Timber Management—to 1943"; A. G. Lindh, inspection report on Bitterroot National Forest, November 24, 1955, NAS 95-60A70, box 10, folder "Inspection—1957."

6. Lawrence W. Zach and S. Blair Hutchison, *The Forest Situation in Ravalli County, Montana,* 13–14.

7. Lawrence W. Zach, "A Half Century of Lumbering in Ravalli County," press release, January 27, 1944, folder "Info on Timber in Bitterroot," 1–2, BNF historical timber records.

8. Ibid., 6.

9. GB to Regional Forester [Evan W. Kelley], January 10, 1944.

10. C. M. Granger to regional foresters, June 21, 1946, NAS 95-63A209, box 8, folder "S—Sales—Policy—1931–1949." Road funding data are from Baker et al., *National Forests of the Northern Region,* 170.

11. P. D. Hanson to Chief, Forest Service, June 14, 1946 [by Axel G. Lindh], NAS 95-63A209, box 8, folder "S—Sales—Policy—1931–1949."

12. P. D. Hanson to Region 1 forest supervisors and district rangers, July 26, 1946 [by C. S. Webb], ibid.

13. A. G. Lindh to GB, November 15, 1946, GBP 10/2.

14. Clary, *Timber and the Forest Service,* 116.

15. Lindh to GB, November 15, 1946.

16. See, especially, Randal O'Toole, *Reforming the Forest Service.*

17. Lindh to GB, November 15, 1946.

18. Brandborg to Regional Forester, n.d., NAS 95-63A209, box 9, folder "Sales—General—1949–1954."

19. GB to Regional Forester, October 10, 1951, NAS 95-60A70, box 9A; "Report of Public Hearing on Certain Timber Access Roads, Bitterroot National Forest," July 2, 1954, NAS 95-60A70, box 7A, folder "Access Road Hearing, July 1954."

20. Miles Romney Jr. to U.S. Forest Service, Darby Ranger Station, July 1, 1954, ibid.; Miles Romney Jr., "The Avenues to Our Future Should Not Be Paved with Past Mistakes" *Western News* (Hamilton, Mont.), June 17, 1954.

21. "Statement by Ravalli County Logging and Lumbering Group," attached as exhibit 6 of "Report of Public Hearing."

22. Stewart Brandborg, telephone interview by author, May 18, 2008; "Bitterroot National Forest: The Year in Review, 1954" [issued February 1, 1955], NAS, Northern Region historical files, box 61.

23. John R. Castles, memo to files, June 28, 1954; GB to Regional Forester, July 9, 1954, NAS 95-63A209, box 9, folder "S—Sales—Bitterroot—General—1957 and 1958."

24. These figures were cited in a forest inspection report filed by A. G. Lindh on November 25, 1955, NAS 95-60A70, box 10, folder "Inspection—1957," and were eventually incorporated into the 1957 revision of the timber-management plan.

25. C. J. Warren to Mike Mansfield, February 2, 1955, NAS 95-63A209, box 9, folder "S—Sales—Bitterroot—General—1957 and 1958."

Chapter 8. The Life of the Community: 1943–1952

1. Brandy's lectures to civic groups are mostly undated but fall within the period 1935–1948. They are an important expression of his underlying philosophy and his views on adult education and community betterment. This example is from GBP 23/2.

2. Melby's role in the Montana Study is discussed in Richard Roeder, "The Genesis of Montana Margins." Additional background comes from Carla Homstad, "Two Roads Diverged: A Look Back at the Montana Study." Melby outlined his hopes for the Forest Service's role in the study in a December 7, 1944, letter to L. A. Campbell of the regional office in Missoula (USFS-NR, file 1680, "Montana Program").

3. Howard, *Montana,* 275.

4. Baker Brownell, "Colonial Economy vs. Balanced Economy," USFS-NR, file 1680, "Montana Program."

5. Hamilton Study Group report and recommendations, July 13, 1945, Montana Study Research Collection, KRTA, series 1, 5/4.

6. Richard W. Poston, *Small-Town Renaissance: A Story of the Montana Study*, 50–61.

7. "'Timber Down the Hill,' Episode Two of *Darby Looks at Itself*," presented December 7, 1945, Montana Study Research Collection, series 1, 5/4.

8. Poston, *Small-Town Renaissance*, 75. McDonald comments: John Coleman, Charles H. McDonald oral history interview, January 22, 1970 (MHS OH-4, side A).

9. Harold F. Kaufman and Lois C. Kaufman, *Toward the Stabilization and Enrichment of a Forest Community*.

10. A. G. Lindh, "Notes by the Forest Service," in ibid.

11. A. G. Lindh to Baker Brownell, August 30, 1946, USFS-NR, file 1680, "Montana Program."

12. Meyer Wolff, "Memorandum on the Projected Montana Study," January 20, 1945, ibid.

13. "Montana Study Research Survives Board Debate," *Great Falls Tribune*, December 19, 1945.

14. Baker Brownell to GB, December 21, 1945, Joseph Kinsey Howard Papers, MHS, 5/2.

15. GB to Howard, September 3, 1948, ibid.

16. University of Montana, "A Proposal for Continuance of the Montana Study," February 1, 1949; George A. Selke to David A. Stevens, April 20, 1949; both in Montana Study Research Collection, KRTA, box 3. Stevens finally rejected the idea in a letter to Selke on October 14, 1949, ibid.

17. C. T. Forster to GB, January 25, 1949. This letter and the following correspondence regarding Brandborg's loyalty board hearing, unless otherwise cited, are from folder "Correspondence Re: Guy M. 'Brandy' Brandborg, 1949 and 1955," McKelvey Papers, KRTA.

18. R. T. Reid to GB, March 28, 1949. Reid was the Agriculture Department's personnel director.

19. GB to Forster, May 6, 1949. Brandy had advocated that the county commissioners make comprehensive soil surveys and adopt zoning requirements to prevent "flagrant misuse" of unsuitable lands—an issue that would remain unsolved and would polarize the Bitterroot Valley during the early twenty-first century.

20. United States Senate, Investigations Subcommittee on Expenditures, *Investigation of Federal Employees Loyalty Program* (Sen. Rep. 1775, 80th Cong., 2nd sess.), 1–3.

21. Brandborg mentioned the earlier investigation in an April 1, 1949, letter to Mike Mansfield, who wrote to the loyalty board in support of Brandy and offered to appear at his hearing.

22. Joseph Kinsey Howard to Charles A. Murray, May 6, 1949. Charles Murray was an administrative assistant to Montana senator James E. Murray.

23. The hearing record was not made public. My account is based on Joseph Kinsey Howard's description of the affair in a letter to Ernest O. Melby, June 7, 1949.

24. Howard to Melby, ibid.

25. Reid to GB, January 3, 1950.

26. Hugh Adair to Zales Ecton, June 4, 1949.

27. GB interview with Mavis McKelvey, May 21, 1975, MHS OH-413-01b, side A.

28. Hanson to GB, February 27, 1952, personal collection of Stewart Brandborg.

29. GB to Hanson [1952], ibid.

30. GB to George V. Ring, October 14, 1952, Nez Perce National Forest history files; GB to George Marshall, August 25, 1953, GBP 9/10.

Chapter 9. Holding the Line: 1948–1958

1. Arnold Bolle, talk given to annual meeting of the Montana Wildlife Federation, Kalispell, Montana, December 1, 1962, Arnold Bolle Papers, KRTA, 21/5.

2. "Conservation Education in the 1951 State Legislature," folder "Miscellaneous," McKelvey Papers, KRTA; Montana Conservation Council Records, KRTA, 4/15.

3. GB, McKelvey interview, May 6, 1975, side A.

4. Howard C. Lee to "Montana Rangers," February 4, 1953, NAS 95-60A70, box 7A, folder "Roads & Trails—Bitterroot—C. Y. 1955."

5. "A Plan: Protection and Development of Wildlife Habitat, Darby District, Bitterroot National Forest" [1955], NAS 95-60A70, box 14, folder "W—Management—Bitterroot—General C. Y. 1957," 25–27.

6. Ibid., 23–24. See also "A Plan Concerning Use, Protection, and Development of Wildlife Habitat, Stevensville District, Bitterroot National Forest, 1957," ibid., 19–20. The economic valuation of forest watersheds is inexact at best, but contemporary assessments typically factor in recreational, municipal, and power-generation uses as well, which would increase their value even further.

7. The Wilson letter is reprinted, in part, in Gerald W. Williams, *The Forest Service: Fighting for Public Lands*, 412–13.

8. Paul W. Hirt, *A Conspiracy of Optimism: Management of the National Forests since World War Two*, 293.

9. "Ravalli County Agricultural Resource Conservation Program" [mimeo, n.d.], GBP 4/11. Brandborg reflected upon his efforts to set up this and other programs in a paper titled "A History of Development and Improvement Efforts in Ravalli County," which he presented to a committee of the Hamilton Chamber of Commerce in 1963 (GBP 19/1).

10. James L. Goodrich (and seven others) to Richard E. McArdle, December 6, 1954, USFS-NR, G. M. Brandborg personnel file. Given Brandy's long history of behind-the-scenes organizing, it is possible that he instigated this unusual letter, although that would have required a high degree of chutzpah even for him.

11. Ron Trosper, telephone interview by author, February 7, 2007.

12. These are in the American Motors Conservation Award Collection of the Denver Public Library, 2/29.

13. Howard Zahniser to GB, March 14, 1958; Brandborg to "Johnnie" [John Craighead], April 7, 1958, both in TWS, series 1, 9/9.

14. Multiple Use–Sustained Yield Act, PL 86-517, enacted June 12, 1960.

15. *Address of Hardin R. Glascock to Forest Land Use Conference, American Forest Products Industries, Inc., Washington, D.C., Sept. 21–22, 1961.*

Chapter 10. Redeeming the Forest: 1955–1962

1. "Region One Timber Cut Sets New Record," news release, USDA Forest Service, Northern Region, February 1, 1955, NAS 95-76B1317, box 1; Richard E. McArdle [by Edward P. Cliff] to Regional Foresters, December 28, 1955, NAS 95-60A70, box 10A, folder "S—Plans—Timber Management—1954, 1955."

2. The Bitter Root Forest Associates appears to be a reconstituted version of the Ravalli County Logging and Lumbering Group that Billings represented the previous year regarding practices in the West Fork. Billings's statement was before a joint hearing of the Legislative Oversight Committee of the Senate Interior and Insular Affairs Committee and the House Subcommittee on Public Works, Government Operations Committee, 84th Cong., 1st and 2nd sess., November 30, 1955.

3. Inspection report filed by A. G. Lindh, November 25, 1955, NAS 95-60A70, box 10, folder "Inspection—1957."

4. What to do with Douglas fir in mixed stands continued to puzzle the regional office's silvicultural staff; in 1955 one forester noted that more than 250,000 acres of commercial ponderosa pine on the Bitterroot were "seral, or...growing temporarily on natural D. fir sites," and would need "a lot of intensive management in stand improvement, planting, etc." to keep the ponderosa growing. In response, a colleague offered that "we all realize that it will take a lot of doing to fight off Douglas fir on north-facing slopes. Sometimes I wonder if it would be desirable to even attempt to eliminate Douglas fir from the ponderosa pine type because of excessive cost. The cost would be greater than the return" (Fred W. Johnson, review of Bitterroot National Forest timber-management plan, November 24, 1954, with response by Corland L. James, January 13, 1955, NAS 95-60A70, box 10A, folder "S—Plans—Timber Management—1954, 1955").

5. The early clearcutting units are listed in the BNF's FACTS timber sale database (formerly TSPIRS).

6. P. D. Hanson to Forest Supervisors [mimeo], NAS 60A70, box 10, folder "S—Improvement—General."

7. Carl Wetterstrom to Regional Forester, January 2, 1957, NAS 95-60A70, box 10, folder "S—Inspection—General—1957."

8. Wetterstrom to Trosper, November 28, 1956, ibid.

9. Wetterstrom to Regional Forester, June 25, 1958, NAS 95-63A209, box 9, folder "S—Sales—Bitterroot—General—1957 and 1958."

10. "Proposed Guidelines for Preparation, Form, and Approval of Timber

Management Plans in Region One, May 10, 1957," NAS 95-60A70, box 10A, folder "Timber Management, 1957."

11. "Timber Management Plan, Bitterroot Working Circle, Bitterroot National Forest, Montana, 1957," USDA Forest Service, Bitterroot National Forest, Government Documents Collection, Mansfield Library, Missoula, ii.

12. Ibid., 12–13.

13. Ibid., 21–23.

14. Clearcutting in Blue Joint drainage: USDA Forest Service, Northern Region, *Management Practices, Bitterroot National Forest: A Task Force Appraisal, May 1969–April 1970*, 91–92. Figures for other sales involving clearcutting are from the Bitterroot's FACTS database.

15. The road-construction estimate was included in Region 1's budget requests submitted to Congress as part of the agency's *Long Range Program for National Forests* (U.S. House of Representatives, Committee of Agriculture, Subcommittee on Forests, 86th Cong., 1st sess., 1959), 160–64, cited in Baker et al., *National Forests of the Northern Region*, table 12.3.

16. Charles L. Tebbe, "The Access Road Situation in Region One," statement before Subcommittee on Roads, Committee on Public Works, U.S. Senate, Missoula, December 14, 1957 (USFS-NR, file 7100 Engineering Operations). By this time the Northern Region had consolidated several of its national forests, which now numbered sixteen.

17. Arnold Bolle outlined the events leading up to the *Full Use and Development* report in his prefatory remarks to a November 14, 1989, oral history interview with Robert Wolf (KRTA OH-227-29, 1–5).

18. USDA Forest Service, Northern Region, *Full Use and Development of Montana's Timber Resources*, xii.

19. Ibid., xiv.

20. Ibid., 1.

21. P. D. Hanson to Herman N. Simpson, June 4, 1956, NAS 95-60A70, box 10, folder S—Cooperation—General—1957"; A. G. Lindh to Stanford Research Institute, October 22, 1954, NAS 95-60A70, box 10, folder "S—Cooperation—General—1954–55–56–57"; Dan Hall, Robert Wolf oral history interview, November 27, 1990, KRTA OH-227-43, 6–7.

22. Michael Frome included an account of the Saddle Mountain fire in *Whose Woods These Are: The Story of the National Forests*, 218–22.

23. "Administrative Fire Analysis, Mine (Sleeping Child) Fire 8/4/61," NAS 95, Region 1 history files, box 63, folder "Historical Management."

24. "'Sleeping Child' Holocaust Sweeps Montana Wilderness"; John McClintic, interview by Dave Filius, February 1977, box "History of Bitterroot Forest & Valley," folder "Sula Area History," 8–9, BNF Archives. McClintic was a rancher in the Sula area.

25. " 'Sleeping Child' Holocaust."

26. Harold Andersen to Regional Forester, November 21, 1962, BNF fire control records, folder "Sleeping Child (Mine) Fire." Region 1's aerial spraying program had debuted on the Bitterroot during Brandy's watch, but in later years he recanted, pleading lack of knowledge of DDT's effects before the publication in September 1961 of Rachel Carson's *Silent Spring*.

27. "Amended Timber Management Plan, Bitterroot Working Circle, Bitterroot National Forest, Montana-Idaho, F.Y. 1966–F.Y. 1972," BNF historical timber records, folder "Timber Management Plans"; Harold Andersen to district rangers, December 26, 1961, ibid.

28. Bob Gilluly, "Operation Firebreak Scheduled in Two Bear Area about Oct. 1," *Ravalli Republican* (now *Ravalli Republic*), September 23, 1966. Mick DeZell observed recently that the young, thickly growing lodgepole pine that regrew in firebreak areas was somewhat fire resistant, much of it withstanding the extensive fires of 2000 (interview by author, July 31, 2008).

29. USDA Forest Service, Bitterroot National Forest, *Timber Management Plan, Bitterroot Working Circle, Bitterroot National Forest, Montana*, 9.

Chapter 11. Staking Out the Selway: 1939–1967

1. In a memo to Evan Kelley in 1940, Brandborg pointed out that the truck trails would require boundary modifications if the area was reclassified under U-1. Meyer Wolff, Kelley's assistant in charge of recreation and lands, replied that reclassification should be delayed in view of the likely controversy it would bring (GB to Kelley, February 13, 1940, and Wolff to GB, February 20, 1940, both cited in A. Moore and Baird, *Wild Places Preserved*, 177–78).

2. Wilderness Society outing: Stewart Brandborg, interview by author, October 12, 2007; Mark W. T. Harvey, *Wilderness Forever: Howard Zahniser and the Path to the Wilderness Act*, 161–62. Harvey Broome devoted a chapter to the outing in his book *Faces of the Wilderness*. Selway logging: William P. Cunningham, "The Magruder Corridor Controversy: A Case History," 40. Cunningham's thesis is the foremost account of the controversy over logging in the Magruder Corridor.

3. Statement of G. M. Brandborg, Selway-Bitterroot wilderness hearing, March 7, 1961, Missoula, LMP 41/3. Brandy's early boundary recommendations do not seem to have survived. The Forest Service gave letter designations (*A* through *F*) for various exclusions from its proposed wilderness area.

4. Area E included 173,000 acres in the Magruder Ranger District of the Bitterroot National Forest, with the remainder in the drainages of Bargamin Creek and Running Creek on the Nezperce National Forest. See "Upper Selway Management Area, Bitterroot National Forest."

5. Bernie A. Swift, memo to files, May 18, 1959, NAS 95-67A136, box 4, folder "S-Plans—Timber Management—Planning—Bitterroot Forest 1958–";

W. H. Johnson to Harold Andersen, January 21, 1963, and Andersen to Regional Forester, January 29, 1963, file 2410 Plans, folder "Magruder Block," BNF Archives.

6. Andersen to Morton R. Brigham, January 5, 1965, SBP 42/1.

7. Forestwide timber sales figures are from "Timber Management Plan for the Bitterroot National Forest, 1966," historical timber files, BNF Archives. Slow Gulch sale: Cunningham, "Magruder Corridor Controversy," 77.

8. Doris Milner, oral history interview by Scott Bischke, December 9, 2002 (MHS OH-2076, tape 1, side A).

9. Doris Milner, oral history interview by Mavis McKelvey, 1975 (KRTA OH-413-03).

10. Clifton R. Merritt, oral history interview by Scott Bischke, December 19, 2002 (MHS OH-2075, tape 2, side B), with supplemental information from Bischke in a telephone interview by author, January 23, 2007; also William Cunningham, telephone interview by author, March 9, 2007.

11. Minutes of Save the Upper Selway Committee, September 20, 1964, Brock Evans Papers, University of Washington Libraries, 12/35. Stewart Brandborg recounted the Wilderness Society's involvement with the Selway committee in an interview with the author, January 25, 2007. He and Clif Merritt composed the Selway brochure and arranged for its printing.

12. Save the Upper Selway Committee, *Save the Wilderness of the Upper Selway* (brochure) (Evans Papers, University of Washington Libraries, 12/35).

13. Doris Milner to Clif Merritt, December 3, 1964, box 12, folder "Upper Selway, 1964—Previous," Clifton R. Merritt Papers, KRTA.

14. Miles Romney Jr., "Save the Upper Selway Wilderness," *Western News* (Hamilton, Mont.), January 27, 1965.

15. "Save Selway for Its Beauty, Recreation—Mrs. Milner Asks," *Ravalli Republican*, February 5, 1965.

16. GB to Merritt, January 11, 1965, box 12, folder "Selway 1965," Merritt Papers, KRTA.

17. Brigham to Rahm, April 13, 1966, Evans Papers, University of Washington Libraries, 12/34. Rahm replaced Boyd Rasmussen in early 1964.

18. Milner to Olsen, January 27, 1965, Arnold Olsen Papers, KRTA, 82/6.

19. Romney to Olsen, May 3, 1965, ibid.

20. Hollingsworth and Billings to Metcalf, LMP 41/3. Andersen's comments are cited in Cunningham, "Magruder Corridor Controversy," 83. Milner to Bowler: January 27, 1965, Bruce Bowler Papers, Idaho State Historical Society, 37/21.

21. Trosper to GB, June 21, 1965, SBP 42/2; Miron Heinselman, *The Boundary Waters Wilderness Ecosystem*, 120–21.

22. Brigham to Roger Pegues, April 13, 1966, also GB note to Pegues, April 1966, both in Evans Papers, University of Washington Libraries, 12/32. Roger Pegues

was Evans's predecessor as the FWOC's Northwest conservation representative in Seattle. Metcalf legislation: Stewart Brandborg to Milner, January 21, 1966, SBP 42/2. Stewart attached his draft of an Upper Selway wilderness bill to a letter to Metcalf, May 26, 1966, Bowler Papers, 37/26.

23. GB to Clif Merritt and Stewart Brandborg, December 23, 1966, folder "Selway 1965," Merritt Papers, KRTA.

24. Metcalf to Freeman, May 24, 1966, SBP 42/2; Cunningham, "Magruder Corridor Controversy," 94.

25. "Statement of G. M. Brandborg, Hamilton, Montana, in Support of Proposals for Wilderness Protection of the Upper Selway River," December 9, 1966, GBP 21/1.

26. Handbill, SBP 63/5. No date or attribution is given.

27. "Statement by Secretary Freeman on the Report of the Review Committee for the Magruder Corridor" [April 20, 1967], Magruder Corridor file, BNF Archives.

28. Selke to Brandborg, June 14, 1967, GBP 20/7.

Chapter 12. A Fighting Democratic Faith: 1964–1969

1. B. K. Monroe, "The Brandy B. K. Knew," *Ravalli Republic*, August 15, 1978.

2. GB to Bowler, December 1966, Bowler Papers, 37/28.

3. Brandy made this comment to Bill Jellison of the Rocky Mountain Laboratory in November 1967 (Ruth Brandborg notes, collection of Stewart Brandborg).

4. The commission consisted of eighteen members appointed by the Senate, the House, and the president. Its report, *One Third of the Nation's Land* (Washington, D.C.: Government Printing Office, 1970), called for a major overhaul of federal land laws and led to the passage of the Federal Land Policy and Management Act of 1976 (PL 94-579, 94th Cong.), which focused on Bureau of Land Management lands. The commission also proposed that the Forest Service be merged with the BLM—which never occurred—and that both agencies be guided by a more production-oriented philosophy.

5. Brandborg to Aspinall, November 5, 1967, GBP 10/6.

6. Sigurd F. Olson to GB, December 3, 1967, ibid.

7. Ruth Brandborg's background is drawn from Rainbolt, "An Elephant in Every Yard" (see chap. 6, n. 8), and from interviews with Stewart Brandborg.

8. Division of Timber Management, Northern Region, functional plan for fiscal year 1963–1964, Intaglio, Inc., Research Collection, KRTA, 5/25.

9. "Amended Timber Management Plan, F.Y. 1966–F.Y. 1972." After minor revisions to Karr's proposal, the forest's allowable cut was set at 63 mmbf, not including the lodgepole-pine type, which was left in the unregulated category.

10. Ray Karr to Harold Andersen, "Management of Softwood Species—Bitterroot," February 17, 1966, BNF historical timber records, folder "Timber Management Plans." Karr based his recommendation for mechanical stripping of the soil surface on research studies at the Boise Basin Experimental Forest in Idaho, which

showed better seedling survival and growth than with hand planting. Machine planting on the Bitterroot was begun in 1962 and was applied to terraced clearcuts in 1964.

11.   In an undated letter that he sent to Lee Metcalf around 1969, Lindh said that "over the years we had very great difficulty in reestablishing forest growth on many severe south facing slopes. I was the one who urged that terracing be tried. Consequently, I cheer today's foresters for these trials.... These are worthy experiments" (LMP 32/1). I am indebted to Ray Abbott, former Sula District forester, and Sonny LaSalle, who worked on the West Fork District as a reforestation crew leader, for their descriptions of the terracing and planting procedure.

12.   USDA Forest Service, Northern Region, *Management Practices, Bitterroot National Forest,* 35.

13.   Bitterroot National Forest annual reports, 1963–1967, NAS 95, Region 1 history files, box 61, folders "BNF—Historical Reports—Forests" and "Bitterroot National Forest—Timber—Historical"; *Forest Patterns: Beauty and Use* [pamphlet], USDA Forest Service PA-679 (Washington, D.C.: Government Printing Office, 1965).

14.   Sonny LaSalle, telephone interview by author, July 23, 2008; Ray Abbott, telephone interview by author, October 17, 2007.

15.   Matthew Hansen, Samuel J. Billings oral history interview, October 4, 1982, MHS OH-421, tape 2, side A.

16.   J. Leonard Bates, "Fulfilling American Democracy: The Conservation Movement, 1907 to 1921," 29. A rebuttal to this interpretation of Progressivism came soon after from Samuel P. Hays, whose book *Conservation and the Gospel of Efficiency* stressed the movement's emphasis on managed resource production. The Progressive movement was broad enough to include adherents of both gospels. Brandborg's social activism expressed his populist leanings, whereas his actions as supervisor showed that he was comfortable working within the scientific-managerial paradigm.

17.   Bates, "Fulfilling American Democracy," 30.

18.   GB to Bolle [February 1967], GBP 19/1.

19.   Bolle to GB, February 25, 1967, ibid.

20.   Statement of Doris Milner, ibid., 147–48.

21.   Baker et al., *National Forests of the Northern Region,* 325; Ray Karr, telephone interview by author, August 8, 2008.

22.   Statement of Richard Schloemer, Victor, Mont., before Senate Subcommittee on Public Lands, hearings on Forest Lands Restoration and Production Act, Senate Bill 1734 (92nd Cong., 1st sess.), August 9, 1971, Portland, Oregon. The Bitterroot eventually acknowledged that it had overcut the Montana portion of the forest: its 1972 multiple-use plan cited "an inability to disperse timber harvest, with clearcutting viewed as the best alternative for concentrating cutting over the

smallest possible area" (USDA Forest Service, Bitterroot National Forest, *Bitterroot National Forest Multiple Use Plan, Part 1, July 17, 1972*).

23. Arnold W. Bolle, William K. Gibson, and Elizabeth Hannum, *The Forest Products Industry in Montana*, 58.

24. Harold F. Kaufman, "Sociology in Forestry," 117, cited in Con H. Schallau, "Sustained Yield versus Community Stability: An Unfortunate Wedding?" 21, 23. Schallau argues that "far from being the means to achieve community stability, sustained yield now competes with it" (ibid., 22).

25. GB to Irving Brant, September 28, 1970, TWS, series 1, 9/10.

26. Curt Meine, "Conservation and the Progressive Movement: Growing from the Radical Center," 180–81.

Chapter 13. Collision Course: 1965–1969

1. Bob Gilluly, "S and W Sawmill Can Produce 100,000 Board Feet Every 8 Hours," *Ravalli Republican*, January 29, 1965. The Intermountain Lumber Company acquired this mill in July 1967.

2. Forest Cooper to Metcalf, February 9, 1965, LMP 41/3.

3. GB to Miles Romney, September 1967(?), Stewart Brandborg Papers, KRTA, box 30, folder "Logging Rav. County."

4. Merrill Tester to Regional Forester, June 2, 1967, file 2470 Silvicultural Practices, folder "Sleeping Child Water Users Association," BNF Archives.

5. Stanton Cooper to Mansfield, November 9, 1966; Sleeping Child Water Users Association to Mansfield, April 29, 1967, ibid.

6. Orville Grossarth to Merrill Tester, May 8, 1968, ibid.

7. "Minutes of First Annual Program Committee Meeting, January 9, 1967," Western Montana Fish and Game Association records, KRTA, 9/17; GB to Romney, February 1967, GBP 5/6.

8. Milner to Metcalf, June 19, 1967, LMP 40/12.

9. GB to Romney, February 1967.

10. John Coleman, "An Interview with Champ Hannon," MHS oral history OH-2, January 21, 1970. Hannon worked on the Bitterroot in various capacities beginning in 1925.

11. McKelvey, "Brandy Peak Dedication" (see chap. 2, n. 6).

12. GB to Metcalf, September 28, 1969, GBP 13/2.

13. Quotation is from Ruth Brandborg's notes, September 25, 1968, personal collection of Stewart Brandborg.

14. Bitterroot Resource Conservation and Development Committee, "Recreation Committee Minutes for October 1, 1968," collection of Doris Milner family.

15. "Project Proposal #168, Recreation Committee, Bitterroot Resource Conservation and Development Program," GBP 19/1.

16. "Minutes of the Program Committee Meeting," Bitterroot RC&D, October 8, 1968, collection of Doris Milner family; Bob Gilluly, "RCD Subcommittee Criticizes Forest Timber Cutting Practices," *Ravalli Republican,* October 9, 1968. In 1970 the Forest Service's Bitterroot Task Force would determine that significant volumes of ponderosa pine had been cut from stands dominated by Douglas fir, leading to an overcut in the pine component (see chapter 14).

17. Tester to Regional Forester, October 9, 1968, Bitterroot Controversy files, BNF Archives.

18. Tester to Regional Forester, November 1, 1968, ibid.; Wilma Henault, "People Employed in Timber Industry Hold Meeting, Protest RCD Logging Study Proposal," *Ravalli Republican,* October 21, 1968.

19. Myron Alteneder, letter to editor, *Ravalli Republican,* October 31, 1968.

20. Jack Evans, letter to editor, *Ravalli Republican,* November 7, 1968.

21. "Three Resolutions Adopted as Sportsmen Meet Monday," *Ravalli Republican,* November 26, 1968; Bolle to GB, January 27, 2009, GBP 1/4.

22. GB to Brock Evans, October 1968, GBP 7/4.

23. Evans recalled the FWOC meeting in an e-mail to the author, December 21, 2008. He also reminisced on the subject as a preface to his personal files on the Bitterroot controversy (Evans Papers, University of Washington Libraries, 14/27).

24. Milner to Pechanec, August 23, 1967 (TWS, series 4, 43/3); Milner to Pechanec, November 5, 1968, BNF historical timber records, folder "Clearcutting Commentary."

25. Pechanec to Milner, November 12, 1968, ibid.

26. Rahm to Popham, May 1, 1969, GBP 2/6. Deputy chief M. M. Nelson, in a December 20, 1968, letter to the Bitter Root Multiple Use Association, stated that the RC&D's study proposal "appears to be generally consistent with the objectives of the Forest Service" and "should materially improve public understanding of our management objectives" (BNF historical timber records, folder "Clearcutting Controversy").

27. Gerald Williams, William A. Worf oral history, May 1, 1990, USFS-NR historical collection, Missoula. Consolidation had reduced the number of national forests in the Northern Region from its former seventeen.

28. GB to Burk, December 2, 1968, GBP 3/6. Burk's journalism career and his involvement in the Bitterroot controversy are analyzed in Christopher T. Ransick, "The Bitterroot Controversy: Dale Burk's Dual Role as Journalist and Activist." Burk spoke with me about his involvement in the Bitterroot controversy and his friendship with Guy Brandborg in a number of wide-ranging conversations from 2006 to 2008.

29. GB to Burk, August 29, 1969, GBP 1/4.

30. Ransick, "The Bitterroot Controversy," 19.

31. Dennis Swibold, "Anaconda Sheds Its Press."

32. Dale A. Burk, "Logger Attacks 'Clear Cut' Logging in Bitter Root,'" *Missoulian*, November 2, 1969.

33. Dale A. Burk, "Bitter Root Logging 'Extractive Industry,'" *Missoulian*, November 4, 1969.

Chapter 14. Engineering the Resistance: 1969–1970

1. K. A. Keeney, memo to record, November 7, 1969, BNF historical timber records, folder "Clearcutting Controversy"; Dale A. Burk, interview by author, August 2, 2007, Missoula.

2. Brock Evans, "Memo from BE to Montana-Bitterroot file," Evans Papers, University of Washington Libraries, 14/27.

3. Dale Burk, interview by author, August 2, 2007; Ruth Brandborg recollections, collection of Stewart Brandborg.

4. Ransick, "Bitterroot Controversy," 21; Burk, interview by author, August 2, 2007.

5. William E. Towell, "The Bridger Controversy"; Gale McGee, introduction to *The Case for a Blue Ribbon Commission on Timber Management in the National Forests* [ed. Laney Hicks], 3–4. The Forest Service's Wyoming study team issued its report, titled *Forest Management in Wyoming*, in 1971 through the Intermountain Region in Ogden, Utah.

6. GB to Otto Teller, September 15, 1969, Evans Papers, University of Washington Libraries, 14/27.

7. Merrill Tester to Teller, October 23, 1969, Bitterroot Controversy files, BNF Archives.

8. Tester to Gerald Bergh, November 29, 1968, Evans Papers, University of Washington Libraries, 14/27; Arnold Bolle, "Background and Effects of *A University View of the Forest Service, 1970–1995*," Bolle Papers, KRTA, 67/6. An edited version of this paper appeared as "Bitterroot Revisited."

9. Dale A. Burk, "Ranchers Fear Watershed Destruction," *Missoulian*, November 6, 1969.

10. Dale A. Burk, "Forestry Requires Long-Term Perspective," *Missoulian*, November 9, 1969. Subsequent articles appeared on November 12 and 13.

11. Dale A. Burk, "Retired Forester Criticizes Bitter Root Practices," *Missoulian*, November 16, 1969. Subsequent articles appeared on November 17 and 18.

12. Edward Cliff to Mansfield, December 4, 1969, GBP 12/6.

13. Bob Gilluly, "Moderate, Extreme Outlooks Balanced," *Ravalli Republican*, December 9, 1969.

14. USDA Forest Service, Northern Region, *Management Practices, Bitterroot National Forest*, 14.

15. Gordon Robinson collected his views on conservative forestry in his book *The Forest and the Trees: A Guide to Excellent Forestry*.

16. Ibid., 70–71.

17. Gordon Robinson, comments on Bitterroot Task Force Report, in *Final Environmental Statement: Management Direction for the Bitterroot National Forest, May 5, 1971.*

18. Craig E. Smith, typescript of speech presented to Hamilton Lions Club, January 6, 1970, W. Leslie Pengelly Papers, KRTA, 7/7.

19. "Darby's Intermountain Mill to Close, 50 Jobs Affected by Shutdown," *Ravalli Republican,* March 27, 1970; "Conservation Leader Attacks Lumber Industry for Overcut," *Missoulian,* April 2, 1970.

20. R. E. Stermitz, "Bitter Root: Shameful Distortion," *Missoulian,* April 7, 1970; Dale A. Burk, "Attack on Former Forest Service Official Follows Statement," *Missoulian,* June 26, 1970.

21. GB, "Those to Blame for the Overcut," *Missoulian,* July 3, 1970.

22. Horace Koessler, "Keeping the Record Straight," *Missoulian,* August 17, 1970.

23. Neal M. Rahm, remarks presented at meeting of Bitterroot Task Force, Hamilton, Montana, May 11, 1970, Evans Papers, University of Washington Libraries, 14/30.

24. Hutchison and Worf remarks, ibid., 12, 29.

25. Ibid.

26. USDA Forest Service, Northern Region, *Management Practices, Bitterroot National Forest,* 66.

27. Ibid., 15.

28. Ibid., 9.

29. Joel Frykman, a consulting forester for the Intermountain Company and a former timber division chief in the Intermountain Region, noted that in his experience, district rangers' and supervisors' personnel developed proposed cutting levels that were then reviewed by regional and Washington office staff. "We found it necessary to reduce most requests by Forest Supervisors because their estimates were usually higher than could be accomplished," he wrote in 1971. "Individual Supervisors may have encouraged higher goals for timber cutting on some Ranger Districts where the supply was abundant, but the goal setting was proposed by the field, and not by upper levels of management." The chief forester, he said, worked primarily to provide financing "for the goals already proposed by the field officers" (Joel L. Frykman, "Review of a Report by a Select Committee of the University of Montana on the Bitterroot National Forest, Montana," NAS Region 1 history files, box 61, folder "BNF—Historical—Clearcutting Controversy 1971–72—2 of 2").

30. USDA Forest Service, Northern Region, *Management Practices,* 50–51, including table 8.

31. Ibid., 100. Bill Worf points out that all of the division heads in Region 1, including the timber staff, knew that more silvicultural and reforestation work needed

to be done, but neither industry nor agency officials in Washington supported the necessary funding. Their goal was to get the cut out, he said, not long-term management (telephone interview by author, October 9, 2009).

32. Evans to Rahm, June 24, 1970, Brock Evans Papers, University of Washington Libraries, 14/27.

33. Aldrich to Rahm, June 29, 1970, ibid.

34. GB to Metcalf, May 18, 1970, GBP 13/1.

35. USDA Forest Service, Northern Region, *Management Practices, Bitterroot National Forest*, 2.

Chapter 15. Under the Microscope: 1970

1. Orville Daniels, interview by author, January 25, 2007, Missoula.

2. Daniels described his initial work on the Bitterroot in a February 19, 1971, talk given to the Intermountain Section of the Society of American Foresters in Missoula (copy provided courtesy of Bitterroot National Forest). During fiscal year 1971 he pulled five timber sales totaling 30.6 mmbf in order to incorporate new environmental safeguards. Most were offered again, but the largest one, the Moose Creek sale in the East Fork drainage, was appealed by the Montana Wilderness Association (John R. Milodragovich to Director, Timber Management, Washington Office, November 12, 1971, NAS 95-76B1317, box 1, folder "2490 Records & Reports FY72—Timber Sale Accomplishment Report").

3. Dale A. Burk, "Coyote Clearcutting Protested," *Missoulian*, November 6, 1970.

4. Dale A. Burk, "Ranchers Claim Watershed Damage from Logging," *Missoulian*, November 1, 1970. The schoolhouse in the lower Sleeping Child valley was the scene of previous meetings between the ranchers and the Forest Service.

5. "Nixon to Ask Increase in Harvest of Timber," *Idaho Statesman*, March 19, 1969.

6. Gordon Robinson, oral history interview by Harold K. Steen, October 3, 1978 (San Francisco: Sierra Club History Committee, in Sierra Club Oral History Series, Bancroft Library, University of California, Berkeley, http://bancroft. berkeley.edu/ROHO/collections/subjectarea/natres/sierraclub.html).

7. The Saylor letter is cited in Jack Shepherd, *The Forest Killers: The Destruction of the American Wilderness*, 84. Saylor spoke at a hearing on the National Timber Supply Act before the House Committee on Agriculture, 91st Cong., 1st sess., February 4, 1970.

8. GB to Mansfield, May 1, 1969; reply, May 12, GBP 12/6.

9. Ray Karr, telephone interview by author, August 6, 2008; Dale A. Burk, "Rahm Acknowledges Some Forest Service Inadequacies," *Missoulian*, April 12, 1970.

10. USDA Forest Service, Northern Region, *Quality in Timber Management: A Current Evaluation*; James Risser, "An Old Forester Speaks Out," *Des Moines Register*, February 16, 1971.

11. USDA Forest Service, Northern Region, *Quality in Timber Management*, 38–39.

12. Ibid., 47–48 (emphasis in the original).

13. Metcalf sent copies of many of the letters he had received to Arnold Bolle, including the first cited here, which came from a Victor resident (and former Forest Service employee) identified only as "Bill" (Bolle Papers, KRTA, 12/14). The second letter is from Keith Evans of Hamilton, November 19, 1970, LMP 37/2.

14. Charles McDonald to Metcalf, November 8, 1969, LMP 37/5.

15. Brandborg occasionally drafted letters for others to sign, but with few exceptions the letters in Metcalf's files on the Bitterroot timber issue appear to be heartfelt and original. Brandy's role as a behind-the-scenes organizer was widely acknowledged, though. When Metcalf sent Brandy a copy of the Bolle Report, he acknowledged that "your letter to me was one of the factors responsible for my original request to Dean Bolle" (Metcalf to GB, November 13, 1970, GBP 13/3).

16. Bolle, "Background and Effects of *A University View of the Forest Service*" (see chap. 14, n. 8).

17. Gerald Williams, Arnold W. Bolle oral history, KRTA OH-249, May 1, 1990, 12–13.

18. Metcalf to Bolle, December 2, 1969, GBP 13/2.

19. GB to Bolle, February 28, 1970, TWS, series 1, 9/9; Bolle, "Background and Effects of *A University View of the Forest Service*."

20. Arnold W. Bolle et al., *A University View of the Forest Service*, 13.

21. Ibid., 17–18.

22. Ibid., 20.

23. Ibid., 20–22. The Select Committee did not identify who wrote the individual sections of its report, but Wambach's correspondence with Bolle at the time of the report's release identifies this as his analysis (Bolle Papers, KRTA, 67/9). See also Richard W. Behan's account of the committee's work in his book *Plundered Promise*, 151–58.

24. Bolle et al., *University View*, 22.

25. Bolle, "Bitterroot Revisited," 170; Bolle et al., *University View*, 24 (emphasis in the original).

26. Bolle et al., *University View*, 24.

27. Clarence Strong and G. M. DeJarnette to Bolle, January 21, 1971, Bolle Papers, KRTA, 67/11.

28. Robert Marshall, *The People's Forests*, 79–80.

Chapter 16. A Function of the University: 1971

1. Bolle oral history interview, 15.

2. Risser, "An Old Forester Speaks Out" (see chap. 15, n. 10); GB to Bolle, November 16, 1970, GBP 17/12; "Mike Frome," 5. Frome lasted just a couple months longer at *American Forests* before William Towell, head of the American Forestry Association, its parent group, pressured the magazine's editor to muzzle the outspoken columnist.

3. Bolle, "Bitterroot Revisited," 170; Dale A. Burk, "Forestry Alumni Condemn and Defend Bolle Report," *Missoulian,* March 4, 1971; Richard E. Shannon, March 5, 1971, Bolle Papers, KRTA, 67/3.

4. Bolle, "Bitterroot Revisited," 170; Behan, *Plundered Promise,* 156; Robert T. Pantzer to Bolle, November 19, 1970, Bolle Papers, KRTA, 67/1.

5. C. Allan Friedrich to Bolle, January 29, 1971, Bolle Papers, KRTA, 67/5. Friedrich's report was *Some Watershed Aspects of Logging on the National Forests of Region One—with Special Reference to the Spruce Program.*

6. John A. Zivnuska to Bolle, December 1, 1970, NAS, Region 1 historical files, box 61.

7. Burk, "Forestry Alumni."

8. Dale A. Burk, Tom Ellerhoff, and Jeanette Ingold, "Neal Rahm and His Forest Service," *Missoulian,* March 21, 1971; Ray Karr, telephone interview by author, August 8, 2008.

9. USDA Forest Service, Northern Region, "Statement of Findings" [1971], Intaglio, Inc., Research Collection, KRTA, series 8, 7/8.

10. Members of the Bitterroot Task Force and the Bolle committee exchanged views at a meeting of the University of Montana Environmental Society on December 11, 1970 ("Public Discussion of Bitterroot Controversy," University of Montana, Mansfield Library, audiotape 308, side A).

11. National Forest Products Association, "Review of Forest Service and University of Montana Committee Reports on the Bitterroot National Forest," in *"Clear-Cutting" Practices on National Timberlands,* by U.S. Senate, Committee on Interior and Insular Affairs, Subcommittee on Public Lands, pt. 1, 1073–1104.

12. USDA Forest Service, Northern Region, *Management Direction for Northern Region.*

13. Ibid., 8, 11, 15.

14. Neal M. Rahm, "Northern Region Emphasis," Intaglio, Inc., Research Collection, KRTA, series II, 7/9.

15. Rahm to Division Chiefs, Forest Supervisors, and Director, EDC, November 25, 1970, attached to USDA Forest Service, Northern Region, *Management Direction for Northern Region.*

16. A transcript of the citizen statements at Rahm's December 8 news conference is attached to his remarks (Intaglio, Inc., Research Collection, KRTA, 7/17).

17. Rahm's memo was reprinted as a preface to *Management Direction for the Bitterroot National Forest, Final Environmental Statement, May 5, 1971,* 2.

18. Ibid., 16.

19. Rahm to Forest Supervisors and Division Chiefs, March 11, 1971, Intaglio, Inc., Research Collection, KRTA, series II, 7/9. Rahm's statement prefaced a series of seminars he held in 1971 to brief his forest officers on the need for public involvement and more effective oversight of timber cutting (Baker et al., *National Forests of the Northern Region,* 271).

20. Burk, Ellerhoff, and Ingold, "Neal Rahm."

21. Ibid.

22. "Regional Program Direction for F.Y. 72," Intaglio, Inc., Research Collection, KRTA, series II, 7/9.

23. USDA Forest Service, Bitterroot National Forest, *Magruder Corridor Resource Inventory,* 22–23; "Management Proposal for the Magruder Corridor, June 1, 1971," BNF Archives.

24. GB to Rahm, December 3, 1970, LMP 32/2.

25. Metcalf to Edward P. Cliff, January 20, 1971, ibid.

Chapter 17. Forestry on Trial: 1970–1971

1. Hicks, *Case for a Blue Ribbon Commission.*

2. Dale A. Burk, "Public Concern and Agency Response," in ibid., 17.

3. Testimony of Edward C. Crafts before the Subcommittee on Forests, House Committee on Agriculture, May 23, 1969, cited in Clifton Merritt, "Wilderness-on-the-Rocks," in ibid., 29.

4. GB, "Historical Perspective," in ibid., 15.

5. GB to Metcalf, May 18, 1970, GBP 13/3. The fight over Anderson's bill (Senate Bill 1820, 81st Cong., 1st sess.) is described in Steen and Guth, *U.S. Forest Service,* 267–68. Mike McCloskey, then executive director of the Sierra Club, wrote in a memoir that the Metcalf bill was intended to tie up timber-industry lobbyists in a defensive battle, thus forestalling their attempts to pass the Timber Supply Act ("Taking Over as Environmentalism Takes Off," 33). The strategy evidently succeeded.

6. Shepherd, *Forest Killers,* 160–62.

7. Edward P. Cliff, "State of the Forest Service, 1971," opening statement at regional foresters and directors meeting, Washington, D.C., January 18, 1971 (Intaglio, Inc., Research Collection, KRTA, series II, 8/3). Cliff gave much the same message to his employees in a memo sent to each agency office in October 1970, which was reprinted in part in *American Forests* 77 (January 1971): 11.

8. GB to Mansfield, May 1, 1969, and January 24, 1970, GBP 12/6; Metcalf to GB, June 16, 1970, GBP 13/2.

9. GB to Bruce Bowler, Bowler Papers, Idaho State Historical Society, 37/30; Bowler reply, September 9, 1970, ibid.

10. Metcalf to Church, August 24, 1970, blind copy in GBP 13/2.

11. Frank Church acknowledged that he scheduled the hearings as a result of requests from concerned citizens and from Senators Metcalf, Mansfield, McGee, and Randolph (Church to Merrill E. Deters, April 29, 1971, Frank Church Papers, Boise State University, series 2.2, 2/7). He also acknowledged Mike Mansfield's role in calling for hearings in a December 11, 1970, letter to Mansfield (Church Papers, Boise State University, series 2.3, 2/3). As Senate majority leader, Mansfield's request carried considerable weight.

12.   Church to Evans, March 11, 1971, Church Papers, Boise State University, series 2.3, 2/6; Kenneth B. Pomeroy to members of the National Council of Forestry Association Executives, January 12, 1971, GBP 13/2. Pomeroy was referring to legislative hearings, of course, not court action.

13.   Risser, "An Old Forester Speaks Out" (see chap. 15, n. 10).

14.   U.S. Senate, Committee on Interior and Insular Affairs, Subcommittee on Public Lands, *"Clear-Cutting" Practices*, 1:3.

15.   Ibid., 67–68.

16.   Evan W. Kelley to E. D. Sandvig, December 20, 1951, in ibid., 385–86. Earl Sandvig had once worked in the Northern Region as a range examiner. In 1951 Ed Cliff removed him from a similar position in the Rocky Mountain Region when his strenuous efforts to curb overgrazing angered livestock interests.

17.   Ibid.

18.   Ibid., 77.

19.   Dale A. Burk, "The Legacy of Lee Metcalf."

20.   U.S. Senate, Committee on Interior and Insular Affairs, Subcommittee on Public Lands, *"Clear-Cutting" Practices*, 1:159.

21.   The Hubbard Brook story and Dr. Curry's involvement are detailed in chapter 6 of Stephen Bocking, *Ecologists and Environmental Politics: A History of Contemporary Ecology*, 130–31.

22.   USDA Forest Service, *National Forest Management in a Quality Environment: Timber Productivity*.

Chapter 18. Reporters to the Scene: 1971–1973

1.   McGee to Church, June 9, 1971; Church reply, June 16, 1971, both in Church Papers, Boise State University, series 2.3, 2/9. McGee's bill for a clearcutting moratorium was Senate Bill 1592, 92nd Cong., 1st sess.

2.   W. D. Hagenstein, "Environmentalists Add Fourth Dimension to Clearcut Harvesting."

3.   Packwood to Church, June 4, 1971, Church Papers, Boise State University, series 2.3, 2/9. Packwood knew the power of the timber industry all too well; his bill to rescue the threatened valley of French Pete Creek in the Cascade Range was bottled up in the Interior Committee, on which Mark Hatfield served.

4.   U.S. Senate, Committee on Interior and Insular Affairs, Subcommittee on Public Lands, *"Clear-Cutting" Practices*, 3:1059–62; Norbert V. DeByle, *Quality of Surface Water—Miller Creek Block, Flathead National Forest, Montana*; Norbert V. DeByle and Paul E. Packer, "Plant Nutrient and Soil Losses in Overland Flow from Burned Forest Clearcuts."

5.   Robert R. Curry, "Geologic and Hydrologic Effects of Even-Age Management on Productivity of Forest Soils, Particularly in the Douglas-Fir Region"; S. P. Gessell, D. W. Cole, and John Turner, "Elemental Cycling and Even-Age

Management." In a pointed reference to Curry's claims, these authors stated that "exaggeration and distortion of the few facts now available will do great damage to a rational approach in resolving natural resource conservation and management" (196). Curry felt that what knowledge was available was sufficiently alarming to merit more intensive study.

6. GB to Metcalf, May 20, 1971, GBP 13/2.

7. John A. Green to R. P. Van Gytenbeek, February 16, 1972; Orville Daniels to Regional Forester, March 7, 1972; both in Bitterroot controversy files, BNF Archives.

8. USDA Forest Service, "Staff Paper on Technical Aspects of Terracing," Bolle Papers, KRTA, series V, 30/4. The paper appears to be among those prepared by Region 1 staff in response to the Bolle Report.

9. "Sen. McGee Shocked with Valley's Clear Cut Scenes," *Western News* (Hamilton, Mont.), August 25, 1971; Burk, "Sen. McGee Views Bare Bitterroot" (see introduction, n. 1); Dale A. Burk, "The Outdoor Picture," *Missoulian*, August 29, 1971.

10. Hill, "National Forests" (see introduction, n. 2); Gladwin Hill, "National Forests: Timber Men vs. Conservationists," *New York Times*, November 15, 1971.

11. This account of the Oh-My-God clearcut is Dale Burk's; another attributes the exclamation to one of the reporters on board the bus as they first encountered the giant opening. See also Orville Daniels's recollection in part 4 of the Forest Service's 2005 centennial film *The Greatest Good*. Reporter Don Schwennesen covered a later visit to the area in his article "Bitterroot Management: Old and New Problems," *Missoulian*, July 4, 1976.

12. James Nathan Miller, "The Crisis of Our National Forests."

13. USDA Forest Service [individual author unknown], "Statement on *Reader's Digest* Article 'Crisis of Our National Forests,'" December 6, 1971, GBP 3/6.

14. George C. Wilson, "Forest Service Fights for Life," *Washington Post*, July 16, 1973.

15. The *Daily Interlake*'s nine-part series ran October 18–27, 1971.

16. "Aerial Vista of Clear-Cut at Head of Sleeping Child Depicts Savagery of Timber Harvesting," *Western News* (Hamilton, Mont.), November 17, 1971.

17. Bob Gilluly, interview by author, July 29, 2009, Anaconda, Montana.

18. William R. Moore, "Let Us Manage Land Together," *Missoulian*, March 10, 1970.

19. William R. Moore, interview by author, September 29, 2007, Condon, Montana. See also "Hunting the Public Interest," address to Society of American Foresters, Northern Rocky Mountain Section, July 1970.

20. Baker et al., *National Forests of the Northern Region*, 257.

21. Brandborg's comments on the meeting with Yurich are from an undated note to Stewart Brandborg, box 31, SBP. Glen Smith was a prominent range conservationist in the regional office; the "Major" was former regional forester Evan Kelley. Yurich replied by letter, January 28, 1972, GBP 17/12. Yurich's statement on

reforestation projects is from Dale A. Burk and Tom Ellerhoff, "Our Forests Are in His Hands," *Missoulian,* April 16, 1972.

22. "Summary of Supervisor-Staff Conference, February 22–25, 1972," cited in Baker et al., *National Forests of the Northern Region,* 273; allowable cut figures are from John Milodragovich's statement before an informal hearing that Montana congressman John Melcher held in Missoula on August 17, 1973 (U.S. House, Committee on Interior and Insular Affairs, Subcommittee on Public Lands, *Damage to Public Lands from Forest Practices or Fluoride Emissions*).

23. J. H. Wikstrom and S. Blair Hutchison, *Stratification of Forest Land for Timber Management Planning on the Western National Forests.*

24. Milodragovich to Regional Forester, April 20, 1972, NAS 95-76B1317, box 1, folder "2470 Silvicultural Practices—Harvest Regeneration Record 1966–1971." The precommercial thinning backlog is taken from Milodragovich's testimony before the August 17, 1973, subcommittee hearing.

25. GB to Metcalf, January 11, 1972, GBP 13/2.

26. Daniels to RC&D Recreation Committee, April 20, 1972; Milner to Charles Butz, May 19, 1972; both in box "Bitterroot Controversy Info," BNF Archives.

27. GB to Burk [1972], GBP 23/4.

28. GB to Metcalf, April 18, 1972, GBP 13/1.

29. Orville Daniels, paper presented to the Intermountain Section of the Society of American Foresters, February 19, 1971, BNF history files.

30. Dale A. Burk, "Bitterroot Revises West Side Management," *Missoulian,* November 14, 1971; "Bitterroot Forest Modifications Seek New Quality Standard," *Missoulian,* November 26, 1972. Milner's statement came at Representative Melcher's August 17, 1973, hearing.

31. Dale A. Burk, "Wounds Taking Time to Heal," *Missoulian,* June 18, 1972.

32. GB to Church, January 21, 1972, Church Papers, Boise State University, series 1.1, 135/16. Brandborg's December 1973 statement to Milner is in the Doris Milner family collection. He did not give the name of the sale.

Chapter 19. Maneuvers and Negotiations: 1971–1974

1. Meeting notes, Softwood Lumber and Softwood Plywood Industry Advisory Committee, May 12, 1971, NAS 95-76B1317, box 1, folder "President's Task Force on Softwood Lumber and Plywood."

2. Dale A. Burk, "President's Panel Holds Secret Session to Coerce Foresters to Abandon 'Quality' Management Plan," *Missoulian,* July 15, 1972; Dale A. Burk, "President's Panel Cancels Public Session," *Missoulian,* July 14, 1972.

3. Dale A. Burk, "Cancellation of Public Involvement Session Shows 'Role of Politics' in Timber Management," *Missoulian,* July 16, 1972.

4. "Timber Industry Blocks Proposed Order to Impose Restraints on

Clear-Cutting," *Wall Street Journal,* January 14, 1972; "A Too Clear-Cut Decision," *New York Times,* January 18, 1972.

5. Wambach's remarks were made at a meeting of the University of Montana's Student Environmental Society December 11, 1970 (Mansfield Library, audiotape 308).

6. McKelvey interview, MHS OH-413-01b, side A.

7. Dale A. Burk, "National Interest Builds in Forest Management," *Missoulian,* September 5, 1971; James Risser, "Culver Asks GAO Probe into Forests," *Des Moines Register,* May 27, 1971; "A Too Clear-Cut Decision."

8. Edward C. Crafts to Church, April 30, 1971, Church Papers, Boise State University, series 2.2, 2/7; "Proposed Subcommittee or Committee Report on Management Practices on Public Lands," Church Papers, Boise State University, series 1.1, 30/14.

9. U.S. Senate, Committee on Interior and Insular Affairs, Subcommittee on Public Lands, *Clearcutting on Federal Timberlands: Report by the Subcommittee on Public Lands to the Committee on Interior and Insular Affairs, United States Senate;* Edward P. Cliff to Frank Church, April 3, 1972, Church Papers, Boise State University, series 1.1, 135/16. Cliff said that the guidelines were "technically sound, and represent a desirable and constructive policy statement for future federal forest land management." His consent is not surprising; according to Arnold Bolle, the final guidelines (in contrast to Ed Crafts's draft proposal) were devised by Leon Cambre, a Forest Service staffer on loan to Metcalf (Bolle, "Bitterroot Revisited," 176n17).

10. Dale A. Burk, "The Outdoor Picture," *Missoulian,* October 17, 1972. Pinchot made his tour on October 3 (Dale A. Burk, "Pinchot Says Bitterroot Timber Use 'Appalling,'" *Missoulian,* October 5, 1972).

11. Burk, "Pinchot Says."

12. GB to Pinchot, November 8, 1972, GBP 17/13.

13. F. Bruce Lamb, "If Only in Clichés, Tell It Like It Is"; Al Wiener, "Gifford Pinchot Would Have Laughed." G. B. Pinchot's rebuttal was printed in the January 1974 issue, p. 3.

14. USDA Forest Service, Northern Region, *USDA Forest Service Environmental Statement, Multiple Use Plan—Moose Creek Planning Unit;* Dale A. Burk, "Moose Creek Plan Delayed by Disputes," *Missoulian,* September 5, 1971.

15. Milton Van Camp to Orville Daniels, August 22, 1972; William Grasser to Daniels, August 11, 1972; both in TWS, series 4, 40/20.

16. "Statement Submitted by G. M. Brandborg at June 2, 1971 Public Hearing on Moose Creek," TWS, series 1, 9/10.

17. GB to Daniels, August 25, 1972, ibid.

18. David A. Adams, *Renewable Resource Policy: The Legal-Institutional Foundations,*

297; J. Michael McCloskey, *In the Thick of It: My Life in the Sierra Club,* 133; John Fedkiw, *Managing Multiple Uses on National Forests, 1905–1995,* 113. Dennis M. Roth argues that chiefs Cliff and McGuire began the RARE program without prodding from the CEQ in order to resolve the uncertainties it faced in allocating roadless lands to timber production (*The Wilderness Movement and the National Forests, 1964–1980,* 36–37).

19.   The agency issued its RARE survey decision in a brief report titled *New Wilderness Study Areas: Roadless Area Review and Evaluation.* The decision in the *Sierra Club v. Butz* lawsuit was issued by the Northern District Court of California on August 29, 1972, before the Forest Service issued its final environmental impact statement on the RARE project in October 1973. See also Roth, *Wilderness Movement and National Forests,* 37.

20.   Milner quotation: Bischke interview, tape 2, side A; Brandborg quotation: McKelvey interview, May 21, 1975, side B.

21.   GB, McKelvey interview, May 6, 1975, side B; ensuing quotations are from Ruth Brandborg's notes, October 17, 1972.

22.   Dale A. Burk, "The Outdoor Picture," *Missoulian,* December 19, 1972.

23.   The text of Brandborg's talk is in the collection of the Doris Milner family.

24.   "Address of Mr. Douglas Scott, Northwest Representative, Sierra Club and Federation of Western Outdoor Clubs, Seattle, Washington," in *Adapting to Environmental Pressures: Response of the Timber Industry,* ed. Stuart U. Rich.

25.   Brandborg's comments are from his November 5, 1967, statement to Wayne Aspinall's Public Land Law Review Commission (GBP 10/6).

Chapter 20. Charting a Workable Future: 1971–1976

1.   The planning directive was issued on November 1, 1971, as title 2100 of the *Forest Service Manual.*

2.   USDA Forest Service, Bitterroot National Forest, *Burnt Fork Unit Plan;* Dale A. Burk, "Forest Service Selects Burnt Fork Plan," *Missoulian,* December 28, 1972.

3.   USDA Forest Service, Bitterroot National Forest, *Bitterroot National Forest Multiple Use Plan, Part 1.* This document bore little resemblance to the detailed forest plans later mandated by the National Forest Management Act.

4.   Ibid., 4–5.

5.   William Grasser to Orville Daniels, September 22, 1972, GBP 16/1.

6.   GB to Metcalf, March 1, 1974, GBP 13/1.

7.   Alan W. Green and Theodore S. Setzer, *The Rocky Mountain Timber Situation, 1970,* 1, 21–22.

8.   Alan G. McQuillan, "Montana Forests: Knowing the Past and Sowing the Future," 5; Richard Manning, *Last Stand: Logging, Journalism, and the Case for Humility,* 31.

9.   Brandborg to Thurman [Trosper] and Don [Aldrich], February 12, 1974, collection of Doris Milner family.

10. Federal Emergency Management Agency, *Flood Insurance Study, Missoula County, Montana, and Adjacent Areas, August 16, 1988;* "Bitter Root Project," http://www.usbr.gov/dataweb/html/bitterrt.html; U.S. Geological Survey, "Montana Flood-Frequency and Basin-Characteristic Data," http://mt.water.usgs.gov/freq?page_type=site&site_no=12344000; GB, "Bitterroot Flood Control Means Protecting Land," *Missoulian,* June 30, 1974; GB to Metcalf, April 23, 1975, SBP 26/5.

11. K. Elder, L. Porth, and C. A. Troendle, "The Effect of Timber Harvest on the Fool Creek Watershed after Five Decades," abstract, 2006, http://adsabs.harvard.edu/abs/2006AGUFM.B21F..01E. The authors wrote, "Annual maximum daily mean flows and instantaneous peak flows average 16% and 18% higher and occur seven days earlier, respectively, than pre-treatment conditions." Half of the forested area was cut, a high percentage compared to total forest removals in the Bitterroot. For an overview of research, see K. Elder et al., "Disturbance and Water-Related Research in the Western United States."

12. Timothy A. Burton, "Effects of Basin-Scale Timber Harvest on Water Yield and Peak Streamflow," paper no. 95146 of the *Journal of the American Water Resources Association* (1997), http://www3.interscience.wiley.com/journal/119177260/abstract?CRETRY=1&SRETRY=0.

13. GB to Metcalf, May 14, 1975, GBP 13/1 (emphasis in the original).

14. Guthrie to GB, August 15, 1974, GBP 9/4, reprinted as "A Voice of Anger and Thunder," in *Big Sky, Fair Land: The Environmental Essays of A. B. Guthrie, Jr.*

15. A. B. Guthrie Jr., speech given to Hamilton League of Women Voters, December 5, 1974, reprinted as "Better to Call It Change," in ibid.

16. Guthrie to GB, May 25, 1974, GBP 9/4.

17. Metcalf to [EPA Administrator] John R. Quarles, April 18, 1975, GBP, 13/4.

18. Bill Jellison, "Notes on Meeting of Concerned Citizens of Ravalli County with Mr. Bruce Parry of EPA, Denver, Colorado, April 17, 1975," SBP 26/5.

19. Brandborg to John Green, February 15, 1975, ibid.

20. Sallie M. Brutto, "Citizens Dismayed at EPA Peek upon Forest Conditions—Denial of Study," *Western News* (Hamilton, Mont.), November 5, 1975; Brandborg's reaction: GBP 9/3.

21. The appellate court decision in the Monongahela case was *West Virginia Division of the Izaak Walton League of America v. Earl Butz,* United States Court of Appeals for the Fourth Circuit, No. 74-1387, decided August 21, 1975.

22. Harold K. Steen, "Gordon Robinson: Forestry Consultant to the Sierra Club," oral history interview, September 20, 1977, Santa Cruz, California (San Francisco: Sierra Club History Committee, 1979), 87–88, 109; Dennis C. LeMaster, *Decade of Change: The Remaking of Forest Service Statutory Authority during the 1970s,* 57.

23. The genesis of the 1976 National Forest Management Act—as Humphrey's legislation was known—is well described in LeMaster, *Decade of Change.*

24. Fedkiw, *Managing Multiple Uses,* 109.

25. National Forest Timber Management Reform Act of 1976, sections 5(a) and 7(c) ("Statement on Introduced Bills," *Congressional Record,* February 4, 1976).

26. Bolle to GB, November 4, 1975, and GB to Bolle, November 12, 1975, both in GBP 2/9; Bolle, oral history interview by Gerald Williams, 24.

27. "Statement of G. M. Brandborg," in *Forest and Rangeland Management: Joint Hearings before the Subcommittee on Environment, Soil Conservation, and Forestry of the Committee on Agriculture and Forestry,* by U.S. Senate, Subcommittee on the Environment and Land Resources of the Committee on Interior and Insular Affairs, 211–13.

28. Statement of Larry B. Blasing, Inland Forest Resource Council, Missoula, in ibid., 878–85.

29. The National Forest Management Act of 1976 (PL 94-588) was adopted as a set of amendments to the Forest and Rangeland Renewable Resources Act of 1974.

30. LeMaster, *Decade of Change,* 69–70, appendix B. According to LeMaster, Metcalf obtained these provisions over the protests of the Forest Service and the timber industry. Robert Wolf explained that the "silviculturally essential" requirement, which Church had introduced at the behest of environmentalists, was dropped to allow a "broader base to the decision and selection process" in designing timber sales and to avoid possible litigation over the more restrictive term (Wolf to Church, August 24, 1976, Church Papers, Boise State University, series 1.1, 62/11).

31. Metcalf to GB, May 10, 1976, GBP 13/3.

32. Robert Wolf, oral history interview by Arnold Bolle, Alan McQuillan, and Dan Hall, April 26, 1989, Missoula (KRTA OH-227-21, 17).

33. "Transcript of Proceedings, Committee on Agriculture and Forestry, United States Senate," Church Papers, Boise State University, series 1.1, 63/6, 29.

34. Don Schwennesen, "2 Retired Foresters Believe National Forests Endangered," *Missoulian,* September 12, 1976.

35. GB, "Criminal Punishment Needed," *Missoulian,* February 6, 1976.

Chapter 21. Legacy of a Conflict: 1976–2006

1. Christine Johnson, "Land Use Planning Urged by Ravalli County Citizens," *Missoulian,* March 1, 1976.

2. Arnold Bolle recalled Brandy's remarks at the dedication of Brandy Peak (McKelvey, "Brandy Peak Dedication" [see chap. 2, n. 6]).

3. Sam Reynolds, "A Giant Man," *Missoulian,* March 14, 1977.

4. Burk and Schwennesen, "New Forestry Leaders Needed" (see introduction, n. 3).

5. Don Schwennesen, "Yurich Leaves Northern Region after Implementing Reform," *Missoulian,* July 5, 1976.

6. Richard Behan has been among the most vociferous of the NFMA's critics; his position is summarized in his 2001 book, *Plundered Promise* (esp. 192–96).

7. Joseph M. Hinson, "National Forest Planning: A Timber Industry Perspective"; Andy Stahl, "The Broken Promises of Forest Planning."

8. Milner to Robert Morgan, July 3, 1977, Milner family collection. Fittingly, a taller peak a few miles to the south is named for Elers Koch, another Bitterroot giant.

9. Vern Hamre to Ruth Brandborg, August 7, 1971, Milner family collection.

10. USDA Forest Service, Northern Region, *Forest Plan, Bitterroot National Forest, September 1987*, III-80. These reductions reflected, if belatedly, the issues raised in Wikstrom and Hutchison's *Stratification of Forest Lands* study released in 1971. From his 1944 economic study to his participation in the 1970 Bitterroot Task Force report, Blair Hutchison made a lasting contribution to the management of the Bitterroot National Forest.

11. USDA Forest Service, Northern Region, *Final Environmental Impact Statement, Bitterroot National Forest Plan*, B-55.

12. USDA Forest Service, Northern Region, *Forest Plan*, table II-1. Sale volumes through the 1970s are from USDA Forest Service, Northern Region, *Proposed Bitterroot National Forest Land Management Plan*, 2006, fig. 2, p. 26. The 1972 plan did not project an annual allowable cut, since the individual unit plans were still under preparation.

13. USDA Forest Service, Northern Region, *Final Environmental Impact Statement*, II-26.

14. Thomas J. Barlow et al., *Giving Away the National Forests: An Analysis of U.S. Forest Service Timber Sales Below Cost.*

15. Jessica Montag and Keith Stockman, *Western Montana Planning Zone Social Science and Economics Specialists' Report*, 137. The cumulative timber harvest level for the period 1988–2007 from the Bitterroot National Forest amounted to 198.6 mmbf of all species—only 30 percent of the allowable sale quantity of 667 mmbf for the same period (USDA Forest Service, Northern Region, *Forest Plan Monitoring and Evaluation Report, Fiscal Year 2007, Bitterroot National Forest*, table 5).

16. The two mills in the Darby area were owned by Stoltze-Conner (the former Del Conner mill) and the Darby Lumber Company. Employment figures are from the Montana Department of Labor and Industries, cited in Charles E. Keegan et al., "Impacts of the 2000 Wildfires on Forest Industry Employment," table 1.

17. Larry Swanson, *The Bitterroot Valley of Western Montana Area Economic Profile*, table 1, p. 18. Income figures are in 1996 dollars. Swanson noted that "while [the forest products] industry has seen considerable decline in employment and labor earnings throughout the larger region and in forest land peer counties, this industry in Ravalli County is as large as in any time in its history." Economist Thomas Michael Power of the University of Montana argues that the West's traditional reliance on resource extraction obscures the increasingly important role

of the new service-based economy. "With economic development," Power writes in his book *Lost Landscapes and Failed Economies: The Search for a Value of Place,* "the role of export activity and even the visibility of the 'export base' begins to decline. Services and goods that were previously imported are produced locally, reducing the need for exports" (143).

18.   For a sample of the extensive news coverage and commentaries on the aftermath of the 2000 fires on the Bitterroot, see Sherry Devlin, "Bitterroot National Forest Issues Final EIS," *Missoulian,* October 11, 2001; Mick DeZell, "Mismanaged Forest to Blame for Fires," *Ravalli Republic,* September 13, 2007; Michael Jamison, "Wildfire's 'Destruction' Crucial to Some Species," *Missoulian,* August 21, 2005; George Wuerthner, "Logging and Wildfire: Ecological Differences and the Need to Preserve Large Fires," 190. An opinion poll conducted in Ravalli County by the Bureau of Business and Economic Research at the University of Montana showed strong support for the BNF's salvage program, with 89 percent of respondents "favoring" or "strongly favoring" timber salvage in burned areas (*Bitterroot Burned Area Recovery Project,* appendix C, http://www.fs.fed.us/projects/documents/ApdxC.pdf).

19.   Mark E. Swanson et al., "The Forgotten Stage of Forest Succession: Early-Successional Ecosystems on Forest Sites."

20.   Native Forest Network, "Restoration or Exploitation: A Hard Look at the Bitterroot 'Burned Area Recovery Plan,'" http://www.nativeforest.org/pdf/Bitterroot_Primer.pdf; Perry Backus, "Bitterroot National Forest Regrowth Patchy 10 Years after Fires," *Ravalli Republic,* September 19, 2010.

21.   Stephen Saunders, Charles Montgomery, and Tom Easley, *Hotter and Drier: The West's Changed Climate;* Ken Gibson et al., *Mountain Pine Beetle Impacts in High-Elevation Five-Needle Pines: Current Trends and Challenges.*

22.   Cole Mayn estimates that half or more of the clearcut and terraced area on the Bitterroot NF exhibits detrimental soil disturbance, primarily compacting. The subsoil grappler is designed to loosen subsurface layers without mixing soil horizons; preliminary tests indicate soil porosity is improved around 40 percent (telephone interview by author, August 11, 2009). See also Rob Chaney, "Starting Over: RMEF, Forest Service Try an Experimental Approach to Create Better Elk Habitat," *Missoulian,* July 12, 2010.

23.   Dave Calkin, "Economic Research Unit Explores Biomass Utilization Opportunities on the Bitterroot National Forest," *Eco Report* (Bitterroot Ecosystem Management Research Project) (Fall 2005). Craig E. Thomas, *Just the Tip…Regurgitations of a Montana Woodsman,* 169–77.

24.   Betsy Cohen, "Schweitzer: Mill Closure Provides Green Energy Opportunities," *Missoulian,* December 23, 2009.

25.   USDA Forest Service, Forest Products Laboratory, "Structural Grading of Logs

from Small-Diameter Trees"; Sherry Devlin, "Biomass Isn't One Size Fits All, Says Report," *Missoulian*, August 1, 2006.

Afterword

1. See, for example, the set of forest-restoration standards promoted by a broad coalition of environmental groups (D. A. DellaSalla et al., "Citizens' Call for Ecological Forest Restoration: Forest Restoration Principles and Criteria"). The authors differentiate between practices they view as ecologically sound, such as removing roads, invasive weeds, and barriers to fish and wildlife migration, and those they regard as shilling for the timber industry, such as heavy postfire salvage logging. The standards also emphasize home owners' responsibility to create defensible space around their buildings.

2. Ray Ring and Carlotta Granstaff, "Forest Service Shuts Down 'Three Old Geezers,'" *High Country News* (Paonia, Colo.), January 23, 2006. The FOB filed a civil discrimination suit in federal court over the incident, but in May 2009 the group agreed to drop the case after the Forest Service promised to allow "thorough and open public debate, including the views of those different or in opposition to their own" (Associated Press, May 13, 2009, cited in http://www.firstamendmentcenter.org/news.aspx?id=21578).

3. As one example, in 1996 the Sierra Club, by vote of its national membership, called for an end to all commercial logging on federal public lands. The new policy, which reflected the antilogging stances taken by many regional activist groups, replaced a much more nuanced statement calling for the maintenance of natural integrity of forest ecosystems, but permitting some logging (see http://www.sierraclub.org/policy/conservation/forest.aspx).

4. LaSalle interview (see introduction, n. 4). By 2009 the Big Sky Coalition had become inactive, but many valley residents are still interested in proceeding with thinning and other hazard-reduction programs.

5. Bitterroot National Forest, "Trapper Bunkhouse Land Stewardship Project, Final Environmental Impact Statement," appendix G, http://www.fs.fed.us/r1/bitterroot/projects/trap_bunk_feis/Appendix%20G.pdf.

6. The 1987 Bitterroot Forest Plan anticipated that about 10 percent of the forest's commercial stands would be managed as "old growth"—a fairly minimal standard. What might the forest look like if 50 percent were the goal—and given time, how much quality lumber might it produce?

7. The Montana Wilderness Association, in particular, has for a number of years engaged certain sawmill owners around the state in a dialogue about timber use versus preservation. One result of these discussions was legislation announced by Montana senator Jon Tester in July 2009 that would set aside some new wilderness areas while mandating (not merely allowing) minimum levels of timber

harvest on several national forests, including the Beaverhead-Deerlodge. The proposed bill would establish 67,500 acres of wilderness on the eastern slope of the Sapphire Range but would not address wilderness or timber harvest on the Bitterroot side. The bill has drawn opposition from groups that favor wilderness protection without an economic quid pro quo. Still, it indicates that some environmental advocates are willing to consider economic issues alongside preservation concerns.

Bibliography

Adams, David A. *Renewable Resource Policy: The Legal-Institutional Foundations.* Washington, D.C.: Island Press, 1993.

Address of Hardin R. Glascock to Forest Land Use Conference, American Forest Products Industries, Inc., Washington, D.C., Sept. 21–22, 1961. Washington, D.C.: American Forest Products Industries, 1961.

American Forestry Association. *Proceedings of the American Forest Conference.* Washington, D.C.: H. M. Suter Publishing, 1905.

Anderson, B. A. "Mushrooms." *Northern Region News* (August 21, 1936).

Arno, Stephen F., and Carl E. Fiedler. *Mimicking Nature's Fire: Restoring Fire-Prone Forests in the West.* Washington, D.C.: Island Press, 2005.

Arno, Stephen F., Carl E. Fiedler, and Matthew Arno. "Giant Pines and Grassy Glades: The Historic Ponderosa Ecosystem, Disappearing Icon of the American West." *Forest History Today* 14 (Spring 2008): 12–19.

Ayers, H. B. *The Lewis and Clarke Forest Reserve.* Washington, D.C.: Government Printing Office, 1900.

Baker, Robert D., Robert S. Maxwell, Victor H. Treat, and Henry C. Dethloff. *National Forests of the Northern Region: Living Legacy.* College Station, Tex.: Intaglio, 1993.

Barlow, Thomas J., Gloria E. Helfand, Trent W. Orr, and Thomas B. Stoel Jr. *Giving Away the National Forests: An Analysis of U.S. Forest Service Timber Sales Below Cost.* Washington, D.C.: Natural Resources Defense Council, 1980.

Barney, Daniel R. *The Last Stand: Ralph Nader's Study Group Report on the National Forests.* New York: Grossman, 1974.

Bateridge, Thomas. "Effects of Clearcuts on Water Discharge and Nutrient Loss, Bitterroot National Forest, Montana." Master's thesis, University of Montana, 1974.

Bates, J. Leonard. "Fulfilling American Democracy: The Conservation Movement, 1907 to 1921." *Mississippi Valley Historical Review* 44 (June 1957): 29–57.

Behan, Richard. *Plundered Province: Capitalism, Politics, and the Fate of the National Forests.* Washington, D.C.: Island Press, 2001.

Bocking, Stephen. *Ecologists and Environmental Politics: A History of Contemporary Ecology.* New Haven: Yale University Press, 1997.

Bolle, Arnold W. "The Bitterroot Revisited: A University [Re]View of the Forest Service." In *American Forests: Nature, Culture, and Politics,* ed. Char Miller, 163–76. Lawrence: University Press of Kansas, 1997.

Bolle, Arnold W., Richard W. Behan, Gordon Browder, Thomas Payne, W. Leslie Pengelly, Richard E. Shannon, and Robert F. Wambach [Select Committee of the University of Montana]. *A University View of the Forest Service.* U.S. Senate, Committee on Interior and Insular Affairs. Senate Document 91-115. Washington, D.C.: Government Printing Office, 1970.

Bolle, Arnold W., William K. Gibson, and Elizabeth Hannum. *The Forest Products Industry in Montana.* Bulletin 31. Missoula: Montana Forest Conservation and Experiment Station, May 1966.

Briegleb, Philip A. *Growth of Ponderosa Pine by Keen Tree Class.* Forest Research Note 32. Portland, Ore.: USDA Forest Service, Pacific Northwest Forest Experiment Station, January 15, 1943.

Broome, Harvey. *Faces of the Wilderness.* Missoula: Mountain Press, 1972.

Burk, Dale. *The Clearcut Crisis: Controversy in the Bitterroot.* Great Falls, Mont.: Jursnick Printing, 1970.

———. *Great Bear, Wild River.* Eureka, Mont.: Stoneydale Press, 1977.

———. "The Legacy of Lee Metcalf." *Living Wilderness* (July 1979).

Butcher, Edward Bernie. "An Analysis of Timber Depredations in Montana to 1900." Master's thesis, University of Montana, 1967.

Calkin, David. *Historic Resource Production from USDA Forest Service Northern and Intermountain Region Lands.* Research Note PNW-RN-540. Portland, Ore.: USDA Forest Service, Pacific Northwest Research Station, 1999.

Clary, David A. *Timber and the Forest Service.* Lawrence: University Press of Kansas, 1986.

Cochrell, Albert N. *The Nezperce Story: A History of the Nezperce National Forest.* Rev. ed. 1960. Reprint, Missoula: USDA Forest Service, 1970.

Crist, Michele R., Thomas H. DeLuca, Bo Wilmer, and Gregory H. Aplet. *Restoration of Low-Elevation Dry Forests of the Northern Rocky Mountains: A Holistic Approach.* Washington, D.C.: Wilderness Society, 2009.

Cunningham, William P. "The Magruder Corridor Controversy: A Case History." Master's thesis, University of Montana, 1968.

Curry, Robert R. "Geologic and Hydrologic Effects of Even-Age Management on Productivity of Forest Soils, Particularly in the Douglas-Fir Region." In *Even-Age Management*, ed. Richard K. Hermann and Denis P. Lavender. Symposium proceedings, August 1, 1972 [location of conference unknown], 137–78. Corvallis: Oregon State University School of Forestry, 1973.

DeByle, Norbert V. *Quality of Surface Water: Miller Creek Block, Flathead National Forest, Montana*. Progress Report Study No. 1605-517. Ogden, Utah: USDA Forest Service, Intermountain Forest and Range Experiment Station, 1971.

DeByle, Norbert V., and Paul E. Packer. "Plant Nutrient and Soil Losses in Overland Flow from Burned Forest Clearcuts." In *Watersheds in Transition: Proceedings of a Symposium, Fort Collins, CO, June 19–22, 1972*, ed. Sandor C. Csallany, Thad G. McLaughlin, and William D. Striffler. Urbana: American Water Resources Association, 1972.

DellaSalla, D. A., et al. "Citizens' Call for Ecological Forest Restoration: Forest Restoration Principles and Criteria." *Ecological Restoration* 21, no. 1 (2003): 14–23.

DeVoto, Bernard. "Sacred Cows and Public Lands." In *The Easy Chair*, by Bernard DeVoto. Boston: Houghton Mifflin, 1955.

Diamond, Jared. *Collapse: How Societies Choose to Fail or Succeed*. New York: Viking, 2005.

Dupuyer Centennial Committee. *By Gone Days and Modern Ways*. Havre, Mont.: Griggs Printing and Publishing, 1977.

Elder, K., et al. "Disturbance and Water-Related Research in the Western United States." In *Proceedings: 2nd Interagency Conference on Research in the Watersheds.* Coweeta Hydrologic Lab, May 15–18, 2006, Otto, N.C. Fort Collins, Colo.: USDA Forest Service, Rocky Mountain Research Station, 2006.

Federal Emergency Management Agency. *Flood Insurance Study, Missoula County, Montana, and Adjacent Areas, August 16, 1988*. Washington, D.C.: Federal Emergency Management Agency, 1988.

Fedkiw, John. *Managing Multiple Uses on National Forests, 1905–1995*. Washington, D.C.: Government Printing Office, 1998.

Friedrich, C. Allan. *Some Watershed Aspects of Logging on the National Forests of Region One—with Special Reference to the Spruce Program*. Missoula: USDA Forest Service, Northern Rocky Mountain Forest and Range Experiment Station, December 1953.

Frome, Michael. *Promised Land: Adventures and Encounters in Wild America*. Knoxville: University of Tennessee Press, 1994.

———. *Whose Woods These Are: The Story of the National Forests*. New York: Doubleday, 1962.

Gessell, S. P., D. W. Cole, and John Turner. "Elemental Cycling and Even-Age

Management." In *Even-Age Management,* ed. Richard K. Hermann and Denis P. Lavender, 179–98. Symposium proceedings, August 1, 1972 [location of conference unknown]. Corvallis: Oregon State University School of Forestry, 1973.

Gibson, Ken, et al. *Mountain Pine Beetle Impacts in High-Elevation Five-Needle Pines: Current Trends and Challenges.* Missoula: USDA Forest Service, 2008.

Glover, James M. *Robert Marshall: A Wilderness Original.* Seattle: Mountaineers, 1986.

Goode, Richard U. "Bitter Root Forest Reserve." *National Geographic,* September 1898, 387–400.

Green, Alan W., and Theodore S. Setzer. *The Rocky Mountain Timber Situation, 1970.* Resource Bulletin INT-10. Ogden, Utah: USDA Forest Service, Intermountain Forest and Range Experiment Station, November 1974.

Gruell, George E., Wyman C. Schmidt, Stephen F. Arno, and William J. Reich. *Seventy Years of Vegetative Change in a Managed Ponderosa Pine Forest in Western Montana.* General Technical Report INT-130. Ogden, Utah: USDA Forest Service, Intermountain Forest and Range Experiment Station, August 1982.

Guthrie, A. B., Jr. *Big Sky, Fair Land: The Environmental Essays of A. B. Guthrie, Jr.* Ed. David Petersen. Flagstaff, Ariz.: Northland Press, 1988.

Hagenstein, W. D. "Environmentalists Add Fourth Dimension to Clearcut Harvesting." *Western Conservation Journal* (May–June 1971): 29–31.

Hartwell, Michael G., Paul Alaback, and Stephen F. Arno. "Comparing Historic and Modern Forests on the Bitterroot Front." In *The Bitterroot Ecosystem Research Project: What We Have Learned,* ed. Helen Y. Smith. Symposium proceedings, May 18–20, 1999, Missoula, RMRS-P-17. Ogden, Utah: USDA Forest Service, Rocky Mountain Research Station, 2000.

Harvey, Mark W. T. *Wilderness Forever: Howard Zahniser and the Path to the Wilderness Act.* Seattle: University of Washington Press, 2005.

Hays, Samuel P. *Conservation and the Gospel of Efficiency: The Progressive Conservation Movement, 1890–1920.* 1959. Reprint, Pittsburgh: University of Pittsburgh Press, 1999.

Heinselman, Miron. *The Boundary Waters Wilderness Ecosystem.* Minneapolis: University of Minnesota Press, 1996.

[Hicks, Laney, ed.] *The Case for a Blue Ribbon Commission on Timber Management in the National Forests.* Denver: Rocky Mountain Chapter of the Sierra Club and Western Regional Office of the Wilderness Society, 1970.

Hinson, Joseph M. "National Forest Planning: A Timber Industry Perspective." *Western Wildlands* 16 (Winter 1990): 23–27.

Hirt, Paul W. *A Conspiracy of Optimism: Management of the National Forests since World War Two.* Lincoln: University of Nebraska Press, 1994.

Homstad, Carla. "Two Roads Diverged: A Look Back at the Montana Study." *Montana: The Magazine of Western History* 53 (Autumn 2003): 16–29.

Horstman, Mary C., and Kristi Whisennand. *The History of Sheep Grazing on the Lolo and Bitterroot National Forests, 1907–1960.* Missoula: USDA Forest Service, Northern Region, 1997.

Howard, Joseph Kinsey. *Montana: High, Wide, and Handsome.* Rev. ed. New Haven: Yale University Press, 1943.

Joslin, Les. *Uncle Sam's Cabins: A Visitor's Guide to Historic U.S. Forest Service Ranger Stations of the West.* Bend, Ore.: Wilderness Associates, 1995.

Kaufman, Harold F. "Sociology in Forestry." In *Research in the Economics of Forestry,* ed. William A. Duerr and Henry J. Vaux. Washington, D.C.: Charles Lathrop Pack Forestry Foundation, 1953.

Kaufman, Harold F., and Lois C. Kaufman. *Toward the Stabilization and Enrichment of a Forest Community.* Missoula: Montana Study, 1946.

Keegan, Charles E., Todd A. Morgan, A. Lorin Hearst, and Carl E. Fiedler. "Impacts of the 2000 Wildfires on Forest Industry Employment." *Montana Business Quarterly* 40 (Autumn 2002): 8–13.

Keen, F. P. "Relative Susceptibility of Ponderosa Pines to Bark Beetle Attack." *Journal of Forestry* 34 (October 1, 1935): 919–27.

Keillor, Steven J. *Cooperative Commonwealth: Co-ops in Rural Minnesota, 1859–1939.* St. Paul: Minnesota Historical Society Press, 2000.

Koch, Elers. *Forty Years a Forester, 1903–1943.* Missoula: Mountain Press, 1998.

———. "The Passing of the Lolo Trail." *Journal of Forestry* 33 (February 1935): 98–104.

Lago, Don. *On the Viking Trail: Travels in Scandinavian America.* Iowa City: University of Iowa Press, 2004.

Lamb, F. Bruce. "If Only in Clichés, Tell It Like It Is." *American Forests* 79 (May 1973): 24–27, 60–61.

Langston, Nancy. *Forest Dreams, Forest Nightmares: The Paradox of Old Growth in the Inland West.* Weyerhaeuser Environmental Books. Seattle: University of Washington Press, 1995.

Leiberg, John B. "Bitterroot Forest Reserve." In *Nineteenth Annual Report of the United States Geological Survey to the Secretary of the Interior, 1897–98.* Pt. 5, *Forest Reserves.* U.S. Department of the Interior, Geological Survey. Washington, D.C.: Government Printing Office, 1899.

LeMaster, Dennis C. *Decade of Change: The Remaking of Forest Service Statutory Authority during the 1970s.* Westport, Conn.: Greenwood Press, 1984.

Lowdermilk, W. C. *Conquest of the Land through 7,000 Years.* Rev. ed. 1953. Reprint, Washington, D.C.: USDA Soil Conservation Service, 1975.

Malone, Michael P., Richard B. Roeder, and William B. Lang. *Montana: A History of Two Centuries.* Seattle: University of Washington Press, 1976.

Manning, Richard. *Last Stand: Logging, Journalism, and the Case for Humility.* Salt Lake City: Peregrine Smith Books, 1991.

Marshall, Robert. "Impressions from the Wilderness." *Living Wilderness* (Autumn 1951).

————. *The People's Forests.* 1933. Reprint, Iowa City: University of Iowa Press, 2002.

McCloskey, J. Michael. *In the Thick of It: My Life in the Sierra Club.* Washington, D.C.: Island Press, 2005.

McCloskey, Mike. "Taking Over as Environmentalism Takes Off." *Forest History Today* 14 (Spring 2008).

McCollister, Charles, and Sandra McCollister. "The Clearwater River Log Drives: A Photo Essay." *Forest History Today* 6 (Fall 2000): 20–26.

McQuillan, Alan G. "Montana Forests: Knowing the Past and Sowing the Future." In *Governor's Conference on the Future of Montana's Forests: Crafting a Vision for Landowners and Managers, May 13–14, 2002,* ed. P. F. Kolb. Missoula: Montana Forest and Conservation Experiment Station, 2003.

Meine, Curt. "Conservation and the Progressive Movement: Growing from the Radical Center." In *Reconstructing Conservation: Finding Common Ground,* ed. Ben A. Minteer and Robert E. Manning. Washington, D.C.: Island Press, 1993.

Meyer, Walter H. *Growth in Selectively Cut Ponderosa Pine Forests of the Pacific Northwest.* USDA Forest Service Technical Bulletin 407. Washington, D.C.: Government Printing Office, 1934.

"Mike Frome." *American Forests* 77 (January 1977).

Miller, Char. "Back to the Garden: The Redemptive Promise of Sustainable Forestry, 1893–2000." *Forest History Today* 6 (Spring 2000).

————. *Gifford Pinchot and the Making of Modern Environmentalism.* Washington, D.C.: Island Press, 2001.

Miller, James Nathan. "The Crisis of Our National Forests." *Reader's Digest,* December 1971, 91–96.

Montag, Jessica, and Keith Stockman. *Western Montana Planning Zone Social Science and Economics Specialists' Report.* Missoula: USDA Forest Service, Northern Region, 2006. http://www.fs.fed.us/r1/wmpz/documents/proposed-plans-psd/zone/docs/soc-econ-assess4.pdf.

Moore, AnneMarie, and Dennis Baird. *Wild Places Preserved: The Story of Bob Marshall in Idaho.* Moscow: University of Idaho Library, 2009.

Moore, Bud. *The Lochsa Story: Land Ethics in the Bitterroot Mountains.* Missoula: Mountain Press, 1996.

Neil, J. M. *To the White Clouds: Idaho's Conservation Saga, 1900–1970.* Pullman: Washington State University Press, 2005.

Nie, Martin. "The Bitterroot Controversy." In *Forests and Forestry in the Americas: An Encyclopedia,* ed. Frederick W. Cubbage. http://64.78.1.15/index.php/Main_Page.

O'Toole, Randal. *Reforming the Forest Service.* Washington, D.C.: Island Press, 1988.

Peterson, Ernst C. "A Thousand Miles of Backpacking." *Living Wilderness* (Summer–Fall 1955).

Pinchot, Gifford. *The Fight for Conservation.* New York: Doubleday, Page, 1910.

Pisani, Donald J. "Forests and Reclamation, 1891–1911." *Forest and Conservation History* 37 (April 1993).

Pollinger, Warren. "Lands of Ravalli County, Montana, and Some Problems in Their Use and Development." In *Forest Lands of the United States: Hearings before the Joint Committee on Forestry, 75th Congress, 3rd sess., on Senate Concurrent Res. 31, Portland, OR, December 12–13, 1939*. Washington, D.C.: Government Printing Office, 1940.

Popovich, Luke. "The Bitterroot: A Fading Polemic." *Journal of Forestry* 73 (January 1976): 39–41.

———. "The Bitterroot: Remembrances of Things Past." *Journal of Forestry* 73 (December 1975): 791–93.

Poston, Richard W. *Small-Town Renaissance: A Story of the Montana Study*. New York: Harper and Brothers, 1950.

Power, Thomas Michael. *Lost Landscapes and Failed Economies: The Search for a Value of Place*. Washington, D.C.: Island Press, 1996.

Pyne, Stephen J. *Year of the Fires: The Story of the Great Fires of 1910*. New York: Viking, 2001.

Rajala, Richard A. *Clearcutting the Pacific Rainforest: Production, Science, and Regulation*. Vancouver: University of British Columbia Press, 1999.

Rakestraw, Lawrence. "Forestry Missionary: George Patrick Ahern, 1894–1899." *Montana: The Magazine of Western History* 9 (1959): 36–44.

Ransick, Christopher T. "The Bitterroot Controversy: Dale Burk's Dual Role as Journalist and Activist." Master's thesis, University of Montana, 1988.

Rich, Stuart U., ed. *Adapting to Environmental Pressures: Response of the Timber Industry*. Eugene, Ore.: Forest Industries Management Center, 1974.

Richey, E. Duke. "Subdividing Eden: Land Use and Change in the Bitterroot Valley, 1930–1998." Master's thesis, University of Montana, 1998.

Robinson, Donald H. *Through the Years in Glacier National Park: An Administrative History*. Ed. Maynard C. Bowers. West Glacier, Mont.: Glacier Natural History Association, 1960. http://www.nps.gov/history/history/online_books/glac/adhi.htm.

Robinson, Gordon. *The Forest and the Trees: A Guide to Excellent Forestry*. Washington, D.C.: Island Press, 1988.

Roeder, Richard. "The Genesis of Montana Margins." In *Writing Montana: Literature under the Big Sky*, ed. Rick Newby and Suzanne Hungers. Helena: Montana Center for the Book, 1996.

Roth, Dennis M.. *The Wilderness Movement and the National Forests, 1964-1980*. [Washington, D.C.]: U.S. Department of Agriculture, Forest Service, 1984.

Runte, Alfred. *Public Lands, Public Heritage: The National Forest Idea*. Niwot, Colo.: Roberts Rinehart, 1991.

Saunders, Stephen, Charles Montgomery, and Tom Easley. *Hotter and Drier: The West's Changed Climate*. Denver: Rocky Mountain Climate Organization and Natural Resources Defense Council, 2008.

Schallau, Con H. "Sustained Yield versus Community Stability: An Unfortunate Wedding?" *Journal of Forestry* 87 (September 1989): 16–23.

Severy, J. W., and W. L. Pengelly. "Montana's Venture in Wildlife Education." In *Transactions of the Twenty-first North American Wildlife Conference.* Washington, D.C.: Wildlife Management Institute, 1956.

Shepherd, Jack. *The Forest Killers: The Destruction of the American Wilderness.* New York: Weybright and Talley, 1975.

Silcox, F. A. "A Challenge." *Service Bulletin* 21 (December 13, 1937). http://www.foresthistory.org/ASPNET/people/Silcox/Silcox.aspx.

———. "A Federal Plan for Forest Regulation within the Democratic Pattern." *Journal of Forestry* 37 (February 1939): 116–20.

———. "Foresters Must Choose." *Journal of Forestry* 33 (March 1935): 198–204.

"'Sleeping Child' Holocaust Sweeps Montana Wilderness." *Western Equipment and Timber News* (Portland, Ore.) (September 1961).

Smith, Helen Y., and Stephen F. Arno. *Eighty-eight Years of Change in a Managed Ponderosa Pine Forest.* Gen. Tech. Report RMRS-GTR-23. Fort Collins, Colo.: USDA Forest Service, Rocky Mountain Research Station, 1999.

Smolinski, Carole Simon, and Don Biddison. *Moose Creek Ranger District Historical Information Inventory and Review, Nez Perce National Forest.* Clarkston, Wash.: Northwest Historical Consultants, 1988.

Stahl, Andy. "The Broken Promises of Forest Planning." *Western Wildlands* (Winter 1990): 28–31.

Steen, Harold K., and Christine Guth. *The U.S. Forest Service: A History.* Seattle: University of Washington Press, 2004.

Stegner, Wallace. *The Uneasy Chair: A Biography of Bernard DeVoto.* New York: Doubleday, 1974.

Swanson, Larry. *The Bitterroot Valley of Western Montana Area Economic Profile.* Missoula: University of Montana, O'Connor Center for the Rocky Mountain West, 2001.

Swanson, Mark E., et al. "The Forgotten Stage of Forest Succession: Early-Successional Ecosystems on Forest Sites." *Frontiers in Ecology and the Environment* (March 2, 2010). http://www.esajournals.org/doi/pdf/10.1890/090157.

Swibold, Dennis. "Anaconda Sheds Its Press." *Montana: The Magazine of Western History* 56 (Summer 2006): 2–15.

Thomas, Craig E. *Just the Tip…: Regurgitations of a Montana Woodsman.* Stevensville, Mont.: Stoneydale Press, 2009.

Toole, K. Ross. *Montana: An Uncommon Land.* Norman: University of Oklahoma Press, 1959.

Toole, K. Ross, and Edward Butcher. "Timber Depredations on the Montana Public Domain." *Journal of the West* 7 (July 1968): 351–62.

Towell, William E. "The Bridger Controversy." *American Forests* 75 (November 1969): 45–46.

USDA Forest Service. *A National Forest Economy: One Means to Social and Economic Rehabilitation, Preliminary Draft.* Washington, D.C.: USDA Forest Service, June 1939.

———. *National Forest Management in a Quality Environment: Timber Productivity.* Washington, D.C.: Government Printing Office, 1971.

———. *New Wilderness Study Areas: Roadless Area Review and Evaluation.* Current Information Report No. 11. Washington, D.C.: USDA Forest Service, October 1973.

USDA Forest Service, Bitterroot National Forest. *Bitterroot National Forest Multiple Use Plan, Part 1, July 17, 1972.* Hamilton, Mont.: USDA Forest Service, Bitterroot National Forest, 1972.

———. *Burnt Fork Unit Plan.* Hamilton, Mont.: USDA Forest Service, 1972.

———. *Magruder Corridor Resource Inventory.* Hamilton, Mont.: USDA Forest Service, Bitterroot National Forest, 1970.

———. *Timber Management Plan, Bitterroot Working Circle, Bitterroot National Forest, Montana.* Hamilton, Mont.: USDA Forest Service, Bitterroot National Forest, 1961.

USDA Forest Service, Forest Products Laboratory. "Structural Grading of Logs from Small-Diameter Trees." In *Tech Line.* Madison, Wis.: USDA Forest Service, Forest Products Laboratory, March 2004.

USDA Forest Service, Northern Region. "The Bitterroot National Forest: In Celebration of a Century of Conservation." Missoula: USDA Forest Service, Northern Region, 1997.

———. *Early Days in the Forest Service.* 4 vols. Missoula: USDA Forest Service, Northern Region, 1944–1976.

———. *Final Environmental Impact Statement: Bitterroot National Forest Plan.* Missoula: USDA Forest Service, Northern Region, 1987.

———. *Forest Plan, Bitterroot National Forest, September 1987.* Missoula: USDA Forest Service, Northern Region, 1987.

———. *Forest Plan Monitoring and Evaluation Report, Fiscal Year 2007, Bitterroot National Forest.* Missoula: USDA Forest Service, Northern Region, 2007.

———. *Full Use and Development of Montana's Timber Resources.* Senate Doc. 9. 86th Cong., 1st sess. Washington, D.C.: Government Printing Office, 1959.

———. *Management Direction for Northern Region.* Missoula: USDA Forest Service, Northern Region, December 1970.

———. *Management Direction for the Bitterroot National Forest, Final Environmental Statement, May 5, 1971.* Missoula: USDA Forest Service, Northern Region, 1971.

———. *Management Practices, Bitterroot National Forest: A Task Force Appraisal, May 1969–April 1970.* Missoula: USDA Forest Service, Northern Region, 1970.

———. *Proposed Bitterroot National Forest Land Management Plan, 2006.* Missoula: USDA Forest Service, Northern Region, 2006.

———. *Quality in Timber Management: A Current Evaluation.* Missoula: USDA Forest Service, Northern Region, July 1970.

————. *Upper Selway Management Area, Bitterroot National Forest.* Missoula: USDA Forest Service, Northern Region, 1965.

————. *USDA Forest Service Environmental Statement, Multiple Use Plan—Moose Creek Planning Unit.* Missoula: USDA Forest Service, Northern Region, 1973.

U.S. House. Committee on Interior and Insular Affairs, Subcommittee on Public Lands. *Damage to Public Lands from Forest Practices or Fluoride Emissions.* Hearings, 93rd Cong., 1st sess. Missoula, Mont., August 17, 1973 [and] Washington, D.C., September 20 and 21, 1973. Washington, D.C.: Government Printing Office, 1973.

U.S. Senate. Committee on Interior and Insular Affairs, Subcommittee on Public Lands. *Clearcutting on Federal Timberlands: Report by the Subcommittee on Public Lands to the Committee on Interior and Insular Affairs, United States Senate.* Committee print, 92nd Cong., 2nd sess. Washington, D.C.: Government Printing Office, 1972.

————. *"Clear-Cutting" Practices on National Timberlands.* Hearings, 92nd Cong., 1st sess., April 5–6, 1971. 3 pts. Washington, D.C.: Government Printing Office, 1971.

————. Subcommittee on the Environment and Land Resources of the Committee on Interior and Insular Affairs. *Forest and Rangeland Management: Joint Hearings before the Subcommittee on Environment, Soil Conservation, and Forestry of the Committee on Agriculture and Forestry.* 94th Cong., 2nd sess., on Senate Bills 2851, 2926, and 3091, March 15, 16, and 22, 1976. Washington, D.C.: Government Printing Office, 1976.

Wiener, Al. "Gifford Pinchot Would Have Laughed." *American Forests* 79 (November 1973): 12–13, 34–37.

Wikstrom, J. H., and S. Blair Hutchison. *Stratification of Forest Land for Timber Management Planning on the Western National Forests.* Research Paper INT-108. Ogden, Utah: USDA Forest Service, Intermountain Forest and Range Experiment Station, 1971.

Williams, Gerald W. *The Forest Service: Fighting for Public Lands.* Westport, Conn.: Greenwood Press, 2007.

Williams, Gerald W., and Char Miller. "At the Creation: The National Forest Commission of 1896–97." *Forest History Today* 11 (Spring–Fall 2005): 32–40.

Wuerthner, George. "Logging and Wildfire: Ecological Differences and the Need to Preserve Large Fires." In *The Wildfire Reader: A Century of Failed Forest Policy,* ed. George Wuerthner. Washington, D.C.: Island Press, 2006.

Zach, Lawrence W., and S. Blair Hutchison. *The Forest Situation in Ravalli County, Montana.* Forest Survey Release no. 21. Missoula: USDA Forest Service, Northern Rocky Mountain Forest and Range Experiment Station, 1943.

Index